Frommer's®

# Nepal

## Here's what the critics say about Frommer's:

"Amazingly easy to use. Very portable, very complete."
—*Booklist*

♦

"The only mainstream guide to list specific prices. The Walter Cronkite of guidebooks—with all that implies."
—*Travel & Leisure*

♦

"Complete, concise, and filled with useful information."
—*New York Daily News*

♦

"Hotel information is close to encyclopedic."
—*Des Moines Sunday Register*

♦

"I use a lot of travel guides when preparing my trips, but I have learned to especially trust Frommer's when it comes to picking lodgings."
—*The Orange County Register*

**Other Great Guides for Your Trip:**

*Frommer's Southeast Asia*

*Frommer's Singapore & Malaysia*

*Frommer's China: The 50 Most Memorable Trips*

# Frommer's®

**4th Edition**

# Nepal

## by Karl Samson
## with Jane Aukshunas

MACMILLAN • USA

## ABOUT THE AUTHORS

**Karl Samson** and **Jane Aukshunas** are a husband-and-wife travel writing team who spent part of their honeymoon trekking in Nepal. Karl, who lived in Asia during his early childhood years, is the team's creative writer and has been writing about Nepal since he made his first trip there in 1986. Though sickness prevented Jane from enjoying her first trek (in 1989), she has returned several times since then to assist with this book and has enjoyed all subsequent treks. Other books by this team include *Frommer's Washington State, Frommer's Oregon,* and *Frommer's Arizona.* Karl is also the author of *Frommer's Great Outdoor Guide to Washington & Oregon.* Though the two have seen Nepal change dramatically over the years, they still find it to be one of the most fascinating countries on Earth.

## MACMILLAN TRAVEL

A Pearson Education Macmillan Company
1633 Broadway
New York, NY 10019

Find us online at **www.frommers.com**

ISBN 0-02-862628-1
ISSN 1055-5439

Editor: Kathy Iwasaki
*Special thanks to Nicole Daro*
Production Editor: Robyn Burnett
Photo Editor: Richard Fox
Design by Michele Laseau
Staff Cartographers: John Decamillis and Roberta Stockwell
Front Cover Photo: Swayambunath Stupa in Kathmandu
Back Cover Photo: Machapuchare in Pokhara
Page Creation: Carrie Allen, John Bitter, and Terri Sheehan

## SPECIAL SALES

Bulk purchases (10+ copies) of Frommer's and selected Macmillan travel guides are available to corporations, organizations, mail-order catalogs, institutions, and charities at special discounts, and can be customized to suit individual needs. For more information write to Special Sales, Macmillan General Reference, 1633 Broadway, New York, NY 10019.

Manufactured in the United States of America

# Contents

# List of Maps

## An Invitation to the Reader

In researching this book, we discovered many wonderful places—hotels, restaurants, shops, and more. We're sure you'll find others. Please tell us about them so that we can share the information with your fellow travelers in upcoming editions. If you were disappointed with a recommendation, we'd love to know that, too. Please write to:

Karl Samson and Jane Aukshunas
*Frommer's Nepal,* 4th Edition
Macmillan Travel
1633 Broadway
New York, NY 10019

## An Additional Note

Please be advised that travel information is subject to change at any time—and this is especially true of prices. We therefore suggest that you write or call ahead for confirmation when making your travel plans. The authors, editors, and publisher cannot be held responsible for the experiences of readers while traveling. Your safety is important to us, however, so we encourage you to stay alert and be aware of your surroundings. Keep a close eye on cameras, purses, and wallets, all favorite targets of thieves and pickpockets.

## What the Symbols Mean

### ✪ Frommer's Favorites

Our favorite places and experiences.

The following abbreviations are used for credit cards:

| | | | |
|---|---|---|---|
| AE | American Express | JCB | Japan Credit Bank |
| DC | Diners Club | MC | MasterCard |
| DISC | Discover | V | Visa |
| EURO | Eurocard | | |

## Find Frommer's Online

Arthur Frommer's Budget Travel Online (www.frommers.com) offers more than 6,000 pages of up-to-the-minute travel information—including the latest bargains and candid, personal articles updated daily by Arthur Frommer himself. No other Web site offers such comprehensive and timely coverage of the world of travel.

# The Best of Nepal

For the first-time visitor (and, I can assure you, for the repeat visitor as well), a trip to Nepal can be an overwhelming experience. Jet lag and culture shock, thin air and smog, streets with no names and gods with many names all conspire to confuse, challenge, and astound visitors to this Himalayan kingdom. Before you immerse yourself in the cultural crossroads that is modern-day Nepal, it pays to have a clear idea of where you are going and what you want to see and do. This chapter will tell you about some of the best experiences that Nepal has to offer so that you can plan a trip that will fulfill your expectations and be suited to your needs. These selections will, among other things, clue you in to which trek might be right for you, which temples you should not miss, where to stay, where to eat, and what to bring home from your visit. After deciding on an itinerary, tap your reserves for all the patience you can muster, and you just might be ready to explore the kingdom of Nepal.

## 1 The Best Treks for Cultural Encounters

- **The Annapurna Circuit:** This 3-week-long trek climbs from lowland villages surrounded by lush fields and forests up through the mountains into the desert-dry trans-Himalayan region that lies on the edge of the Tibetan Plateau and then back again. Along the way, trekkers pass through the villages of several ethnic groups. See chapter 10.
- **The Jomosom Trek:** If you don't have enough time to do the entire Annapurna circuit, this trek provides almost as much cultural diversity. At the start of the trek, you pass first through Brahmin and Chhetri villages, then Gurung and Magar villages, and finally, along the Kali Gandaki, Thakali villages. See chapter 10.
- **Upper Mustang:** Until the 1990s, the isolated region of the Kali Gandaki valley known as Upper Mustang was closed to trekkers due to its sensitive location next to the Tibetan border. Today, however, if you can afford the $700 trekking permit, you can venture into this arid and remote region, which is home to a relatively undisturbed Tibetan culture. See chapter 10.

- **Jiri to Namche Bazaar:** Most people heading to the Solu-Khumbu region are intent only on getting a close-up glimpse of Mount Everest and often take a plane into Lukla. However, the trail from Jiri to Namche, though not long on mountain views, does pass through numerous interesting villages that are now visited by a small number of trekkers each year. See chapter 10.

## 2  The Best Treks for Mountain Views

- **Annapurna Sanctuary:** Set at 13,000 feet in an amphitheater surrounded by half a dozen peaks more than 21,000 feet tall, Annapurna Sanctuary is the endpoint of what might be the single most view-intensive trek in Nepal. With 360 degrees of mountains and massive glaciers around you, the view from this high, grassy valley is both awesome and relatively easy to achieve. See chapter 10.
- **Gokyo:** Located within a few days' trek of Everest Base Camp and Kala Pattar, Gokyo actually has better views. From the summit of 17,990-foot Gokyo Ri, you can see Everest, Cho Oyu, Nuptse, Lhotse, and Makalu. See chapter 10.
- **Kala Pattar:** Those who make the arduous trek up to this 18,190-foot peak near Everest Base Camp are rewarded with some of the best views of Mount Everest without climbing the mountain itself. Also visible from this peak are more than half a dozen other high peaks that make for a very impressive 360-degree panorama. See chapter 10.
- **Ghorapani to Ghandruk:** If you want to get the most mountain views in the least amount of time, the trek up from Naya Pul to Ghorapani and then over to Ghandruk should satiate your desire for Himalayan vistas. From the sunrise above Ghorapani to the in-your-face view of Machhapuchhare and Annapurna South from Chomrong, this trek does not disappoint. See chapter 10.

## 3  The Best Short Treks

- **Ghorapani-Ghandruk Loop:** This 5- to 6-day trek takes in some of the best views in Nepal, includes a day of hiking through a beautiful rhododendron forest, and also passes through a few interesting villages, including the large and prosperous Gurung village of Ghandruk. See chapter 10.
- **Jomosom to Muktinath and Back:** If your time is short but you want to see some of the most interesting villages in Nepal, fly in and out of Jomosom and spend 4 or 5 days trekking the desert-dry upper reaches of the Kali Gandaki River valley. Here, in a landscape that's similar to Tibet's, are several villages of flat-roofed, stone-walled houses. See chapter 10.
- **Lukla to Namche Bazaar and Back:** If you are dead set on seeing Mount Everest from the ground and have only a few days to spare for a trek, you can realize your dream by flying in and out of Lukla and then hiking 2 days up to Namche Bazaar. From a hill above this large Sherpa village, there is an excellent view up the valley to Mount Everest. See chapter 10.
- **The Jomosom Trek (abbreviated):** If you have a week to spare and you're in good shape, you should be able to make the trek up to Jomosom and return by plane. Or you could fly into Jomosom and then walk out. Either way, you won't have time to dawdle, but you'll take in some great scenery and many interesting villages. See chapter 10.

## 4 The Best Outdoor Activities Other Than Trekking

- **Mountain Biking Down from Nagarkot:** With its abundance of trails and dirt roads, Nepal is an ideal place to go mountain biking. However, with a landscape that is anything but flat, pedaling here often takes a lot of stamina. This ride, however, is all downhill. There are mountain views at the top and temples at the bottom. See chapter 5.
- **White water Rafting:** All those mountains, all that snow melt. There *must* be great white water rafting here. There is, and "great" doesn't quite describe it. Class IV and V whitewater abounds, and rafting trips can be as long as 10 days. Sure, there are shorter trips and less-demanding rapids, but Nepal really isn't the place for beginners. See chapters 5 and 7.
- **Hot-Air Ballooning over the Kathmandu Valley:** There are excellent views of the Himalayas from the Kathmandu Valley, and those views are even better from a hot-air balloon 3,000 feet above the valley floor. The views of the valley itself are fascinating as well. See chapter 5.
- **Bird Watching:** With more than 800 species of birds recorded here, Nepal is a birders' paradise. In the Kathmandu Valley alone, more than 500 species have been sighted. So in just a couple of weeks of intensive birding, it's possible to add 300 or 400 birds to your life's list. See chapters 5, 7, and 8.
- **In Search of Rhinos and Tigers and Wild Elephants:** Royal Chitwan National Park is the most convenient place in Nepal to see wild Indian one-horned rhinoceroses; tigers are sometimes seen here as well. In Royal Bardia National Park you can see rhinos and tigers, *and* wild Asian elephants. See chapter 8.

## 5 The Best Mountain Views for Non-trekkers

- **From the Everest Mountain Flight:** Maybe you don't have the time to trek to the Everest region, or maybe trekking just isn't your idea of a good time. Whatever the reason, if you aren't going to see Mount Everest from the ground, you can still see it through the window of a plane. See chapter 5.
- **From Nagarkot:** Although you can see a few Himalayan peaks from Kathmandu, for a truly memorable panorama try spending the night at this collection of lodges on a ridgetop at the eastern edge of the Kathmandu Valley. You can see for miles and miles and miles, and from a nearby viewing tower, you can see all the way to Everest. See chapter 6.
- **From Dhulikhel:** The view from this village on the rim of the Kathmandu Valley is almost identical to that from Nagarkot, which is actually visible from Dhulikhel. See chapter 6.
- **From Pokhara:** Be sure to stock up on Tiger Balm before going to Pokhara. You'll need it for the sore neck you'll get staring up at Machhapuchhare and the Annapurnas. And whatever you do, don't sleep through dawn any morning you're here; the morning light show on the Himalayas is splendid. See chapter 7.
- **From an Annapurna Flight:** While the Annapurna massif and adjacent Machhapuchhare aren't as well known as Mount Everest, they are certainly just as impressive. If you want to get a close-up view of these peaks without breaking a sweat try this mountain flight. See chapter 7.

## 6  The Best Temples & Shrines

- **Swayambunath:** Atop a hill on the west side of the Kathmandu Valley stands a hemispherical Buddhist shrine, which is topped by a gilded box. The eyes of the Buddha gaze out from the top of the stupa. It is these eyes that have become the quintessential symbol of Nepal. See chapter 5.
- **Boudhanath:** Located on the east side of Kathmandu and similar in design to Swayambunath, this large Buddhist stupa is particularly sacred to Tibetans, who circumambulate the shrine, sometimes prostrating themselves as they go. Shops full of Tibetan antiques surround the shrine, and beyond these shops are numerous Tibetan Buddhist monasteries. See chapter 5.
- **Pashupatinath:** Dedicated to Shiva in his incarnation as lord of the animals, Pashupatinath is Nepal's holiest and most important Hindu temple and is located on the east side of Kathmandu. The site of open-air cremations and a temporary home to dreadlocked, ganga-smoking Shaivite *sadhus* (holy men), this temple complex is always bustling with activity. See chapter 5.
- **Patan's Golden Temple:** Shiny with gilded metalwork, this Buddhist temple, not far from Patan's Durbar Square, displays some of the finest religious art in the Kathmandu Valley. Just don't be alarmed by the rats that have free range of the temple compound. See chapter 5.
- **Patan's Krishna Temple:** Though well known in the West (thanks to The Beatles and the hippies of the 1960s), the Hindu god Krishna is not worshiped by many in Nepal. However, on Patan's Durbar Square stands an elaborate stone Krishna temple unlike any other in the Kathmandu Valley. See chapter 5.
- **Patan's Mahaboudha Temple:** Packed into a tiny courtyard, this towering temple is covered with thousands of terra-cotta tiles, every one of which bears an image of the Buddha. See chapter 5.
- **Bhaktapur's Nyatapola Temple:** Set atop a five-tiered platform and topped by five roofs, this pagoda-style temple is the most perfectly symmetrical and balanced of all the Hindu temples in the Kathmandu Valley. See chapter 5.
- **Budhanilkantha:** Located on the north side of the Kathmandu Valley, Budhanilkantha enshrines the largest, and one of the most unusual, stone statues in Nepal. The stone carving depicts the Hindu god Vishnu sleeping on a bed of snakes. See chapter 6.

## 7  The Most Interesting Villages & Towns

- **Bhaktapur:** Extensively restored through a German aid project, Bhaktapur is the best preserved of the Kathmandu Valley's three cities, and with traffic restricted in the old neighborhoods, it is a much more enjoyable place to explore than Kathmandu or Patan. See chapter 5.
- **Panauti:** Situated on the eastern edge of the Kathmandu Valley, this remote riverside town has an interesting temple complex that has been under restoration for several years. See chapter 6.
- **Kirtipur:** This hill town, on the south side of the Kathmandu Valley, was the last kingdom to hold out against King Prithvi Narayan Shah in the 18th century. Today, Kirtipur is seldom visited by tourists, but it has great views and is filled with narrow lanes and has almost no cars. See chapter 6.

- **Gorkha:** It was from this hill town, midway between Kathmandu and Pokhara, that Prithvi Narayan Shah launched his campaign to unify Nepal. His fort still stands high on a hilltop above the town itself. See chapter 7.

## 8  The Best Things to Bring Home from Your Visit

- **A Tibetan Carpet:** Hand-knotted wool carpets are thick, warm, and inexpensive, and though they are both bulky and heavy, you can easily get the standard 3-foot by 6-foot carpet into your checked luggage.
- **Thangkas:** All over Kathmandu and Bhaktapur, you'll see artists creating these traditional Buddhist religious paintings. Often unbelievably detailed, these scroll paintings depict various Tibetan Buddhist deities, as well as the wheel of life and medical texts.
- **Your Own Personal God or Goddess:** Should you find yourself desiring your own personal statue of Ganesh, Manjushri, Vishwarupa, Avalokiteshwara, or any other deity from the Buddhist or Hindu pantheons of Nepal, step into any store selling cast-metal figurines of the gods, and you are certain to find the one you seek.
- **Tea:** Both Nepali and Indian teas are available in Kathmandu and are fresher and cheaper than at home. Pick up some tea masala (spice mix), and you'll be able to make your own fragrant and flavorful milk tea.
- **Saffron and Other Spices:** Though it isn't grown in Nepal, saffron is readily available in the spice markets of Kathmandu and is probably a lot cheaper than it is back home. Cardamon and masala mixes are also worth buying.
- **Embroidered T-shirts:** Pick a design from the images on the walls (or bring your own), and in 24 hours, one of Kathmandu's embroidery shops can whip up a colorful machine-embroidered T-shirt. They're cheap and they make great compact gifts.
- **Incense:** There's nothing like incense wafting through your house to take you immediately back to the streets and temples of Kathmandu. For less than $1 a box, you can conjure up the essence of Nepal whenever you need to.
- **A Healthy Intestinal Tract:** Forget the souvenirs and handicrafts. The single most important thing to bring back from Nepal is your health. Watch what you eat and don't forget to wash those hands (your mother was right)!

## 9  The Best Museums

- **The Patan Museum, Patan:** This is Nepal's newest major museum and it's housed in part in Patan's former royal palace. The building has been expertly restored and the museum displays, aimed as much at foreign visitors as at Nepalis, are professionally mounted and highly informative. See chapter 5.
- **The National Museum, Kathmandu:** Although the displays at this museum are not nearly as well lit as those at the Patan Museum, the collections of Hindu and Buddhist iconography is the finest in the country, an excellent introduction to the kingdom's religious heritage. See chapter 5.
- **Natural History Museum, Pokhara:** The collection of butterflies and moths, assembled over many years by a British entomologist, is absolutely fascinating. See chapter 7.
- **Mustang Eco-Museum, Jomosom:** Located in the remote village of Jomosom, on the edge of the Upper Mustang region, this small museum provides an excellent

introduction to the area, which centuries ago grew wealthy from the salt and grain trade between Tibet and India. Until recently, Upper Mustang was closed to foreigners. See chapter 10.

## 10  The Most Unusual Nepali Experiences

- **Animal Sacrifices at Dakshinkali:** If you thought animal sacrifices went out with the Old Testament, think again. There are still Hindu gods and goddesses that must be propitiated with blood. Dakshinkali, on the south side of the Kathmandu Valley, is the most popular animal sacrifice site, with both Hindu Nepalis and tourists. A very macabre cultural experience. See chapter 6.
- **Open-Air Cremations at Pashupatinath:** Though it may seem insensitive and voyeuristic to attend the cremation of a stranger, the lively atmosphere at Pashupatinath, Nepal's most important Hindu temple, soon dispels any apprehensions. Stoned-out holy men, barking dogs, and belligerent monkeys give the entire experience a very surreal quality. See chapter 5.
- **Catching a Glimpse of a Living Goddess:** Statues of gods and goddesses abound in Kathmandu, but there's a real live goddess, too. She goes by the name Kumari and lives in a historic building on Kathmandu's Durbar Square, where she can sometimes be seen glancing out a window. See chapter 5.
- **Watching the Nightly Fruit Bat Fly-Out in Kathmandu:** Although their numbers are dwindling (possibly due to the increase in air pollution), there is still a large population of huge fruit bats living near the Royal Palace in Kathmandu. Each evening at dusk, they leave their treetop roosts and wing out over the valley. Watch them from the roof of your hotel. See chapter 5.
- **Getting Your Forehead Plastered by a Sadhu:** Sooner or later it will happen to you. Some smiling, ash-besmeared character, perhaps with dreadlocks and nothing on but a loin cloth, is going to dig into his bucket of red paste and slap some on your forehead. This is not an assault, but a blessing. By the way, the old guy will want a tip for his troubles.
- **The Steamy Gupteshwor Mahadev Cave in Pokhara:** If your past experience with caves has been one of cold, damp places, check out this one on the south side of Pokhara. Not only does it feel like a sauna inside, but a natural Shiva lingam (phallus) discovered in the cave has made it a very powerful shrine. See chapter 7.
- **Riding an Elephant in Search of Rhinos and Tigers and Bears, Oh My!:** You might not see anything but a few deer, but still, riding an elephant through the tiger-infested jungles of Asia will have you rereading Kipling's *Jungle Book*. See chapter 8.

## 11  The Best Luxury Hotels

- **Yak & Yeti** (Kathmandu; ☎ 977/1-248999): Located just off Kathmandu's most upscale shopping street, the Yak & Yeti is a far more formal place than the name might imply. Excellent restaurants, attractive gardens, two swimming pools, a casino in an old palace, and first-class service make this the best hotel in Kathmandu. See chapter 4.
- **Soaltee Crowne Plaza Kathmandu** (Kathmandu; ☎ 977/1-272555): With spacious grounds, a swimming pool amid neatly manicured gardens, a casino,

and no less than four excellent restaurants, the Soaltee has long been the hotel of choice for visiting heads of state. See chapter 4.

- **Radisson Hotel Kathmandu** (Kathmandu; ☎ 977/1-411818): Though not completely finished when inspected, this new luxury hotel looked as if it would be Kathmandu's first hotel to have a truly contemporary international feel about it. See chapter 4.
- **Dusit Thani Fulbari Resort Hotel** (Pokhara; ☎ 977/61-23451): With sprawling grounds, its own golf course, and a cliff-edge setting, this new luxury hotel is the first golf resort in Nepal. Whether or not you have any interest in playing golf in the Himalayas, the setting and the views are spectacular. See chapter 7.
- **Shangri-La Village Pokhara** (Pokhara; ☎ 977/61-22122): With excellent views of the mountains, a resort-like feel, good restaurants, and plenty of Nepali character in its contemporary design, this Pokhara hotel is, all things considered, the most enjoyable hotel in the country. See chapter 7.

## 12 The Hotels with the Best Views

- **The Everest Hotel** (Kathmandu; ☎ 977/1-488100): From the upper floors of this seven-story hotel, there are good mountain views to the north. If you get a room on a lower floor, head up to one of the rooftop restaurants. See chapter 4.
- **Hotel Himalaya** (Patan; ☎ 997/1-523900): Located on a hill between Kathmandu and Patan's Durbar Square, this hotel has a good view over the rooftops of Kathmandu to the distant Himalayas. You can take in the view from the dining room upstairs from the lobby, too. See chapter 4.
- **Club Himalaya Nagarkot Resort** (Nagarkot; ☎ 977/1-290868): This luxurious hotel is perched on a ridge above the Kathmandu Valley and offers not only the best mountain views in the area, but also the only indoor pool in Nepal. See chapter 6.
- **Tiger Tops Pokhara Village** (Pokhara; ☎ 977/1-411225): Set on a high ridge about 30 minutes east of Pokhara, this rustic lodge is built to resemble a hill village and has hot tubs, as well as excellent views. See chapter 7.
- **Fish Tail Lodge** (Pokhara; ☎ 977/61 20071): This lodge sits on the shore of Phewa Lake, is tucked up against a forest preserve, and is reachable only by a hand-pulled raft or rowboat. With its memorable views of the Himalayas, it was long the best hotel in Pokhara. Now there are more luxurious hotels in town, but none has the adventurous feel of Fish Tail Lodge. See chapter 7.
- **Hotel Everest View** (Shyangboche; ☎ 977/1-224854): Coffee, tea, or oxygen? Those are the basic refreshments at this 13,000-foot hotel on a ridge only a few miles from Mount Everest. Though it costs a small fortune to stay here, if you want to get close to The Mountain and still be sitting in the lap of luxury (well sort of), this is your only choice. See chapter 10.

## 13 The Best Hotels for Nepali Character

- **Dwarika's Kathmandu Village Hotel** (Kathmandu; ☎ 977/1-470770): Merging luxurious accommodations with historic architectural salvages from old buildings all over the Kathmandu Valley, Dwarika's has created a setting both historical and modern. No other hotel in Nepal manages to immerse its guests in such fascinating surroundings. See chapter 4.

- **Hotel Shanker** (Kathmandu; ☎ **977/1-410151**): Kathmandu is full of old European-inspired palaces dating back to the late 19th and early 20th centuries. The Shanker is the only hotel that was once such a palace. It is by no means a luxurious hotel, but the faded glory of this anomalous building is intriguing. See chapter 4.
- **Hotel Vajra** (Kathmandu; ☎ **977/1-272719**): Something of a cultural center for Kathmandu, the traditionally inspired architecture of this hotel sets it apart from the dozens of characterless ones in nearby Thamel. Terraced gardens, little Hindu shrines tucked here and there, and buildings of brick, marble, and carved wood create something of a village feel. See chapter 4.
- **Summit Hotel** (Patan; ☎ **977/1-521810**): Located in Patan and with an excellent view across all of Kathmandu, this hotel is set amid attractive gardens and draws on traditional Kathmandu architectural details for its design. Some guest rooms even have traditional brick floors, and there is lots of carved wood around the premises. See chapter 4.
- **The Fort Resort** (Nagarkot; ☎ **977/1-290869**): Perched high on a ridge at Nagarkot, The Fort is a modern hotel built in the style of Kathmandu's traditional Newari homes. Not only do you get character here, but you also get an outstanding view of the Himalayas. See chapter 6.
- **Kantipur Temple House** (Kathmandu; ☎ **977/1-250131**): This is the first new moderately priced hotel in Kathmandu to be built in the traditional style of the old city. Looking like a cross between a town house and a temple, the Kantipur House is new enough that it hasn't yet worked out all its kinks, but for atmosphere, convenience, and economy, it can't be beat. See chapter 4.

# 14  The Best Kathmandu Valley Budget/Moderately Priced Hotels

- **Astoria Hotel** (Kathmandu; ☎ **977/1-428810**): Located in a quiet residential neighborhood, this small hotel has the feel of a bed-and-breakfast. The organic vegetable garden out back supplies the hotel's tiny French restaurant. See chapter 4.
- **Hotel Excelsior** (Kathmandu; ☎ **977/1-411566**): Set in the heart of Thamel, Kathmandu's main tourist neighborhood, the Excelsior offers rooms that are as comfortable and spacious as those in area hotels charging three times as much. See chapter 4.
- **Kathmandu Guest House** (Kathmandu; ☎ 977/1-413632): Since way back in the hippie days of the 1960s, this budget hotel, housed partly in a historic European-influenced mansion, has been the favored address of budget travelers in Kathmandu. It's still a great place to stay and there are always plenty of interesting people hanging out in the lobby, garden, and front courtyard. See chapter 4.
- **Hotel Sunset View** (Kathmandu; ☎ 977/1-480057): Situated in a quiet residential neighborhood not far from the airport, this hotel is surrounded by Japanese gardens and has views over the rooftops of Patan. Though the hotel is not large, it has two restaurants, one of which serves Japanese food. See chapter 4.
- **Nagarkot Farmhouse Resort** (Nagarkot; ☎ 977/1-228087): Set high on a ridge above the Kathmandu Valley and under the same management as the Hotel Vajra, this place is more rustic lodge than resort. Nonetheless, it is a memorable and atmospheric place from which to enjoy views of the Himalayas and do a bit of hiking. See chapter 6.

## 15 The Best Restaurants

- **Chez Caroline Café Restaurant and Pâtisserie** (Kathmandu; ☎ 263070): Located in the elegant Baber Mahal Revisited shopping/dining arcade, this casual little open-air French cafe serves excellent sandwiches and desserts. See chapter 4.
- **Ghar-e-Kabab** (Kathmandu; ☎ 221711): This restaurant on Durbar Marg has for years served the best Indian food in Kathmandu. The chicken tikka almost melts in your mouth. See chapter 4.
- **Yin Yang Restaurant** (Kathmandu; ☎ 425510): With an attractive little terrace, this Thamel Thai restaurant does a very respectable job of duplicating the vibrant flavors of Thai food. See chapter 4.
- **Thamel House** (Kathmandu; ☎ 410388): For traditional Nepali food in a restored historic home, Thamel House is convenient, economical, and not overly touristy. The food goes beyond basic *dal bhat tarkari,* and service is usually very good. See chapter 4.
- **Bukhara** (Kathmandu; ☎ 272550): Located at the Crowne Plaza Soaltee hotel, this outpost of an upscale Indian restaurant chain brings Moghul cuisine to Kathmandu. The decor is as exotic as you could hope for on a trip to the Himalayas. See chapter 4.
- **Al Fresco** (Kathmandu; ☎ 272550): Sometimes, even in far-off Nepal, you just have to have some good pasta, and this is the place to get it in Kathmandu. Located in the Crowne Plaza Soaltee, Al Fresco uses primarily imported ingredients, which are what makes the food here so much better than that at other Italian restaurants around town. See chapter 4.
- **The Chimney Room** (Kathmandu; ☎ 248999): Inspired by Boris's, the first restaurant to open in Kathmandu years ago, The Chimney Room, located inside the Yak & Yeti Hotel, serves Russian specialties such as borscht, Chicken Kiev, stroganoff, and shashlick. See chapter 4.
- **Fuji Restaurant** (Kathmandu; ☎ 225272): Imagine eating Japanese food in a historic gambling pavilion that is reached by a footbridge over a small pond and looks as if it were moved to Kathmandu from the back gardens at Versailles. Eclectic and very memorable. See chapter 4.
- **Mike's Breakfast** (Kathmandu; ☎ 424303): Although Mike's is in fact open for lunch and dinner too, it is at breakfast that this place really shines. Bottomless cups of coffee (a rarity in Nepal) and huge breakfasts are the perfect way to start a serious day of temple touring. See chapter 4.
- **Caravanserai Café** (Pokhara; ☎ 22122): Located at the Shangri-La Pokhara Village hotel, this restaurant offers great prices, a beautiful setting, and reasonably professional service. Although there isn't a view of the mountains, the food makes up for this shortcoming. See chapter 7.

# 2

# Getting to Know Nepal

Nepal, bordered on the north by the Tibetan Autonomous Region of China (Tibet), and on the east, south, and west by India, is a small, mountainous kingdom 550 miles long and 90 to 150 miles wide (about the size of Iowa or England). Roughly rectangular in shape, the country follows the line of the Himalayas from southeast to northwest and is one of the few landlocked countries in the world.

Home to the highest peak on earth and almost completely closed to the outside world from the mid–19th century until the early 1950s, Nepal, a mysterious land shrouded in myths and legends, has long beckoned to adventurers and mountaineers. When this tiny Himalayan kingdom finally opened its borders to the outside world, some of the first visitors were mountain climbers headed for Mount Everest.

By the early 1970s, Nepal had, however, been discovered by a very different sort of traveler—globe-trotting, backpack-toting hippies. The word had gotten out that in Nepal, hashish was legal and the cost of living was dirt cheap. Kathmandu became a Himalayan Haight Ashbury. The hippies eventually headed home to Europe and North America when their funds ran low, and they spread the word about living among the peaceful people and snowcapped peaks of Nepal. Tales of the mystic East sent seekers of enlightenment to India and Nepal. Although the image of a Westerner asking about the meaning of life from a holy man on top of a mountain has become a cliché, people do journey to Nepal seeking spiritual guidance from Buddhist lamas.

Today, Nepal is a popular adventure-travel destination for both the backpacker and the well-financed expeditioner. It also has far more to offer than just the chance to hike in the Himalayas. As overwhelming as they may be, Nepal's mountains are just a backdrop for the country's diverse and complex cultural landscape. The peoples of Nepal have been molded by their environment; their religions, agriculture, architecture, and very lives have been dictated by the mountains. The Nepali people are what make a trip to Nepal a truly unique experience.

While Nepal is a fascinating country, it is also one of the poorest countries in the world, and is dealing with the problems faced by other developing nations—overpopulation, pollution, deforestation, and the lack of safe drinking water. Political and geographic isolation had combined to keep Nepal separate from the world until less than 50 years ago, so today the nation is rapidly trying to catch up.

However, Himalayan villages still live by the rhythms of the seasons, and the land is farmed by hand with the help of oxen and buffalo. Overpopulation has forced Nepal to decimate its forests both for firewood and for access to more arable land. In Kathmandu, Nepal's capital, sacred cows still sleep in the streets, and ash-besmeared Hindu holy men still beg for alms outside temples dedicated to an unfathomable pantheon of gods. There are also traffic jams and smog, computers and Coca-Cola. Nepal is not now and never was Shangri-la, but the tiny country on the rooftop of the world has captured the collective Western imagination. Trekkers, mountain climbers, and spiritual pilgrims continue to beat a path to Nepal, and what they find is a country trying to strike a balance between the 19th and the 20th centuries.

# 1 The Natural Environment

The Himalayas are among the youngest mountains on earth, and they are still gaining elevation today, though the forces of erosion tend to counterbalance any potential gains. According to current theories of plate tectonics, the Himalayas have developed in several stages. They began forming some 60 million years ago when the Indian subcontinent collided with the Eurasian continent. At the time these two continents collided, the land now known as Nepal lay at the bottom of the prehistoric Tethys Sea, where a thick layer of sedimentary rock had formed. Today, fossils from this ancient sea floor can be found throughout the Himalayas, even on the slopes of Mount Everest itself. In this first stage of mountain building, a massive buckling and uplifting of the landscape took place, forming a low mountain range to the north of today's Himalayas.

During the next phase, which began some 10 to 15 million years ago and is known as the Main Central Thrust, the land was thrust up to form the mountain range where the Himalayas now stand. Initially this mountain range was not nearly as tall as today's mountains and developed slowly enough that rivers flowing through the previously formed mountains, in what is now Tibet, continued to flow south, cutting through the newly formed mountain range. Several of these ancient rivers still flow through the Himalayas. One of them, the Kali Gandaki, flows between Annapurna I and Dhaulagiri, two of the highest peaks on earth, and has cut the deepest river gorge on earth.

In the third formative phase, which began only about 500,000 to 600,000 years ago, the Himalayas were pushed upward to much greater heights. The evidence of this phase can be seen in the Kali Gandaki Valley, near the village of Jomosom, where outstanding examples of folded and uplifted rock are exposed on the steep valley walls. This last phase took place so quickly that some of the rivers were dammed by the rising land, forming large lakes. The Kathmandu Valley was once a lake that later drained or dried up. During roughly this same period and perhaps as recently as 200,000 years ago, the Mahabharat Range was also formed. This low range parallels the main Himalayas and effectively blocks the southward flow of most rivers. Today only three rivers (the Karnali, the Kali Gandaki, and the Kois) cut through the Mahabharat Range, and all other rivers to the north feed into these three rivers.

As the tallest mountains on earth, the Himalayas are, due to their great size, the reason for the two distinctly different climates found in Nepal. On the southern slopes, rising air in the late spring draws moisture north from the Bay of Bengal, initiating the annual monsoon. For 4 months or more, rains are steady, sometimes torrential, on the southern slopes of the Himalayas. However, because of their great height, these mountains very effectively wring nearly every drop of moisture from the clouds. Nothing is left for the lands on the north side of the Himalayas, and thus the far side of the mountains and all of the Tibetan Plateau are a high desert.

# Nepal

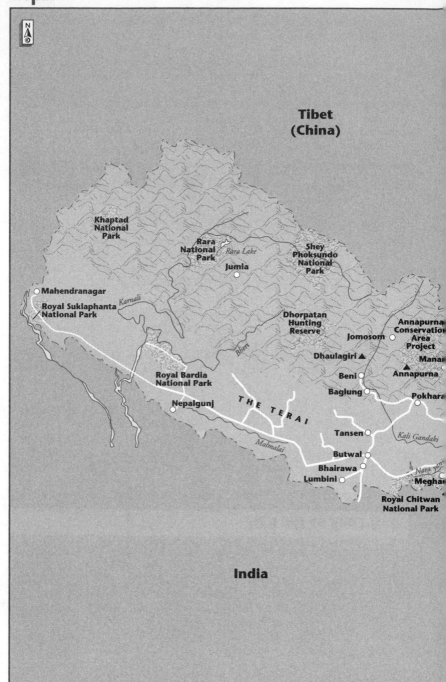

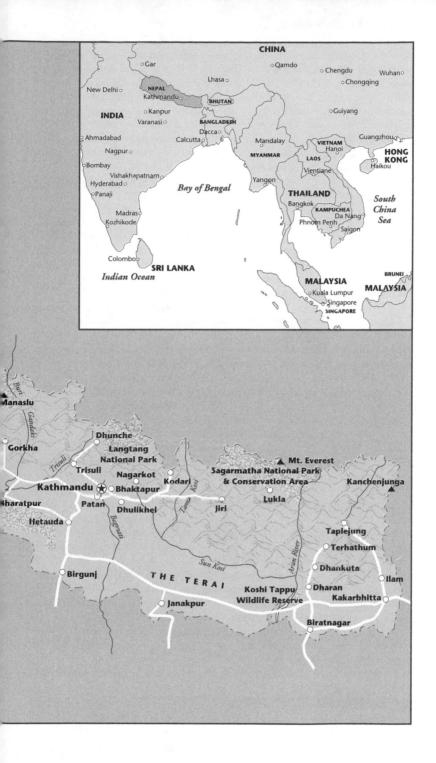

Just as the Himalayas determine the climate on either side of the range, so, too, are they responsible for the great biological diversity in Nepal. With elevations ranging from near sea level to 29,028 feet, Nepal has a wider scope of climatalogical zones than anywhere else on earth. Here you can find subtropical lowlands (Nepal is on the same latitude as Florida), temperate forests, arctic-like alpine regions, and high desert conditions. In addition to this elevation-based diversity are countless microclimates. In some places the variations in habitats are so pronounced that you can stand in a damp, dark forest on the north side of a ridge and stare across a river at a hillside so sunbaked that it can support only cactus and other xeriphitic plant species.

The lowlands of the Terai, perhaps because they were so sparsely populated with humans until about 30 years ago, support the greatest numbers of large mammals. Several national parks and wildlife reserves preserve the Terai's subtropical hardwood forests, dominated by mahogany-like sal trees and kapok (silk cotton) trees, and vast expanses of grasslands. Due to this diversity of habitats, the region's national parks are home to such endangered species as **Bengal tigers, leopards, clouded leopards, Indian one-horned rhinoceroses,** and wild **Asian elephants.** The Terai is also home to no fewer than four species of **deer** and three species of **antelope.** Several species of **monkeys** also live in this region. The last small herd of wild **water buffalo** in Nepal is to be found in Koshi Tappu Wildlife Reserve, and the **Indian bison** or **gaur** lives in Royal Chitwan National Park. While the **Bengal tiger** is the most feared of the animals in this region, most people here agree that it is the **sloth bear** that is the most aggressive. With their long claws, these small bears eat termites, which they get at by tearing apart large termite mounds. **Hyenas** and **wild boars** also inhabit this region. The rivers of the Terai are home to not only man-eating marsh mugger **crocodiles,** but also long-nosed fish-eating **gharial crocodiles,** and the rare Gangetic **dolphin.**

The Mabhaharat Range and the midland valleys do not support as much wildlife as does the Terai, in large part because of human habitation in this region. However, it is in this region that the greatest diversity of **bird** species is to be found. Some 500 of Nepal's more than 800 bird species have been reported in the Kathmandu Valley alone. The most conspicuous wild mammals of this region are **rhesus macaque monkeys,** which inhabit many temple compounds, where they scavenge food offerings and beg for handouts.

While the high Himalayas are not nearly as hospitable as the lower elevations of Nepal, they still manage to support a surprising number of large mammals. Among them are several hoofed mammals, including **blue sheep, ghorals, Himalayan tahrs, serows,** and **musk deer** (unusual for having tusks). Blue sheep and Himalayan tahrs both inhabit the highest alpine regions and are prey for the elusive **snow leopard.** Serows, a goat-antelope, and the goatlike ghoral both live at lower elevations. Himalayan black **bears** and **wolves** and the rare **red pandas** also live in these high mountains, but are rarely seen. Much more common are **stone martens** and common **langurs,** long-haired, long-tailed monkeys. And of course, these mountains are also home to the elusive **yeti.** While oak and pine are among the dominant tree species throughout the lower elevations of this region, at higher elevations there are firs and junipers. In the middle elevations, at around 8,000 to 10,000 feet, you'll see the huge **rhododendron** trees that produce, in spring, Nepal's national flower, the *laligurans.*

## 2 The Regions in Brief

Though most foreigners associate Nepal only with the Himalayas, its elevation varies from 29,028-foot Mount Everest to a low of only 220 feet above sea level in the southern part of the country. Between these two extremes lie two low mountain ranges and the midland valleys, which are home to the majority of the population.

**The Himalayas**    The Himalayas, the highest mountain range on earth, comprise approximately one-third of Nepal's landmass and form the country's northern border with Tibet. These mountains range in elevation from about 10,000 feet to 29,028 feet and are among the youngest mountains on earth. This sparsely populated region of the country is the destination of most trekkers and is what most people imagine when they think of Nepal. The Himalayas are further divided into the inner valleys, which are drier than the southern slopes of the mountains, and the trans-Himalayan region, which is a high desert.

**The Midlands**    Located between 3,000 and 10,000 feet above sea level, the midland of Nepal, also known as the *pahar* zone, is characterized by numerous fertile valleys and a fairly temperate climate. It is in this region that most of Nepal's major cultural developments have taken place. The **Kathmandu** and **Pokhara Valleys** are the two most populous valleys of the region, and it is here that most travelers spend the majority of their time when they are not trekking. It comes as a great surprise to most first-time visitors that the Himalayas are not visible from most of Kathmandu. Kathmandu lies in a valley surrounded by high hills. You must ascend a bit from the valley floor before more than just the tips of a few peaks become visible.

**The Mahabharat Range**    This mountain range, which rises as high as 9,000 feet (2,744m), parallels the Himalayas and is bordered on the north by the midlands and on the south by the inner Terai (duns). The mountains are still heavily forested, though the valleys are entirely under cultivation, as are many of the slopes. It is through this range that you must travel to get from Kathmandu or Pokhara to Royal Chitwan National Park, and it is in these mountains that most of the best rafting rivers are found.

**The Terai**    Extending as low as only 220 feet above sea level and comprising roughly 17% of Nepal's landmass, the Terai lies along the edge of the **Gangetic Plain.** Hot and humid for much of the year, this lowland region was once sparsely populated due to the high incidence of malaria. However, since the 1960s, when a mosquito-control program using DDT was implemented (and which is still in place), the Nepali government has turned the Terai into the country's main industrial and agricultural region. Today, this is the fastest-growing part of the country both economically and with regard to population. There are still large stands of hardwood forests here, and several national parks and preserves provide protection for the abundant wildlife, which includes Indian one-horned rhinos, Bengal tigers, leopards, wild water buffalo, and Asian bison. The Terai is further divided into two sections that are divided by the Churia Hills.

**The Churia Hills**    This range of low hills extends up to an elevation of around 3,000 feet (915m) and parallels the Indian border, forming a natural barrier between the two countries. In Royal Chitwan National Park, a densely forested tract of the Churia Hills has been preserved and is home to tigers and wild elephants.

## 3  Nepal Today

Despite what you might come to believe after thumbing through a few trekking-company catalogs, Nepal is not Shangri-la. Nor are yaks, ponies, or your own two feet the predominant means of transport here. In one form or another, Nepal has most of the supposed modern conveniences of the developed nations (sport utility vehicles, the

Internet, CNN, and Coca-Cola). It also has most of the social and environmental problems as well (overpopulation, smog, and deforestation). While close to 10% of the land has been set aside in national parks, a high birthrate is putting great pressures on the land in what has always been a primarily agricultural society. Nepal today is no Shangri-la, but it is still a fascinating and beautiful country able to claim what no other nation on earth can claim: the world's highest mountains.

Two-thirds of the country is taken up by the rugged Himalayas, and consequently, the kingdom's 22 million inhabitants live off a relatively small percentage of the landmass. In recent years, the lowlands (yes, this mountainous kingdom does have flat plains, too) have supported most of Nepal's industrial development and population growth. The sprawling cities of this region, rarely visited by foreigners, have far more in common with India than they do with the Nepal of the hills and mountains.

Despite the industrialization of the Terai, Nepal continues to bank on its vast hydroelectric potential as a means of generating foreign revenue. India is the intended customer for electricity that will be generated by various hydro projects throughout the country. These projects are now beginning to come into conflict with the Nepal's small but significant rafting industry. The same rivers that offer the highest hydroelectric potential also provide some of the best whitewater rafting in the world. The recent damming of the Kali Gandaki, near Pokhara, has shortened and potentially eliminated what previously was one of the most popular rafting rivers in the country.

Hydroelectricity aside, Nepal remains one of the poorest countries on earth, and many people are dissatisfied with the pace of economic change in Nepal. Despite the conversion within the past decade to a democratic form of government, several years of ineffectual coalition governments have left the people somewhat disenchanted with the idea of democracy. In the hills of west-central Nepal, a Maoist insurrection has been growing, with rebels targeting police and military personnel. This insurrection prompted the U.S. government, in late 1998, to prohibit its employees stationed in Kathmandu from traveling outside the capital by road. At press time, the Maoists were still active, though generally not in areas frequented by travelers or trekkers.

Since Nepal opened its borders to foreign visitors in the early 1950s, the World Wide Web has done more for tourism than anything else. Today, nearly every little hotel and trekking company seems to have e-mail and often its own Web site. Whereas mail can take weeks between Nepal and the United States or Europe and phone links can be abysmal, drop a line by e-mail and you'll likely hear back within the day. In Kathmandu and Pokhara there are now numerous e-mail centers and cybercafes where you can log on to the Internet for a few cents a minute.

In the hills, big changes continue along the main trekking routes. Roads have pushed deeper and deeper into the mountains, shortening many treks. Be sure to find out the currently recommended starting point for any trek before you set out. In the valley of the Kali Gandaki, which is the most popular trekking route in the country, nearly every village now has electricity provided by small hydroelectric projects. While this means a more comfortable life for Nepalis, it also means that powerlines are now part of the views of the Himalayas. Expect to find everything from satellite TVs to electric irons to vacuum cleaners in lodges along this route, and many larger villages now have a telephone. Despite the availability of electricity, wood continues to be the primary cooking fuel in many hill villages, and deforestation continues at an alarming rate. Along with deforestation come landslides and erosion, both of which reduce the amount of arable land.

Trekking lodges continue to get larger and more comfortable, with many now boasting rooms with private bathrooms and even Western-style sit-down toilets that sometimes really flush! The immense popularity of both Jon Krakauer's best-seller *Into Thin Air* and the IMAX Everest movie has done much to increase the popularity of trekking in the Everest region. Expect larger-than-ever crowds in the wake of all this media coverage of the world's highest peak.

Down in the lowlands of the Terai, Chitwan seems to have reached critical mass as far as the number of lodges, both inside and outside the park, is concerned. Some upgrading is going on in the village of Sauraha just outside the park, but for the most part there have been no new tourism developments here in nearly a decade. However, elsewhere in the Terai there have been some big changes. Royal Bardia National Park has seen a proliferation of lodges in recent years and is quietly becoming *the* national park to visit, especially if you want to see a tiger or wild elephants. In the far-eastern Terai, there are also now two lodges adjacent to Koshi Tappu Wildlife Reserve, which is noteworthy for being one of the best bird-watching spots in the country.

## 4  A Look at the Past

Nepal's precarious position between two of the world's political giants—India and China—has dictated its history for centuries. The early history of Nepal is inextricably interwoven with Hindu and Buddhist mythology, and consequently it is often difficult to discern what is historical fact and what is myth.

**Reality or Myth?**   There is evidence that as early as 700 B.C., people were living in the Kathmandu Valley. The two Indian epics *Ramayana* and *Mahabharata* both mention the Kirantis, who lived in the mountains north of India—an area that coincides with the Kathmandu Valley. A fifth-century inscription at Changu Narayan, a remote and little-visited, though fascinating, temple in the Kathmandu Valley, indicates that the Kiranti dynasty lasted from the eighth century B.C. to the third century A.D. The Kirantis may themselves have been descendants of an even older dynasty, the Ahirs, shepherds who supposedly were the first rulers of the Kathmandu Valley. Over the centuries, there were successive migrations into the mountains by refugees, nomads, and conquering armies from Tibet, India, and even Central Asia. Both the Ahirs and the Kirantis are likely to have migrated into the mountains as well.

**The Enlightened One**   From a global perspective, the most significant event in Nepal's history was the birth of Prince Siddhartha Gautama, around 563 B.C. in the Shakya kingdom of Kapilvastu in the lowlands of Nepal (near present-day Lumbini). Siddhartha Gautama, at age 29, renounced his claim to the throne of his kingdom and became a wandering ascetic searching for a way to end all human suffering. After wandering for 6 years and practicing all types of accepted spiritual pursuits of the time, he sat down under a *bo* (banyan or pipal) tree to meditate. During this meditation, the prince found the answer he had been seeking. From that point on, he was known as the Buddha (the Enlightened One), and within a few centuries, his doctrine had spread throughout much of India and Nepal.

In 250 B.C., the Indian emperor Ashoka, who had converted to Buddhism after conquering most of northern India, made a pilgrimage to Lumbini. There he erected a stone pillar with an inscription commemorating the birth of the Buddha. The pillar was not rediscovered until 1895, at which time its inscription led to the discovery of other ruins in the area. Recent excavations at Lumbini, now a cultural and religious park, have unearthed another inscribed stone, which might have also been left by Ashoka. Today, the Ashoka pillar is one of Lumbini's major attractions. According to legends, Ashoka continued to Kathmandu and erected four *stupas* (reliquary shrines) at the four corners of Patan, where the Buddha is said to have visited briefly. Although there is no record of either of these visits, the stupas can still be seen.

## Dateline

- **7th or 8th c. B.C.** The Kiranti settle in Kathmandu Valley.
- **563 B.C.** Prince Siddhartha Gautama born in Lumbini.
- **250 B.C.** Emperor Ashoka of India makes pilgrimage to Lumbini; visits Kathmandu Valley.
- **ca A.D. 200** Licchavi dynasty begins in Kathmandu Valley.
- **460** King Manadeva I records construction on Swayambunath Stupa and has Boudhanath Stupa erected.
- **879** End of Licchavi dynasty. Beginning of Thakuri dynasty.
- **Late 10th c.** Kathmandu founded.
- **1200** Start of Malla dynasty.
- **1346** Swayambunath Stupa destroyed.
- **Mid–17th c.** Swayambunath Stupa rebuilt.
- **1696** Temple built at Pashupatinath.
- **1769** Prithvi Narayan Shah unifies Nepal.
- **1792** Nepal loses war with Tibet.
- **1815** Nepal loses war with British.
- **1816** First British resident arrives in Kathmandu.
- **1846** Jung Bahadur Rana seizes power. Ranas rule the country until 1951.
- **1854** Nepal goes to war with Tibet.
- **1924** George Mallory disappears near the summit of Mount Everest.
- **1934** Earthquake shakes Kathmandu Valley, destroying temples and other sites.
- **1951** King Tribhuvan restored to the throne; declares Nepal a democratic country.

*continues*

From the second century to the ninth century A.D., the Kathmandu Valley was ruled by the Licchavi dynasty. Several stone inscriptions, the earliest historical records in Nepal other than the Ashokan pillar and stone at Lumbini, date from this period, and the most important of these can be seen at **Changu Narayan Temple,** mentioned above. In A.D. 460, King Manadeva of the Licchavi dynasty is said to have erected **Boudhanath Stupa** and had construction done on **Swayambunath Stupa.** Whether these projects were actually carried out by Manadeva is still a matter of speculation. What is certain, however, is that during the Licchavi period, stone carving became an accomplished art form in the Kathmandu Valley, and many statues remain from this period. Look for these at Changu Narayan, at Um Maheshwar Temple in Patan, and in the National Museum in Kathmandu.

By the end of the ninth century A.D., the Thakuri dynasty, of which little is known, had developed in the Kathmandu Valley. This dynasty left as its most important legacy the founding of the city of Kathmandu at the confluence of the Vishnumati and Bagmati Rivers.

Sometime around 1200, the first of the Malla kings came to power in the Kathmandu Valley. Under the Mallas, who ruled until the middle of the 18th century, art and, especially, architecture flourished in the Kathmandu Valley. In each of the valley's main cities—Kathmandu, Patan, and Bhaktapur—Malla kings erected grand palaces and ornate temples. Seemingly enamored of their own wealth and good taste, these kings even erected statues of themselves. These palaces, temples, and kingly statues now compose the bulk of the historic structures on the Durbar Squares of the three cities. However, as glorious as the reigns of the Malla kings were, these kings were still only the rulers of a small, albeit very important, portion of present-day Nepal.

**The Unification of Nepal**   Prior to the 18th century, Nepal was a patchwork of tiny independent kingdoms, but in 1769, Prithvi Narayan Shah conquered the tiny kingdoms of the Kathmandu Valley and completed his quest to unify Nepal. Part of his reason for uniting Nepal was to create a strong defense against the encroaching British, whom the king saw as a threat. The East India Company was firmly in control of India by this time, and British soldiers guarded the Nepal-India border. In 1767, Prithvi Narayan Shah's troops defeated a British regiment and seized a considerable number of weapons. Under the successors of Prithvi Narayan Shah, a period of expansionism ensued during the latter part of the 18th century. However, the Nepali army suffered a defeat at the hands of the Chinese in 1791 and again in 1792 after Nepal invaded Tibet.

In 1814, 39 years after the death of Prithvi Narayan, the Nepali army attempted to enlarge Nepal's borders into India. It took 2 years for the British troops to defeat them, much longer than they had anticipated. The British developed such respect for the fighting abilities of these rugged soldiers that they have recruited them ever since. The peace treaty signed with Britain at the end of this war effectively set the boundaries of present-day Nepal.

From the time of Nepal's unification, there was an ongoing struggle between the various royal families who had been conquered by Prithvi Narayan. By the middle of the 19th century, the Kathmandu Valley's Rana family had begun to wield a great deal of political influence, and in 1846, Jung Bahadur Rana seized power from the reigning king and installed himself as prime minister for life. The position of prime minister became hereditary, effectively replacing the lineage of the royal family, and members of the Rana family ruled the country for the next century. During this time the Shah royal family was left intact but did not have any power.

- **1956** Nepal joins the United Nations.
- **1959** First parliament elected; later the same year it is dissolved.
- **1962** New constitution and panchayat system of government introduced.
- **1972** King Birendra ascends the throne.
- **1990** King allows political parties and democratic elections.
- **1996** Twelve people die attempting to climb Mount Everest.
- **1998** Maoist rebels escalate small-scale insurrection in central Nepal.
- **1999** George Mallory's body discovered near the summit of Mount Everest.

Despite the remoteness and isolation of Nepal, the Ranas quickly developed relations with Europe and became infatuated with all things European. The traditional architecture of the Kathmandu Valley was abandoned in favor of European neoclassical aesthetics as the Ranas attempted to duplicate the excesses of European royalty. Today, the Kathmandu Valley is filled with dozens of palaces, mansions, and other buildings that are glaringly out of place.

**The Nationalist Movement**   During the 1930s and 1940s, there was growing discontent with the ruling Rana regime. When India gained independence in 1947, the Ranas lost the British support they had enjoyed for many years. The nationalist movement that had started in India spilled over into Nepal with the formation of the Nepali Congress party. In 1950, this party spearheaded a revolution against the Rana regime. At about the same time, the powerless King Tribhuvan Bir Bikram Shah sought refuge in India. In 1951, the Indian government helped negotiate a cease-fire, and the monarchy was restored to power with King Tribhuvan on the throne. A coalition Rana-Nepali Congress cabinet was also formed.

Over the next 8 years unsuccessful attempts were made at forming a democratic government. In 1959, a new constitution went into effect, and in that year the Nepali Congress party won the majority of the votes. King Mahendra, who had succeeded his father, King Tribhuvan, in 1955, immediately came into conflict with this popularly elected government and dissolved the cabinet in 1960. In 1962, the king introduced a new constitution and a new form of government called the *panchayat*. This system banned all political parties, prohibited organized opposition, and effectively consolidated all real power in the hands of the king by creating village and city councils that could make recommendations to the king but could not actually pass laws.

In early 1990, widespread dissatisfaction with the panchayat system, along with the initiation of the democratic process in Eastern Europe, brought about organized protests throughout Nepal. Banned political parties, with assistance from political parties of neighboring Asian countries, held a conference in Kathmandu. The result was a demand for a democratic form of government and an end to the ineffective panchayat system. Bloody protests and rioting broke out in early April 1990. These protests soon led to King Birendra Bir Bikram Shah's announcement that a new constitution would be drafted and that a multiparty democratic political system would be established, effectively changing the kingdom's system of government to a constitutional monarchy with the king as head of state.

The first elections were held in 1991, with Nepal's communist party making a strong showing. In 1994, the communist party gained a plurality of seats in parliament, and Nepal became the first post–Cold War country to elect a communist government. However, the communists did not gain the majority in the parliament and were forced to form a coalition government, which did not last. Since then several more coalition governments have come and gone, none of which has been able to govern successfully. The people of Nepal seem to be tiring of these unsuccessful attempts at democratic rule, and hopes were high at press time that general elections called for May of 1999 would finally bring to power a single party that could unify the government. However, there are others in the country—Maoist communists— who have already given up on democracy and have taken up arms. In the west central hills of Nepal, a growing Maoist insurgency threatens to undermine Nepal's newfound democratic government. This armed rebellion is currently small, and outbreaks of violence are scattered. Although the police and army have been the targets up to this point, it is worth checking with your embassy to find out the current status of the Maoist uprising before planning a trip to Nepal in upcoming years.

# 5 Art

Virtually all of Nepal's art, except for works by a handful of little-known contemporary artists, is religious in nature and expresses both Hindu and Buddhist iconography. Religious expression in art has taken the form of stone, wood, terra-cotta, and metal statuary, as well as paintings on canvas and paper. Much of this artwork is on display in temples and palaces throughout the Kathmandu Valley and other parts of the country. There are also five museums in the Kathmandu Valley devoted to the art of Nepal (one in Kathmandu, one in Patan, and three in Bhaktapur).

The oldest existing works of art in Nepal are **stone statues** dating from the first century A.D. Stone carving flourished during the period of the Licchavi dynasty. There are several fifth- and sixth-century statues and reliefs on display at the National Museum, and several others can be seen at Changu Narayan, a temple in the eastern part of the Kathmandu Valley. The massive statue of the Reclining Vishnu at Budhanilkantha, north of Kathmandu, also dates back to this period.

The Malla dynasty, which lasted from 1200 to 1769, witnessed a flowering of the arts, primarily in the 17th and 18th centuries. **Sculptures** of Buddhist and Hindu deities in bronze, wood, and terra-cotta from this period are on display at the National Museum. **Repoussé,** a style of metalworking in which sheets of brass or gilded copper are beaten into relief designs, reached a peak during the Malla period and is best represented by the Golden Gate in Patan. Arguably the most famous works of art in Nepal are the **erotic roof struts** on many of the country's pagoda temples. These carved wooden struts display men, women, and animals in various graphically erotic poses.

*Thangkas,* painted scrolls used by Buddhist monks for meditation and religious ceremonies, are another art form that has become popular. These colorful scrolls, often minutely detailed, depict Buddhist deities, the Buddhist wheel of life (depicting life on earth, in heaven, and in the realms of hell), and various aspects of Tibetan medicine. The National Museum, the National Art Gallery, and the Patan Museum all have collections of thangkas. In Kathmandu, Patan, and Bhaktapur, there are also thangka galleries and studios where you can see artists at work. You may notice that the currently popular styles differ somewhat from the style of the 18th- and 19th-century thangkas in the valley's museums.

The **decorative arts** have long been a part of Nepali culture, and almost no household item went undecorated until the recent advent of plastic and mass production. Water pots, vases, and pitchers, traditionally made of brass and copper, were often decorated with simple patterns. The Brass and Bronze Museum in Bhaktapur has a representative collection of such items. **Wood carving,** which was centered in Bhaktapur, was used on everything from butter churns and knife scabbards to windows and door frames. Today, the roof struts and windows of the Malla period are among the main tourist attractions of the Kathmandu Valley. The peacock window on Bhaktapur's Pujari Math, a former Hindu priests' home and now the National Woodcarving Museum, is considered the finest example of the wood-carver's art, though the windows on the Kumari Bahal on Kathmandu's Durbar Square are even more beautiful.

One unusual form of folk art still practiced today is the painting of bicycle rickshaws, trucks, and buses with colorful designs and sometimes even landscapes. Keep your eyes open for such rolling artwork as you walk the streets of Kathmandu.

## 6  Architecture

Art and architecture overlap in Nepal, where temples and palaces are decorated with intricately carved windows, sculptural roof struts, and repoussé metalwork facades. The red brick and dark hardwood construction of densely packed neighborhoods has led many Western visitors to compare the cities of the Kathmandu Valley to medieval European cities. This architectural style is characteristic of the Newars, the ethnic group that has traditionally lived in the Kathmandu Valley. **Newari architecture** is Nepal's most distinctive architectural style. The rosy glow of pink brick homes dotting the terraced fields of the Kathmandu Valley at sunset is one of the valley's most memorable images, especially when seen from a plane.

Newari architecture reached its zenith under the Malla kings in the 17th and 18th centuries, and it is from this period that most of the Kathmandu Valley's most important buildings date. Since palace architecture was based on standard home styles, with one or more courtyards, it was in temple architecture that Newari architects experimented. **Temple architecture** in Nepal embraces a number of styles, though the most notable and beautiful is the **pagoda** style. Nepali tradition holds that pagoda architecture originated in Nepal. The style was later copied in Lhasa, Tibet, from where it made its way to China. Pagodas in Nepal have between one and five roofs, though there are only three pagodas in the Kathmandu Valley with five roofs. The Nyatapola Temple in Bhaktapur, a five-roofed temple atop a five-tiered pyramid base, is considered the most beautiful, symmetric, and graceful temple in Nepal. The Basantapur tower, within the Hanuman Dhoka Palace on Kathmandu's Durbar Square, is the only pagoda that can be climbed, and in fact not all pagodas have floors that correspond to their many roofs.

Most pagodas and buildings are constructed from brick, which, until recently, was the most common building material in the middle elevations of Nepal. However, a few temples are built in the *shikhara* style of architecture from northern India. These temples are usually plastered and whitewashed or made of stone. The Mahaboudha Temple in Patan is the most ornate shikhara-style temple in the Kathmandu Valley.

Two of Nepal's most important architectural constructions are the stupas of Swayambunath and Boudhanath. *Stupas* are large hemispherical mounds that represent the Buddha and his teachings. In some ways they resemble the pyramids of Egypt or pre-Columbian America, though they have never been used as tombs. Smaller stupas credited to Indian emperor Ashoka stand at the four corners of Patan. *Chaityas,* much smaller than stupas, are small spire-shaped shrines often found in courtyards in Buddhist neighborhoods of the Kathmandu Valley. *Chortens,* which are found in the Buddhist villages of the high mountains, are similar to chaityas, though they are usually a bit larger and are erected not in courtyards but at important religious sites.

Over the centuries, major earthquakes have repeatedly hit the Kathmandu Valley. In 1934, a devastating quake razed most of the temples and palaces in the valley. Since then, most, but not all, of the valley's damaged historic buildings have been reconstructed. However, the reconstruction did not always exactly duplicate the original architecture, as is the case with the Mahaboudha Temple in Patan. When reconstruction of this temple was completed, there were enough of the original bricks left over to build another small temple immediately adjacent to the main temple. The Bhaktapur Development Project, a German-funded program, has restored more than 100 buildings in Bhaktapur, making this city a showcase of Newari architecture. In Panauti, a small town in the southeast corner of the Kathmandu Valley, a joint French-Nepali project has been busy restoring an extensive temple complex.

Though Newari architecture predominates in the Kathmandu Valley, styles vary outside the valley. In the lowlands of the Terai, the Tharu people build their huts almost exclusively with grasses, using a mixture of mud and cow dung to seal the walls. In the high elevations of Solu-Khumbu, home of the Sherpas, most homes are built of stone; even the roofs are made of slate. This ethnologic architectural diversity is one of the reasons that a trek through the hills and mountains of Nepal is so fascinating.

A footnote worth mention is the construction of dozens of European-style neoclassical palaces and residences in Kathmandu during the late 19th and early 20th centuries. Examples include the Gaddi Baithak on Kathmandu's Durbar Square, the Shanker Hotel, the old wing of the Hotel Yak & Yeti, the recently restored Baber Mahal Revisited shopping center, the minaret-like Bhimsen Tower near the Kathmandu General Post Office, and even the Kathmandu Guest House. These buildings were constructed during the Rana regime when members of the Rana family traveled to Europe and became infatuated with what they saw. Nepal's coffers were emptied to erect these stuccoed, pilastered, and shuttered excesses, and today these buildings are nearly as interesting as the more traditional Newari temples and palaces.

## 7  Nepal: Asia's Religious Crossroads

With nearly 90% of the population claiming to be Hindu, Nepal calls itself the world's only Hindu kingdom. However, in Nepal there is a fine line between Hinduism and Buddhism. Many temples and shrines that are ostensibly dedicated to Hindu deities are frequented by Buddhists as well. Overlapping both of these religions is Tantrism, which in the West is often misconstrued as a religion based on sex. Tantrism is a set of prescribed formulas calling on physical and moral precepts such as meditation, yoga, and magic formulas to understand the interconnectedness of all spiritual and physical existence. It is Tantrism that has given Nepal many of its more frightening deities such as Bhairav and Kali.

## HINDUISM

Hinduism is a polytheistic religion that had its origins between 4,000 and 5,000 years ago in northern India. It is based primarily on moral codes published thousands of years ago in the *Vedas*, as well as precepts set forth in other ancient books such as the *Puranas, Upanishads, Bhagavad Gita,* and *Ramayana.* At the heart of Hindu beliefs are three major gods: Brahma (the creator), Vishnu (the preserver), and Shiva (the destroyer). With less power, but often of more personal significance for individuals, are the thousands of (some say one million) lesser gods.

Most Westerners find Hinduism confusing because of this plethora of gods. What causes much of the confusion is that many gods are worshiped in different incarnations (avatars). These different incarnations represent different valuable attributes, as do most Hindu gods. To further confuse matters, each god has his consort and vehicle (animal or being) upon which he travels.

With thousands of gods to choose from, it is not surprising that Hinduism has divided into numerous sects that focus on specific gods. The largest sects in Nepal are the Shaivites (followers of Shiva), Vaishnites (followers of Vishnu), Shaktas (followers of Shakti), and Ganpatyas (followers of Ganesh).

**Shiva**    In Nepal, Shiva is the most revered Hindu god, and he is most commonly worshiped in the form of the Shiva lingam, a phallic symbol that is usually displayed atop a base called a yoni, which is symbolic of female genitals. Shiva lingams sometimes have four or even five faces on them. Nepal's most famous Shiva lingam, which has five faces on it, is at Pashupatinath Temple in Kathmandu. Pashupati, the lord of the animals, is an incarnation of Shiva. Another of Shiva's incarnations, Natraj, also called the dancing Shiva, is rarely depicted in Nepal. More often, however, Shiva appears in his terrifying aspect as Bhairav. There are several famous images of Bhairav in Kathmandu, including the Kal Bhairav and Seto Bhairav of Hanuman Dhoka Square and the Akash Bhairav in Indrachowk. Parvati is Shiva's consort, and Nandi the bull is his vehicle. A statue of Nandi stands in front of nearly every temple containing a Shiva lingam.

The cult of Shiva is one of the largest Hindu cults, and wandering Shaivite ascetics known as sadhus are a common sight around Pashupatinath Temple. During the annual festival commemorating Shiva's birthday, pilgrims from all over Nepal and

### The Caste System

The caste system, though now officially illegal in Nepal, has been an integral part of Hinduism since its inception. This class system divides society into very rigid strata based on the types of work performed by members of the caste. Under Brahmanic law, there are four basic castes. **Brahmans** are the priest caste, **Chhetris** the warrior caste, **Vaisyas** the merchants and artisans, and **Sudras** the farmers. Formerly it was impossible for a person from a lower class to aspire to a job reserved for people of a higher class. Thus, members of society were kept in their places. Today, even though the caste system is not as rigid as it once was, people of lower castes are rarely able to improve their socioeconomic status due to the deeply ingrained restrictions of the system.

India visit Pashupatinath. Among these pilgrims are many holy men who paint themselves with ashes, perform yogic feats, and sleep on beds of nails. Shaivite sadhus can be recognized by the trident they carry, a symbol of Shiva.

**Vishnu**   Vishnu (also called Narayan in Nepal) has appeared on earth in nine incarnations (and is predicted to return again in a 10th incarnation). These include Krishna (well-known in the West because of his followers, who are commonly called Hare Krishnas); Narsimha (half-man and half-lion); Rama (hero of the epic *Ramayana*); the Buddha (there is frequent overlap of Buddhism and Hinduism in Nepal); Matsya (a fish that saved a famous holy man from a flood); Varaha (a boar that defeated the demon Hiranyaksha); Kurma (a turtle that whipped the ocean into nectar for the gods); Vamana (a dwarf who overcame the demon Bali); and Parashurama (a brahman who defeated warriors). Vishnu is often depicted with four arms, which hold a conch shell, a wheel, a club, and a lotus bud. Changu Narayan and Budhanilkantha, both in the Kathmandu Valley, are the two holiest Vishnu shrines in Nepal. The king of Nepal is also said to be an incarnation of Vishnu.

Vishnu's consort is Laxmi, who is worshiped as the goddess of wealth in Nepal. Each year on Deepawali during the Tihar festival, usually held in October, Nepalis put candles in their doorways and windows to light the way to the family money box for Laxmi, who visits earth on that day. Vishnu's vehicle is the half-man, half-bird Garuda, who is often seen kneeling in front of temples dedicated to Vishnu.

**Ganesh**   Ganesh, the elephant-headed god of wisdom and good fortune, is the son of Shiva and Parvati. According to tradition, Ganesh was born a normal child while his father was away on a long journey. When Shiva returned, he suspected his wife of infidelity and chopped off Ganesh's head with such force that he was unable to find it. When Parvati told him Ganesh was his son, Shiva took the head of the first animal he spotted and affixed it to the body of his child. This figure is one of the most commonly worshiped gods in Nepal because he is credited with removing obstacles and protecting people on journeys. In the belief that Ganesh will intercede on their behalf, people even visit Ganesh shrines before going to worship other gods. Ganesh shrines seem to be everywhere in Kathmandu, though the one most revered is behind the Kasthamandap building just off Durbar Square.

**Parvati**   Shiva's consort has developed her own following of worshipers. She is depicted in both benevolent and wrathful incarnations, though the terrifying incarnation as Durga or Kali is much more common. The Dakshinkali Temple just outside the Kathmandu Valley is known for the animal sacrifices that are regularly performed there. The annual Dasain festival is dedicated to Parvati's terrifying attributes, and during the festival, many goats and water buffalo are sacrificed.

**Hanuman**   In the Indian epic *Ramayana,* when Rama's wife, Sita, is kidnapped, Hanuman the monkey king plays an important role in rescuing her from the evil Ravana and is seen as an ever-faithful servant. A statue of Hanuman guards the old royal palace on Kathmandu's Durbar Square and even lends its name to the palace and square, which are both called Hanuman Dhoka (gate). Over the years people worshiping this statue have smeared it with red paste so that it is no longer recognizable as Hanuman. (Smearing red powder or paste is a standard form of showing respect or worshiping a deity.)

## BUDDHISM

Buddhism had its beginnings in southern Nepal and northern India about 2,500 years ago. It is based on the teachings of the Buddha, who was born Prince Siddhartha Gautama in present-day Lumbini, Nepal, around 563 B.C. The prince led a very sheltered life until he was 29 years old, when he saw for the first time the suffering of old age and death. The sight of so much suffering deeply affected him, and he left his wife and family to become a wandering ascetic searching for a way to end all suffering. For 6 years the prince wandered, studying every contemporary religion and spiritual discipline without success. On the verge of giving up, he sat beneath a bo tree and, during meditation, discovered the way to end suffering. From this time on he was called the Buddha, "The Enlightened One."

His realizations became known as the four noble truths and the eightfold path to enlightenment. The four noble truths are that life is full of pain and suffering, pain and suffering is caused by desires and attachments, there is a way to end pain and suffering, and the way to end pain and suffering is through the eightfold path of Buddhism. The eightfold path consists of the right views, right intent, right speech, right conduct, right livelihood, right effort, right mindfulness, and right meditation.

Today, Buddhism is divided into two main schools, called Hinayana or Theravada and Mahayana. Hinayana Buddhism adheres more closely to the original teachings of the Buddha and emphasizes the quest for personal enlightenment (nirvana). Mahayana, on the other hand, emphasizes the individual's responsibility to help others to achieve nirvana. A person who follows this path becomes a *bodhisattva,* an enlightened being who remains on earth to help others achieve nirvana. Mahayana Buddhism is the type followed by most Nepalis. Tibetan Buddhism is a form of Mahayana Buddhism, whose spiritual leader is the Dalai Lama. Tibetan Buddhism is a synthesis of Buddhism and an older Tibetan religion called Bon. There are four major Tibetan Buddhist sects: Gelugpa, Nyingmapa, Kargyupa, and Sakyapa. All four sects are represented in Nepal by various monasteries, with the greatest concentration of monasteries in the vicinity of Boudhanath Stupa near Kathmandu. Tibetan Buddhism is also known as Vajrayana Buddhism and Lamaism. Among Nepal's ethnic groups that profess Buddhism as their faith are the Tamangs, Gurungs, Newars, and Sherpas.

## 8  The Many Faces of Nepal

Nepal, a natural barrier between two giant countries—China to the north and India to the south—is a meeting point of races. From India came the Indo-Aryan or Caucasoid peoples, and from Tibet came Mongoloid or Tibeto-Burman peoples. Consequently, the ethnic makeup in Nepal is as varied as the geography, and the cultural and social life is complex and diverse. There are 35 distinct ethnic groups and castes, each with its own specific customs. These groups are primarily differentiated by dialect, geography, religion, and dress. The people of Nepal can be divided into three main categories: Hindu castes, ethnic groups of the lowlands and middle hills, and northern border people. The Hindu castes are Indo-Aryan, while the border peoples—Sherpas, Bhotiyas, and Tamangs—are purely Tibeto-Burman. The Newars, Rais, Limbus, Gurungs, and Magars, who inhabit the middle hills, are a mixture of the two races.

The Brahmans and Chhetris, high Hindu castes, tend to dominate politics. Brahmans have traditionally been the priests of Hindu society and can be recognized by the long thread they wear over their left shoulder. Chhetris are the warrior class. Both the royal family and the Ranas, who ruled Nepal for more than a hundred years, are of the Chhetri caste.

The ethnic groups of the middle hills predate the Hindu castes, who migrated north from the plains of India. These groups inhabit different regions of the middle hills, and within a single region they may live at different elevations. The Newars live primarily in the Kathmandu Valley. Much of the art and architecture that is identified as Nepali is more specifically Newari. The Gurungs inhabit the higher hills of central Nepal near Pokhara. They are primarily farmers and shepherds, and they practice both Hinduism and Buddhism, depending on where they live. Many Gurkha soldiers are Gurungs. The Magars, primarily Hindus, follow a similar lifestyle, farming the lower hills of the same parts of central Nepal. The Thakalis, who are Buddhists, live almost exclusively in the Thak Khola Valley near the upper reaches of the Kali Gandaki River, which flows down from Tibet. Though they once controlled the salt trade with Tibet, they are now international traders and innkeepers. The Rais and Limbus live in eastern Nepal, where they practice a mixture of Buddhism and Hinduism. The Tamangs are a primarily Buddhist ethnic group from the hills near Kathmandu. Today, many of them work as porters.

A number of ethnic groups live in the lowland Terai region, the largest of which is the Tharu people. The Tharus are an aboriginal people who are subsistence farmers and who practice an animist religion with Hindu influences. The people in villages surrounding Chitwan National Park are Tharus. In the eastern Terai there are several more distinct ethnic groups, though their numbers are much smaller than those of the Tharus. There are also a few Muslims living along the Indian border.

In the high mountains of the northern border region live the Sherpas and the Bhotiyas, people of Tibetan stock who practice Buddhism. Sherpas inhabit the Solu-Khumbu region and have become associated with mountaineering and trekking in Nepal. Since the first Western expeditions set out to climb Mount Everest, Sherpas have led the way, carried the loads, cooked the food, and often climbed side by side with famous mountaineers. Sherpas and Bhotiyas are primarily shepherds and farmers who survive in a harsh environment where a single crop of potatoes or barley is grown by irrigating rocky fields. The term "Bhotiya" means "people of Tibet" and is used to describe both the native ethnic groups and more recent Tibetan immigrants.

Buddhism, Hinduism, and a synthesis of the two religions dictate much of the cultural and social life in Nepal. Almost nothing is done without first making an

## The Yeti

Among the world's best loved and most persistent legends is that of the yeti— the abominable snowman. The latter term for these beasts comes from a British report in the late 1800s that referred to the "abominably smelling man of the snows," a loose translation of the Sherpa term for a yeti. Is the yeti fact or fiction? In the absence of a live specimen or verifiable remains of a yeti, no one is sure.

Stories of the yeti originated in the Solu-Khumbu region near Mount Everest. This area is home to the Sherpa people, who have frequently reported seeing or hearing yetis. Though the Sherpas have no doubt about the existence of the human-like animal, scientists are very skeptical. As recently as the mid-1970s, a Sherpa woman was reportedly attacked by a yeti, and several yaks were said to have been killed by a yeti in a separate incident. Several yeti expeditions have been mounted since the 1960s, including one led by Sir Edmund Hillary. These expeditions did not turn up anything more than questionable footprints. Supposed yeti relics—scalps and a skeleton of a hand—at a pair of monasteries in the Khumbu region were declared to be fakes after analysis by Western authorities, but nonetheless, some of these were stolen in 1991. Today, the legend of the yeti lives on.

offering to the appropriate god, and throughout the year religious celebrations and festivals are held to honor the various gods. Several Hindu festivals include animal sacrifices, and though to Westerners these sacrifices seem a bit barbaric, for many Nepali families such an occasion is one of the few times a year when there is meat on the table.

Among all ethnic groups and religions, arranged marriages are still the norm in Nepal. Marriages may be arranged as early as birth (sometimes even earlier), though it is more common to make the arrangements when the boy and girl are in their teens. Polygamy, though officially illegal, is still practiced by some groups. Polyandry, the taking of more than one husband (usually brothers) by a woman, is also still practiced by some people of the northern border regions. This tradition originated among the Tibetan peoples because men were often gone for many months on trading expeditions.

## 9  Recommended Books & Films

### BOOKS

For such a small country, Nepal has been the subject of a surprising number of books. Many of the titles listed here either are not available or are difficult to find in the United States and England. However, they are generally widely available in bookshops in Kathmandu and Pokhara.

**Mountaineering & Trekking**    *Into Thin Air* (Anchor Books, 1998) by Jon Krakauer. This immensely popular best-seller provides a heart-wrenching account of the tragic events that took place on Mount Everest in the spring of 1996. A dozen people died that year in the worst Everest climbing season on record. *The Climb: Tragic Ambitions on Everest* (St. Martin's, 1998) by Anatoli Boukreev and G. Weston Dewalt. Also on Mount Everest in the spring of 1996, Boukreev provides his own account of the tragedy.

*Annapurna* (The Lyons Press, 1997) by Maurice Herzog. Written by one of the world's most renowned climbers, this is an account of the first ascent of Annapurna I, which was the first 8,000-meter (26,000-ft) peak to be scaled. The book is very readable and provides excellent background on the Annapurna region. Incidentally, this expedition was mounted from the north side of the peak, not from Annapurna base camp in the Annapurna Sanctuary.

*The Seven Mountain-Travel Books* (Mountaineers Books, 1991) by H. W. Tilman. In the late 1940s and early 1950s, H. W. Tilman, Nepal's first trekker, explored the hills and mountains of Nepal. This is a reprinted version of Tilman's account of his exploration.

**Trekking & Rafting Guides**    *Trekking in the Nepal Himalaya* (Lonely Planet, 1997) by Stan Armington. Compact and concise, this is an easy-to-follow guidebook for independent trekkers doing teahouse treks. All the major trekking routes are covered by Armington, who has operated his own trekking company since 1971.

*A Guide to Trekking in Nepal* (Mountaineers Books, 1997) by Stephen Bezruchka. For many years this has been the definitive trekker's handbook. This extremely detailed book's only fault is that the trekking times listed are much faster than most independent trekkers tend to hike. Bezruchka is a doctor, and the health-care chapter of this book is particularly thorough.

*Trekking in the Everest Region* (Trailblazer Publications, 1998) by Jamie McGuinness. If you're heading only to the Everest region and don't want to carry a trekking guide to the whole country, this is a good book to use. Detailed area maps.

*Trekking in the Annapurna Region* (Trailblazer Publications, 1996) by Bryn Thomas. Likewise, this book is a good choice for anyone heading only to the Annapurna region. Detailed area maps.

*Trekking Peaks of Nepal* (Mountaineers Books, 1998) by Bill O'Connor. If you have already done a few treks in Nepal and are looking for something more challenging, pick up a copy of this book, which provides route descriptions for most of Nepal's trekking peaks—mountains that can be scaled with a minimum of equipment.

*White Water Nepal* (Menasha Ridge Press, 1997) by Peter Knowles and David Allardice. Anyone serious about rafting or kayaking in Nepal should check out this book, which is full of detailed descriptions of Nepal's rivers and also includes all the information you'll need to mount your own paddling expedition.

**Travelogues, Essays & General Nonfiction**　*Travelers' Tales Nepal* (Traveler's Tales Guides, 1997) edited by Rajendra S. Khadka. With essays by Jimmy Carter, Stan Armington, Jan Morris, Jeff Greenwald, and dozens of other people who have spent time in Nepal, this book offers excellent background reading for anyone preparing for a trip to Nepal. The essays reflect a wide spectrum of experiences that give the reader some idea of what to expect from this unpredictable country.

*The Snow Leopard* (Penguin Books, 1996) by Peter Matthiessen. This book combines science, religion, and philosophy in an extremely readable work. Matthiessen here writes of his trip with George Schaller to the Dolpo region of Nepal. Matthiessen's search for the elusive snow leopard parallels his own search for spiritual fulfillment.

*Shopping for Buddhas* (Lonely Planet, 1996) by Jeff Greenwald. The quest for the perfect Buddha statue becomes an obsession with Greenwald in a travelogue that uses shopping as a metaphor for the spiritual quest that brings many travelers to Nepal.

*The Violet Shyness of Their Eyes: Notes from Nepal* (Calyx Books, 1993) by Barbara J. Scott. This book gives a woman's perspective on life and travel in Nepal. Scott's book is based on a year she spent living and working in Nepal.

*Nepali Aama: Life Lessons of a Himalayan Woman* (Anchor Books, 1995) by Broughton Coburn. Originally published in 1982, this book is about the relationship between Coburn, a Peace Corps volunteer in the 1970s, and his Nepali *aama* (mother), who looked after him when he lived in a loft above her water buffalo shed. Coburn also wrote *Aama in America: A Pilgrimage of the Heart* (Anchor Books, 1995). Years after his stint as a Peace Corps volunteer, Coburn brought his aama to the United States to share his country with her. This book chronicles their travels across America.

*Video Night in Kathmandu* (Vintage, 1989) by Pico Iyer. In the title essay from his insightful and incisive collection of essays, Iyer cuts through the surface of Kathmandu's mysterious image to find that Nepalis are crazy about Rambo and that the drugged-out hippies of the 1960s have been replaced by trekking yuppies. A bit dated but still fun. Iyer also wrote *Tropical Classical* (Vintage Departures, 1998), which is a collection of essays including a lone piece set in Nepal. This essay focuses on experiences surrounding the filming of Bernardo Bertolucci's movie *Little Buddha*.

*Himalayan Odyssey* (Laurel Books, 1990) by Parker Antin and Phyllis Wachob Weiss. This is an account of a 6-month trek through remote sections of west Nepal that, at the time, were off-limits to trekkers. Antin's trek was filled with mishaps and misadventures. Hopefully your own trek will not be like his.

**Natural History**　*Stones of Silence* (University of Chicago Press, 1988) by George Schaller. On the same trip on which Peter Matthiessen based his book *The Snow Leopard*, George Schaller was busy studying the rare blue sheep. His studies of the blue sheep, which are actually not sheep but goat-antelopes, culminated in this, his own account of the trip to Dolpo.

*Vanishing Tracks* (Arbor House/William Morrow, 1989) by Darla Hillard. If you are inspired to learn more about snow leopards after reading Matthiessen's book, then try this account of Hillard's 4 years studying snow leopards in the more remote reaches of Nepal.

*Mammoth Hunt: In Search of the Giant Elephants of Nepal* (Harper Collins, 1997) by John Blashford-Snell and Rula Lenska. Pursuing reports of a giant bull elephant in the far western corner of Nepal, explorer Blashford-Snell went in search of what turned out to be the largest Asian elephant on earth. Also made into a documentary.

**Religion**    *Himalayan Pantheon, A Guide to the Gods and Goddesses of Nepal* (Book Faith India, 1998) by Daniel B. Haber. This booklet, available in Kathmandu, though not exactly thorough, is a concise and readable introduction to the often inscrutable iconography of Nepal.

*Short Description of Gods, Goddesses and Ritual Objects of Buddhism and Hinduism in Nepal* (Handicraft Association of Nepal). This is an indispensable illustrated guide to the myriad religious iconography the visitor will encounter in Nepal. You'll find this book in most Kathmandu bookshops. Make it one of your first purchases when you arrive. You'll get much more out of your trip.

*The Festivals of Nepal* (Calcutta: Rupa & Co., 1988) by Mary Anderson. Hardly a day passes in Nepal without some festival being celebrated somewhere in the country. This book will help you to understand these sometimes-bizarre, often-baffling celebrations.

**Coffee-Table Books**    *Caravans of the Himalaya* (National Geographic Society, 1994) by Eric Valli and Diane Summers. This beautifully photographed book chronicles the caravans of the remote Dolpo region to the north of the Annapurna region.

*Honey Hunters of Nepal* (Harry N. Abrams, 1988) by Eric Valli and Diane Summers. This book documents Nepal's daring honey hunters who scale cliffs with homemade ropes to collect the large honeycombs of wild bees.

*Kathmandu, The Forbidden Valley* (Time Books International, 1990). Of the many coffee-table books about Nepal, this is the most beautiful. Stunning photos and plenty of historical and cultural information make this book a good memento of a trip to Nepal.

**Fiction**    *Lost Horizon* (Pocket Books) by James Hilton. Though it is not specifically about Nepal, this novel is inextricably interwoven with Western images of Nepal. The tale of a tranquil Himalayan valley is an endearing classic.

*Escape from Kathmandu* (Unwin Paperbacks, 1990) by Kim Stanley Robinson. This is a lighthearted romp through modern-day Nepal. Fun reading on a trek.

## FILMS

The most important film to be shot in Nepal in recent years has been the Everest IMAX film, which was made during the ill-fated 1996 spring climbing season. This documentary about climbing Mount Everest is about as close as you can get to feeling like you have actually been there.

Bernardo Bertolucci's *Little Buddha* tells the story of both the Buddha's life and the contemporary search for a reincarnate Tibetan lama. Filmed partly on location in the Kathmandu Valley, it includes many scenes shot in the city of Bhaktapur. Several other films in recent years have also focused on Tibetan Buddhism, including *Seven Years in Tibet* (which was actually filmed in South America) and *Kundun*. James Hilton's novel *Lost Horizon* has been filmed twice, though the original version made in 1937 is infinitely better than the musical remake of 1973.

# 3

# Planning a Trip to Nepal

Planning a trip to Nepal is not as easy as planning a vacation in Hawaii or Europe. Nepal is one of the most distant destinations on earth if you are starting your trip from North America, and it takes almost 2 days just to get there. A trip to this Himalayan kingdom requires a great deal of advance planning. You should set aside plenty of time to make all the necessary arrangements to ensure your journey is as enjoyable as possible.

When should I go? How do I get there? What do I need to pack? Where should I stay? What kind of restaurants are there? What should I see? These are some of the questions that this chapter will answer. It will also answer equally important questions about immunizations and visas. Planning a trip can be exciting, especially a journey to somewhere as remote as Nepal. By reading through this chapter, you will be better prepared for Nepal—and hopefully have a much easier trip.

## 1 Visitor Information & Entry Requirements

### VISITOR INFORMATION

The Nepali government does not maintain any foreign visitor information centers, and getting any useful information from the visitor bureau in Nepal is unlikely. Your best bet for information before leaving home will be this book and the Internet. The World Wide Web has been a real boon for the Nepal tourism industry, and because this country has long been a passionate subject for people who have traveled here, there are also lots of specialty sites that focus on travel to Nepal. Post a question about Nepal at some of these sites, and you're likely to get dozens of responses from people who have recently returned.

Internet sites with useful information on Nepal include the following:

**www.travel-nepal.com** (lots of Nepal links)
**www.webnepal.com** (general info and Nepal links)
**www.south-asia.com** (general information and news, lots of links)
**www.visitnepal.com** (hotel and restaurant information)
**www.info-nepal.com** (general information and news)
**www.catmando.com** (lots of good general information)
**travel.state.gov/nepal.html** (U.S. Department of State site for travel warnings and current travel conditions)

The **Himalayan Explorers Club,** P.O. Box 3665, Boulder, CO 80307 (☎ **303/ 494-9656;** fax 303/494-8822; e-mail: www.hec.org), is another good source of information on Nepal. The club sends out both printed and online newsletters full of current information on Nepal, offers various travel and accommodations discounts, and operates a clubhouse in Kathmandu. Club membership is $30 a year.

You could also take a look at some of the books listed under "Recommended Books & Films" in chapter 2 (see page 27). Other possible sources of information are some of the adventure-travel companies listed under "The Active Vacation Planner," in this chapter. These companies will be happy to send you information on their trips to Nepal, and from their brochures, you may be able to cull a bit of useful information— you'll certainly get a good idea of what the country looks like.

Another possibility is to contact the nearest Nepali embassy and ask whether they have any brochures available, but don't count on it. In the United States, the **Nepali embassy** is located at 2131 Leroy Place NW, Washington, DC 20008 (☎ **202/ 667-4550** or 202/667-4552; fax 202/667-5534; e-mail: nepali@erols.com); in the United Kingdom, the embassy is at 12A Kensington Palace Gardens, London W8 4QU (☎ **171/229-1594** or 171/229-6231; fax 171/792-9861).

Your local library is another good source of information. There are frequent articles about Nepal in travel magazines and travel sections of newspapers. Check back issues or look in the *Readers' Guide to Periodical Literature.*

## ENTRY REQUIREMENTS
### DOCUMENTS

**Passport**    All foreign nationals, with the exception of Indian nationals, need a valid **passport** (check its expiration date). Safeguard your passport in an inconspicuous, inaccessible place like a money belt. If you lose it, visit the nearest consulate of your native country as soon as possible for a replacement. Passport applications are downloadable from the Internet sites listed below.

**For Residents of the United States**    If you're applying for a first-time passport, you need to do it in person at one of 13 passport offices throughout the United States; a federal, state, or probate court; or a major post office (though not all post offices accept applications; call the number below to find the ones that do). You need to present a certified birth certificate as proof of citizenship, and it's wise to bring along your driver's license, state or military ID, and Social Security card as well. You also need two identical passport-sized photos (2 in. by 2 in.), taken at any corner photo shop (not one of the strip photos, however, from a photo vending machine).

For people over 15, a passport is valid for 10 years and costs $60 ($45 plus a $15 handling fee); for those 15 and under, it's valid for 5 years and costs $40. If you're over 15 and have a valid passport that was issued within the past 12 years, you can renew it by mail and bypass the $15 handling fee. Allow plenty of time before your trip to apply; processing normally takes 3 weeks but can take longer during busy periods (especially spring). For general information, call the **National Passport Agency** (☎ 202/647-0518). To find your regional passport office, call the **National Passport Information Center** (☎ 900/225-5674; http://travel.state.gov).

**For Residents of Canada**    You can pick up a passport application at one of 28 regional passport offices or most travel agencies. The passport is valid for 5 years and costs $60. Children under 16 may be included on a parent's passport but need their own to travel unaccompanied by the parent. Applications, which must be accompanied by two identical passport-sized photographs and proof of Canadian citizenship, are available at travel agencies throughout Canada or from the central **Passport Office, Department of Foreign Affairs and International Trade,** Ottawa, ON K1A 0G3 (☎ **800/567-6868;** www.dfait-maeci.gc.ca/passport). Processing takes 5 to 10 days if you apply in person, or about 3 weeks by mail.

**For Residents of the United Kingdom**   As a member of the European Union, you need only an identity card, not a passport, to travel to other EU countries. However, you *will* need a passport to enter Nepal. To pick up an application for a regular 10-year passport (the Visitor's Passport has been abolished), visit your nearest passport office, major post office, or travel agency. You can also contact the London Passport Office at ☎ **0171/271-3000** or search its Web site at www.open.gov.uk/ukpass/ukpass. htm. Passports are £21 for adults and £11 for children under 16.

**For Residents of Ireland**   You can apply for a 10-year passport, costing IR£45, at the Passport Office, Setanta Centre, Molesworth Street, Dublin 2 (☎ **01/671-1633;** www.irlgov.ie/iveagh/foreignaffairs/services). Those under age 18 and over 65 must apply for a IR£10 3-year passport. You can also apply at 1A South Mall, Cork (☎ **021/ 272-525**), or over the counter at most main post offices.

**For Residents of Australia**   Apply at your local post office or passport office, or search the government Web site at www.dfat.gov.au/passports/. Passports for adults are A$126 and for those under 18 are A$63.

**For Residents of New Zealand**   You can pick up a passport application at any travel agency or Link Centre. For more info, contact the Passport Office, P.O. Box 805, Wellington (☎ **0800/225-050**). Passports for adults are NZ$80 and for those under 16 are NZ$40.

**Visa**   It is necessary to have a visa to visit Nepal. To obtain a visa you must present your passport; two passport-size photos; a completed visa application form; and $15 for a 15-day visa, $25 for a 30-day visa, $40 for a 30-day double-entry visa, or $60 for a 60-day multiple-entry visa. A visa obtained in this way must be used within 6 months. If you do not happen to live near a Nepali embassy or consulate, first write and request a copy of the visa application form, and then send this, your passport, and your two passport-size photos via registered mail with a self-addressed, stamped envelope for the return of the passport. On the Internet, you can download a visa application form at **www.undp.org/missions/nepal/visa_app.htm.** Visas generally take from 1 to 2 weeks, depending on the type of mail used.

The following are Nepali embassies and missions that can provide visas:

**In the United States:** 2131 Leroy Place NW, Washington, DC 20008 (☎ **202/ 667-4550** or 202/667-4552; fax 202/667-5534; e-mail: nepali@erols.com).

**In the United Kingdom:** 12A Kensington Palace Gardens, London W8 4QU (☎ **171/229-1594** or 171/229-6231; fax 171/792-9861).

**At the United Nations:** 820 Second Ave., 17th Floor, New York, NY 10017 (☎ **212/ 370-3988**).

The following are Nepali honorary consulates general that provide information, visa applications, and visas:

**In Canada:** 310 Duport St., Toronto, ON M5R 1V9 (☎ **416/865-0210**).

**In Australia:** Level 13, 92 Pitt St., Sydney NSW 2000 (☎ **612/9233-6161**); Suite 1, Level 3, 277 Flinders Lane, Melbourne VIC 3000 (☎ **613/9650-6683**); 16 Robinson St., Nedlands, Western Australia 6009 (☎ **618/9386-2102**).

Alternatively, you can obtain a visa upon arrival in Nepal. Visa application forms can be found in the arrivals hall at the airport. If you are entering overland, the border immigration desk should have copies of the visa application form. Visas must be paid for in U.S. dollars even in Nepal, and you will need two passport-sized photos of yourself.

---

**Travel Tip**

---

Take along plenty of passport-sized photos of yourself. You'll need two for a visa, one for a visa extension, and two for every trekking permit you request. You can also get passport photos made cheaply in both Kathmandu and Pokhara.

---

**Visa Extensions**    If you plan to stay longer than allowed on your original visa, you'll have to get a visa extension. You are allowed to stay in Nepal for a total of 120 days per calendar year (although under extenuating circumstances it's sometimes possible to stay for 150 days). Visa extension fees are $1 per day. To obtain a visa extension you will need to go to either the Kathmandu or the Pokhara Department of Immigration Office and fill out a visa extension form. You must then present your passport, one passport-sized photo, and the visa extension form.

**Department of Immigration Offices**    In Kathmandu, the office is at No. 10 Baneswor, Prabha Kanhaiya Complex (☎ **977/1-494273** or 977/1-494337). This office is on the east side of Kathmandu on the road that runs between the Everest Hotel and the International Convention Center. In Pokhara, the office is just off the traffic circle at the far east end of the lakeside. It is west of the Hotel Tragopan and east of the Hotel Pumari (☎ **977/61-21167** or 977/61-20028).

## CUSTOMS

In addition to personal affects, each visitor to Nepal may bring into the country duty-free 200 cigarettes or 50 cigars, 1.15 liters of hard liquor or 12 cans of beer, one still camera and 15 rolls of film, one movie camera or one video camera, one radio, one portable music system, a laptop computer, and one walking stick. When leaving the country, your bag may be inspected by Customs. It is illegal to remove most Nepali antiques from the country. If you have made any purchases that might be considered antique or that even looks old, you should have them inspected and stamped by the Department of Archaeology (see "Shopping" in chapter 5).

**Import Restrictions**    Returning **U.S. citizens** who have been away for 48 hours or more are allowed to bring back, once every 30 days, $400 worth of merchandise duty-free. You'll be charged a flat rate of 10% duty on the next $1,000 worth of purchases. Be sure to have your receipts handy. On gifts, the duty-free limit is $100. You cannot bring fresh foodstuffs into the United States; tinned foods, however, are allowed. For more information, contact the **U.S. Customs Service,** 1301 Constitution Ave. (P.O. Box 7407), Washington, DC 20044 (☎ **202/927-6724**), and request the free pamphlet *Know Before You Go.* It's also available on the Web at www.customs.ustreas.gov/travel/kbygo.htm.

---

## 2 Money

The Nepali rupee (abbreviated Rs) is divided into 100 paisa. There are coins of 5, 10, 25, and 50 paisa (though it is unlikely you will see many of these), and also of 1 and 5 rupees. Paper money comes in denominations of 1, 2, 5, 10, 20, 25, 50, 100, 500, and 1,000 rupees.

At press time, $1 was worth about 66 rupees, and this was the exchange rate used throughout this book. By the time you reach Nepal, the exchange rate will probably have changed, and you may get more rupees for each dollar. However, prices are likely to remain unchanged, because as the rupee is devalued, prices go up. Officially, you can change foreign currency only at a hotel, bank, or currency exchange office.

---

**Travel Tip**
_____

You should remember two things when carrying out cash transactions in Nepal: Hang onto your small bills, and don't take torn notes. Merchants rarely have small bills, and even if they do, they don't want to relinquish them. Making a purchase or paying for a service in Nepal becomes a game of trying to see who will give up their small bills. You should always start by offering a note that is larger than your purchase and insisting that you have nothing smaller. Very large bills are almost worthless for making small purchases. A 1,000- or 500-rupee note is generally useful only for paying hotel bills or making large purchases. Ask the bank to give you 100-rupee notes or smaller. It is especially important to carry lots of small bills if you do a lodge-to-lodge trek. There is an acute change shortage in the hills.

---

Unofficially, a black market flourishes and offers a slightly higher rate, especially for large-denomination U.S. dollars. Changing money on the black market is, however, illegal, even though many people do so. Your hotel is likely to be the most convenient place to change money, though hotel exchange rates tend to be a bit lower than those you'll get at a currency exchange office or bank. Be sure to keep foreign exchange encashment receipts whenever you change money. You'll need these in order to exchange any excess rupees you happen to have when it comes time to leave the country. Banks will convert only a maximum of 10% of the total amount you have exchanged.

   _Note:_ There are no ATMs (Automated Teller Machines) in Nepal at the current time.

**TRAVELER'S CHECKS**   Traveler's checks can easily be exchanged for Nepali rupees at banks and hotels. Even some shopkeepers will accept traveler's checks,

---

## What's That on That Rupee Note Anyway?

All bank notes in Nepal have a picture of the king on them. However, they also have many important other Nepali images. These include the following:

**1 rupee:** Musk deer, Ama Dablam peak, and Pashupatinath temple

**2 rupees:** Leopard, Jayabagesori Temple (near Pashupatinath), Vajra Jogini statue (this note is sometimes called a _chituwa,_ which is Nepali for leopard)

**5 rupees:** Yaks, Mount Everest, and Kathmandu's Taleju Temple

**10 rupees:** Shiva/Garuda statue from Changu Narayan, black buck antelope

**20 rupees:** Sambar deer, Patan's Krishna Mandir

**25 rupees:** A cow, Machhapuchhare, Hanuman Dhoka Palace, Singha Durbar

**50 rupees:** Himalayan thar (mountain goat), Janaki Mandir

**100 rupees:** Indian one-horned rhinoceros, Nyatapola Temple, mountains, Shakyamuni Buddha statue (this note is sometimes called a _gaida,_ which is Nepali for rhinoceros)

**500 rupees:** Tengboche Monastery, Ama Dablam peak, two tigers, Dakini statue

**1,000 rupees:** An elephant, Swayambunath Stupa, Manjushri statue (this note is sometimes called a _hatti,_ which is Nepali for elephant)

## The Nepali Rupee, the U.S. Dollar & the British Pound

At press time $1 = approximately Rs66 (or Rs1 = 1.5¢), and this was the rate of exchange used to calculate the dollar values given in this book (rounded to the nearest nickel). The British pound = Rs110. These rates fluctuate from time to time and may not be the same when you travel to Nepal. Therefore, the following table should be used only as a guide:

| Rs | U.S. | £ | Rs | U.S. | £ |
|-----|------|------|-------|-------|-------|
| 1 | .015 | .010 | 300 | 4.55 | 2.75 |
| 5 | .075 | .05 | 400 | 6.05 | 3.65 |
| 10 | .15 | .10 | 500 | 7.60 | 4.55 |
| 50 | .75 | .45 | 1,000 | 15.15 | 9.10 |
| 75 | 1.14 | .70 | 2,000 | 30.30 | 18.15 |
| 100 | 1.52 | .90 | 2,500 | 37.90 | 22.70 |
| 200 | 3.03 | 1.80 | 3,000 | 45.45 | 27.25 |
| 250 | 3.78 | 2.25 | 5,000 | 75.75 | 45.40 |

though technically this is illegal, as is changing traveler's checks on the black market. Traveler's checks in U.S. and Canadian dollars and pounds sterling are the most easily exchanged, but don't count on being able to change a traveler's check in a small-town bank. It is always best to carry enough rupees for the duration of your trip if you are doing a lodge-to-lodge trek. However, banks in Jomosom, Tatopani, and Namche Bazaar (on the two most popular trekking routes) will usually change them.

**CREDIT CARDS**  American Express, MasterCard, and Visa credit cards are widely accepted in Nepal at tourist hotels and more-expensive restaurants. In Kathmandu, many shops that sell primarily to tourists also accept credit cards. Before paying for a hotel room with a credit card, be sure to find out if the hotel charges extra for using a credit card. This is a common practice in Nepal.

## 3 When to Go

Most travelers to Nepal are coming here to see the Himalayas, so it's important to visit during the time of year when the mountains are not hidden behind thick clouds or veils of haze. The most popular time to visit is during October and November. In these months following the end of the monsoon, the skies clear and the temperatures are mild—perfect trekking weather. However, if you don't like crowds, this is not the time to come. Kathmandu hotels stay packed, and the most popular trekking routes become human highways.

From December through February, the crowds thin out. Though it rarely even gets to freezing in the Kathmandu Valley, it can be quite cold at the higher elevations. However, it doesn't get so cold that a good sleeping bag and a down jacket won't keep you warm. Winter snowstorms can be a problem for trekkers, so it's important to keep a close eye on the weather and plan for a couple of snow days during any winter trek. Down in the Terai, this is the best time to see wildlife, such as rhinos, in the national parks.

March and April are the second-most-popular months for trekking. The weather is once again mild (and can be hot at lower elevations), the mountains are still in view, and, best of all, the rhododendron trees are in bloom in the hills. The flowers of these trees, called *laligurans* in Nepali, are the country's national flower.

May through September are the monsoon months in Nepal. During this time thick clouds obscure the Himalayas from view, and torrential rains cause frequent landslides. The monsoons also bring out the leeches and make trekking during this time of year an absolutely miserable experience (though there aren't any crowds and the landscape is lush and green). The monsoon season is, however, one of the best times to visit the remote, desert-like regions along the Tibetan border, including Mustang and Dolpo.

## CLIMATE

Nepal ranges from an elevation of 220 feet above sea level in the Terai to 29,028 at the top of Mount Everest. Between these two extremes, the rugged topography of peaks, ridges, and valleys creates a variety of climates and microclimates. Temperatures vary as much with elevation as with time of year. In the Terai, days are warm even in January and December, whereas in the high Himalayas, the snow remains year-round.

There are, however, two distinct seasons: the rainy **monsoon season** and the **dry season.** The monsoon begins as early as late April or early May in the Kathmandu Valley, and as late as mid-June in the Terai. Rains, though not as torrential as farther south in India, are constant and steady. This is the main growing season in Nepal and the time of year with the fewest visitors. The rains continue until mid-October with a gradual slacking off beginning as early as late September. With the end of the monsoon, the cool, dry season begins.

Mid-October to mid-December is the **prime time** to visit Nepal, whether you're trekking or simply sightseeing. The sky is a clear blue, and the mountains are visible almost daily. Temperatures even at 13,000 feet rarely go below freezing during the day, and in the Kathmandu Valley it can be warm enough for shorts and T-shirts. From mid-December to late January, there is a slight chance of frost in the Kathmandu Valley, and it can get well below freezing higher up in the mountains. There is still good trekking at lower elevations, and fewer people visit at this time. This is my favorite time to visit, though the country is quite dry and brown by November. From February to March, the weather begins to warm up, and the skies are sometimes cloudy, although there are still quite a few clear days. March to April is the second-most-popular time for trekking, though haze often obscures the mountains and it can be much too hot to trek at lower elevations. In May the weather even in Kathmandu or Pokhara can be uncomfortably hot, and in the Terai temperatures it can reach more than 110°F.

### Average Monthly Temperature & Rainfall In Kathmandu

|                  | Jan | Feb | Mar | Apr | May | June | July | Aug | Sept | Oct | Nov | Dec |
|------------------|-----|-----|-----|-----|-----|------|------|-----|------|-----|-----|-----|
| Avg. High (°F)   | 66  | 68  | 77  | 86  | 86  | 86   | 86   | 84  | 81   | 73  | 73  | 68  |
| Avg. Low (°F)    | 36  | 39  | 46  | 52  | 61  | 68   | 70   | 68  | 66   | 59  | 39  | 36  |
| Rainfall (in.)   | 1.9 | .4  | .6  | .2  | 5.8 | 5.3  | 12.9 | 8.1 | 7.8  | 1.7 | 0   | 0   |

# HOLIDAYS

There are more than 35 days of official government holidays each year in Nepal, and most of these are religious in nature. The sheer number of Hindu deities that must be honored is the cause of this holiday calendar. Add to the numerous Hindu holidays, the Buddhist holidays, and days of national significance, and hardly a week goes by without a major holiday or festival. Since most of these holidays are based on the phases of the moon, the date on which they fall changes from year to year. In addition, many shops close for several days on either side of the official holiday date.

If you wish to plan your visit to coincide with a particular festival, contact a Nepali embassy or one of the tourist information centers in Nepal to determine the specific date for the year you are traveling.

## NEPAL CALENDAR OF EVENTS

February

- **Shivaratri,** Pashupatinath. Devout Hindus come from all over Nepal and India to celebrate the birthday of the god Shiva. Many *sadhus* (mendicant ascetic holy men) make the pilgrimage to Pashupatinath, where they collect alms.
- **Tibetan New Year,** Boudha. Attended by Buddhists from Nepal and Tibet, the religious festivities include the raising of prayer flags, masked dances by lamas, prayers, and blessings.

March

- **Holi** (also called Fagu), all over Nepal. This festival, a celebration of the victory of Narsimha, a half-man–half-lion incarnation of Vishnu, over the demon Hiranyakashipu, is marked by the throwing of colored powders and colored water on everyone and everything in sight. Keep your camera covered. Full moon of March (sometimes late February).

April

- **Bisket,** Bhaktapur. This weeklong festival marks the beginning of the new year. A huge chariot, containing statues of the gods Bhairav and Bhadrakali, is pulled through the streets of the city and down to the bank of the Hanumante River.

May

- **Buddha Jyanti,** throughout Nepal. This festival, associated with pilgrimages to important Buddhist shrines, celebrates the birthday of the Buddha. Swayambunath and Boudhanath are particularly busy during this festival.
- **Rato Machendranath Jatra,** Patan. Machendranath is the patron deity of the Kathmandu Valley, and during this monthlong festival, the image of the Rato Machendranath is pulled through the streets of Patan in a huge wooden chariot. The festival is held to ensure a good monsoon for the rice crop.

July

- **Janai Purnima,** at Khumbheshwar Temple in Patan and Gosainkund Lake in Gosainkund. High-caste Hindus, including Brahmins and Chhetris, replace the sacred thread that they wear over their left shoulders. *Jhankris* (medicine men) perform dances.

August

- **Gaijatra,** Kathmandu Valley. Called the Festival of Cows, Gaijatra is an 8-day-long celebration to honor dead relatives. People who have had a death in the family within the past year bring a cow (either real or someone in costume) to participate in the festival. Festivities take place on the valley's three Durbar Squares.

- **Krishnastami,** Patan. In celebration of the Hindu god Krishna's birthday, there is a nightlong vigil, with much music and singing, at the stone Krishna Mandir in Patan.
- **Teej,** Pashupatinath. This is a woman's festival during which women go to bathe in the holy waters of the Bagmati River at Pashupatinath Temple.
- **Chaitra Dasain,** all over Nepal. A smaller version of Dasain, which is held in September or October (see below), Chaitra Dasain is marked by many animal sacrifices.

September
- **Indra Jatra,** Kathmandu and all over Nepal. This 7-day festival, in celebration of Indra, the god of rain, marks the end of the monsoon and the beginning of the dry season. During the festival, the Kumari (living goddess; is paraded through Kathmandu aboard her chariot, and blessed homemade beer is drunk through a straw in the mouth of the giant mask of the White Bhairav on Hanuman Dhoka Square. Newari dances are performed in the Durbar Square nightly.

October
- **Haribhodini Ekadashi,** Budhanilkantha, Changu Narayan, and Pashupatinath. This 10-day festival celebrating Vishnu's awakening from a 4-month nap is marked by pilgrimages to various Vishnu shrines and temples around the Kathmandu Valley. Late October or early November.
- **Dasain,** all over Nepal. Also known as Durga Puja, this is Nepal's biggest festival and goes on for 2 weeks. It is also one of the most gruesome festivals on earth, with goats, water buffaloes, and yaks being slaughtered by the thousands in the name of worshiping the goddess Durga. Blood from these sacrificial animals is scattered on everything from images of the goddess Durga to Royal Nepal Airlines' jets. This is the single-most-important festival in Nepal.
- **Tihar,** all over Nepal. Sort of a combination of Christmas, New Year's, the Fourth of July, and Halloween, this festival is also called the Festival of Lights. Lasting 5 days, Tihar starts out with the worship of crows (food is put out for the birds). The next day, dogs are worshiped (marigold garlands are hung round their necks, and red powder is placed on their foreheads). On the third day, Nepali new year's eve, cows get the marigold garlands and red powder (and also rings of paint on their sides). Also, on this day, houses and businesses are covered with candles and Christmas lights, and paths are traced to the family or business money box so that the goddess Laxmi will bless the house or business and help it to prosper in the upcoming year. The fourth day is new year's day (Deepawali) and is the day of worshiping yourself. On the fifth day, brothers are worshiped by their sisters. Early to mid-month.

November
- ✪ **Mani Rimdu,** Tengboche Monastery, Solu-Khumbu. Masked dances are performed by monks, who are celebrating the triumph of Buddhism over the ancient Bon religion, at a remote Buddhist monastery near Mount Everest. Full moon in November.

December
- **Bala Chaturdashi,** Pashupatinath. In memory of dead relatives, people from all over the Kathmandu Valley visit this temple to light candles and then scatter

seeds in the Mrigasthali forest on the hill across the river from Pashupatinath. There is much singing and dancing by pilgrims late into the night.

# 4  The Active Vacation Planner

Although the mountains are more than enough for most people, there is more to a Nepal adventure vacation than trekking or mountain climbing. This country has some of the best **bird watching** and **white-water rafting** in the world, and with each passing year, new **mountain-biking** routes are being explored.

There is now a lodge east of Kathmandu near the Tibetan border that caters specifically to adventure travelers. **The Borderland,** Thamel (P.O. Box 13558), Kathmandu (☎ **977/1-425836;** fax 977/1-435207; e-mail: resort@tibet-border.wlink.com.np), offers trekking, mountain-biking, rafting, and rock-climbing tours in conjunction with various local companies. The lodge is rustic, and because of the type of people it attracts, it is usually a pretty lively place.

Also, if you're interested in exploring the national parks of the Terai region, **Explore Nepal,** Kamaladi (P.O. Box 536), Kathmandu (☎ **977/1-247078** or 977/1-247079; fax 977/1-224237; e-mail: explore@mos.com.np), offers a variety of tours taking in Chitwan, Bardia, Koshi Tappu, and Sukila Phanta Wildlife Reserve.

## BIRD WATCHING

With numerous climatic zones, from steamy lowlands to alpine aeries, Nepal is a bird-watcher's paradise. Royal Chitwan National Park alone is the home to more than 450 species of birds. Serious birders will want to pick up a copy of *The Book of Indian Birds* (Bombay Natural History Society, 1996) by Salim Ali, and check out *Birds of Nepal* (if it's back in print) as soon as they arrive in Kathmandu. Armed with one of these excellent field guides, you will be able to add dozens, if not hundreds, of bird sightings to your life's list while you are in Nepal.

There is good birding in the Kathmandu Valley at Phulchok (see "Bird Watching" in chapter 5 for details). In Pokhara, there is good birding near the dam on Phewa Lake. However, the best birding in the country is down in the national parks of the Terai region. Royal Chitwan National Park, Royal Bardia National Park, and Koshi Tappu Wildlife Reserve are the best bird-watching locations, and all lodges at these parks provide experienced guides to help those unfamiliar with the birds of the sub continent. For more information on birding in the Terai, see chapter 8.

## JUNGLE SAFARIS (WILDLIFE VIEWING)

The lowland forests of Nepal's Terai region, though not really jungles, are full of rare wildlife, including Bengal tigers, Indian one-horned rhinoceroses, and wild Asian elephants. These animals can often be seen in various national parks and wildlife preserves in this region. The most popular and most easily accessible wildlife-viewing area is Royal Chitwan National Park, which has numerous lodges both within and just outside the park. Here you can explore the park on the back of an elephant, by Land Rover, or by dugout canoe. More remote and less crowded is Royal Bardia National Park, created to protect tigers and home to wild elephants and Gangetic dolphins. At Koshi Tappu Wildlife Reserve, bird watching is the most popular activity, though there are also Gangetic dolphins and rare wild water buffalo. For more information on these parks and this reserve, see chapter 8.

## MOUNTAIN BIKING

Nepal and mountain biking are naturals, but not exactly in the way most people at first think. Before you start planning to ride your bike to Mount Everest, you should realize that trails in Nepal are not the sort of trails you're familiar with back home. Trails are often relentlessly steep (no switchbacks here), and stone stairways are commonplace. Although every year there are people who mountain-bike along the main trekking routes, they usually end up hiring a porter to carry the bike much of the way. Still, there are sections of remote single-track trail that are so utterly awesome that it more than makes up for not being able to ride more than 50% or 75% of a trail.

This said, there are countless miles of trails and quiet mountain backroads that are ideal for mountain biking. Currently the most popular areas are around the rim of the Kathmandu Valley and around Pokhara. However, there is the entire country still to be explored, and for the adventurous mountain biker, Nepal is still terra incognita waiting to be explored.

Currently, two companies in Kathmandu offer mountain-bike trips ranging in length from 1 to 12 days. Both of these companies also offer trips across Tibet. See "Outdoor Activities" in chapter 5 for more information. A few international adventure-travel companies also offer bike tours in Nepal. See below for details.

## MOUNTAINEERING/TREKKING PEAKS

So, you've read Jon Krakauer's *Into Thin Air,* and instead of convincing you once and for all that climbing mountains, especially big Himalayan mountains, is crazy, it has you itching to bag some peaks. Well, as long as you are in good physical shape, have a bit of mountain-climbing experience, and have plenty of cash, you too can climb mountains in Nepal, even Mount Everest. Numerous adventure-travel companies all over the world mount guided expeditions to peaks in Nepal every year. These range from relatively easy (and relatively inexpensive) ascents of "trekking peaks" to full-blown Everest expeditions. Plan ahead, though. The peaks of Nepal are so popular that many of them are booked years in advance by expeditions from all over the world.

For most people, the **trekking peaks** are sufficient challenge to satisfy the desire to have climbed a Himalayan peak. Trekking peaks are peaks that have been designated by the Nepali government as easy enough to be climbed without the aid of a full-scale expedition. However, don't get the idea that a trekking peak is just another easy stroll in the hills. The 18 designated trekking peaks range in height from 18,325 feet (5,587m) to 21,625 feet (6,654m). Most of these peaks require technical climbing experience and equipment, but some of them are easy enough to summit that it's possible to organize your own expedition. To find out about all the requirements and permits necessary for climbing one of these peaks on your own, contact the **Nepal Mountaineering Association** on Nagpokhari, Naxal (P.O. Box 1435), Kathmandu (☎ 977/1-411525; fax 977/1-416278). Permits cost $150 to $300 depending on the height of the mountain you intend to climb.

Expeditions to Nepal's 135 official **mountaineering peaks** require long and serious planning, large amounts of equipment and supplies, and usually dozens of porters, cooks, and Sherpas as support. Consequently, these expeditions are the realm of professional expeditions and adventure-travel companies. Even a small expedition can cost thousands of dollars, and the expedition permit alone can cost as much as $70,000 (for Mount Everest). For more information on mountain climbing in Nepal, contact the **Nepal Mountaineering Association,** Nagpokhari, Naxal, Kathmandu (☎ 977/1-411525; fax 977/1-416278), or the **Ministry of Tourism & Civil Aviation, Mountaineering Division,** Singha Durbar, Kathmandu (☎ 977/1-241909).

The best way to climb any of the trekking peaks, and the only way to climb the mountaineering peaks, is on an organized expedition. Many of the major trekking companies offer trips to various trekking peaks each year (see "Adventure-Travel Companies" below).

> **Factoid**
>
> Nepal is home to 8 of the world's 14 peaks that are over 8,000 meters (26,000 ft) tall, and within 20 years of opening its doors to the outside world in 1951, all of Nepal's 8,000-meter peaks had been scaled.

## TREKKING

Trekking (derived from a South African Boer word) is just another name for hiking in the mountains. It can be anything from an overnight jaunt to a 2-month-long expedition. Treks vary from simple lodge-to-lodge hikes at relatively low elevations to fully catered trips with dozens of porters, guides, and cooks doing all the work for you. There are treks of all lengths and difficulties, and trekkers, especially those doing lodge-to-lodge treks, can choose to walk as little or as much as they want each day. Consequently, nearly anyone visiting Nepal can do a little trekking if they wish.

Because trekking is the single-most-popular form of outdoor activity in Nepal and is the reason a large percentage of visitors come to Nepal, it is covered extensively in the last two chapters of this book. See chapter 9 for in-depth information on planning a trek; see chapter 10 for descriptions of trekking routes. See "Adventure-Travel Companies," later in this chapter, for recommendations on international trekking companies; see chapter 9 for a list of recommended Nepali trekking companies.

## WHITE-WATER RAFTING

With hundreds of rivers tumbling down out of the Himalayas, Nepal is one of the finest white-water rafting destinations on earth. There is a wide range of rafting opportunities for everyone from novices to seasoned paddlers, though the majority of the rafting trips recommended here are only for people with previous rafting experience. Trips of from 1 to 10 days are possible.

There is a wide range of rates for rafting trips, depending on the length of the trip, the starting point, and the mode of transportation to the put-in point (buses are cheaper than private cars). One- and two-day trips on the Trishuli River are the most common and are operated by dozens of companies, many of which, especially in Kathmandu's Thamel neighborhood, advertise rafting trips starting as low as $15 for a day on the river. However, be aware that you get exactly what you pay for. If you opt for the cheapest trip possible, you'll likely be dealing with some fly-by-night company that uses thirdhand rafts (probably not self-bailing ones, either), battered wooden paddles, and inexperienced guides. Considering that rafting the rivers of Nepal can include life-or-death situations, it makes sense to pay a little bit extra to go with a reliable company. See the list below.

Some questions to ask before signing on for a rafting trip include these: How do we get to the put-in point—bus or car? How old is the raft? Is it self-bailing? Are the paddles wooden or plastic? How old are the life jackets? Are helmets provided? What sort of food will be served? What sort of beverages? How much experience does the river guide have, and is he trained in first aid and CPR?

For information on rafting companies in Kathmandu and Pokhara, see "Outdoor Activities" in chapters 5 and 7. For companies outside Nepal that offer rafting trips, see the list below.

### THE RIVERS

**Trishuli**   Class III and IV. This is the closest rafting river to Kathmandu and is by far the most popular river in Nepal. The Trishuli's popularity makes it rather crowded, and its proximity to the highway between Kathmandu and Pokhara means this is not exactly a wilderness trip. However, there are plenty of exciting rapids, especially in the upper stretch of the river. Rafting companies offer trips of 1 to 4 days on this river.

**Bhote Kosi**   Class IV to V. For experienced paddlers only, the Bhote Kosi is a wild and steep river located near the Tibetan border (*Bhote Kosi* means Tibet River). Although this run is short and some companies break the trip into two stretches (one above the dam and one below the dam), it is some of the most intense water in Nepal.

**Kali Gandaki**   Class III to IV+. Located near Pokhara, the Kali Gandaki was for many years a favorite rafting river for 5-day trips. However, the construction of a dam has shortened these trips to 3 days, and some companies have quit running the river altogether.

**Sun Kosi**   Class IV to V. This is the quintessential Nepal wilderness rafting trip and is considered one of the top-10 rafting trips in the world. Trips generally last 10 days, with 2 days in transit to and from the river. The trip covers 169 miles of river, and on the way back there is a stop at Chitwan National Park.

**Seti**   Class II and III. Flowing out of the Pokhara Valley, the Seti River is the easiest and warmest river regularly run in Nepal. Because it is such a relatively easy river, it is ideal for beginners and is frequently used for kayaking classes. More of a float trip than a white-water rafting expedition, the Seti is mostly about scenery. Trips on this river usually last 3 days and finish only an hour from Chitwan National Park.

**Karnali**   Class IV to V. Located in remote western Nepal, the Karnali, which flows down to Bardia National Park, requires a 2-day trek just to get to the put-in. Once on the river, you're faced with 102 miles of white water, including 40 major rapids. Trips usually take 11 or 12 days from start to finish and include 6 days on the river.

## ADVENTURE-TRAVEL COMPANIES

Nepal is one of the most popular adventure-travel destinations in the world, and there are hundreds of companies that specialize in trips to this tiny Himalayan kingdom. Nepal's adventures are of four major types: **trekking, white-water rafting, mountain biking,** and **jungle safaris.** It is quite possible and commonplace to combine several of these adventurous activities into one trip. Companies offering trekking, rafting, mountain biking, and jungle safari trips in Nepal include the following.

### IN THE UNITED STATES

**Above the Clouds,** P.O. Box 398, Worcester, MA 01602-0398 (☎ **800/233-4499** or 508/799-4499; fax 508/797-4779; www.gorp.com/abvclds.htm; e-mail: sconlon@world. std.com). Trekking.

**Adventure Center,** 1311 63rd St., Suite 200, Emeryville, CA 94608 (☎ **800/227-8747** or 510/654-1879; fax 510/654-4200; www.adventure-center.com; e-mail: tripinfo @adventure-center.com). Trekking, rafting, jungle safaris.

**Geographic Expeditions,** 2627 Lombard St., San Francisco, CA 94123 (☎ **800/ 777-8183** or 415/922-0448; fax 415/346-5535; www.geoex.com; e-mail: info@geoex. com). Trekking, jungle safaris.

**Himalayan Travel,** 110 Prospect St., Stamford, CT 06901 (☎ **800/225-2380** or 203/359-3711; fax 203/359-3669; www.gorp.com/himtravel/htm; e-mail: worldadv @netaxis.com). Trekking, mountaineering, rafting, jungle safaris.

**Journeys,** 107 April Dr., Suite 3, Ann Arbor, MI 48103 (☎ **800/255-8735** or 313/665-4407; fax 313/665-2945; www.journeys-intl.com; e-mail: info@journeys-intl.com). Trekking, rafting, jungle safaris.

**KE Adventure Travel,** P.O. Box 10538, Aspen, CO 81612 (☎ **800/497-9675** or 970/925-6704; www.keadventure.com; e-mail: ketravel@rof.net). Trekking, mountaineering expeditions, rafting, jungle safaris.

**Ker & Downey Nepal,** 13201 NW Freeway, Suite 800, Houston, TX 77040 (☎ **800/324-9081** or 713/744-5244; fax 713/895-8753; e-mail: legendary@tfcomp.com). Luxury lodge treks, rafting, jungle safaris.

**Lute Jerstad Adventures International,** P.O. Box 19537, Portland, OR 97280 (☎ **503/244-6075;** fax 503/244-1349). Trekking, rafting, jungle safaris. Their office will be moving to Canby, Oregon, within the year.

**Mountain Madness,** 4218 SW Alaska St., Suite 206, Seattle, WA 98116 (☎ **800/328-5925** or 206/937-8389; fax 206/937-1772; www.mountainmadness.com; e-mail: mountmad@aol.com). Trekking, mountaineering, jungle safaris.

**Mountain Travel Sobek—The Adventure Company,** 6420 Fairmount Ave., El Cerrito, CA 94530 (☎ **888/687-6235;** fax 510/525-7710; www.mtsobek.com; e-mail: info@mtsobek.com). Trekking expeditions, jungle safaris.

**Overseas Adventure Travel,** 625 Mt. Auburn St., Cambridge, MA 02138 (☎ **800/221-0814** or 617/876-0533; fax 617/876-0826). Trekking, rafting, jungle safaris.

**Snow Lion Expeditions,** Oquirrh Place, 350 South 400 East, Suite G2, Salt Lake City, UT 84111 (☎ **800/525-TREK** or 801/355-6555; fax 801/355-6566; www.snowlion.com; e-mail: info@snowlion.com). Trekking, mountaineering, bicycle touring, Buddhist pilgrimages.

**Wilderness Travel,** 1102 Ninth St., Berkeley, CA 94710 (☎ **800/368-2794** or 510/558-2488; fax 510/558-2489; www.wildernesstravel.com; e-mail: info@wildernesstravel.com). Trekking, mountaineering programs, jungle safaris.

## IN THE UNITED KINGDOM

**Classic Nepal,** 33 Metro Ave., Newton, Alfreton, Derbyshire DE55 5UF (☎ **01773/873497;** fax 01773/590243; www.himalaya.co.uk; e-mail: classicnepal@himalaya.co.uk). Trekking, mountaineering expeditions, rafting, jungle safaris.

**Crusaders,** 57-58 Church St., Twickenham TW1 3NR (☎ **0181/892-7606;** fax 0181/744-0574; www.crusadertravel.com; e-mail: info@crusadertravel.com). Trekking, rafting, jungle safaris.

**Encounter Overland Expeditions,** 267 Old Brompton Rd., London SW5 9JA, United Kingdom (☎ **0171/370-6845;** fax 0171/244-9737; www.encounter.co.uk; e-mail: adventure@encounter.co.uk). Trekking, rafting, jungle safaris.

**Exodus,** 9 Weir Rd., London SW12 0LT (☎ **0181/675-5550;** fax 0181/673-0779; www.exodustravels.co.uk; e-mail: sales@exodustravels.co.uk). Trekking, rafting, jungle safaris, mountain biking.

**Explore Worldwide,** 1 Frederick St., Aldershot, Hants GU11 1LQ (☎ **01252/760000;** fax 01252/760201; www.explore.co.uk/; e-mail: info@adventureworld.com.au). Trekking, rafting, jungle safaris.

**Himalayan Kingdom Treks,** 20 The Mall, Clifton, Bristol BS8 4DR (☎ **0117/923-7163;** fax 0117/974-4993; e-mail: 101460.2022@compuserve.com). Trekking, rafting, jungle safaris.

**Himalayan Kingdoms Expeditions,** 45 Mowbray St., Sheffield S3 8EN (☎ **0114/276-3322;** fax 0114/276-3344; www.hkexpeds.demon.co.uk; e-mail: expeditions@hkexpeds.demon.co.uk). Mountaineering expeditions.

**KE Adventure Travel,** 32 Lake Rd., Keswick, Cumbria CA12 5DQ (☎ **017687/73966;** fax 017687/74693; www.keadventure.com; e-mail: keadventure@enterprise.net). Trekking, mountaineering expeditions, rafting, jungle safaris.

**Sherpa Expeditions,** 131a Heston Rd., Hounslow, Middlesex TW5 0RD (☎ **0181/ 577-2717;** fax 0181/572-9788; www.sherpa-walking-holidays.co.uk/; e-mail: sherpa. sales@dial.pipex.com). Trekking, rafting, jungle safaris.

## IN AUSTRALIA & NEW ZEALAND

**The Classic Safari Company,** Level 11, 456 Kent St., Sydney, NSW 2000 (☎ **612- 9263-3311;** fax 612-9267-3047; e-mail: adventure@africatravel.com.au). Trekking, jungle safaris.

**HKE Jagged Globe,** P.O. Box 133, Hampton, Victoria 3188 (☎ **03-9533-5588;** fax 03-9533-5599; e-mail: gsports@ocean.com.au). Trekking, mountaineering programs.

**Peregrine Travel,** 258 Lonsdale St., Melbourne VIC 3000 (☎ **03-9662-2700;** fax 03-9662-2422; www.peregrine.net.au; e-mail: travelcentre@peregrine.net.au); also at Level 5, 38 York St., Sydney NSW 2000 (☎ **02-9290-2770;** fax 02-9290-2155; e-mail: peresyd@iaccess.com.au); and 1st Floor, 862 Hay St., Perth WA 6000 (☎ **08-9321-1259;** fax 08-9481-7375; e-mail: plambert@tpg.com.au). Trekking, mountaineering, rafting, jungle safaris.

**Ultimate Descents,** P.O. Box 208, Motueka, New Zealand (☎ **64/3-528-6363;** fax 64/3528-6792). Rafting, kayaking.

# 5  Learning Vacations

## SPIRITUAL STUDY & YOGA

For centuries, India, Nepal, and Tibet have been well-known as mystical destinations for spiritual seekers. The Beatles made spending time in an *ashram* (center for religious studies) the "in" thing to do in the 1960s, and ever since then people have been flocking to this part of the world to find enlightenment. The frequently seen cartoon of some poor lost soul climbing to the top of a mountain to ask a famous yogi the *Big Question*—What is the meaning of life?—may well have originated in Nepal. This country is a crossroads, a meeting ground of two of the world's great religions—Buddhism and Hinduism. There aren't any Hindu ashrams in Nepal that I know of (India has cornered that market), but those interested in studying Tibetan Buddhism, meditation, or yoga have come to the right place.

**Kopan Monastery,** P.O. Box 817, Kathmandu (☎ **977/1-481268**), is a Tibetan Buddhist monastery located a couple of miles north of Boudha in the Kathmandu Valley. Home to more than 150 young monks and nuns from Nepal and Tibet, it is also a center for Westerners seeking to learn more about Buddhism. Throughout the year the monastery offers many short courses, and every November, there is an extensive month long course that includes daily teachings and meditation instruction. This course is extremely rigorous (for part of the course you are prohibited from speaking, get only one meal a day, and have your sleep limited), and there is intense pressure on participants to become practicing Buddhists. The course costs $276, including teachings, all meals (vegetarian), and a bed in a dormitory.

The **Kathmandu Centre of Healing,** Maharajgunj (☎ **977/1-413094** or 425946; www.ancientmassage.com; e-mail: kch@mos.com.np), is affiliated with Kopan Monastery and offers short courses and weekly teachings on meditation, Hatha yoga, and massage. The **Himalayan Buddhist Meditation Centre,** Kamaladi Ganesthan (☎ **977/ 1-221875;** fax 977/1-251409; www.dharmatours.com/hbmc; e-mail: hbmc@mos.com. np), offers residential courses in Buddhism and also short workshops. Bulletin boards around Kathmandu (and specifically at the Nepalese Kitchen Restaurant near Chhetrapati) usually have notices for courses in Buddhist studies being held in Boudha, the center for Tibetan Buddhism in Nepal and home of many monasteries.

All over Thamel, Kathmandu's budget travelers' neighborhood, there are signs advertising yoga instruction. Any of these instructors should be able to teach you quite a bit of yoga in a short time, and fees are very reasonable. The **Patanjali Yoga Center,** Chhauni, Museum Road (☎ **977/1-278437** or 271767; fax 977/1-245231), near the National Museum, offers daily classes. They welcome students at all levels.

## LEARNING NEPALI

It takes extra effort to learn some Nepali, but if you have the time, the rewards are worth it. Nepalis are truly pleased when they find out that you speak a bit of their language. Learning a little Nepali helps greatly in understanding the Nepali culture and opens doors to long-lasting friendships. The **Kathmandu Institute of Nepali Language,** Jyatha, Thamel (☎ **977/1-225777** or 977/1-229294; Fax 977/1-416500), offers classes from 1 week to 3 months. **Bala Ram Thapa,** P.O. Box 3785, Kathmandu (☎ **977/1-330120**), a language instructor who has had 16 years' experience with the U.S. Peace Corps, offers one-on-one instruction at your residence for a reasonable fee.

# 6  Health, Insurance & Other Concerns

## STAYING HEALTHY

What follows is meant to be used for general guidance only; consult your doctor or local international health clinic for details.

### COLDS & RESPIRATORY ILLNESSES

During the winter months, colds are probably the most common illness in Nepal, and within a few days of arriving in Kathmandu, most people have either developed a full-blown cold or have developed the Kathmandu cough. This latter malady is brought on by the dust and smog that plague this city. Kathmandu is the dustiest city we've ever been in, and the dust can be very irritating to the eyes, nose, and throat. Some people choose to wear aspirators (face masks) or bandannas to keep out the dust. Face masks are sold in Kathmandu pharmacies and other shops frequented by tourists. Though a cold is likely the worst thing that you'll come down with in Nepal, there are quite a few other illnesses you should know about and take precautions against.

### VACCINATIONS & PROPHYLAXIS

Nepal does not require any vaccinations for entry. However, Nepal is one of the poorest countries in the world, and consequently hygiene and medical-care standards are very low. In some areas of the country there is only one doctor for every 100,000 people. Diseases associated with poor sanitation, often considered tropical diseases, are commonplace in Nepal. There are vaccines that prevent most of these diseases, and because some of the vaccines require a series of treatments over several months, you should contact your local public health department at least 6 months before your planned trip to Nepal. In the United States, you can also get information from the **International Travelers' Hotline** at the **Centers for Disease Control** in Atlanta (☎ **888/232-3228;** www.cdc.gov).

For travel to Nepal, the following **vaccinations** are recommended: typhoid, tetanus, diphtheria, and polio. Also, if you were born after January 1, 1957, you should make sure you have been immunized against measles. Malaria tablets (if you are visiting the Terai), the hepatitis A vaccine, and a vaccination against meningo-coccal meningitis are also advised.

In Kathmandu the best and most reliable sources of information are either the CIWEC Clinic or the Nepal International Clinic, both of which have e-mail addresses and both of which can tell you which immunizations they currently recommend (for contact information, see below).

One problem with contacting your county health board for information is that, unless you live in a major metropolitan area, the chances of their having vaccinations for tropical diseases are slight. You might have to drive to the nearest city, pay an initial-visit fee to see a doctor, and then pay astronomical fees for the vaccinations, which often are not covered by health insurance. Although costly and time-consuming, this may be necessary.

Booster shots, for those who have traveled in the tropics before, can be obtained conveniently and relatively cheaply in Kathmandu at two clinic that are staffed by Western or Western-trained medical staff. **Nepal International Clinic** (☎ 977/ **1-412842** or 434642; fax 977/1-419713; e-mail: basnyat@npl.healthnet.org) is located on Naxal near the south gate of the current royal palace, and the **CIWEC Clinic** (☎ **977/1-228531** or 241732; www.bena.com/ciwec; e-mail: advice@ciwecpc.mos. com.np) is off Durbar Marg near the Hotel Yak & Yeti. All of the immunizations for the various diseases listed below are available at either of these clinics, and both use disposable needles and vaccines manufactured in Europe or North America.

**Cholera**   Cholera is a bacterial infection spread by contaminated water. The main symptom is severe diarrhea. Cholera is quite common in Nepal, especially during the monsoon season, although tourists rarely contract it. Cholera vaccinations are no longer recommended, but if you should develop severe diarrhea accompanied by nausea, vomiting, cramps, and dizziness, you should suspect cholera and seek medical attention immediately.

**Hepatitis A**   Infectious hepatitis (Type A) is common in Nepal. It is characterized by extreme fatigue and jaundice (yellowing of the skin and eyes) and is spread by conta-minated food and water. There is now a vaccine against this type of hepatitis. For full immunization, you need to receive injections spaced 6 months apart.

**Hepatitis B**   This viral disease is spread primarily by sexual or blood contact with an infected person and is often fatal. A vaccine is available against this disease, though tourists' chances of contracting hepatitis B are quite low. The vaccine is taken in a series of three injections over 6 months.

**Japanese Encephalitis**   This is another mosquito-borne disease found in the lower elevations of Nepal. It is most common during the monsoon season and the beginning of the dry season. You are at greatest risk if you spend more than 3 weeks in the Terai region of Nepal, especially in a rural area such as Chitwan National Park. The vaccine is given as a series spaced over several weeks.

**Malaria**   Malaria is a mosquito-borne disease that occurs in the Terai region of Nepal, where several national parks are located. It is characterized by high fever, chills, and general malaise. The species of mosquito that transmits malaria is active only from dusk to dawn, so take extra precautions at these times. Wear a long-sleeve shirt, long pants, and socks to cover as much of your skin as possible. Use mosquito repellent on any exposed skin. If possible, sleep under a mosquito net, or burn mosquito coils, which are available at most general stores in Nepal. There is no immunization against malaria, but a prophylaxis can reduce or prevent the outbreak of the disease. Chloro-quine is still the accepted prophylaxis in Nepal (in other countries the disease has developed resistance to chloroquine). If you should contract malaria, the standard treatment is Fansidar. However, Fansidar can cause severe side effects; consult your doctor before taking it. Mefloquine is also effective in chloroquine-resistant areas, but it also has side effects, though not as extreme as those of Fansidar.

**Meningococcal Meningitis**   Outbreaks of meningitis have occurred in Kathmandu in recent years, and protection against this often-fatal disease is highly recommended. Meningococcal meningitis is a bacterial infection that affects the central nervous system. The immunization is usually very expensive in the United States, but it can be had for a fraction of the cost in Kathmandu.

**Polio**   Though it is no longer a significant threat in most developed nations, polio is still common in Nepal. You'll need to update your childhood immunization series of three doses. The oral vaccine is still commonly used. If you did not receive a series of polio vaccinations as a child, consult your doctor as far in advance of your departure as possible.

**Rabies**   Rabies is fairly common in Nepal and it's commonly carried by dogs and monkeys. Extreme caution should be taken around these animals. Do not feed temple monkeys! If not treated promptly, rabies is fatal. A vaccine is available, and though it will not prevent you from getting rabies if you are bitten by a rabid animal, it will give you more time to seek medical attention. This preexposure vaccine is given as a series of three shots spaced over 1 month. The shots are generally recommended only for people who plan to spend several months or longer in an area where they might be exposed to rabies.

If you have not had the preexposure vaccine and you are bitten by a possibly rabid animal, thoroughly rinse the wound with running water for 20 minutes. Immediately seek medical attention. If you are trekking, you must find the nearest two-way radio and request a helicopter evacuation to Kathmandu, where you should immediately begin the series of injections to prevent the onset of rabies.

**Tetanus-Diphtheria**   Tetanus (lockjaw) can easily be contracted from cuts and scratches, especially puncture wounds. The immunization, which is generally given in conjunction with a diphtheria immunization, is good for up to 10 years.

**Typhoid**   Spread by contaminated food and water, typhoid is a bacterial infection characterized by high fever. Typhoid is common in Nepal, and vaccination is highly recommended. You'll need to have it several months before leaving for Nepal.

## WATER PURIFICATION

The majority of illnesses in Nepal are spread by unsanitary conditions, particularly contaminated water. Consequently, it is important to take special precautions to ensure that your drinking water is safe. The best precaution is not to drink any water unless you have purified it yourself, or know that it has been boiled. Do not drink tap water; even bottled water in Nepal is suspect because bottles, especially out on the trekking routes, are sometimes refilled with unsafe water.

Water purification can be done in a number of ways, but **boiling** it for 20 minutes is the most common method. This is generally not something you can do yourself, and not something you can count on a Nepali to do for you—boiling water for 20 minutes will seem like a waste of precious fuel. Milk tea is the most common drink in Nepal and it's made with boiled water, though whether it has been boiled long enough to kill bacteria and other organisms is never certain. There is a risk with drinking tea, but a relatively low one.

A much better method of purifying water is with **iodine,** though some people don't like the taste of iodized water. Iodine, which is a poison and should never be taken internally at its full strength, comes in solutions of varying strengths. Use 8 drops of tincture of iodine (a 2% solution) or 4 drops of Lugol's solution (the most common form of iodine in Nepal) to sterilize a quart or liter of water.

Water-purification **tablets** are another option. There are two types available, but only one of them, tetraglycine hydroperioiodide, is effective for purifying water in Nepal. Chlorine tablets, which are the most common form of water-purification tablets, are *not* effective at killing amoebic cysts.

Portable water **filters,** which have become popular among backpackers in the United States, will filter out bacteria, amoebas and their cysts, and giardia and their cysts, but not the hepatitis virus. With this limitation, these filters are useless in Nepal, where hepatitis is prevalent. However, a two-stage filter which filters and iodinizes water is effective against the hepatitis virus. Look for these filters at large camping-supply stores.

## DIARRHEA

The best way to avoid developing diarrhea during your visit to Nepal is to avoid eating raw vegetables and unpeeled fruits and to drink only treated water, hot drinks, or bottled drinks (avoid ice). Plenty of soft drinks are available, as well as bottled water (mineral water), sparkling water (soda), beer, and juices. You will find that any restaurant in Kathmandu that caters to tourists will claim to use boiled and filtered water and will also claim to treat its vegetables with a sterilizing solution. This is usually true and you can usually get away with eating salads and drinking iced drinks at these establishments. However, there are still risks involved. Why take a chance on getting diarrhea just so you can eat a pile of shredded cabbage and a slice of tomato (this is what most salads consist of in Nepal)? If you're at the start of a trip, it pays to be cautious. Remember that almost no one leaves Nepal without having some sort of stomach problems, so plan a few sick days into your schedule if you can. Though you may be tempted, you should also avoid cheesecakes and meringue pies while in Nepal. Salmonella bacteria favor these two items.

The next-most-important thing to remember is to wash your hands before you eat. This may sound simple, but it is not always easy, especially when you're trekking. Nepalis always wash their hands, or at least rinse them, before eating because they eat with their fingers. Moist towelettes or sterilizing gel will be invaluable.

Unfortunately, what is commonly contracted in Nepal is not always the simple traveler's diarrhea that goes away after a few days. Doctors in Nepal clinics have found that the majority of cases of diarrhea require treatment with antibiotics. If you develop diarrhea, it is very important to drink enough fluids to avoid dehydration. Packets of oral rehydration salts added to drinking water will help to replenish salts and electrolytes lost by your body. These packets are readily available for only a few cents per package all over Nepal. In the West, the same salts are difficult to find and are often very expensive.

There are a number of ways to deal with diarrhea, depending on its severity. The first line of defense should be Pepto-Bismol tablets, which are unavailable in Nepal, so be sure to bring some from home. If the diarrhea becomes so severe that it is difficult to stay hydrated, an antidiarrheal drug such as Imodium, Lomotil, or codeine can be taken. Such drugs are not antibiotics and only treat symptoms, but they're particularly helpful if travel is necessary. If diarrhea is due to food poisoning, though, these drugs can be harmful. Remember, too, that codeine is a narcotic and can become addictive if taken over a long period.

**Bacterial Diarrhea**   Of all the possible causes of diarrhea, bacterial infect the most common. This is caused by a proliferation of a usually harmless form coli bacteria. Because E. coli in Nepal has developed a resistance to the antibiotic sulfamethoxazole-trimethoprim (SMZ-TMP), which is marketed in the United States under the trade names of Septra and Bactrim, the most common way to treat bacterial diarrhea in Nepal is with Norfloxacin or Ciprofloxacin (both readily available).

**Amoebic Dysentery**   Though this is one of the most dreaded of diseases among travelers to the tropics, amoebas can be easily treated if diagnosed. The problem is that amoebas are often difficult to detect. If left untreated, they will migrate to the liver and cause damage, so it is very important that you let your doctor know that amoebic dysentery is a possibility should you develop diarrhea after leaving Nepal. Symptoms of amoebic dysentery include abdominal pain, diarrhea (frequently with blood or pus in the stool), lethargy, and fever. In Nepal, the recommended treatment for amoebic dysentery is tinidazole (marketed in Nepal as Tiniba). In the United States, where tinidazole is not available, Flagyl is the recommended drug.

**Giardiasis**   Another cause of long-term diarrhea, giardiasis is caused by a protozoan and is quite common in Nepal. Giardiasis is spread by water and food that has been contaminated with the cysts of the giardia organism; it has an incubation period of 7 days. Therefore, if you develop diarrhea on your second or third day in Nepal, giardiasis is not the cause. Giardiasis has been frequently associated with the passing of gas and burps that smell like rotten eggs. Though this is often true, it is not always the case. More common symptoms of giardiasis are a violent bubbling in the intestines accompanied by pain in the upper part of the abdomen. Diarrhea may come and go and often occurs only in the morning. Because the giardia protozoa live in the upper intestines, they are very difficult to detect in a stool sample, and people often go undiagnosed for months because the symptoms can be similar to those of many other illnesses. Remember that the incubation period for giardia is about 1 week, and should you develop diarrhea after returning home, it is important that you tell your doctor that giardiasis is a possibility. In the United States, giardiasis is usually treated with the drug Flagyl, but in Nepal, the recommended treatment is tinidazole (marketed as Tiniba).

**Food Poisoning**   Salmonella is the most common cause of food poisoning in Nepal. It is caused by a bacteria found in chickens and therefore in egg products. Fresh-cooked eggs are rarely a problem, but dishes such as cheesecake and meringue pie commonly support the growth of salmonella. It's best to avoid these two treats. The symptoms of salmonella are severe stomach cramps, diarrhea, vomiting, fever, and chills. Luckily, these all pass within 24 hours. Antidiarrheal drugs such as codeine, Imodium, and Lomotil should never be taken if salmonella poisoning is suspected. The salmonella bacteria secretes a poison as it passes through your body—slowing its progress will only make you sicker. To treat salmonella, drink as much liquid as possible.

## ALTITUDE SICKNESS

Altitude sickness (also called acute mountain sickness, or AMS) is an illness caused by the lack of oxygen at high altitudes. Anyone planning a trek in Nepal should become familiar with the symptoms, causes, and cures for this easily avoidable and sometimes fatal illness. Though altitude sickness generally does not occur below 10,000 feet, some people may suffer minor symptoms as low as 8,000 feet. Symptoms of altitude sickness include headaches, fatigue, lassitude, coughing, shortness of breath, loss of appetite, nausea, reduced urine output, heavy legs, and a drunken gait. Being physically fit is no guarantee that you will not develop symptoms. Having been to high elevations in the past without developing symptoms is no guarantee that you will not develop altitude sickness at the same elevation or even lower on a subsequent trip. There is no way to predict who will and who will not be struck with this illness, but trekkers who are overexerting themselves and are panting and breathless may be more susceptible. Someone who staggers into camp far behind the rest of the group is also a likely candidate. The best advice is to take it easy. Carry a light pack. Walk slowly.

Trekkers who spend several days hiking up to an altitude of 10,000 or 11,000 feet are less likely to develop altitude sickness than those who fly into the high-altitude airstrips at Lukla, Jomosom, and Manang. It can be very dangerous to fly into an elevation higher than 10,000 feet, such as the airstrip at Shyangboche above Namche Bazaar. It is very important for trekkers who fly in to spend 1 or 2 days acclimatizing to the elevation. Acclimatization is best done by resting for part of the day and perhaps taking a short hike to a higher elevation and then returning to the elevation at which you will be sleeping. This is the climb-high, sleep-low theory, and it should be used throughout high-altitude treks. *The rule of thumb:* Try not to ascend more than 1,000 feet per day when you are above 9,000 or 10,000 feet. Also, when you are above 10,000 feet, you should sleep for 2 nights at the same elevation for every 3,000 feet you ascend.

The first signs of impending altitude sickness are headache, extreme fatigue, shortness of breath, and loss of appetite. If these symptoms appear, you should not continue climbing until after acclimatizing for 1 or 2 days. Once the symptoms disappear, it is safe to continue. If the symptoms do not disappear, or get worse, descent to a lower elevation will be necessary.

Symptoms of worsening altitude sickness include increasing tiredness, severe headaches, vomiting, and loss of coordination. These are symptoms of high-altitude cerebral edema (HACE), an extreme form of acute mountain sickness. Acute mountain sickness is the result of fluid collecting between cells in the body, particularly in the brain and lungs. HACE, the accumulation of fluid in the brain, can cause death within 12 hours if symptoms are ignored. Increasing shortness of breath, coughing (sometimes with pink sputum being coughed up), and tiredness are symptoms of high altitude pulmonary edema (HAPE), which is the accumulation of fluid in the lungs. If nothing is done to alleviate the symptoms of HAPE, the person suffering from this form of altitude sickness can drown in the fluid collecting in the lungs.

One very important symptom of acute mountain sickness is loss of coordination. If someone is staggering or seems to be walking as if they are drunk, acute mountain sickness should be suspected. A good test is to ask the affected person to walk a straight line, placing one foot directly in front of the other without staggering or losing balance. If the person cannot perform this task, he or she should descend immediately. Anyone who just wants to lie in his or her sleeping bag should be made to perform this test and, if unable to walk without staggering, should be immediately evacuated to a lower elevation. Descending could mean the difference between life and death.

If the symptoms of HACE or HAPE occur, the person must descend immediately, and never alone. Descent should continue until the symptoms begin to decrease; this usually occurs within 1,000 to 1,500 feet. The affected person should descend slowly and avoid overexertion. It is always best to recognize symptoms early so the sick person can descend under his own volition, and while it is still light outside. If the person is unconscious, a yak, pony, or porter can usually be hired for transport to a lower elevation.

Those trekking with a group often have the hardest time dealing with altitude sickness. Group treks are usually on a tight schedule, and no one wants to have to cut their trek short because they are feeling badly. Don't let peer pressure get to you, and don't take chances. If you aren't feeling well, stop climbing. Don't try to keep up with the others.

People with heart disease or respiratory problems are advised not to attempt to trek to high elevations. Pregnant women should also stay below 12,000 feet. Children are more susceptible to altitude sickness and should be watched closely for any symptoms. Infants, who cannot tell you when they are feeling bad, should not be taken to high elevations. Also, sleeping pills and sedatives should not be taken at high altitudes because they slow breathing and may lead to altitude sickness. Drinking alcohol at high altitudes can also be dangerous and will, at the least, make you drunker faster than you ever thought possible.

**The Himalayan Rescue Association,** Jyatha, Thamel, P.O. Box 4944, Kathmandu (☎ 977/1-262746; e-mail: hra@aidpost.mos.com.np), located south of Tridevi Marg, is a nonprofit organization that is working to reduce the number of casualties among trekkers and mountain climbers in Nepal. Founded in 1973, the organization operates two rescue posts that are staffed by volunteer doctors during the main trekking seasons. One post is at Pheriche on the way to Everest Base Camp, and the other is in Manang at the foot of Thorong Pass. At the association's main office in Kathmandu, you can learn more about altitude sickness. They also have a bulletin board that is used by independent trekkers looking for trekking companions, and log books filled with descriptions of treks written by people who have stopped by the HRA office.

## INSURANCE

**Health/Accident**    Check your health-insurance policy before you leave your home country to make sure you are covered while traveling abroad. Medicare does not cover U.S. citizens traveling in Nepal. While you're in Nepal, the most important type of insurance to have is a policy that pays for emergency evacuation. The hospitals in Nepal are frightfully far behind Western standards, and most foreigners living in Nepal go to Bangkok or Singapore when they need medical treatment. If there is enough time, you should try to get to one of these cities before having any type of emergency surgery performed. Evacuation insurance is especially important for trekkers, and most major trekking agencies will not take you on a trek unless you can show proof that you have insurance to pay for emergency evacuation from the mountains. Helicopter rescue flights cost $600 to $1,400 per hour. Most helicopter rescues take 2 to 3 hours, so you are looking at a bill of $1,200 to $4,200. Before a helicopter will be sent to rescue you, you usually must prove that you can pay for the service. An insurance policy is sufficient proof. Among the reputable issuers of travel insurance are:

**International SOS Assistance,** P.O. Box 11568, Philadelphia, PA, 19116 (☎ **800/ 523-8662** or 215/244-1500; fax 215/244-0165; www.intsos.com; e-mail; individual@ intsos.com), is a travel-assistance company. They offer many services, including emergency evacuation, medical insurance for travelers, hospital admission, 24-hour hotline, return of unattended minors, return of remains, and trip cancellation. They offer special rates for couples and families.

**Travel Guard International,** 1145 Clark St., Stevens Point, WI 54481-9970 (☎ **800/ 826-1300;** fax 800/955-8785), offers a policy that includes medical coverage, emergency evacuation, trip cancellation and interruption, baggage protection, and accidental death insurance. Supplemental trip cancellation and baggage loss insurance may also be purchased.

**Travelex,** P.O. Box 9408, Garden City, NY 11530-9408 (☎ **800/228-9792**), offers different travel insurance policies for 1 day to 6 months. Coverage includes medical, emergency evacuation, baggage loss, trip cancellation or interruption insurance, and flight insurance against death or dismemberment.

**Access America Inc.,** 6600 W. Broad St., Richmond, VA 23230 (☎ **800/424-3391** or 804/285-3300), offers policies similar to those offered by Travelex; **Wallach & Company,** 107 W. Federal St., Suite 13, Middleburg, VA 20117 (☎ **800/237-6615**), offers medical insurance only.

**Loss/Theft**    They can ruin your vacation if they happen, and no one wants to think about them, but loss and theft of baggage do happen. If you're taking expensive trekking equipment or cameras, be sure to check your homeowner's, condo, co-op, or renter's insurance policy to make sure that it covers theft of your belongings when you're traveling abroad. If it does, be sure you know what sort of documentation you'll need and how soon you will have to contact the insurance company after the theft occurs. If you do not have this kind of insurance, consider taking out a policy against loss, theft, or damage. **International SOS Assistance, Travel Guard International, Travelex,** and **Access America Inc.,** above, all offer insurance against loss, theft, or damage of your baggage.

**Cancellation**    If there's some possibility that you will not be able to make your trip, consider trip-cancellation insurance. It will enable you to get a refund for the price of your ticket or entire tour package should you have to cancel at the last minute. Several of the insurance companies mentioned above offer this type of insurance.

## 7  What to Pack

**CLOTHING**    Nepal is a mountainous tropical country, which means that you may experience great climatic extremes. In October, which is one of the prime trekking months in Nepal, it can be hot enough to swim in Kathmandu or Chitwan while there are snowstorms raging in the high mountains. Be prepared for these extremes. Also, keep in mind that your wardrobe is likely to be quite different depending on whether you are trekking or just sightseeing. If you plan to trek, your single-most-important article of clothing will be a well-broken-in pair of comfortable hiking boots with good ankle support.

In general, one of the most important items is a pair of sturdy, enclosed walking shoes. The streets of Nepal are very bad and very dirty, and there are rarely sidewalks. You'll want to keep your feet as well protected as possible. As far as clothing is concerned, you should probably bring at least three changes of clothes since it often takes more than 24 hours to have clothes washed and dried. Casual clothing is the norm in Nepal, and the only place you might want to wear something dressy is at an expensive hotel restaurant. Thermal underwear is a necessity in winter months and when trekking, as are wool socks and a wool sweater (plentiful and inexpensive in Kathmandu) or fleece jacket. Thermal underwear also comes in handy if you go rafting; it helps retain body heat and dries out quickly. A down jacket is compact, lightweight, and warm, whether you are going trekking or not. A hat with a visor is invaluable while trekking, and in winter or when trekking, a warm hat and gloves or mittens can make the difference between being comfortable and freezing. If you are going to Chitwan in search of tigers and rhinos, remember to bring some khaki, brown, or green clothing so you won't be too conspicuous. A poncho or a good rain jacket can come in handy any time of year. Quick-drying nylon shirts and nylon pants with legs that zip off to convert the pants into shorts are also quite handy to have along.

**OTHER ITEMS**    In addition to the clothing mentioned above, here are some other items you might want to bring (for more suggestions, see the first-aid kit recommendations in chapter 9):

**Antibacterial Hand Gel**    This stuff is absolutely invaluable for cleaning your hands when there is no water around.

**Backpacking Towel**    These compact and highly absorbent synthetic chamois towels don't take up much space and can come in quite handy.

**Bandana or Scarf**    These can be used as face masks to keep out dust and diesel fumes.

**Binoculars**    If you are a bird-watcher, you will want to bring along your binoculars and take a trip to Chitwan National Park, home to more than 400 species of birds. Binoculars are also great to have while trekking.

**Camera & Film**    Nepal is one of the most photogenic places on earth. Film is readily available throughout Nepal, even at shops in remote villages along the main trekking routes. In Kathmandu and Pokhara, it is about the same price or a little cheaper than in the United States. Though print films (Fuji and Kodak) are the most commonly available, Ektachrome and Fujichrome slide film can also be purchased.

**Dropper Bottle**    A small bottle with a built-in dropper is a good way to carry iodine, which is probably the best way to purify water in Nepal. Though iodine is available in Nepal, it comes poorly packaged in bottles that almost always leak.

**Earplugs**    Barking dogs can ruin a night's sleep even in Kathmandu's most expensive hotels; consequently, earplugs are invaluable.

**Flashlight**    The electricity is regularly shut off in Kathmandu, and out on the trail there sometimes isn't any electricity at all. Headlamp-type flashlights are the best choice since they allow you to have your hands free (especially important when using outhouses while trekking).

**Handkerchief**    Runny noses are a fact of life in Nepal. You can avoid the problem of what to do with all that messy tissue paper by carrying a handkerchief.

**Insect Repellent**    You might not need this if you are in Nepal during the main trekking seasons, unless you visit one of the national parks in the Terai region.

**Lip Protection**    The winter climate in Nepal can be dry and cold, and up in the mountains, it is often very windy. Take along something to protect your lips from drying and cracking.

**Moist Towelettes**    A package of disposable moist towelettes is great for cleaning hands when no soap and water are handy when trekking.

**Pepto-Bismol**    Unavailable in Nepal, these tablets are about the best thing you can take for a simple upset stomach and are considered invaluable by many.

**Plastic Bags** (zipper type)    Sealable plastic bags are great for keeping camera equipment, electronics, and important papers dry.

**Sleeping Bag**    A down-filled bag is the best since it is lightweight, compact, and warm. A bag may also come in handy if you're traveling on the cheap; budget hotels often don't provide enough blankets. If you are trekking, you will definitely need a warm sleeping bag.

**Sunglasses**    The sun is bright, and in the snowfields at high altitudes, the glare can cause snow blindness.

**Sunscreen**   Despite the cool weather, this is still the tropics, and the sun can be intense. Apply sunscreen to your face and hands, especially at higher elevations.

**Swiss Army Knife**   These all-purpose utility knives are invaluable.

**Umbrella**   If you are visiting during the rainy season, an umbrella is an absolute necessity.

**Water Bottle**   With your own water bottle and iodine, you can have purified water no matter where you are.

## 8  Tips for Special Travelers

**FOR TRAVELERS WITH DISABILITIES**   Though a few of the more expensive hotels are becoming aware of the needs of travelers with disabilities, Nepal in general is not an easy country for people with disabilities to get around in. Sidewalks, where they exist, sometimes have curbs more than a foot high. Streets are uneven, potholed, muddy, and crowded. Temples and other buildings of interest to visitors almost always have steps, if not a steep stairway.

This said, there is at least one company that offers tours to Nepal for travelers with disabilities. **Accessible Journeys,** 35 W. Sellers Ave., Ridley Park, PA 19078 (☎ 800/ 846-4537 or 610/521-0339; fax 610/521-6959), operates tours to Nepal and India for those with mobility impairments.

For more general information, contact **Mobility International USA,** P.O. Box 10767, Eugene, OR 97440 (☎ 541/343-1284; www.miusa.org; e-mail: miusa@igc. apc.org), a membership organization that promotes international educational exchanges for people of all disabilities and ages. Although they do not offer trips to Nepal, this organization is a good source of general information and referrals. For a $35 membership fee, you receive a quarterly newsletter and access to a referral service.

In the United Kingdom, general information about travel for people with physical disabilities is available from the **Royal Association for Disability & Rehabilitation** (RADAR), 12 City Forum, 250 City Rd., London EC1V 8AF (☎ 0171/250-3222; fax 0171/250-0212). This organization publishes fact sheets and books that can be useful to anyone with disabilities planning a trip to Nepal or anywhere else.

For more helpful information on travel for the disabled, check out the Web site **www.access-able.com.** Here you'll find forums, bulletin boards, organizations, publications, and travel agents specializing in disabled travel arrangements. Agents are also listed for Great Britain and Australia.

**FOR SENIORS**   With each passing year, we have been meeting more and more older travelers in Nepal, and as is the case with younger travelers, most seem to be coming here with the specific goal of trekking. Although it's a strenuous activity, trekking may be far less difficult than it sounds if you are in good health and are accustomed to walking regularly. If you set your own pace or opt for a group trek with others in the same age range, you should have no problem. However, there are still some things to be aware of before buying your plane ticket to Kathmandu.

Nepal is about halfway around the world from North America, which means that jet lag can be extreme. Since there are no direct flights to Nepal from the United States, you must stop for a night's rest en route. This will help to combat jet lag, but it can still take more than a week to overcome your jet lag once you arrive in Nepal. Therefore, it is essential to take it easy for the first few days.

Before you head to Nepal, it is a good idea to have a physical exam. Medical care is far from adequate in Nepal, and even a minor medical emergency could prove life-threatening here. Also, if you suffer from heart disease of any sort, consult your

## Travel Tip

Store photocopies of important documents, such as your passport, visa, airline tickets, and insurance certificates, in a separate place from the originals. Also, remember to keep your traveler's check numbers in a different place from the actual checks.

---

doctor before planning a trek that will take you to high elevations. Altitude sickness can be particularly dangerous for anyone with a prior heart condition.

Be sure to pack an adequate supply of all of the medications you normally take, and know their generic names. If you lose your medications or run out, Nepali pharmacists are more likely to know the drug by its chemical name than by its U.S. trade name. Though many prescription drugs are available over the counter for much less money than in the United States, you can't count on a Nepali pharmacy to carry the wide variety of medications available in the United States. It is also a good idea to carry a spare set of glasses and keep one pair in a safe place such as the hotel safe-deposit box, in case your first pair gets lost or broken.

When making an airline reservation, always inquire about senior-citizen discounts. Many seniors travel to Nepal with an organized tour. Most of these tours are combined India and Nepal trips that add a few days in Kathmandu and perhaps Chitwan National Park onto the end of the trip, but **Overseas Adventure Travel,** 625 Mt. Auburn St., Cambridge, MA 02138 (☎ **800/221-0814** or 617/876-0533; fax 617/876-0826), offers lodge-to-lodge trekking in Nepal for older active travelers.

If you want something more than the average guided tour, **Elderhostel,** 75 Federal St., Boston, MA 02110-1941 (☎ **877/426-8056;** www.elderhostel.org), arranges study programs for those age 55 and over (and a spouse or companion of any age) in the United States and in 77 countries around the world, including Nepal. Most courses last about 3 weeks, and many include airfare, accommodations in student dormitories or modest inns, meals, and tuition. Write or call for a free catalog, which lists upcoming courses and destinations.

If you are not already a member, the **American Association of Retired Persons (AARP),** 601 E St. NW, Washington, DC 20049 (☎ **800/424-3410** or 202/434-2277), is a good source of information for senior citizens. Membership is only $8 for a married couple. **AARP** can also provide travelers with a list of travel suppliers, such as airlines, hotels, and vacation packagers who offer discounts to members. **Travel Companion Exchange,** P.O. Box 833, Amityville, NY 11701 (☎ **516/454-0880**), provides listings of possible travel companions who often specify special interests, age, education, and location. At press time prices were $99 for a 6-month membership and newsletter (soon going up to $159 for a 1-year membership), and $48 per year for the bimonthly newsletter only. Sample issues cost $6. Because this newsletter comes out frequently, information presented on cut-rate airline fares is timely and useful.

For a useful Web site with information on senior travel, check out **www.accessable. com** (see description above).

**FOR SINGLE TRAVELERS**    Single travelers need never travel alone in Nepal unless that is truly what they want. The Thamel neighborhood, frequented by budget travelers, is a spot for independent travelers who hang out in the cafes, restaurants, and pubs. The most popular restaurants are often so crowded that single travelers are seated together at the same table—a great way to meet people. There are also a number of bulletin boards around Thamel that serve as clearinghouses for people seeking trekking companions.

Trekking agencies in Nepal will often allow single travelers to join groups that have already arranged a trek if it is agreeable with the trekking party. Other companies have regularly scheduled treks and white-water rafting trips that solo travelers can join. Still, other adventurous types set off for the trekking trails alone (not advisable) and meet up with fellow trekkers en route to the trailhead. I have done this myself and have found trekking companions before ever setting foot on the trail. Solo U.S. citizens in Nepal often find themselves spending time with Canadians and other English-speaking folks from Britain, New Zealand, and Australia.

If you prefer to make arrangements for a traveling companion before leaving home, **Travel Companion Exchange,** P.O. Box 833, Amityville, NY 11701 (☎ **516/454-0880**), can help you find someone who shares the same interests. This agency publishes a bimonthly newsletter. As a member, you will receive the newsletter and listings of personal profiles of other members (see "For Seniors," above, for details).

Nepal is still a very safe country for single travelers of either sex. You should be generally quite safe anywhere in Kathmandu, Pokhara, or any other small town or village. The only exception is on the trekking trails. In the past few years, there have been increasing numbers of robberies and even occasional murders of lone trekkers. *Do not trek alone!* Always find a companion, whether it is another trekker, a porter, or a guide.

**FOR FAMILIES**    There are a lot of things to consider before taking children to Nepal, but one consideration stands out above all others. Have your children had all of their childhood vaccinations? If not, you could be risking your children's health and possibly their lives by taking them to Nepal. Childhood diseases that have long been controlled in developed nations are still widespread in Nepal. See "Health, Insurance & Other Concerns," earlier in this chapter, for more information on which diseases are problems in Nepal. Children are also more susceptible to, and more severely affected by, gastrointestinal illnesses, which are very common in Nepal. Diarrhea is one of the main causes of child deaths in Nepal. Carry antibacterial hand gel or moist towelettes at all times so you can clean your children's hands whenever necessary. This is the first line of defense against stomach bugs.

One of the hardest parts of a family trip to Nepal is the plane ride. It takes well over 24 hours of flying, plus an overnight stop somewhere, to reach Nepal. That's a long time for a child to be stuck in a plane. Be sure to pack plenty to entertain the young ones. Also, bring along your kids' favorite snacks, since airline food may not appeal to them. Some airlines have special meals for children; be sure to ask when making your reservations. It's a good idea to have kids carry their own little day pack filled with books, crayons, paper, and small toys. They'll feel right at home once they arrive in Kathmandu, where virtually all visitors wear day packs everywhere they go.

Don't bother bringing a stroller to Nepal; it will only be an inconvenience on the uneven streets. A better choice is a child carrier that you wear on your back. Outdoor supply stores now sell well-designed baby packs that combine storage space with a seat for the baby. These are an excellent idea if you plan to go trekking with a child too small to walk all the time. Keep in mind, though, that children this young are more susceptible to altitude sickness.

You won't find disposable diapers in Nepal. In fact, most children in Nepal don't wear diapers at all, or pants for that matter, until they are old enough to be toilet trained. You may have to rely on cloth diapers and have them washed daily.

Most hotels allow children under age 12 to stay free in your room if you don't request an extra bed. Bring along sleeping bags and mats for the kids to sleep on. Only a few of the most expensive hotels in Nepal have any facilities for children, so you might want to pick a hotel that has some sort of garden for the kids to play in. Most

Nepali children speak some English, often more than adults, and with so many English-speaking children, your kids will likely find playmates wherever they go. Also, Nepali adults are usually fascinated with Western children and enjoy interacting with them.

Be sure that your children always carry a photocopy of their passport so that if they should get lost, whoever finds them will know which local authorities to contact. Another good idea is to tie a whistle around a young one's neck so that if the child gets lost she can blow on it. Many of the streets in Kathmandu are so crowded that a child could be only a few feet away from you and be unable to see you.

**FOR STUDENTS**    Though a student ID card won't get you any discounts in Kathmandu, it can save you a bundle on your air ticket. The best resource is the **Council on International Educational Exchange,** or CIEE. They can set you up with an ID card (see below), and their travel branch, **Council Travel Service (☎ 800/226-8624;** www.ciee.com), is the biggest student travel-agency operation in the world. It can get you discounts on plane tickets, rail passes, and the like. From CIEE you can obtain the student traveler's best friend, the $18 **International Student Identity Card** (ISIC). It's the only officially acceptable form of student identification, good for cut rates on plane tickets and other discounts. It also provides you with basic health and life insurance, evacuation insurance, and a 24-hour help line. If you're no longer a student but are still under 26, you can obtain a **GO 25 card** from the same people, which will get you the insurance and some of the discounts.

In Canada, **Travel CUTS,** 200 Ronson St., Suite 320, Toronto, ON M9W 5Z9 (☎ 800/667-2887 or 416/614-2887; www.travelcuts.com), offers similar services. **Campus Travel,** 52 Grosvenor Gardens, London SW1W 0AG (☎ 0171/730-3402; www.campustravel.co.uk), opposite Victoria Station, is Britain's leading specialist in student and youth travel.

## 9  Getting There

### BY PLANE

The single-most-important thing to know about flying to Nepal is that with relatively few flights into the country, seats book up months in advance during the peak trekking season (Oct and Nov). March and April can also be difficult months for getting a confirmed seat, but not nearly as difficult as in the fall. Try to make reservations at least 6 months in advance, especially if you want to fly on Thai Airways or Singapore Airlines. By July or August, you'll find that nearly every flight into the country during this period is wait-listed. Royal Nepal Airlines, which is infamously unreliable, is usually the last airline to fill up.

There are no direct flights from the United States to Nepal, so unless you fly Thai Airways, Singapore Airlines, or Pakistan International Airlines, you're going to have to change airlines somewhere en route, usually in London or Delhi if you are eastbound or in Bangkok or Singapore if you are westbound. You'll also have to spend a night somewhere en route—Bangkok, Singapore, Karachi, and Delhi are the usual overnight stops. Whether you choose to get a room for the night or stay at the airport is up to you. If you opt for a room, try to get a discount of some sort through your airline. If you have a few days to spare, you can usually schedule a stop in Europe or Southeast Asia at no additional charge on the airfare. If you are traveling through Delhi, it's a good idea to have an Indian visa, even if you aren't planning to leave the airport. We've had reports of people being refused onward passage because they didn't have a visa, even though they were only transiting through the airport.

## THE AIRLINES & THE ROUTES

**From North America**   Only three airlines have service between the United States and Nepal. **Thai Airways** (☎ 800/426-5204) flies from Los Angeles via Bangkok. **Singapore Airlines** (☎ 800/742-3333) flies from Los Angeles, San Francisco, New York, and Vancouver via Singapore. **Pakistan International Airlines** (☎ 800/221-2552) flies from New York via Karachi. However, by changing airlines somewhere en route, you have plenty of other choices; major American and Canadian airlines can get you to Asia or Europe, where you can connect to Kathmandu-bound flights.

**From London**   Royal Nepal Airlines, Biman Bangladesh Airlines, Qatar Airways, and **Pakistan International Airlines** all fly from London to Nepal. Alternatively, you can fly to Delhi and then transfer to an airline with service to Nepal.

**From Europe**   Royal Nepal Airlines flies from London, Frankfurt, and Paris. **Transavia** has flights from Amsterdam. **Austrian Airlines** has flights from Vienna. **Aeroflot Russian Airlines** flies from Moscow.

**From Australia**   Singapore Airlines and **Thai Airways International** both have connecting flights from Australia to Nepal. **Qantas** flies to Bangkok, where you can transfer to **Thai** or **Royal Nepal Airlines.**

**From Asia**   Royal Nepal Airlines flies from Delhi, Calcutta, Mumbai (Bombay), Bangkok, Hong Kong, Osaka, and Singapore. **Thai Airways** flies from Bangkok. **Singapore Airlines** flies from Singapore. **Biman Bangladesh Airlines** flies from Dhaka. **India Airlines,** Air India's domestic carrier, flies from Calcutta, Delhi, and Varanasi. **Pakistan International Airlines** flies from Karachi. **China Southwest Airlines** flies from Lhasa, Tibet. **Druk Air (Royal Bhutan Airlines)** flies from Paro, Bhutan, and Delhi.

**From the Middle East**   Royal **Nepal Airlines** flies from Dubai. **Gulf Air** flies from Abu Dhabi. **Qatar Airlines** flies from Doha, Qatar.

## FINDING THE BEST AIRFARE
### Full Fares

**Coach**   Coach fares are full-price tickets with no advance-purchase requirement. The tickets are refundable, and you can change your date of departure. However, these two slight advantages over an APEX fare do not outweigh the great cost difference that often applies. Currently, full coach fares are around $4,500 from the west coast of the United States and around $5,000 from the east coast.

**Business Class**   You get slightly larger seats, better meals, and more attentive service in business class, which might be just what you want on such a long trip. Currently, business-class fares are about $4,000 from the west coast and $5,100 from the east coast.

**First Class**   If you need a large seat, gourmet meals, and personal service, you are going to pay considerably more on a flight to Nepal. At press time first-class seats from the west coast were about $8,000; add $100 more from the east coast.

### Advance-Purchase Excursion Fares (APEX)

These are the lowest regular airfares, and they usually have restrictions on when you can fly and how far in advance you must pay for your ticket. APEX fares usually carry stiff cancellation penalties, and departure dates cannot be changed after you pay for your ticket. However, with these restrictions, you can save several hundred dollars over the regular economy airfare. At press time a round-trip APEX fare was between $1,500 and $1,800 from either the west or the east coast of the United States.

**Consolidators**   Consolidators, also known as bucket shops, are a good place to find low fares. Consolidators buy seats in bulk from the airlines and then sell them back to the public at prices below even the airlines' discounted rates. You can find their ads, usually just a list of destinations and prices, in the Sunday travel sections of major city newspapers. The list of prices is usually just a come-on and often does not include taxes and surcharges. However, when all the charges are added in, these tickets are often cheaper than what you will get by going directly to the airlines. At press time, west-coast bucket shops were selling tickets for about $1,000 to $1,500 from west-coast cities to Nepal.

Bucket-shop tickets are often nonrefundable or carry a stiff penalty for cancellation, and initial departure dates usually cannot be changed once the ticket is issued. Before you pay, ask for a confirmation number from the consolidator and then call the airline itself to confirm your seat. Be prepared to book your ticket with a different consolidator—there are many to choose from—if the airline can't confirm your reservation.

**Council Travel** (☎ 800/226-8624; www.counciltravel.com) and **STA Travel** (☎ 800/781-4040; www.sta.travel.com) cater especially to young travelers, but their bargain-basement prices are available to people of all ages. **Ticket Planet** (☎ 800/799-8888) specializes in round-the-world tickets. **Travel Bargains** (☎ 800/AIR-FARE; www.1800airfare.com) was formerly owned by TWA but now offers the deepest discounts on many other airlines, with a 4-day advance purchase. Other reliable consolidators include **1-800-FLY-CHEAP** (www.1800flycheap.com) and **TFI Tours International** (☎ 800-745-8000 or 212/736-1140), which serves as a clearinghouse for unused seats. There are also "rebaters" such as **Travel Avenue** (☎ 800/333-3335 or 312/876-1116) and the **Smart Traveller** (☎ 800/448-3338 in the United States or 305/448-3338), which rebate part of their commissions to you.

**Cheap Airlines**   There are a couple of reliably cheap airlines for flights into Nepal from Asian cities or Europe: **Biman Bangladesh Airlines** (☎ 888/702-4626) and **Pakistan International Airlines (PIA)** (☎ 800/221-2552).

**Internet Reservations**   The Internet is now becoming the best place to search for cheap fares, although it's still wise to compare your findings with the lowest published fare. A few of the better-respected virtual travel agents are **Travelocity** (www.travelocity.com) and **Microsoft Expedia** (www.expedia.com). Just enter the dates you want to fly and the cities you want to visit, and the computer roots out the lowest fares (sometimes).

## OVERLAND
### BY BUS/TRAIN FROM INDIA

There are six official border crossings with India, and at all of them there are usually Nepali buses to meet you. However, wherever you happen to cross the border, you still have a long and bumpy ride to Kathmandu or Pokhara. Overlanding from India to Nepal is quite inexpensive and for this reason is common among budget travelers who have been exploring India. From Delhi, most people opt to go partway by train (to Gorakhpur) and then transfer to a bus bound for the Indian border town of Sunauli. Once across the border into Bhairawa, Nepal, there are local buses to Pokhara and Kathmandu. It is possible to take a deluxe bus from Delhi, India, to Kathmandu. The entire trip takes about 1½ days and costs less than $20.

### BY BUS FROM TIBET

Although time-consuming, it is possible to travel overland from Lhasa, Tibet. There are regularly scheduled buses to the Nepali border, but most travelers opt to hire a bus, truck, or Land Rover to make the journey to the Nepali border crossing at Kodari. From Kodari, you must catch a local Nepali bus for the rest of the trip to Kathmandu. This trip takes from 3 days to 1 week.

## PACKAGE TOURS

Few package tours go only to Nepal, unless they also include a bit of trekking, rafting, or a jungle safari. If you simply want to do some sightseeing and admire the Himalayas from afar, you will probably have to visit Nepal as part of an India-Nepal tour. These tours are offered by several companies, and your local travel agent should be able to find one that best suits your needs. Among the most reliable companies offering tours that include Nepal in the itinerary are the following:

### IN THE UNITED STATES

**Abercrombie & Kent,** 1520 Kensington Rd., Oak Brook, IL 60523-2141 (☎ 800/323-7308 or 630/954-2944; fax 630/954-3324; www.abercrombiekent.com; e-mail: info@abercrombiekent).

   **Esplanade/Swan Hellenic,** 581 Boylston St., Boston, MA 02116 (☎ 800/426-5492 or 617/266-7465).

   **Sita World Travel, Inc.,** 8125 San Fernando Rd., Sun Valley, CA 91352 (☎ 800/421-5643 or 818/767-0039; fax 818/767-4346; www.sitatours.com).

   **Smithsonian Institution,** Study Tours and Seminars, 1100 Jefferson Dr. SW, MRC 702, Washington, DC 20560 (☎ 202/357-4700; fax 202/633-9250).

### IN THE UNITED KINGDOM

**Abercrombie & Kent,** Sloane Square House, Holbein Place, London SW1W 8NS (☎ 0171/730-9600; fax 0171/730-9376).

   **Crusaders,** 57-58 Church St., Twickenham TW1 3NR (☎ 0181/892-7606; fax 0181/744-0574; www.crusadertravel.com; e-mail: info@crusadertravel.com).

   **Encounter Overland Expeditions Ltd.,** 267 Old Brompton Rd., London SW5 9JA (☎ 0171/370-6845; fax 0171/244-9737; www.encounter-overland.com; e-mail: adventure@encounter.co.uk).

   **Explore Worldwide,** 1 Frederick St., Aldershot, Hants GU11 1LQ (☎ 01252/760000; fax 01252/760201; www.explore.co.uk/; e-mail: info@adventureworld.com.au).

## 10  Getting Around

### BY PLANE

Until a few years ago, Royal Nepal Airlines (RNAC), the national carrier, was the only airline operating in Nepal. RNAC was legendary for its inefficiency, and a trip to their office in Kathmandu was often a Kafkaesque nightmare. However, there is now plenty of competition from private airlines. The easiest way to make flight reservations is through a travel agency in Kathmandu or Pokhara, but should you wish to contact an airline directly, here are the phone numbers in Kathmandu (see chapter 7 for details): **Buddha Air** ☎ 977/1-417802 or 418864; **Cosmic Air** ☎ 977/1-246905 or 247485; **Gorkha Airline** ☎ 977/1-423137 or 428286; **Lumbini Airways** ☎ 977/1-483381; **Necon Air** ☎ 977/1-473860 or 480565; **RNAC** ☎ 977/1-226574 or 977/1-220757, at the airport 977/1-470919; and **Yeti Airways** ☎ 977/1-421215 or 421147.

   It is not usually possible for a foreign travel agent to book domestic flights. If you want to book a domestic flight before your arrival in Nepal, try contacting a Kathmandu travel agent such as **Natraj Tours & Travel,** Ghantaghar, Kamaladi (☎ 977/1-222014 or 977/1-222532), or **Nepal Travel Agency,** Ramshahpath

(☎ 977/1-430188 or 977/1-431013). If you are unable to make a reservation before arriving in Nepal, do so as soon after your arrival as possible, especially in the busy months of October and November, when all the domestic flights get booked up quickly.

Flight schedules in Nepal change frequently, and flights are often canceled due to bad weather, especially in early October when the monsoon is still lingering. It is very common for flights out of Lukla to be canceled for several days in a row. This is one of the times when it is helpful to be on an organized trek; these groups generally have more clout and get on the planes before independent trekkers. Keep this in mind if you are planning to go trekking in the Everest region. Try not to make any reservations for a week after your scheduled return flight from Lukla just in case weather and a logjam of trekkers force you to walk out or sit in Lukla for several days.

In recent years, **helicopters,** because they can fly in worse weather and lower and slower than fixed-wing airplanes, have been the preferred mode of travel to Lukla and Shyangboche (both in the Solu-Khumbu region near Mount Everest). This means that if you are scheduled to fly out of either of these airstrips and cloudy weather sets in, you are more likely to get out on time if you have a reservation on a chopper. However, in 1998, noncharter helicopter flights were banned at these airstrips for safety reasons. Expect the ban to be lifted in coming years. Helicopter airlines come and go with alarming regularity in Nepal, so check with a travel agency in Kathmandu for current information.

## BY BUS

In Nepal, if there is a road, it is served by a bus or some other vehicle carrying paying passengers. Buses in Nepal are slow, crowded, cramped, dirty, smoky, and decrepit, and they frequently break down. The roads are potholed, winding, and often closed by landslides. This combination makes for some of the hardest traveling in the world. You might get the impression that we don't like traveling by bus in Nepal—you are absolutely correct. If you can afford to avoid the buses here, by all means do so. If your budget requires you to travel by bus, at least try to take the better buses when possible. There are several "tourist buses" operating between Kathmandu and Pokhara. Almost any hotel or travel agency in either city will make a reservation on one of these buses. They are slightly more expensive than the regular bus service (say, $3 instead of $1.50), but they offer more leg room and wider seats, and take fewer hours (say, 7 or 8 instead of 10 or 12) to cover the 200 kilometers. Regular buses throughout Nepal are incredibly cheap. You can get a 16-hour ride for less than $2 (though you will cover only 125 miles).

All local buses in Nepal make frequent tea stops at filthy roadside teahouses. Due to the lack of hygiene at these places, we don't recommend eating anything that doesn't come wrapped, bottled, or inside a peel (bananas and mandarins). These truck stops usually do not have toilets other than the nearest bushes. I always bring my own snacks and a bottle of water when traveling by bus, and you'd be wise to do the same. Tourist buses, on the other hand, usually stop at relatively pleasant rest areas where tea and food are usually laid out for a quick feeding of the hungry passengers.

Trekkers will find that newer roads leading up into the mountains to trailheads are often served only by jeeps and trucks. These vehicles are always overloaded and can be extremely uncomfortable. If you have the time to take an alternative walking route, I recommend that you do so.

## BY TAXI/CAR

There are no self-drive car rentals in Nepal. All cars are rented with a driver, which has two benefits: You don't have to deal with the chaotic driving of Nepali bus, truck, and taxi drivers, and you can enjoy the amazing scenery. Almost every hotel, no matter whether it is a budget guest house or a deluxe hotel, will be able to arrange a hired car (or taxi) and driver for you. It generally costs around Rs1,200 ($18.20) to Rs1,500 ($22.75) to hire a taxi for the day in Kathmandu or Pokhara. However, if you plan to travel out of either Kathmandu Valley or Pokhara Valley, this price will go up, and you may have to negotiate over who will pay for the gas. To hire a taxi, car, or minivan to take you to Pokhara will cost between $60 and $80. This can be a cost-effective way to travel between the two cities. It is faster than the bus, is less expensive than flying, and allows you to see some of the countryside up close.

In Nepal, as in India and other countries influenced by the British Empire, you drive on the left side of the road with the steering wheel on the right. Since you won't be driving yourself, most driving rules are of no concern. However, one rule bears mentioning: Do not hit a cow! Should you rent a motorcycle, this could be very important to you. Cows are sacred, and there are stiff jail sentences for anyone convicted of hurting or killing a cow in Nepal. And cows, for some reason, love to sleep in the middle of roads!

## BY MOTORCYCLE

If you are an experienced motorcyclist (off-road experience comes in handy), a motorcycle can be a good way of getting around in Nepal. Motorcycles are available for rent in Kathmandu's Thamel neighborhood and Pokhara's Lakeside neighborhood. They usually rent for Rs400 ($6.05) to Rs500 ($7.60) per day plus gasoline (petrol), which at press time was selling for around $2.40 per gallon. These motorcycles are generally 100 to 175cc bikes, which means they don't have much power and aren't very good for long trips. However, they work well for day trips.

## SUGGESTED ITINERARIES

The following itineraries are basically for someone who wants to experience the highlights of Nepal. If, however, your main interest is trekking, you can cut back your time in Kathmandu and skip Royal Chitwan National Park entirely to get in more days on the trail. Even in a week's visit, it is possible to get a taste for trekking with a 1- to 3-night trek.

### If You Have 1 Week

**Days 1–3**    Explore the Kathmandu Valley. Visit Kathmandu's Durbar Square on your first day; Patan, Pashupatinahht, and Boudhanath on your second day; and Bhaktapur, Changu Narayan, and Nagarkot (for mountain views) on your third day.

**Days 4–5**    Ride elephants and search for rhinos, tigers, and bears at either Royal Chitwan or Royal Bardia National Park. Stay at one of the many lodges in or near the park. Proceed to Pokhara on day 6.

**Days 6–7**    Explore Pokhara (maybe take a taxi up Sarangkot Hill). The next morning, after catching the sunrise over the Himalayas, return to Kathmandu. Visit Swayambunath at sunset.

### If You Have 2 Weeks

**Days 1–4**    Explore the Kathmandu, taking in the sights mentioned above and also visiting some of the more remote temples in the valley. Spend the night at Nagarkot or Dhulikhel.

**Days 5–7**  Spend 2 days rafting on the Trishuli River between Kathmandu and Chitwan National Park, and then explore the park, searching for rhinos and tigers and bears amid the park's forests and grasslands.

**Days 8–9**  Visit Pokhara and take in the astonishing sunrise view of the Himalayas, maybe take a scenic flight, and explore a bit of the valley.

**Days 10–13**  Take a 4-day trek out of Pokhara.

**Day 14**  Return to Kathmandu.

**If You Have More Than 2 Weeks**

For the best treks in Nepal, you'll need a minimum of a week and as much as 17 or 18 days, so if you have more than 2 weeks for a trip to Nepal and trekking is your prime interest, you can do just about any of the most popular treks.

## 11  Tips on Eating in Nepal

Most Nepalis eat only two real meals each day (for breakfast they will often have only sweet milk tea and fried dough). The first significant meal comes around 10am, and dinner is usually eaten between 6 and 7pm. Lunch and dinner for most of the population consists of rice, lentils, and vegetables. However, in the higher elevations where rice does not grow, potatoes and barley are substituted. Because cows are sacred, beef is not eaten in Nepal (although at more-expensive restaurants beef imported from India is served). In the absence of beef, water buffalo is the most popular meat, though it is relatively expensive. Goat, chicken, and pork are eaten, but again these are all expensive. Most Nepalis are restricted to a vegetarian diet for financial reasons.

Nepali food is similar to simple Indian food in that it relies on chilies, garlic, and onions for flavoring. *Dal bhat,* which is Nepali for lentils and rice, is the mainstay of the Nepali diet and can be good, bad, or mediocre. It is traditionally accompanied by fried vegetables and some spicy pickled vegetable (*achar*). Few restaurants in Nepal serve Nepali food because it has developed a bad name due to the generally insipid renderings of dal bhat that get served to tourists and trekkers. However, Nepali dishes, including dal bhat when well prepared, are quite delicious. While western desserts such as chocolate cake and apple pie dominate dessert menus in Nepal, one local dessert to watch for is *sikarni,* an ambrosial yogurt dessert that shows up on menus in Nepali/Tibetan restaurants. See "Menu Items" in the Appendix of this book (page 289).

Tibetan food is slightly more common on menus partly because of the mysterious cachet that Tibet still enjoys. There are several Tibetan dishes you may encounter in

---

### Some Nepali Food Customs

Hindus consider food contaminated or polluted if it has been touched by a Westerner since Westerners are casteless. Do not offer to share your food if you have already taken a bite, and do not touch cooked food that is intended for other people. Wait to be served rather than serving yourself, because this would contaminate the meal for everyone else. Also, remember that you should use only your right hand for eating. When sharing water with Nepalis, pour the water into your mouth without touching your lips to the water bottle or pitcher. Do not throw garbage into any household cooking fire in Nepal. The flame is considered sacred by many of the country's people.

restaurants in Kathmandu, in Pokhara, and on the trail. *Thukpa* is a vegetable-noodle soup. *Momos* and *kothays* are meat- or vegetable-stuffed dumplings similar to Chinese potstickers. Momos are steamed, and kothays are fried.

## FAST FACTS: Nepal

**American Express**    Nepal's only American Express office is in Kathmandu (see "Fast Facts" in chapter 4 for details).

**Business Hours**    On Saturday, the Nepali weekend, government offices and many businesses are closed. Banks: Sunday to Thursday 10am to 2:30pm in summer (10am to 2pm in winter), Friday 10am to 12:30pm; bars: closing time is 10pm or midnight; offices: Sunday to Thursday 10am to 5pm in summer (10am to 4pm in winter), Friday 10am to 3pm; stores: daily 10am to 7pm (tourist shops often open earlier and stay open later). Many businesses and some shops close for an hour at lunch.

**Car Rentals**    See "Getting Around," earlier in this chapter.

**Climate**    See "When to Go," earlier in this chapter.

**Currency**    See "Money," earlier in this chapter.

**Customs**    See "Visitor Information & Entry Requirements," earlier in this chapter.

**Documents Required**    See "Visitor Information & Entry Requirements," earlier in this chapter.

**Drug Laws**    Though marijuana and hashish were once legal in Nepal, today you can be jailed for possession of even small amounts. Many drugs that are available only by prescription in the West are available over the counter in Nepal, and you can save a substantial amount of money by stocking your trekking first-aid kit here instead of at home.

**Drugstores**    Known as pharmacies, chemists, and dispensaries, drugstores in Nepal are usually tiny shops stocked floor to ceiling with boxes and bottles. Tell the proprietor what you need, and he will get it for you.

**Electricity**    The current in Nepal is 220 volts/50 cycles, and it is not very reliable. There are regular blackouts in Kathmandu.

**Embassies & Consulates**    Embassies and consulates are all located in Kathmandu. See "Fast Facts" in chapter 4 for details. The U.S. Embassy strongly recommends that U.S. citizens register with the U.S. embassy in Nepal upon arrival in case the embassy needs to contact you in the event of an emergency. Also, a stolen or lost passport can be replaced more quickly if you have previously registered with the Embassy. Registration can be done by e-mail at usembcon@mos.com.np. Consult the U.S. State Department site for details.

**Emergencies**    See the Kathmandu and Pokhara chapters for phone numbers to call in the event of an emergency.

**Etiquette**    It is customary to remove one's shoes before entering a Nepali household or temple. You should walk clockwise around Buddhist temples, stupas, mani walls, and chortens. Many Hindu temples are off-limits to non-Hindus. When giving or receiving something, use your right hand or both hands (touching your left hand to your right wrist when giving or receiving money is a traditional Nepali way of using both hands). It is also customary to eat with your right hand only. Do not point your finger or your feet at people or religious objects. Do not throw garbage in cooking fires, which are considered sacred. Do not offer a Hindu a bite of food if you have already taken a bite yourself. Likewise, do not touch food that is meant for someone else.

**Holidays**   See "When to Go," above, in this chapter.

**Information**   See "Visitor Information & Entry Requirements," earlier in this chapter.

**Language**   Though Nepali is the national language, more than a dozen other languages are spoken. The *Nepali Phrasebook,* published by Lonely Planet, is useful and readily available. You'll find that people in the tourism and trekking businesses generally speak English (as well as several other languages). Off the main trekking routes and in jobs not related to tourism, English is much less widely spoken.

**Liquor Laws**   Liquor laws are lax in Nepal. If you look old enough, you'll get served.

**Mail**   Letters take anywhere from 2 to 6 weeks to get to the United States or Canada. A postcard to the United States, Canada, or Australia costs Rs15 (23¢), and letters start at Rs20 (30¢); to Great Britain, 12Rs (18¢) and Rs18 (27¢), respectively.

You can get stamps at post offices, at bookshops, and often at hotel reception desks, though you'll pay a little extra at the latter two. EMS, Express Mail Service provided by the post office, is usually a dependable way to mail documents and small packages. To ship a package from Nepal, you must show your passport, have your package inspected by Customs, and then have the package sealed. This takes time and money at every step. It is much easier and only slightly more expensive to let a reliable shipping agent take care of your shipping. Airmail can take about a week, whereas sea mail can take as long as 3 months. For more information about shipping, see "Shipping It Home," under "Shopping," in chapter 5.

**Maps**   Bookshops in Kathmandu and Pokhara have a wide variety of maps (though few of them are very detailed) in a range of prices. The Nepal and Pokhara maps printed by the Swiss company Karto Atelier are among the best maps available and, in Nepal, sell for a little more than $10 (though they aren't easy to find). The tourist office in Kathmandu sometimes has free Nepal and Kathmandu maps available, and the tourist information center in Pokhara hands out free maps to that city. The best trekking maps are the German-made Schneider maps. These are expensive and hard to find in Kathmandu, but they may be available from a good map store in your home country. The best commonly available trekking maps are those of the Nepa Maps series, which are designed by an Italian mapmaker. These maps are only slightly more expensive than other maps and are readily available in bookshops in the Thamel district of Kathmandu.

**Medical Emergencies**   See the individual chapters for phone numbers to call in the event of an emergency. Since medical facilities in Nepal are far below Western standards, most Westerners who need major medical attention fly to Bangkok or Singapore.

**Newspapers/Magazines**   *The Rising Nepal* and *The Kathmandu Post* are Nepal's English-language daily newspapers and cover international and national news; in addition, the *International Herald Tribune* and *USA Today* are available daily. *Nepal Traveller* and *Travellers' Nepal* are very informative English-language magazines for tourists. Asian editions of *Time* and *Newsweek*, which tend to focus on Asian news, are available, as are *The Economist* and other British and European magazines. These publications are sold at bookshops in Kathmandu and Pokhara.

**Photographic Needs**   Kodak and Fuji print and slide films are both readily available in Nepal (even in remote villages on main trekking routes) and are usually quite a bit cheaper than they are in the United States. Before going to Nepal, you might invest in a polarizing filter if your camera will accept one. At high altitudes and in snowy areas, a polarizer will eliminate glare, make blues richer, and reduce contrast. Before heading out on the trail, be sure you have an extra battery (available in Kathmandu). When you're departing Nepal through Tribhuvan International Airport, it is important to remember that the X-ray machines used on checked baggage are *not* film-safe.

**Police**   Police are rarely in evidence outside cities in Nepal. Should you need the police while traveling between cities, go to the nearest town or village and ask for the local police officer (who, unfortunately, will likely not speak English). While trekking, you can contact the police through check posts along the route.

**Restrooms**   You won't find many public restrooms in Nepal. For Nepalis, almost any spot somewhat removed from public view makes a convenient public toilet, and you are expected to follow suit. This can be very inconvenient for women when shrubbery is unavailable to hide behind. I suggest wearing a long skirt when traveling long distances by bus or car. This will provide a semblance of modesty should you need to relieve yourself en route. In cities such as Kathmandu and Pokhara, there are toilets in all restaurants and in the lobbies of more-expensive hotels. The Nepali word for toilet is *charpi,* and in English you should ask for the toilet, not the restroom.

**Safety**   Nepal is relatively safe. However, the crime rate has been rising in recent years. Therefore, you should never trek alone. Take extra precautions with your valuables when traveling on crowded buses, where you are easy prey to pickpockets. I suggest always keeping your money (preferably traveler's checks), passport, and airline tickets in a money belt or neck bag worn under your clothes. Try to avoid displaying large amounts of money in public. Also, backpacks and items from backpacks do sometimes get stolen off bus roofs (especially on the bus to Jiri). Make sure your bag is securely fastened to the luggage rack, and don't leave anything of value in it. Better yet, buy a second bus ticket for your backpack and put it in the seat next to you.

**Taxes**   There is a 10% Value Added Tax on hotel rooms and restaurant meals. This tax is calculated on top of the 2% Tourism Service Charge, which is just a tax by another name. At the airport, there is a Rs1,000 ($15.15) international departure tax and a Rs100 ($1.50) domestic departure tax.

**Telephone & Fax**   The telephone system in Nepal is surprisingly good. The dial tone is a bit lower, slower, and softer than that heard on U.S. telephones, but otherwise it is similar. Rapid beeps mean that the line is busy. In Kathmandu, all phone numbers now have six digits; in Pokhara they have five digits. Elsewhere the number may be less than five digits. When dialing Nepal from another country, you must dial the country code (977) and the city code (Kathmandu,

1; Pokhara, 61) and then your number. When dialing long-distance within Nepal, you must first dial zero, then the city code, and then the number you are trying to reach. Many hotels now offer international direct dialing. For the international operator dial 186.

You won't find pay phones in the usual sense, but almost any shopkeeper in Kathmandu or Pokhara who can afford a phone operates it as a pay phone for residents of the neighborhood. You'll often see such phones sitting in a wooden box on store counters. A local phone call usually costs two or three rupees.

Telephones now exist even in many remote villages on the major trekking routes, though some of these are solar-powered and work only when the sun is shining. When you're out on the trail, it can be reassuring to know that a telephone is only a few hours' (or at most just a couple of days') walk away.

**Time Zone**   Nepal is one of the few countries in the world that does not base its clock on an even-hour difference from Greenwich mean time. Instead, Nepal takes its time from the number of hours and minutes' difference between Greenwich and Kathmandu. Thus the country is 5 hours and 45 minutes ahead of Greenwich mean time, 10 hours and 45 minutes ahead of eastern standard time, and 15 minutes ahead of India. Nepal is 1 hour and 15 minutes behind Thailand, 2 hours and 15 minutes behind China (except between Apr and Sept, when it is 3 hr and 15 min behind).

**Tipping**   Tipping was not common in Nepal until introduced by Western tourists, and still it is done only in hotels and restaurants frequented primarily by tourists or to compliment good service. Suggested amounts for tips: airport porters expect Rs20 to Rs25 (30¢ to 40¢); hotel staff (in more expensive hotels), Rs10 to Rs20 (15¢ to 30¢) per day (look for a tip box on the reception desk); waiters, 10% (but only in expensive restaurants such as those at luxury hotels); service personnel, 10%; taxi drivers, round up by Rs5 (8¢); trekking porters and rafting staff, roughly 1 day's wages per week of service.

**Water**   Water in Nepal is not safe to drink unless purified in some way. See "Health, Insurance & Other Concerns," earlier in this chapter, for details.

**Yellow Pages**   Your hotel or a nearby telephone communications office will most likely have either a tourist phone directory, in English, with yellow pages called *All Nepal Tourism Information & Telephone Guide*, or *Nepal's Business Directory*, both published annually.

# 4 Settling into the Kathmandu Valley

**K**athmandu. The very name conjures up images of snow-covered peaks, snake charmers and mountaineers, holy men and sacred cows. Perhaps no other city on earth has seemed so mysterious. This city, capital of the Himalayan kingdom of Nepal, lies in a wide valley hidden behind a wall of nearly impenetrable mountains. Today, winging into Kathmandu on an international flight, the Mahabhaharat Range slides by below as the Himalayas shimmer in the distance. The jumbled landscape doesn't give the appearance that it could ever provide a level surface large enough to land a Boeing or Airbus. Then, as the peaks below grow uncomfortably close to the belly of the plane, mountainsides give way to gentler slopes and terraced hillsides, which are dun-colored in the post-monsoon months favored by trekkers. Brick houses dot the fields of a seemingly idyllic rural setting. Suddenly the city comes into view—uniformly brown and low-rise, it sprawls across the valley floor. There's a quick glimpse of a huge white hemisphere in the distance, and suddenly the plane is on the runway. The passengers breathe a communal sigh of relief for having safely landed amid the Himalayan peaks. The excitement is palpable as passengers wait to deplane. Through the door lies Kathmandu, city of mystery, the most exotic city in Asia.

However, as feet hit tarmac, the reality of modern-day Kathmandu immediately comes to bear. The arrivals hall is a zoo and no one seems to know what to do. Guards want to inspect your bags as you *leave* the arrivals hall. Outside, hordes of taxi drivers, porters, and hotel touts block the exit door. Beyond the airport gates, the streets are chaotic at best. Clouds of blue-black smoke billow from diesel trucks, buses packed like sardine cans stop in the middle of the road, cows wander aimlessly, and horns blare incessantly. The smoke of funeral pyres mingles with the stench of garbage. Women in colorful saris dash out of the way of your careening taxi as it bounces upon potholes large enough to swallow a car.

However, once you have settled into your hotel, you can venture out onto the streets of old Kathmandu, where a different picture slowly begins to emerge. Kathmandu is a city of alleyways leading into the unknown, a city where roadside shrines are sprinkled with marigold petals and aging temples double as produce markets. Strange odors— a mélange of incense, cow dung, and rotting garbage—drift through the streets. Eerie discordant music—the tinny jangling of cymbals, the drone of a harmonium, the pulse of drums—might fill a nearly deserted square at nightfall as musicians sit hunched over their ancient instruments on the floor of a tiny temple. In the market, vendors swaddled in woolen shawls sit behind baskets full of mandarins and radishes. Kathmandu has been called a medieval city, and it is hard not to think of it as such as you wander its back streets. The lanes are narrow, and in the oldest parts of town, there is little traffic (though the few cars and motorcycles that venture into these ancient alleys make frequent use of their horns). People do the heavy work here, not vehicles. They carry heavy-laden baskets on their backs or slung from poles across their shoulders. Perhaps time has not completely stood still in Kathmandu, but it certainly has not passed as swiftly as it has in other parts of the world.

For more than a hundred years Kathmandu was cut off from the outside world by a government that wished to keep the country isolated. When the royal family was restored to power in the mid-1950s, Nepal opened its borders and the painful process of entering the 20th century began. Today, Kathmandu has much of the Western world's technology, but alas, many of its environmental and social woes as well. There are cars and computers, fax machines and factories, cellular phones and satellite TV. There are also traffic congestion and smog, deforestation and unemployment. However, with the help of the West, Nepal is working to overcome these problems. Kathmandu is certainly no Shangri-la, but it is one of the world's most fascinating cities, nonetheless.

Arriving in Kathmandu is a full-on sensory assault—an experience never to be forgotten. It becomes immediately obvious that you have arrived in a different world. Don't be unprepared. Read this chapter and you'll know what to expect and what to do. Preparation won't lessen the sensory overload, but it may help you to cope.

# 1 Orientation

## ARRIVING

**BY PLANE** Immediately upon arrival in Kathmandu, you will begin to understand that dealing with the Nepali government bureaucracy is an arduous, often-frustrating task. Cultivate patience.

Because Nepali rupees are not available outside of Nepal, the very first thing you'll need to do is change some money at one of the currency exchange desks right inside the door of the arrivals hall. Exchange rates here are about the same as you'll get at banks and exchange offices outside the airport. Be sure to hang onto your receipt; you'll need it if you have to change any money back at the end of your visit.

Next, you'll need to fill out an embarkation card if you did not already do so on the plane. Now is also the time to get a visa if you did not obtain one before leaving home. There should be both embarkation cards and visa application forms somewhere in the arrivals hall, but don't expect anything here to be marked or have any semblance of order. A 15-day visa costs $15 and a single-entry 30-day visa costs $25. With forms in hand and U.S. dollars with which to pay your visa fee (U.S. dollars are all they'll accept here), take a place in the correct line. There are separate lines for those who already have visas and for those who are applying for visas at the airport.

When you have completed these formalities, proceed downstairs to baggage pickup. Customs will then inspect your bag. You must have all bags, even carryons, inspected and marked before you can leave the terminal. Beyond the baggage pickup and before exiting the building, you'll find the airport's tourist information desk, where you can pick up a map and brochures. If you don't have a room reservation yet, the staff at this desk will call around for you.

---

**Travel Tip**

When you're arriving in and departing from Nepal through Tribhuvan International Airport, it is important to remember that the X-ray machines used on checked baggage are not film-safe.

---

Next comes the hard part—negotiating a taxi into town. The easiest way to get to your hotel is to let the hotel know (by mail, phone, fax, or e-mail) when you will be arriving and on what flight, and ask them to send a car or van to pick you up. Most hotels offer this service either free or for about the going rate of a taxi. If you haven't made arrangements with a hotel, the next-easiest way to get into town is to pay for a fixed-rate taxi before you even leave the arrivals building. You'll find the taxi desk near the visitor information desk. The fare into town is Rs200 ($3.05). These are your two best options, especially if you've been in transit for more than a day and are suffering from jet lag and sleep deprivation.

If, however, you want to save a dollar and throw yourself immediately into bargaining mode, step through the doors to the outside world without a taxi voucher in hand. Taxi drivers, porters, and touts will descend on you like vultures, pulling at your bags and demanding the name of your hotel. If you don't give them a name, they'll start trying to sell you some obscure hotel. A tout, for those who have never encountered one, is a person who is paid on a commission basis to take you to a particular hotel (or shop or whatever). A shrewd bargainer might be able to negotiate a fare of Rs125 to Rs150 ($1.90 to $2.25). Good luck!

Although there are public buses into town, they aren't likely to take you anywhere near your hotel and are overcrowded even when you aren't dragging any luggage. Don't even consider this option.

When departing, be sure to first ask at your hotel whether they offer airport transfers. If they do, this is your best bet for getting to the airport. Otherwise, you'll have to go out on the street, find a taxi, and negotiate a rate. Of course, by this time you should be an old hand at negotiating taxi fares. Shoot for Rs100 ($1.50) to Rs150 ($2.25).

**BY BUS**   If you are arriving in Kathmandu for the first time by bus, you are probably coming from either India or Pokhara. If you're coming from India, your bus will most likely let you off at the Gongabu Bus Park on Ring Road north of Thamel (Kathmandu's main budget-accommodations neighborhood). From here, it's a 10-minute taxi ride to Thamel. If you happen to be coming into town on a tourist bus from either Pokhara or Chitwan, you will be let off at the intersection of Kantipath and Tridevi Marg on the eastern edge of the Thamel neighborhood.

## TOURIST INFORMATION

The **Department of Tourism** operates two information centers in Kathmandu: at the airport (☎ 977/1-470537) and just off Durbar Square on New Road (☎ 977/1-220818). They are both open Sunday to Thursday from 10am to 6pm and on Friday from 10am to 4pm. You are more likely to find brochures and maps at the airport information desk, which also specializes in providing information on hotels and guest houses. The downtown office usually has brochures during the peak seasons, though they are often reluctant to hand them out. Either of these desks can help you with general questions. Your hotel staff, travel agencies, and both *Travellers' Nepal* and *Nepal Traveller* magazines, which are sometimes available at hotels in Kathmandu, are also all good sources of information.

# CITY LAYOUT

**MAIN ARTERIES & STREETS**   Kathmandu can be easily divided into two distinct sections: old Kathmandu and new Kathmandu. Old Kathmandu is a maze of narrow streets, even narrower alleys, and interconnected courtyards of various sizes. The best way to get around in old Kathmandu is on foot. Even a bicycle is not very successful at negotiating these crowded streets. New Kathmandu, on the other hand, consists of much wider streets and avenues, many of which are one-way and almost all of which are now frighteningly congested and very dangerous to cross on foot. Be very careful when crossing, even at crosswalks. Remember: pedestrians *never, never, never* have the right of way in Nepal.

At the center of the city are **Ratna Park** and the **Tundikhel,** which together form a large expanse of grass that is used primarily as a military parade ground. A small part, however, is used by the general public for grazing goats, children flying kites, and teenagers playing soccer. The Tundikhel is divided by only a few streets and, consequently, it is difficult to get from one side to the other. Down the east side of this green area runs an extension of **Durbar Marg,** the city's upscale shopping street. The extension is one-way heading south for nearly a mile without any way of getting to the other side of the Tundikhel. On the west side of the Tundikhel, with northbound one-way traffic, is **Kantipath.** Farther to the north Kantipath becomes **Lazimpat.** About midway up the Tundikhel on the west side, **New Road** (which was built many years ago after a devastating earthquake) leads off to the west and continues for half a mile to **Durbar Square.** The famous **Freak Street** runs south from New Road just before you get to Durbar Square.

Durbar Square is at the very heart of old Kathmandu. The road that angles northeast from Durbar Square is the main market street of Kathmandu and connects back to Kantipath. If you angle to the left off of this street at the first intersection north of Durbar Square, you will be on a narrow street that leads to the **Thamel** neighborhood. From Thamel's main square (which long ago was the only place referred to as Thamel), **Tridevi Marg** leads east to Kantipath, with the extension of this road connecting to Durbar Marg.

Circling the two cities of Kathmandu and Patan is the **Ring Road,** from which main roads lead off to other towns and cities. The road to Bhaktapur, Dhulikhel, Nagarkot, Tibet, and Jiri (trailhead for the Everest trek) begins in the southeast corner of the city. The road to Pokhara and Chitwan National Park starts in the southwest part of the city. The road to Budhanilkantha is an extension of Lazimpat, which is an extension of Kantipath. The road to Boudhanath begins in the northeast corner of the city, and the road to Balaju, Kakani, and Trisuli Bazaar begins in the northwest.

**Finding an Address**   Kathmandu just might be the most difficult city in the world when it comes to finding an address. There are neither street names nor address numbers on buildings. This lack of a system dates back to when Kathmandu was just a small town and there was no such thing as mail. To this day nothing has been done to improve the situation, although businesses now use post office boxes to get around the problem.

Addresses do not list streets but rather neighborhoods, and neighborhoods may take their names from squares, temples, important buildings, or some other significant landmark. Thamel is a good example of this. Thamel is the address given for dozens of hotels, restaurants, and businesses located on different streets all over Kathmandu's main tourist neighborhood. Whereas traditionally Thamel referred to the immediate neighborhood of a single square, it now refers to an expanding tourist district where businesses come and go with amazing regularity. Finding an address in Thamel is a nightmare. Often the only way to find a business is to call for directions, and more often than not, if you are anywhere nearby when you call, the business will send someone to get you and lead you there. Business cards or brochures will almost always have a map showing you how to find the establishment. Otherwise, you'll have to go to the general neighborhood of the address and start asking shopkeepers if they know where to find the business you are looking for. For assistance in locating businesses mentioned in this chapter, we have often included a readily identifiable landmark as a reference point. Good luck!

**Street Maps**    The tourist information desk at the airport hands out free maps of Kathmandu, as do most hotels and travel agencies. None of these maps is very good. Bookstores around Thamel also sell Kathmandu maps, but for the most part they are not much better than the free maps.

## NEIGHBORHOODS IN BRIEF

**Thamel**    This is Kathmandu's main budget-accommodations neighborhood, and nearly every street is lined with cheap hotels and restaurants, interesting shops, and trekking agents. It's a real scene, and the crowds and constant noise can really frazzle the nerves after only a short time. Thamel begins 1 block west of the north end of Kantipath on the street known as Tridevi Marg. The area from Jyatha on the south to Lekhnath Marg on the north and over to Paknajol on the west is all considered Thamel, though the neighborhood seems to extend its boundaries every year.

**Durbar Marg**    Durbar Marg runs south from the gates of the Royal Palace and is Kathmandu's main upscale shopping and hotel street. Lining this wide avenue, you'll find expensive restaurants, deluxe hotels, and shops selling jewelry, imported clothing, and Tibetan antiques. Durbar Marg shops now seem to appeal primarily to Indian tourists, and aside from the antiques stores, there isn't much to see on this street.

**Durbar Square**    The heart of old Kathmandu, Durbar Square is home to one of the greatest concentrations of temples, shrines, and old palaces found in the world. Although by day it is overrun with tourists, taxis, curio sellers, and cycle rickshaws, it is still the single-most-important stop on any visit to Kathmandu. You'll find Durbar Square at the western end of New Road, which has its start at the Tundikhel.

**Freak Street**    Well-known in the days when Kathmandu was the hippie capital of the world, Freak Street is no longer the budget traveler's main lodging area in Kathmandu. However, shops and very cheap guest houses still line this street just south of Basantapur Square, which itself is at the southeast corner of Durbar Square.

**Patan (Lalitpur)**    Though it is actually a separate city, Patan, which is also known as Lalitpur, is divided from Kathmandu only by the Bagmati River. Patan has its own Durbar Square and old city area, as well as the Patan Industrial Estate and the Tibetan Refugee Camp. The city is known for its metalworkers, and their shops abound in the area near the Temple of 1,000 Buddhas.

**Bhaktapur (Bhadgaon)**    Located 9 miles east of Kathmandu, Bhaktapur is the third major city of the Kathmandu Valley and is the best preserved. In order to continue the ongoing preservation of Bhaktapur, visitors must now pay a fee to enter the older parts of the city. Bhaktapur is known for its wood-carvers and thangka painters.

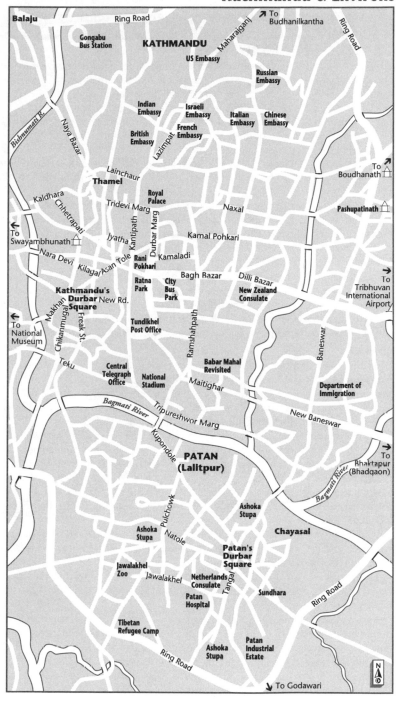

Balaju

Ring Road

To
Budhanilkantha

Gongabu
Bus Station

**KATHMANDU**

Maharajganj

Ring Road

US Embassy

Russian
Embassy

Bishnumati R.

Naya Bazar

Indian
Embassy

Israeli
Embassy

Italian
Embassy

Chinese
Embassy

Lazimpat

British
Embassy

French
Embassy

Lainchaur

To
Boudhanath

**Thamel**

Kaldhara

Royal
Palace

Naxal

Pashupatinath

Chhetrapati

Tridevi Marg

Durbar Marg

Kantipath

To
Swayambhunath

Jyatha

Kamal Pohkari

Nara Devi

Kilaga/Asan Tole

Rani
Pokhari

Kamaladi

Kamaladi

Bagh Bazar

Dilli Bazar

To
Tribhuvan
International
Airport

Makhan

**Kathmandu's
Durbar
Square**

New Rd.

Ratna
Park

City
Bus
Park

New Zealand
Consulate

Chikanmugal

Baneswar

To
National
Museum

Freak St.

Tundikhel
Post Office

Ramshahpath

Teku

Central
Telegraph
Office

National
Stadium

Babar Mahal
Revisited

Maitighar

Department of
Immigration

Bagmati River

Tripureshwor Marg

New Baneswar

Kupondole

**PATAN
(Lalitpur)**

Bagmati River

To
Bhaktapur
(Bhadqaon)

Ashoka
Stupa

Pulchowk

**Chayasal**

Ashoka
Stupa

Natole

**Patan's
Durbar
Square**

Jawalakhel
Zoo

Jawalakhel

Netherlands
Consulate

Tangal

Sundhara

Ring Road

Patan
Hospital

Tibetan
Refugee Camp

Ashoka
Stupa

Patan
Industrial
Estate

Ring Road

To Godawari

N

## 2  Getting Around

### BY PUBLIC TRANSPORTATION

**BY BUS**   There are basically three types of public buses: full-size buses, minibuses, and three-wheeled tempos. However, they are all, for the most part, rolling sardine cans, especially the minibuses and tempos, which are built for people with an average height of about 5 feet, 2 inches. It is nearly impossible to get a seat on any sort of bus unless you get on at the very start of the route, and consequently, even a short ride can be a traumatic experience. For this reason, buses are best avoided, though they are very cheap. Most buses begin their routes from the City Bus Park on the east side of the Tundikhel, south of Durbar Marg. Bhaktapur buses are an exception. These buses leave from Bagh Bazaar, east of Ratna Park and a long block north of the City Bus Park.

The electric buses that operate between Kathmandu and Bhaktapur are an exception. These buses are usually crowded only at rush hour and are an economical way to get to and from Bhaktapur. The only drawback is that they leave from just east of the traffic circle near the National Stadium, which is a long way from Thamel or Durbar Marg.

In some parts of town there are three-wheeled tempos that operate on a fixed route in the same way that buses do. These tempos have two bench seats behind the driver and are usually blue or white. The white tempos are electric and are known as *safa* (clean) tempos. Most tempos start their routes from Kantipath, just north of the General Post Office or from Bag Bazaar, on the south side of Rani Pokhari, which is at the north end of the Tundikhel.

**BY TAXI**   Taxis can be found, among other places, in front of all major hotels, at major intersections in Thamel, and along Durbar Marg. They are also easily hailed on any major street. Though taxis do have meters, it is very difficult to get the drivers to use them. Consequently, you will be forced to bargain for the price of a ride. Be sure to settle on a price before getting into the cab. Offer about half of whatever price the taxi driver asks for. The price you settle on will likely be above what you would pay on the meter, but there's not much you can do about this. If you should convince a driver to use his meter, the flag-drop rate is Rs7 (10¢); the fare increases by Rs2 (3¢) every 200 meters. After 9pm, add 50% to the meter fare. Most of the major hotels also have their own private taxis, though these are more expensive than regular cabs. If you need a taxi at night and can't find one on the street, call the **Night Taxi Service** (☎ 224374).

Hiring a taxi by the day or half day can be one of the best ways to see a lot of the Kathmandu Valley. By hiring the taxi for the day, you won't have to worry about finding another taxi whenever you're done exploring one sight and want to move on to another. Having the taxi prearranged can also help you avoid wasting time as you explore the valley. Expect to pay between Rs1,000 ($15.15) and Rs1,500 ($22.75) to hire a taxi for the day.

**Auto-rickshaws,** also known as meter tempos or tuk-tuks, are rounded, black, three-wheeled motorcycle-rickshaws that operate as taxis. These vehicles are second only to diesel trucks and buses in the amount of exhaust fumes they spew out and are a major contributing factor to the air-pollution problem in the Kathmandu Valley. For this reason, they should be used only as a last resort. Besides, they're miserably uncomfortable. Tempo fares are generally about half that of a taxi for a comparable trip.

*A suggestion:* If you're taking a taxi to or from Thamel and you don't have a lot of luggage, you'll be doing your part to lessen the chaos, congestion, and noise in the neighborhood if, instead of making the taxi driver negotiate the narrow, pedestrian-clogged streets of Thamel, you get in or out on Tridevi Marg (the wide street leading into Thamel). You may have to walk a few blocks, but with one less taxi in the neighborhood, your walk will be a little less traumatic.

**BY CYCLE RICKSHAW**    For short trips in the old neighborhoods of Kathmandu, a bicycle rickshaw is your best bet other than walking. Early mornings, before the streets get too congested, are the best time to make bicycle rickshaw excursions. Because cycle rickshaws are narrower than a taxi, they can negotiate many streets that a taxi would have difficulty getting through. A cycle rickshaw can carry two people and baggage (if the bags aren't too heavy). Rates are negotiable, and you must be sure to agree on the fare before getting in. Bargain hard—drivers know that tourists can pay more, and they charge accordingly. A trip between Durbar Square and Thamel will cost about Rs30 (45¢). For many people, riding in one of these human-powered vehicles is the very essence of traveling in Asia.

**BY CAR**    Car rentals in the familiar sense are not available in Nepal. You cannot rent a car that you drive yourself; car rentals here include the car *and driver.* Official car rentals, available through hotels and some major travel agencies, can range in price from $25 to $80 per day. However, since you are, in effect, hiring a taxi when you rent a car in Nepal, you'll save money by simply negotiating with a taxi driver for a day's hire of his taxi. See "By Taxi," above for details on hiring a taxi by the day.

**BY MOTORCYCLE**    For the adventurous who have previous riding experience, a motorcycle is a good way to explore the less developed corners of the Kathmandu Valley, though just getting out of the city is an absolute nightmare. Be sure to get helmets, and make sure the horn works. Be aware that it is a criminal offense to injure a cow, and you are likely to encounter quite a few cows on the roads as you travel around the valley. You'll find numerous motorcycle-rental stands around Thamel. Expect to pay between Rs400 ($6.05) and Rs500 ($7.60) per day, plus gas, which currently costs Rs40 (60¢) per liter.

**BY BICYCLE**    Until the past few years, bicycles were one of the best and most popular ways of getting around Kathmandu and the rest of the valley. However, with increased traffic congestion and the clouds of exhaust that go with the ever-growing number of motorcycles, cars, trucks, and buses on the road, bicycles are now neither a very safe nor a very pleasant way to get around. However, should you feel like taking to the streets of Kathmandu, you can rent a low-quality mountain bike for between Rs75 ($1.15) and Rs100 ($1.50).

The most important thing to look for when renting a bicycle is a good bell. If the bell isn't loud and easy to ring, find another bike. Bells are the only way of clearing the streets in front of you. They work especially well on children playing in the street but are totally ineffective in moving sleeping cows. If the bell is in good working order, check to see if other important features—such as the brakes—are functioning. Give the bike a test ride; if the seat isn't right, have it adjusted.

**ON FOOT**    In Kathmandu's old city, your feet are often the only feasible means of getting around. In the market area north of Durbar Square, the crowds of people are usually so dense that it is impossible to even get a bicycle through the streets. It is about a 20-minute walk from Durbar Marg or Thamel to Durbar Square. Swayambunath is a 30- to 45-minute walk. Keep in mind that the streets of Kathmandu are rough, uneven, and often filled with garbage and cow dung. I suggest sturdy walking shoes.

## FAST FACTS: Kathmandu

**American Express**    The American Express office (☎ **977/1-227635** or 977/ 1-226172; www.catmando.com./yeti-travels) is located just around the corner from Durbar Marg at the opposite end from the Royal Palace. Open Sunday to Thursday from 10am to 5pm, Friday from 10am to 4:45pm. The office is closed for lunch between 1 and 2pm. If you have an account with American Express, you may receive mail at this office.

**Baby-sitters**    Major hotels in Kathmandu offer baby-sitting services, but other than that, you'll have to take the little ones with you.

**Business Hours**    See "Fast Facts: Nepal," in chapter 3.

**Car Rentals**    See "Getting Around," earlier in this chapter.

**Climate**    See "When to Go," in chapter 3.

**Country & City Codes**    Nepal's country code is **977;** Kathmandu's city code is **1.** If you are calling Kathmandu from within Nepal, dial 0 first and use only the city code. If calling from outside Nepal, dial 977, then 1, and then the local phone number.

**Currency Exchange**    Officially, you can change foreign currency only at a hotel, bank, or currency exchange office. Unofficially, a black market flourishes and offers a slightly higher rate, especially for large-denomination U.S. bills. Changing money on the black market is, however, illegal, even though many people do so. Your hotel is likely to be the most convenient place to change money, though the exchange rates tend to be a bit lower than those you'll get at a currency-exchange office or bank.

The next-best place to change money is at one of the currency-exchange offices in Thamel. These either charge a small service fee or discount the official bank exchange rate. Either way, you don't lose much, and it can be fun to shop around for the best rate. The few banks around town that do change money usually have long lines and are the worst places to go to. Always get a receipt so you can change rupees back to foreign currency when you leave Nepal. You will be allowed to change back only 10% of the money you converted into rupees.

**Dentist**    For the names of English-speaking dentists in Kathmandu, contact your embassy or consulate.

**Doctor**    For the names of English-speaking doctors, contact your embassy or consulate.

**Drugstores**    Drugstores in Kathmandu are known as chemists or pharmacies. They are usually little hole-in-the-wall places crammed with prescription medicines. Most drugs you might need for your trekking first-aid kit are available here at much lower prices than in the United States, and without a prescription. You'll find several pharmacies on the periphery of Thamel (one on the street leading north from Thamel's main square and another about a third of the way between Thamel and Durbar Square) There's also one on the corner of Kantipath at Rani Pokhari (the square pond with the island temple).

**Embassies/Consulates**    Before going in person, it's best to call the embassy or consulate to find out when it is open.

**Australian Embassy,** Bansbari (north of Ring Road on an extension of Maharaj-gunj) (☎ 977/1-371678 or 977/1-371466).

**British Embassy,** Lainchaur (on the road to the left of the Hotel Ambassador), Lazimpat (☎ 977/1-411590 or 977/1-410583).

**Canadian Consulate,** Lazimpat (☎ 977/1-415193 or 977/1-415389).

**Chinese Embassy,** Baluwatar (☎ 977/1-411740 or 977/1-411958).

**Indian Embassy,** Lainchaur (☎ 977/1-410900 or 977/1-414990).

**New Zealand Consulate,** Dilli Bazaar (☎ 977/1-412436).

**Thai Embassy,** Bansbari (☎ 977/1-371410 or 977/1-371411).

**United States Embassy,** Pani Pokhari (an extension of Lazimpat) (☎ 977/1-411179 or 977/1-412718).

**Emergencies**    **Fire:** ☎ 101 for fire brigade. **Tourist Police:** (English-speaking) ☎ 247041, 220818, or 429750 (Thamel); or ☎ 100. **Ambulance:** ☎ 211959 or 228094 (Nepal Red Cross).

**Eyeglasses**    Optic Palace, Jamal, Ranipokhari (☎ **226673**), open Sunday to Friday from 8am to 7:30pm, can replace or repair your glasses in 2 or 3 days. It's a good idea to travel with spare eyeglasses to avoid being without a pair in case yours cannot be replaced. Contact lenses can be problematic if you are planning a long trek. Fingers tend to stay dirty, and the risk of eye infections is great.

**Hospitals/Clinics**    Should you become seriously ill while in Nepal, the recommended procedure is to get yourself to Bangkok or Singapore as quickly as possible. Both of these destinations have many excellent hospitals where the quality of care is equal to that in any Western hospital. Consult your embassy in either of these destinations for a recommendation. If an emergency arises that precludes evacuation, your best choice is the **Patan Hospital,** Lagankhel, Patan (☎ **522295** or 522266), which is under the supervision of Western doctors. For less-serious illnesses there are two excellent clinics: CIWEC, Durbar Marg near Hotel Yak & Yeti (☎ **228531** or 241732), which is staffed by Western or Western-trained doctors and nurses; and **Nepal International Clinic,** Naxal (☎ **412842** or 434642), located 1½ blocks past the main entrance to the current Royal Palace, at the top of Durbar Marg. The latter clinic is operated by a U.S. board-certified internist and is staffed by Westerners.

**Information**    See "Visitor Information," "Entry Requirements," & "Money," in chapter 3.

**Laundry & Dry Cleaning**    Your hotel is the place for having laundry or dry cleaning done, since there are no self-service laundries in Kathmandu. I don't recommend bringing any clothes that require dry cleaning; if you do, it's better to wait and have your clothing cleaned back home.

**Lost Property**    Your only real chance of recovering lost items is to post notices in restaurants around town and hope that your lost item was found by someone who reads English. If you'd like to report a lost or stolen wallet or purse to the police, take someone who speaks English and Nepali with you; very few police officers speak English.

**Luggage Storage**    Virtually all hotels offer luggage storage while you're off trekking, and it's usually free. I have found that stored luggage is safe even in budget hotels.

**Newspapers & Magazines**    Kathmandu's English-language daily newspapers are the *Rising Nepal* and *The Kathmandu Post.* Both papers carry some international news. At bookshops in Thamel and at major hotels, you'll find the

*International Herald Tribune, USA Today,* and Asian editions of *Time* and *Newsweek.* Many British and European magazines are also available in Thamel bookshops.

**Photographic Needs**   There are several camera shops in Thamel and along New Road just east of Durbar Square. These shops offer 1-hour film processing and carry most common films, with the exception of Kodachrome. Prices are often cheaper than what you would pay at home, but be sure to check the expiration dates. Most types of camera batteries are also available.

**Police:** (English-speaking) ☎ **247041,** 220818, or 429750 (Thamel). Or ☎ 100.

**Post Office**   The Kathmandu G.P.O. is on Sundhara beside the Bhimsen Tower (easily spotted minaret-like tower in the middle of town) on the corner of Kantipath, 1 long block south of New Road (☎ **227499** or 225145). Open Sunday to Thursday from 10am to 5pm and Friday from 10am to 3pm. Stamps may be purchased from 7am to 5pm. If you want to receive mail while in Nepal, have it sent (c/o) Kathmandu G.P.O., Kathmandu, Poste Restante. The Poste Restante room is open Sunday to Thursday from 10am to 4pm, and Friday from 10am to 3pm. To mail a package out of Nepal, you must send it from the Foreign Post Office, Sundhara, beside the G.P.O. It's open Sunday to Thursday from 10am to 5pm, Friday from 10am to 2pm. Because it is complicated and not always reliable to send packages overseas from the post office, we recommend using a private shipping company. See "Shopping" in chapter 5 for details. However, for documents and small packets, Express Mail Service (EMS), provided by the post office, is usually dependable.

**Restrooms**   Public restrooms are rare in Kathmandu. You'll find them in restaurants and some hotel lobbies. Don't be surprised if an otherwise very Western-looking establishment has only an Asian-style squat toilet. The common term for a restroom in Nepal is *toilet* (or *charpi* in Nepali).

**Safety**   Kathmandu is still a surprisingly safe city, even at night. However, this does not mean you can be careless with your money, passport, and other valuables. I suggest always carrying tickets, money, and passport in a money belt or neck bag that can be worn under your clothing. Carry only as much cash as you expect to spend during any foray out of your hotel. Keep this money separate from your money belt so that you don't reveal the location of your valuables to curious eyes.

**Taxes**   On hotel and restaurant bills in Nepal, you will usually pay a 2% Tourism Service Charge (TSC) and, on top of this, a 10% Value Added Tax (which is levied even on the 2% TSC). The airport departure tax is Rs1,000 ($15.15) on international flights and Rs100 ($1.50) for domestic flights.

**Taxis**   See "Getting Around" in this chapter.

**Telephone/Fax/E-mail**   There are dozens of communications centers conveniently located in the Thamel neighborhood. At any of these offices, you can make a phone call or send a fax for around Rs170 to Rs185 ($2.60 to $2.80) per minute. Thamel also has numerous communications centers from which you can send e-mail for around Rs8 (12¢) per minute. For information on using the telephone in Nepal, see "Country & City Codes," above.

**Television**   There is only one Nepali television station. However, most hotels now get satellite cable television (if not in the rooms, at least on a lobby television) that includes CNN and the BBC World News.

**Useful Telephone Numbers**   International operator: ☎ **186** or 187; English-speaking directory assistance: ☎ **197**.

# 3  Accommodations

Kathmandu has one of the widest ranges of room prices of any city in the world. You can get a room for $2 a night, or one for $200 a night. However, the vast majority of the city's hotel rooms fall within a range from about $15 to $85. Within this price range, the best deals are to be had in the $25 to $50 range. For a rate higher than $50, you're probably paying for unnecessary upgrades such as air-conditioning (not needed in trekking seasons) and a television (not nearly as entertaining as the streets of Kathmandu). Consequently, you won't find many hotels in the moderate range listed here. I have found that most Kathmandu hotels in this price range are rather shabby and overpriced for what you get. If you want the comfort normally expected in the moderate price range, try a deluxe room in an inexpensive or budget hotel.

In the expensive and very-expensive ranges, you will be paying for the amenities you would expect in top-notch hotels. These hotels usually have a swimming pool and other exercise facilities, as well as several restaurants and bars. However, conditions in Nepal conspire to confound hoteliers, and you may be slightly disappointed in the quality of even the most expensive rooms in Kathmandu. Trust that regardless of any shortcomings you might encounter, you are still experiencing the best that Nepal has to offer.

Because Kathmandu has long been a favorite destination of backpack travelers, there is an abundance of inexpensive hotels. I have found that one of the most important factors when choosing an inexpensive hotel is a quiet location. I have chosen hotels with this in mind so that your sleep will be as undisturbed as possible.

There are a few things to keep in mind when booking a hotel room in Kathmandu. Most hotel rooms come with two twin beds. If you want a double bed, be sure to request it. Also, during the busy trekking-season months of March, October, and November, the best hotels in Kathmandu stay booked up. If you are planning to visit during any of these months, reserve your room as far in advance as possible. This applies to both expensive and inexpensive hotels. The flip side of this is that room rates are very flexible. It is often possible to get a 20 to 30% discount even in the busy seasons. It's usually easier to get such discounts at less-popular and new hotels.

Hotel bills (except in the cheapest of budget accommodations) must be paid with foreign currency. I have listed the prices in this guide in U.S. dollars only, which is how you will be billed. Two separate taxes will also be tacked onto your hotel bill: a 2% Tourism Service Charge and a 10% Value Added Tax, which is calculated on top of the 2% TSC. When planning your budget, keep these numbers in mind; these taxes will add a considerable amount to your total bill. Also, when booking a room, be sure to ask if there is an extra charge for paying with a credit card. Although this practice is officially prohibited by credit-card companies, it is a common practice in Nepal.

Because of the torrential rains that occur during the monsoon season, carpets are often musty with mildew even in the most expensive hotels. To mask unpleasant odors, hotels often use liberal doses of mothballs, which smell just about as bad as the mildew. If your room smells bad, try asking for a different room. Also, you should be aware that barking dogs are a problem throughout Nepal and often keep people awake even at Kathmandu's most expensive hotels. Bring earplugs even if you are normally a heavy sleeper.

In the listings below, the "Very Expensive" category includes hotels charging more than $150 per night for a double room; the "Expensive" category includes hotels charging between $100 and $150; the "Moderate" category includes hotels charging $40 to $99; and the "Inexpensive" category includes hotels charging less than $40. Unless otherwise noted, all rooms have private bathrooms.

Most hotels don't charge for children under 12 staying in their parents' room. Also, hotels in Kathmandu generally don't charge for local phone calls. If you're heading off on a trek, you can usually store your luggage free at your hotel, and your belongings are usually quite safe.

Phone numbers listed here include both the Nepal country code and the Kathmandu city code. When calling from within Kathmandu, it is necessary only to dial the last six digits.

## THE DURBAR MARG AREA

Durbar Marg, Kathmandu's most upscale shopping street, leads south from the gates of the Royal Palace. Along this street you'll find several top-end hotels, as well as several excellent restaurants.

### VERY EXPENSIVE

✪ **Hotel Yak & Yeti.** Durbar Marg (P.O. Box 1016), Kathmandu. ☎ **977/1-248999** or 977/1-240520. Fax 977/1-227781 or 977/1-227782. E-mail: reservations@yakandyeti. com. 289 units. A/C MINIBAR TV TEL. $175–$240 double; $325–$600 suite. AE, DC, JCB, MC, V.

If money is no object and you need all the amenities of a full-service hotel, then the Yak & Yeti is the place to stay in Kathmandu. Situated on a lane off Durbar Marg, the hotel incorporates a restored 19th-century palace, which now houses two restaurants, several grand banquet halls, and the Casino Royale. In the lobby, granite floors, carved wood pillars, and gleaming brass and copper provide a suitably exotic feel, and through a wall of glass you can see the hotel's extensive gardens.

If you desire modern conveniences, request one of the deluxe rooms in the new wing, which are the hotel's most comfortable though they lack Nepali character. The older rooms, though not as comfortable, have more character. Try to get a room facing the garden.

**Dining/Diversions:** The Chimney Room restaurant is known for its Russian dishes, while Naachghar, a fabulously ornate Indian restaurant in the old palace wing, features Nepali cultural performances nightly (see "Dining," below, for details on both restaurants). For casual dining, there's the Sunrise Café, and in the lobby, there's a piano bar. The hotel's Casino Royale is the most impressive casino in the city.

**Amenities:** Two swimming pools, tennis courts, sauna, steam bath, whirlpool spa, fitness center, jogging trail, 24-hour room service, currency exchange, laundry/ dry-cleaning service, safe-deposit box, tour/travel desk, massages, shopping arcade, beauty parlor, baby-sitting, business center.

### EXPENSIVE

**Hotel de L'Annapurna.** Durbar Marg (P.O. Box 140), Kathmandu. ☎ **977/1-221711,** or in the U.S. and Canada 800/458-8825, or in the U.K. 0800/282699. Fax 977/1-225236. E-mail: a'purna@taj.mos.com.np. 160 units. A/C TV TEL. $130–$160 double; $225–$325 suite. AE, DC, JCB, MC, V.

A longtime favorite with tour groups, the Annapurna is set back a bit from Durbar Marg, and though it is nowhere near as atmospheric as the nearby Yak & Yeti, it offers

# Kathmandu Accommodations

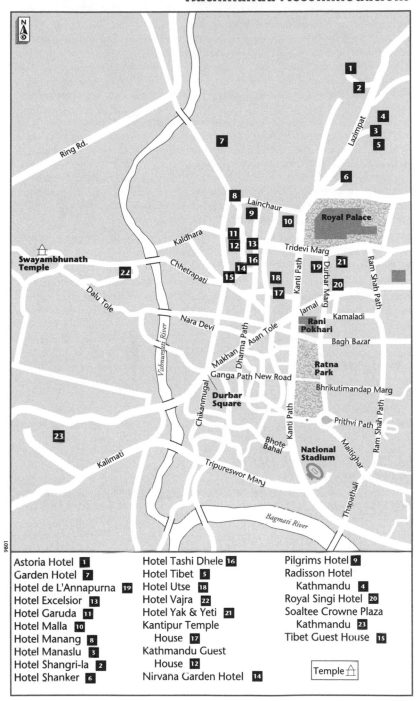

Astoria Hotel **1**
Garden Hotel **7**
Hotel de L'Annapurna **19**
Hotel Excelsior **13**
Hotel Garuda **11**
Hotel Malla **10**
Hotel Manang **8**
Hotel Manaslu **3**
Hotel Shangri-la **2**
Hotel Shanker **6**

Hotel Tashi Dhele **16**
Hotel Tibet **5**
Hotel Utse **18**
Hotel Vajra **22**
Hotel Yak & Yeti **21**
Kantipur Temple House **17**
Kathmandu Guest House **12**
Nirvana Garden Hotel **14**

Pilgrims Hotel **9**
Radisson Hotel Kathmandu **4**
Royal Singi Hotel **20**
Soaltee Crowne Plaza Kathmandu **23**
Tibet Guest House **15**

Temple 🏛

both a good location and more reasonable rates. A pool, an excellent Indian restaurant, and Kathmandu's best pastry shop are the highlights here. Decor throughout the hotel includes an odd mix of Nepali and European pieces.

The standard rooms were recently renovated and now are as comfortable as the more expensive rooms. These latter rooms have marble bathrooms and window seats with bolsters. Some of the standard rooms overlook the hotel's minimal gardens and are worth requesting.

**Dining/Diversions:** Ghar-e-Kabab is the hotel's superb Indian restaurant (see "Dining," below for details). Downstairs from Ghar-e-Kabab are the pastry shop and a coffee shop. The hotel also has a Chinese restaurant. In the lobby, there's a small bar overlooking the hotel's pool, and in the adjacent lounge there's live jazz music most nights. The hotel's Casino Anna is a throwback to the 1970s in a small town in Nevada.

**Amenities:** Swimming pool, health club with sauna, tennis courts, 24-hour room service, laundry/dry-cleaning service, travel agency, car rentals, massages, billiard room, shopping arcade, barbershop, beauty salon, business center.

**Royal Singi Hotel.** Lal Durbar, Kamaladi (P.O. Box 13168), Kathmandu. ☎ **977/1-424190** or 977/1-424191. Fax 977/1-424189 or 977/1-425802. E-mail: hotel@rsingi.wlink.com.np. 89 units. A/C TV TEL. $100–$130 double; $200 suite. AE, MC, V.

Nondescript in design and decor, this newer high-rise hotel may not surround you with Himalayan atmosphere, but it offers a better value than other nearby top-end hotels. It's located just off Durbar Marg, which means the upscale shops and restaurants are only a block away. A waterfall fountain at the back of the lobby is the highlight of the hotel's common areas, and though guest rooms lack Nepali character, they are comfortable and clean.

**Dining/Diversions:** There are an attractive coffee shop, a dining room serving the standard Kathmandu please-everyone menu, and, up on the seventh floor, a Chinese restaurant with a good view of the city. There's also a small bar.

**Amenities:** 24-hour room service, safe-deposit boxes, currency exchange, travel/tour desk, laundry service. There are also plans to add a swimming pool, a health club, a beauty parlor, and a business center.

# LAZIMPAT, THE DIPLOMATIC DISTRICT
## VERY EXPENSIVE

✪ **Radisson Hotel Kathmandu.** Lazimpat (P.O. Box 2269), Kathmandu. ☎ **977/ 1-411818** or 977/1-423888. Fax 977/1-411720. E-mail: radkat@mos.com.np. 178 units. A/C MINIBAR TV TEL. $175–$250 double; $300–$600 suite. AE, MC, V.

This is the first Kathmandu hotel to come close to meeting international standards and being truly contemporary. What this means is that service is excellent and furnishings and fixtures throughout the hotel are imported and of high quality (most of the other luxury hotels have had to make do with poorly made Indian and Nepali fixtures). However, along with international standards comes a generic feel that leaves guests wondering whether they're in Houston, London, or Kathmandu. If you don't like surprises in your hotel, this is the place for you.

The deluxe rooms are the best deal; the very luxurious bathrooms have polished granite counters, makeup mirrors, telephones, and hair dryers. Other amenities include in-room safes, ironing boards and irons, and coffeemakers—basically everything you'd expect at a first-class hotel in North America. However, what you won't find anywhere else are the Himalayan mountain views that you get from the upper floors of this hotel.

**Dining/Diversions:** Although it was still not fully operational at the time of my visit, the hotel was about to open a "rustica" style Italian restaurant. A casual cafe in the lobby and a small bar were already open. There were also plans for a poolside cafe.

**Amenities:** 24-hour room service, concierge, laundry/valet service, travel/tour desk, gift shop, business center. The swimming pool and a health club with sauna, whirlpool, and massage were still not completed at the time of my visit.

## EXPENSIVE

✪ **Hotel Shangri-la.** Lazimpat (P.O. Box 655), Kathmandu. ☎ **977/1-412999.** Fax 977/1-414184. E-mail: hosang@mos.com.np. 86 units. A/C MINIBAR TV TEL. $130 double; $250 suite. AE, JCB, MC, V.

Set behind a high wall that protects it from the noise on busy Lazimpat, the three-story Shangri-la has some of the prettiest gardens of any hotel in the city, and for this reason alone it is a good value. The back garden, with its colorful bougainvillea vines, is the favored public area for relaxation. A four-headed-snake fountain serves as the focal point for the garden, and off to one corner is a swimming pool modeled after a traditional Nepali public bathing fountain. Don't forget to request a room that faces the garden.

Rooms are basic, though some have the carved wooden lattices in the windows that are characteristic of Nepali architecture. Each room has a pair of comfortable chairs and a marble-topped table, but the carpeting is worn and needs replacing. Bathrooms are small but come with tubs.

**Dining/Diversions:** There are a French and a Chinese restaurant here, but it is the garden cafe that is often the most appealing place to eat. There's also a bar just off the lobby.

**Amenities:** Swimming pool, fitness center with sauna, 24-hour room service, courtesy airport and city shuttles, currency exchange, laundry/dry-cleaning service, safe-deposit boxes, shopping arcade, business center, beauty salon, baby-sitting.

✪ **Hotel Shanker.** Lazimpat (P.O. Box 350), Kathmandu. ☎ **977/1-410151** or 977/1-410152. 104 units. A/C TV TEL. $105 double; $125 suite. AE, JCB, MC, V.

For bizarre atmosphere, it's hard to beat the Hotel Shanker. Located just north of the present Royal Palace, this hotel is housed in a European-style 19th-century palace. This is one of the many such architectural excesses around town, and it will likely have you thinking of King Louis XIV rather than the Himalayas. The imposing white structure, with arched windows, stately columns, and ornate cornices, is set in a neatly manicured garden that is the largest and perhaps the nicest in Kathmandu.

Unfortunately, a renovation has left the interior of the hotel anything but palatial. Rooms vary considerably and none is exactly luxurious. However, some rooms have more character than others. Several front rooms have low arched windows and painted plasterwork moldings, an indication that this floor was created when an extra floor was constructed in a high-ceilinged hall. If you don't mind surprises and feel adventurous, give this place a try.

**Dining/Diversions:** The hotel's Kailash restaurant is set amid the crystal and plasterwork of one of the old palace's grandest banquet halls, and is almost reason enough to stay here. However, don't expect to be impressed by the food. There is a dark little bar up a few steps from the lobby.

**Amenities:** Room service, currency exchange, laundry/dry-cleaning service, travel agency, shopping arcade.

## MODERATE

**Hotel Tibet.** Lazimpat (P.O. Box 7956), Kathmandu. ☎ **977/1-429085** or 977/1-429086. Fax 977/1-410957. E-mail: hotel@tibet.mos.com.np. 55 units. TV TEL. $70–$80 double; $110 suite. AE, MC, V.

Located just outside the gate of the new Radisson Hotel Kathmandu, the Hotel Tibet offers moderate rates in a quiet location. Still, it is only a few minutes' taxi ride from the bustle and shopping in the Thamel district. As soon as you step through the front door, you'll be surrounded by Tibetan-style decor, with ornately carved wood throughout the lobby. In the guest rooms, you'll also find Tibetan rugs (though little else to remind you of Tibet). With the deluxe rooms you'll be paying for air-conditioning, which really isn't necessary most of the year; go with the superior rooms. There's a rooftop Tibetan restaurant with nice views of the valley. Amenities include currency exchange, safe-deposit boxes, laundry/dry-cleaning service, and a meditation center.

## INEXPENSIVE

✪ **Astoria Hotel.** Lazimpat (G.P.O. Box 981), Kathmandu. ☎ **977/1-428810.** Fax 977/1-416719. E-mail: nepcraft@mos.com.np. 13 units. TEL. $35–$60 double. AE, DC, JCB, MC, V.

Located on a quiet residential street, this small hotel has the feel of a Nepali bed-and-breakfast and is a welcome change from the dozens of characterless urban hotels in the Thamel neighborhood. With its small French restaurant serving organically grown vegetables straight out of the hotel garden, the Astoria is certainly far more hotel than what you get at higher rates elsewhere in the city. Standard rooms are a very good deal, but if you absolutely must have a TV, minibar, and hair dryer, you'll have to opt for one of the more expensive deluxe rooms. Though low-key, the hotel is run efficiently and is a friendly place to park yourself for either a few days or a few weeks. There's even a playground in the garden, which makes this a good choice for families with small children. Currency exchange, laundry/dry cleaning, room service, and safe-deposit boxes are all available. About the only drawback is that it is about a 5-minute walk out to the main road to get a taxi.

**Hotel Manaslu.** Lazimpat, Kathmandu. ☎ **977/1-410071** or 977/1-413470. Fax 977/ 1-416516. 53 units. TEL. $33–$45 double. Special rates for diplomatic corps and employees of international aid organizations. AE, JCB, MC, V.

If you don't mind being a bit out of the tourist mainstream, the Hotel Manaslu makes a good, economical choice. Located down a winding lane adjacent to the huge new Radisson hotel, the Manaslu has a peaceful front garden that's great for a quiet lunch or afternoon tea. The low prices, quiet setting, and comfortable rooms make this a good value. Many rooms are quite large, and all have wall-to-wall carpeting and plenty of windows. Some have tubs in the bathroom, whereas others have only a shower. The restaurant/bar, decorated in traditional Newari style, serves Indian and continental cuisine. Room service, currency exchange, laundry and dry-cleaning service, and bicycle and car rentals are all available.

## THAMEL

This is Kathmandu's main tourist neighborhood, and it's jam-packed with cheap hotels and restaurants, as well as street after street of shops catering exclusively to budget travelers, trekkers, and other tourists. It's definitely a scene here, and it can be hard to take after a few days; but if you want to be where the action is, and where the services you'll need are located, this is where to stay.

## EXPENSIVE

**Hotel Malla.** Lekhnath Marg (G.P.O. Box 787), Kathmandu. ☎ **977/1-418383** or 977/1-418385. Fax 977/1-418382. E-mail: malla@htlgrp.mos.com.np. 195 units. A/C MINIBAR TV TEL. $146–$170 double; $190–$250 suite. Children under 12 stay free in parents' room. AE, DC, MC, V.

Located on the northern edge of the Thamel neighborhood (and almost across the street from the Royal Palace), the Malla is noteworthy primarily for its pleasant garden and convenient location. The shops and crowded streets of Thamel are only a 5-minute walk away, but the garden (complete with a miniature Buddhist shrine) offers a tranquil escape from the chaos beyond the garden wall. Rooms are comfortable, though cramped, and have large windows and an innocuous international pastel decor that will do nothing to remind you of where you are.

**Dining/Diversions:** Dining options include an Italian restaurant, a Chinese restaurant, a combination continental and Indian restaurant, and a coffee shop that overlooks the garden. There are also a lobby bar and a poolside bar.

**Amenities:** Swimming pool, fitness center, whirlpool, sauna, steam room, 24-hour room service, laundry/dry-cleaning service, currency exchange, travel agency, shopping arcade, beauty parlor, barbershop, business center.

## MODERATE

**The Garden Hotel Kathmandu.** Naya Bazar, Thamel (P.O. Box 5954), Kathmandu. ☎ **977/1-411951,** 977/1-411131, or 977/1-426949. Fax 977/1-418072. E-mail: garden@wlink.com.np. 50 units. A/C TV TEL. $90 double. AE, MC, V.

This hotel does indeed have a garden (and swimming pool), and for these reasons alone it is worth choosing it over comparably priced hotels in the area. However, it's situated on a steep road, which is a 15-minute walk from the heart of Thamel. So if you don't expect to do any garden sitting or swimming, the rates are pretty steep for what you get. The standard rooms are cramped and have small bathrooms with tubs but no counter space. In the deluxe rooms, you get air-conditioning (rarely necessary during trekking months), slightly more space, and a marble bathroom counter. The hotel's restaurant serves standard Kathmandu international cuisine. There is also garden terrace dining, and a small bar off the lobby. Other amenities include 24-hour room service, airport transfers, safe-deposit boxes, laundry/valet service, travel/tour desk, currency exchange, and bicycle rentals.

**Hotel Manang.** Paknajol, Thamel (P.O. Box 5608), Kathmandu. ☎ **977/1-410993** or 977/1-419247. Fax 977/1-415821. E-mail: htlmnang@vishnu.ccsi.com.np. 55 units. A/C TEL. $65–$90 double. AE, DC, JCB, MC, V.

The Manang is a six-story hotel offering simple, moderately comfortable accommodations; located in Thamel's north end. Deluxe rooms have minibars and are a bit larger than standard rooms, but they aren't really worth the additional cost. The marble-floored lobby is a showcase of Newari wood carving with an eye-catching front desk of brick and wood. Most of the business here is from tour groups that get big discounts. There are an underground restaurant across the parking lot from the front door, a coffee shop just off the lobby, and a rooftop restaurant/bar with a good view of the city and mountains. Amenities include 24-hour room service, a travel/tour desk, currency exchange, laundry/valet service, and safe-deposit boxes.

✪ **Kantipur Temple House.** Chusyabahal, Jyatha Tole (P.O. Box 14229), Kathmandu. ☎ **977/1-250131.** Fax 977/1-250078. E-mail: kantipur@tmplhouse.wlink.com.np. 32 units. $50–$85 double. MC, V.

As beautiful as the traditional architecture of Kathmandu is, distressingly few modern hotels have been built to reflect this classic style. This hotel is one of the few exceptions, and the only such hotel in a central location. Situated on the southern edge of Thamel, a block away from a 17th-century monastery currently under renovation, the Kantipur House is a narrow, four-story brick building that conjures up old Kathmandu with its carved windows, brick walls, and traditionally inspired bathing fountain. The rooms are by far the most memorable ones in Thamel. There are baskets (or basket-pattern ceramic pots) for shades on the bedside lamps, rattan furniture, locally made wool rugs, Nepali art, block-print bedspreads, plenty of space, exposed brick walls, and either parquet floors or carpeting. Rooms on the north side of the hotel overlook the trees and gardens that surround the adjacent parliament building. At the time of my visit, the hotel was not quite completed, and there were plans to add an elevator and a rooftop restaurant and bar.

**Nirvana Garden Hotel.** Thamel, Chhetrapati (P.O. Box 5728), Kathmandu. ☎ 977/1-256200 or 256300. Fax 977/1-260668. E-mail: nirvana@wlink.com.np. 60 units. TV TEL. $40–$70 double. AE, MC, V.

While the rooms here aren't among the better values in Kathmandu, the hotel's attractive gardens (complete with artificial waterfall) go a long way toward making up for any shortcomings the rooms might have. Tibetan tables and carpets in the lobby add a touch of the exotic, but because the hotel is popular with tour groups, the lobby always seems to be packed with people. The deluxe rooms are definitely the more livable of the Nirvana Garden's rooms and have balconies and big bathrooms (with tubs and windows). The cheaper rooms have poorly constructed furniture, carpets that could use cleaning, and small Asian-style bathrooms. There is a Kathmandu-standard restaurant on the premises, and meals can be served out in the garden. There's also a rooftop terrace for taking in the view across the valley. Amenities include room service, currency exchange, safe-deposit boxes, and laundry/dry-cleaning service.

## INEXPENSIVE

✪ **Hotel Excelsior.** Narsingh Camp Thamel (P.O. Box 9432), Kathmandu. ☎ 977/1-411566 or 977/1-220285. Fax 977/1-410853. E-mail: excel@wlink.com.np. 51 units. TV TEL. $25–$40 double. AE, MC, V.

By far the best deal in the inexpensive range of hotels, the Excelsior is located in the heart of Thamel behind the popular Pumpernickel Bakery. When you walk up the marble stairs and into the marble-floored lobby, you won't believe that a hotel this attractive could be so inexpensive. The staff is very friendly, and they stay busy keeping the hotel in tip-top shape. Rooms have parquet floors, large windows, twin beds with wool blankets, large wardrobes, a desk and chairs, and large bathrooms. The deluxe rooms are slightly larger than the standard rooms and have balconies and bathtubs. A few rooms have air-conditioning. Room service is available, and there is a small restaurant just off the lobby. Services include laundry, currency exchange, luggage storage, safe-deposit boxes, and airport transfers.

**Hotel Garuda.** Thamel (P.O. Box 1771), Kathmandu. ☎ 977/1-416340 or 977/1-414766. Fax 977/1-413614 or 977/1-472390. E-mail: garuda@mos.com.np. 34 units. $13–$36 double. AE, JCB, MC, V.

Long a favorite of mountaineering expeditions and mentioned by Jon Krakauer in *Into Thin Air*, the Garuda stays packed throughout the main trekking seasons. However, if you contact them several weeks before your arrival, they can usually come up with a room. Located a few hundred feet north of the entrance to the Kathmandu Guest

House, the Garuda offers surprising quality at low rates. The rooms are clean and comfortable and have daily maid service. Some rooms have balconies, though these tend to be on the front of the hotel, making them also the noisiest rooms. Try to get a room on the north side; these have the best views. There are also good views from the roof of the hotel. A restaurant that serves standard Thamel international food and a small deli/bakery are on the premises. Room service, laundry service, luggage storage, safe-deposit boxes, and a travel agency are all available.

**Hotel Tashi Dhele.** Thamel (P.O. Box 7247), Kathmandu. ☎ **977/1-217446.** Fax 977/1-260402. 24 units. $25–$30 double. No credit cards.

Located down an alley just south of Thamel's main square, the Tashi Dhele is partially hidden behind a row of shops and is thus somewhat protected from the noise of the street. This noise insulation is one of the hotel's greatest assets. Most rooms are quite large, some have balconies, and all are carpeted (though the carpet needs replacing). The more-expensive rooms have telephones and televisions. Amenities include laundry service, safe-deposit boxes, airport transfers, luggage storage room, and free bicycle rentals.

**✪ Hotel Utse.** Jyatha, Thamel, Kathmandu. ☎ **977/1-257614,** 977/1-228952, or 977/1-226946. Fax 977/1-257615. E-mail: utse@wlink.com.np. 52 units. TEL. $20–$29 double. AE, JCB, MC, V.

With its ornate and exotic lobby designed to resemble a Tibetan Buddhist temple or Tibetan home, the Utse is one of the most atmospheric budget hotels in Kathmandu, and it is also one of the city's best values. There are Tibetan carpets in the halls, as well as in the deluxe rooms. Some rooms even have thangkas (Tibetan religious paintings) on the walls. One of the highlights of the hotel is a roof garden complete with lawn, a refuge when Kathmandu's noise and dust start getting you down. The standard rooms are of medium size and have parquet flooring, whereas the deluxe rooms are a bit larger and have carpeting. These latter rooms also have televisions and tubs. The restaurant here is well-known for its excellent Tibetan meals and is packed most nights. Services include free airport transfers, room service, luggage storage, safe-deposit boxes, and laundry service.

**✪ Kathmandu Guest House.** Thamel (P.O. Box 2769), Kathmandu. ☎ **977/1-413632** or 977/1-418733. Fax 977/1-417133. E-mail: kgh@thamel.mos.com.np. 120 units (90 with private bathroom). $8–$10 double without bathroom, $12–$60 double with bathroom. AE, MC, V.

Among inexpensive accommodations, the Kathmandu Guest House, set back from the street down a long driveway, is legendary, and consequently is almost always packed. Plan well ahead if you want to stay at this Kathmandu institution, which started out catering to hippies back in the 1960s (even The Beatles stayed here). Part of the hotel is housed in an old palace, though several new wings have been added over the years, creating a hodgepodge of rooms. The charm of this sprawling complex lies in the surprising variety of accommodations available in one place and the interesting mix of travelers who take up temporary residence here. The lobby, which is surprisingly elegant for a hotel in this price range, and the quiet courtyard garden are popular gathering spots and seem to always be filled with people on long trips around the world or those who have spent years exploring Asia. Laundry service, currency exchange, travel agency, and luggage storage are available.

**Pilgrims Hotel.** Thamel (P.O. Box 3872), Kathmandu. ☎ **977/1-416910.** Fax 977/1-424943. E-mail: hotel@pilgrims.wlink.com.np. 21 units (15 with bathroom). TEL. $10 double without bathroom, $15–$20 double with bathroom; $30 suite. AE, MC, V.

What makes this hotel truly special is the management's interest and dedication to the arts—visual, literary, and performing. There is a plethora of old photos, old prints, modern posters, and other framed artworks all over the hotel. It is operated by the owners of the popular Pilgrims Book House and is located up the road that leads north out of Thamel's main square. The hotel offers fairly clean, carpeted rooms. Those with private bathrooms are slightly larger than those without, and some rooms feature unusual octagonal windows. In addition to the lobby restaurant, there is a garden dining area.

**Tibet Guest House.** Chhetrapati, Thamel (P.O. Box 10586), Kathmandu. ☎ 977/1-251763 or 977/1-260556. Fax 977/1-260518. E-mail: tibet@guesths.mos.com.np. 55 units (47 with attached bathrooms). $11 double with shared bathroom; $19–$29 double with private bathroom. AE, MC, V.

Fairly large for a budget hotel, the Tibet Guest House has for many years been one of Thamel's more popular lodgings. Throughout the hotel are touches of Tibetan decor, including Tibetan rugs in the guest rooms. Rooms range from small, simple rooms with shared bathrooms to larger deluxe rooms with air-conditioning and televisions. The rooftop terrace is a good escape from the street-level noise. There's a Tibetan-inspired restaurant on the premises, and a terrace dining area is located outside the hotel's front door. Room service, a laundry service, and complimentary airport transfers are available.

## KATHMANDU'S EAST SIDE (NEAR PASHUPATINATH, BOUDHANATH & THE AIRPORT)
### VERY EXPENSIVE

✪ **Dwarika's Kathmandu Village Hotel.** Battisputali (P.O. Box 459), Kathmandu. ☎ 977/1-470770 or 977/1-473725. Fax 977/1-471379. E-mail: dwarika@mos.com.np. 70 units. $155–$195 double. AE, MC, V.

Located on the east side of Kathmandu near Pashupatinath, Nepal's most sacred Hindu temple, Dwarika's is by far Nepal's most interesting and unusual hotel. If you enjoy staying in historic hotels, then Dwarika's is for you. The hotel's two-story buildings were constructed in the traditional Newari style, and most rooms incorporate antique architectural details. A recent expansion has added what are the city's most luxurious and contemporary guest rooms (and some of the most expensive).

Among the interesting details incorporated into various rooms are block-printed bedspreads and curtains, antique carved windows, beamed ceilings, basket lamps, and bronze statues. Antique wood carvings are complimented by an abundance of modern woodworking, including chairs, mirror frames, ceiling light fixtures, windows, doors, and desks. Newer rooms also have marble and parquet floors and double sinks. The newest wing features extra-large rooms with luxurious bathrooms that have slate floors and walls, double sinks, double tubs, and separate showers.

**Dining/Diversions:** Dwarika's caters primarily to tour groups, and the restaurants reflect this. One serves expensive (for Nepal) multicourse feasts amid classic Nepali surroundings. Dinner here is more an event than a meal. The other restaurant, though very attractive, serves uninspired dishes at high prices. There's also a lounge with plenty of Nepali character and a terrace for alfresco breakfasts.

**Amenities:** Currency exchange, travel/tour desk, laundry service, souvenir shop.

✪ **The Everest Hotel.** New Baneswor (P.O. Box 659), Kathmandu. ☎ 977/1-488100 or 977/1-488099. Fax 977/1-490288 or 977/1-488130. E-mail: everest@vishnu.ccsl.com.np. 160 units and suites. A/C MINIBAR TV TEL. $160–$170 double; $350 suite. AE, DC, JCB, MC, V.

Adjacent to Kathmandu's convention center and not far from the airport, the Hotel Everest provides some of the best mountain views of any hotel in the city. (Be sure to request a room on an upper floor on the north side of the hotel.) Even though the location is not convenient to the city center, it is a good base for exploring both Bhaktapur and Patan. While the hotel itself is generically international in design, doormen and bellhops in Tibetan felt boots should provide an immediate sense of place. A recent renovation has given the guest rooms new carpets, silk curtains, and a vaguely neo-Italianate look. Maybe not what you were expecting in Nepal but pleasant enough.

**Dining/Diversions:** The hotel's many restaurants were in a state of flux during my visit, but you can expect to find a rooftop Chinese restaurant with excellent views, an atmospheric restaurant serving regional cuisines, and a casual coffee shop and poolside dining terrace. There's even a disco here (one of the few in the city) and a casino.

**Amenities:** Swimming pool, health club, tennis court, room service, laundry/dry-cleaning service, travel/tour desk, currency exchange, courtesy airport transfers, courtesy city shuttle, shopping arcade, barbershop, beauty parlor, baby-sitting.

## MODERATE

✪ **Hotel Sunset View.** New Baneswor (P.O. Box 1174), Kathmandu. ☎ **977/1-480057** or 977/1-482172. Fax 977/1-482219. E-mail: sunset@wlink.com.np. 31 units. TEL. $66–$70 double; $99 suite. AE, JCB, MC, V.

Operated by a Nepali-Japanese family and set down a dirt lane only a few hundred yards from the Everest Hotel, the Sunset View is one of the most peaceful, moderately priced hotels in Kathmandu. It lives up to its name with an excellent western view over the rooftops of Patan. Surrounded by beautiful Japanese gardens, the hotel has the feel of a contemporary home. There are several styles of rooms; some have sleeping lofts that make them ideal for families. The suite is a real bargain: It has a high ceiling, a large patio, a huge marble bath, and even a refrigerator. There's a small Japanese restaurant across the garden from the main house and a second, larger dining room in the main building. Laundry service, safe-deposit boxes, and currency exchange are all available.

## INEXPENSIVE

**Hotel Padma.** Boudha (G.P.O. Box 13823), Kathmandu. ☎ **977/1-479052** or 977/1-470957. Fax 977/1-481550. 12 units. TV TEL. $25–$35 double. JCB, MC, V.

There are few hotels anywhere in Nepal that offer as interesting a view as the one from the front windows of this hotel. Ask for a front-side room and you'll be seeing eye to eye with the Buddha. Not only do you get to gaze out your window at Boudhanath, the country's largest stupa, but you also can take in all the hustle and bustle as devout Tibetan Buddhists circumambulate the shrine. Although this hotel is fairly new, the rooms, which are quite comfortable, have an oddly modern Asian style (ca. 1960). There's a second-floor restaurant, and meals and drinks are also served on the rooftop terrace. Room service, laundry service, currency exchange, and safe-deposit boxes are all available.

**Pema Lhamo Guest House.** Boudha, Phoolbari, Kathmandu. ☎ **977/1-480493.** Fax 977/1-487545. 17 units (4 with attached bathroom). $7 double with shared bathroom; $10 double with private bathroom. No credit cards.

If you're in Kathmandu to brush up on your Buddhism, you'll likely be doing your study in the Boudha area. And if you're on a tight budget, this basic guest house is a good choice because it is only a short walk from the stupa. Located down a meandering lane northeast of the stupa, its dark green facade is hard to miss. Rooms are large, are carpeted, and are fairly clean.

# KATHMANDU'S WEST SIDE
## Very Expensive

✪ **Soaltee Crowne Plaza Kathmandu.** Tahachal (P.O. Box 97), Kathmandu. ☎ **977/ 1-272555** or 977/1-27399. Fax 977/1-272205 or 272203. E-mail: crowneplaza@shicp. com.np. 298 units. A/C MINIBAR TV TEL. $180–$250 double; $400–$775 suite. AE, DC, EU, MC, V.

This is one of Kathmandu's oldest luxury hotels and, until the completion of the new Hyatt Regency near Boudhanath, is the largest hotel in the city. As such, this hotel has for years played host to visiting heads of state and large conferences. Consequently, the individual traveler can easily get lost in the shuffle here. However, with four excellent restaurants, attractive gardens, a swimming pool, and a casino, you probably won't mind returning to your hotel at the end of the day. The hotel's biggest drawback is that it is not convenient to any of the city's attractions, shopping areas, or restaurants.

Though the older rooms here are a bit worn, they provide a bit more Nepali atmosphere than the newer guest rooms, which feature generic international decor. There are intricately carved dark-wood lattices framing the large windows, many of which have excellent views of the mountains. In the tile bathrooms, you'll find plenty of counter space, telephones, and hair dryers.

**Dining/Diversions:** Two Indian restaurants, one with evening Nepali cultural shows; an Italian restaurant; a French restaurant; and a coffee shop provide enough dining options to make up for the hotel's inconvenient location. There's a bar in the lobby, and in a separate building, you'll find Casino Nepal.

**Amenities:** A heated outdoor swimming pool (with interesting Nepali-style water fountains), health club with sauna and steam bath, tennis courts, 24-hour room service, courtesy city shuttle and airport transfer, currency exchange, car rental, travel agency, laundry/dry-cleaning service, baby-sitting, shopping arcade, beauty parlor, barbershop, business center.

## Inexpensive

✪ **Hotel Vajra.** Bijeswori (P.O. Box 1084), Kathmandu. ☎ **977/1-272719**, 977/ 1-271545, 977/1-271819, or 977/1-271824. Fax 977/1-271695. E-mail: vajra@mos.com. np. 54 units (46 with private bathroom). $16 double without bathroom, $38–$61 double with bathroom; $90 double suite. AE, MC, V.

The Vajra is one of those rare finds in Nepal—a hotel that actually reflects Nepali culture. Located near Swayambunath Stupa, and set amid lush gardens, the hotel's brick buildings exhibit the traditional architecture of Kathmandu, and there are ornate wood details throughout, as well as murals by local artists. The Vajra is also a cultural center housing an art gallery, a theater, and a library with books on such subjects as Tibetan Buddhism, Nepali natural history, Himalayan art, and regional exploration.

While the rooms are not quite as impressive as the grounds and public areas, they are still a cut above those in other hotels in this price range. The $60 deluxe rooms in the new wing are the most luxurious (with lattice ceilings, brick walls, and marble floors), but the less expensive "super rooms" are also a good bet. The least expensive rooms are a bit funky, though fun if your standards aren't too high. The hotel's Rooftop Gardens, Sunset Bar, and Pagoda Bar (with walls of windows and a painted ceiling based on traditional Tibetan Buddhist designs) are all great places for lunch or a drink. The Explorer's Restaurant, on the ground floor, offers a good breakfast buffet.

Laundry service, currency exchange, bicycle rentals, safe deposit, luggage storage are available.

## PATAN

Though officially a separate city, Patan (also known as Lalitpur) is now more a suburb of Kathmandu. Should you choose to stay in Patan, you will be a 15- to 20-minute taxi ride away from Kathmandu's old city, but close to Patan's equally fascinating old neighborhoods.

### EXPENSIVE

✪ **Hotel Himalaya.** Sahid Sukra Marg (P.O. Box 2141), Lalitpur, Kathmandu. ☎ **997/ 1-523900.** Fax 977/1-523909. E-mail: himalaya@lalitpur.mos.com.np. 100 units. A/C MINIBAR TV TEL. $120 double; $350 suite. AE, DC, JCB, MC, V.

Located on the main road between Kathmandu and Patan, this hotel boasts the best mountain scenery of any hotel in the valley. However, it was looking somewhat worse for wear on my last visit, and shrubs in the hotel's garden had almost completely obscured the views from the lobby. Still, roughly half the rooms (those on the garden side) have good views, and for this reason, the Hotel Himalaya is worth considering. Guest rooms are comfortable (if without much character) with large windows to allow for maximum mountain views—you won't forget where you are.

**Dining/Diversions:** The hotel's main dining room, serving Indian food, is on the second floor. The views of the mountains make this a good choice for lunch. A coffee shop and bar are located downstairs.

**Amenities:** Swimming pool, 24-hour room service, laundry/valet service, complimentary city shuttle, currency exchange, safe-deposit boxes, travel desk, baby-sitting, tennis court, shopping arcade, beauty parlor, barbershop, business center.

### MODERATE

**Hotel Narayani.** Pulchowk, (P.O. Box 1357), Kathmandu. ☎ **977/1-525015.** Fax 977/ 1-521291. E-mail: info@nbe.pc.mos.com.np. 87 units. A/C TV TEL. $85 double; $125 suite. AE, DC, JCB, MC, V.

Located up the hill from the Hotel Himalaya, within easy walking distance of Patan's Durbar Square, the Hotel Narayani is an older hotel that has an attractive lobby, but with rooms that don't live up to that same standard. Old beds, old bedspreads, and old carpets all add up to a sense that this hotel is overpriced for what you get. However, the large garden and swimming pool somewhat make up for the shortcomings of the rooms. If you think you'll spend time lounging by the pool, you might want to consider staying here. Amenities include room service, currency exchange, laundry service, safe-deposit boxes, luggage storage, beauty salon, and souvenir shops.

✪ **Summit Hotel.** Kopundol Height (P.O. Box 1406), Kathmandu. ☎ **977/1-521810** or 977/1-524694. Fax 977/1-523737 or 977/1-535221. E-mail: summit@wlink.com.np. 75 units (61 with private bathrooms). $25–$35 double with shared bathroom, $70–$95 double with private bathroom; $135 apartment (lower rates are for summer months). AE, MC, V.

With an excellent view across the valley to the Himalayas, this two-story brick hotel, located on a winding lane in a quiet residential neighborhood, is one of your best choices. If you like hotels that sacrifice a few comforts for a solid sense of place, the Summit will likely meet with your approval. The decor incorporates Nepali crafts and traditional Kathmandu Valley architectural designs, including ornately carved railings and pillars reminiscent of local palaces and temples. The Summit surrounds a lush

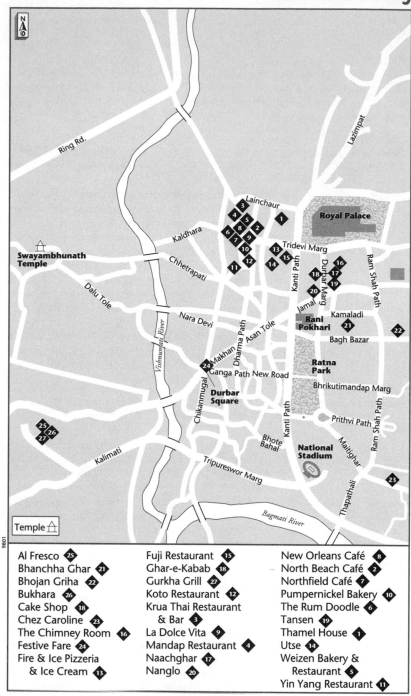

Al Fresco 25
Bhanchha Ghar 21
Bhojan Griha 22
Bukhara 26
Cake Shop 18
Chez Caroline 23
The Chimney Room 16
Festive Fare 24
Fire & Ice Pizzeria
&  Ice Cream 13

Fuji Restaurant 15
Ghar-e-Kabab 18
Gurkha Grill 27
Koto Restaurant 12
Krua Thai Restaurant
&  Bar 3
La Dolce Vita 9
Mandap Restaurant 4
Naachghar 17
Nanglo 20

New Orleans Café 8
North Beach Café 2
Northfield Café 7
Pumpernickel Bakery 10
The Rum Doodle 6
Tansen 19
Thamel House 1
Utse 14
Weizen Bakery &
Restaurant 5
Yin Yang Restaurant 11

garden filled with colorful flowers and shady trees. The best values are the least expensive rooms with private bathrooms. Each of these rooms overlooks the garden; the floors are made of the traditional brick tiles that have been used in local homes for centuries. The more expensive rooms are larger and have better views.

With exposed brick walls, a beamed ceiling, traditional brick-tile floors, and an old Newari-style carved lattice window, the hotel's small restaurant has a very Nepali feel to it. In the adjacent bar, long couches covered with pillows are a great place to relax by a cozy fire. There are dinner barbecues on Friday for Rs500 ($7.60). Amenities include a swimming pool, currency exchange, and airport transfers.

## BHAKTAPUR

Bhaktapur is the best-preserved city in the valley, but there are, unfortunately, very few places to stay, and all of these are suited for budget travelers. However, if budget accommodations don't bother you, I can't overemphasize how different it is to stay in Bhaktapur than in Kathmandu. In Bhaktapur, you can stay right on Durbar Square and not have to constantly deal with the nightmarish traffic that has made Kathmandu almost unbearable. Excellent day hikes can also be started or finished in Bhaktapur, which makes a stay here something of a throwback to slower times in the Kathmandu Valley.

### INEXPENSIVE

**Bhadgaon Guest House.** Taumadhi Square, Bhaktapur-11. ☎ **977/1-610488.** Fax 977/1-610481. 9 units. $15 double. No credit cards.

Located only 50 feet away from the Nyatapola Cafe, this budget hotel is the best you'll find in Bhaktapur. Guest rooms, though small and with tiny bathrooms, are carpeted and have platform beds. From the rooftop restaurant, you can see the Himalayas over Bhaktapur's rooftops. However, the most compelling reason to stay here is the opportunity to step out of the hotel in the morning to a view of the Nyatapola Temple.

**Golden Gate Guest House.** Durbar Square (P.O. Box 21), Bhaktapur. ☎ **977/1-610534.** Fax 977/1-611081. 15 units (6 with private bathroom). Rates: $5.30 double with shared bathroom, $9.85 double with private bathroom. No credit cards.

This guest house is nothing special, but it is only steps away from Durbar Square and the famous Golden Gate, from which the guest house takes its name. Double and triple rooms, with cement floors, are large, though very basic, and contain only beds. Some of the rooms have small balconies. From the roof, there is a nice view of Bhaktapur and the valley.

**Shiva Guest House.** Bhaktapur Durbar Square, Bhaktapur-11. ☎ **977/1-613912.** Fax 977/1-610740. 11 units (none with bathroom). $8–$10 double. No credit cards.

Its ideal location overlooking Durbar Square makes this one of the best budget accommodations in the valley. Rooms are simply furnished with twin beds and little else, but they are clean. The traditional brick-tile floors of the Kathmandu Valley are cold in the winter but very attractive. On the top floor there is a cozy cafe with an international menu.

## 4 Dining

Though you probably won't return from Nepal raving about the meals you had, you can get good food at very reasonable prices. In fact, you will have a very hard time spending more than $15 or $20 on dinner. For $10 you can dine in the best restaurants in Nepal, and for as little as $3 you can get a steak dinner at a budget restaurant. In my opinion, the city's best meals are served at its many Indian restaurants, one or two of which serve meals as delicious as you're likely to find anywhere in the world. Service, on the other hand, leaves much to be desired at even the best restaurants. *Please be patient.*

For visitors with a sweet tooth, Kathmandu is the cake-and-pie capital of Asia, and it is very tempting to sample your way through the desserts of Thamel. Be forewarned: Those outlandishly iced cakes and mountain-peak meringue pies are usually a disappointment unless you've been traveling through India for a few months. Also, keep in mind that salmonella bacteria grow very well in meringue and cheesecake.

Wine is relatively expensive in Nepal because it is all imported. A glass of the least expensive wine can cost Rs300 ($4.55) in a restaurant where a steak dinner costs only Rs250 ($3.80). Local beer, on the other hand, is relatively cheap.

## THE DURBAR MARG & NAXAL AREAS

In addition to the restaurants listed here, you'll find Kathmandu's best pastry shop on Durbar Marg. **The Cake Shop** (☎ **221711, ext. 4114**), is affiliated with the Hotel de l'Annapurna and is just outside the hotel's front gate. The chocolate truffle and opera cakes are wonderful, and a welcome change from the almost-always disappointing pastries in Thamel.

## EXPENSIVE

**Bhojan Griha.** Dilli Bazaar. ☎ **416423** or 411603. Reservations recommended for groups. Set dinner Rs1,000 ($15.15). AE, MC, V. Daily 6:30pm–midnight. NEPALI.

Located 2 long blocks east of Durbar Marg, Bhojan Griha is one of the copy-cat restaurants that has cashed in on the concept of Nepali cuisine served in historic surroundings. In this case, the setting is a neoclassical mansion built a century ago for the priest-counselor to the royal family. The building was saved from demolition by the opening of this restaurant, and visitors now have yet another Rana-period architectural anomaly to visit in Kathmandu. Set meals are the norm here, and cultural performances are part of the experience. There's a tea pavilion out front where you can sample Nepali tea from the country's Ilam tea-growing region. It's all a bit touristy, but the restaurant provides not only a chance to sample the best of Nepali cooking, but also a glimpse into one of Nepal's most unusual historical periods.

✪ **The Chimney Room.** Hotel Yak & Yeti, Durbar Marg. ☎ **248999** or 240520. Reservations recommended. Main dishes Rs325–Rs1,200 ($4.90–$18.20). AE, DC, JCB, MC, V. Daily 6:30–11pm. RUSSIAN/CONTINENTAL.

Originally known as the Yak & Yeti Restaurant and located in another hotel, the Chimney Room was founded by a famous Russian expatriate, Boris Lissanevitch, who resided in Kathmandu for many years. With brick walls and high ceilings, the restaurant has the feeling of a rathskeller and takes its name from a large copper and brass chimney over a circular hearth in the middle of the restaurant. In the winter, roaring fires and stiff drinks help keep the chill away as you wait to be seated. Though some say meals aren't up to their old standards, the Russian specialties introduced by Boris are still popular. Start with a bowl of thick rich borscht, and follow with chicken Kiev, beef Stroganoff, or jumbo prawn shashlik. You'll find all of these dishes on other menus in town, but nowhere are they prepared better than here. Desserts aren't as wonderful as they look, and wine is expensive because of import duties; but cocktails made with local liquor are most reasonable.

# Patan Accommodations & Dining

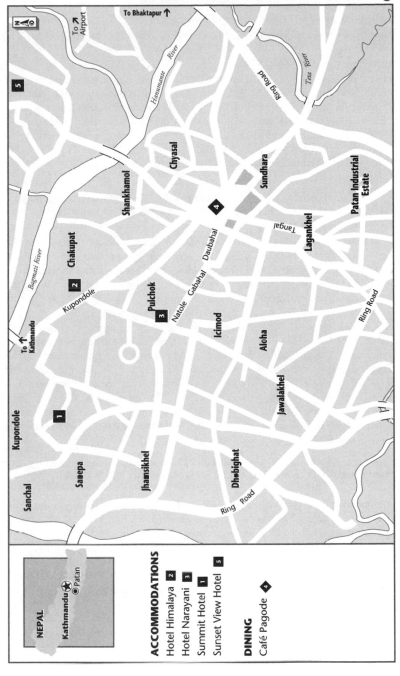

To Bhaktapur ↑

To ↗ Airport

Himmante River

Ring Road

Teta River

Bagmati River

Chyasal

Sundhara

Patan Industrial Estate

Shankhamol

Tangal

Lagankhel

Chakupat

Kupondole

Pulchok

Natole Cabahal Daubahal

Icimod

Aloha

Ring Road

To ↖ Kathmandu

Jawalakhel

Kupondole

Sanchal

Saaepa

Jhamsikhel

Dhobighat

Ring Road

**NEPAL**

Kathmandu ✪ ● Patan

**ACCOMMODATIONS**

Hotel Himalaya 2

Hotel Narayani 3

Summit Hotel 1

Sunset View Hotel 5

**DINING**

Café Pagode 4

95

## MODERATE

**Bhanchha Ghar.** Kamaladi. ☎ **225172** or 228723. Reservations recommended. Set meal Rs800 ($12.10). AE, MC, V. Daily 11am–10:30pm. NEPALI.

Bhanchha Ghar caters primarily to group tours and, with its nightly "cultural program," can seem a bit touristy. However, it was the first Kathmandu restaurant to specialize in serving elaborate Nepali fixed dinners in a restored historic building, a concept that has been copied in recent years. The restaurant is housed in a restored 100-year-old Rana residence, and guests sit on the floor on colorful pillows arranged around low tables. Though there is an à la carte menu, most people order the fixed menu, which includes a couple of flavorful and spicy meat dishes, rice, lentils, two fragrant vegetable dishes, Nepali-style pickles, dessert, tea or coffee, and a glass of *rakshi* (local moonshine).

○ **Fuji Restaurant.** Kantipath. ☎ **225272.** Main dishes Rs140–Rs350 ($2.10–$5.30); set meals Rs450–Rs600 ($6.80–$9.10). No credit cards. Tues–Sun 11:30am–9:30pm. JAPANESE.

This is one of my favorite restaurants in Kathmandu. It's located far back from Kantipath behind a row of offices, and it is a good place to come for seclusion and beautifully prepared Japanese food. The building that houses Fuji was once a Rana gambling hall and dance pavilion; the red brick facade with its white trim seems transported directly from Europe. A pond surrounds the restaurant, and you must walk across a wooden bridge to reach the front door. A large terrace built over the pond, provides a few outdoor tables and for a truly unique dining experience, one table is set on its own private island. Inside, amid the high ceilings and painted plasterwork of past grandeur, there is a small bar, a teppanyaki bar, and a main dining area with large French doors opening onto the pond. The food is light and flavorful with many dishes served in fragrant broths. You'll find all your favorites with the exception of sushi and sashimi; it's not possible to get fish fresh enough for these dishes. The most popular menu offerings are the set lunches and dinners (torimeshi bento is a good deal) that come with many different appetizers, braised vegetables, yakitori, steamed egg custard, tempura, sukiyaki, rice, miso soup, pickles, and fruit.

○ **Ghar-e-Kabab.** Durbar Marg. ☎ **221711.** Reservations recommended for dinner. Vegetable dishes Rs170–Rs190 ($2.60–$2.90); main dishes Rs250–Rs600 ($3.80–$9.10). AE, DC, MC, V. Lunch daily noon–2:30pm; dinner daily 7–10:30pm. INDIAN.

Affiliated with the Hotel de l'Annapurna and located upstairs from the hotel pastry shop, Ghar-e-Kabab has long been one of Kathmandu's best Indian restaurants. The chicken tikka, a boneless chicken tandoori, served here is so succulent and tender that it almost melts in your mouth. You can watch this and other tandoori dishes being baked in the restaurant's glass-walled tandoori show kitchen. The different *nans* (tandoori-baked breads) and *parathas* (fried breads) are the perfect accompaniment to an order of chicken tikka. To start out, be sure to try the papri chaat, a unique melange of flavors and textures. The tomato-coconut soup is delicious, and the *saag* (spinach) is the best you'll ever taste. As one of Kathmandu's top restaurants, Ghar-e-Kebab attracts both well-heeled Nepalis and tourists in the know. In the evenings there is live traditional Indian music to accompany dinner. Unfortunately, service here can be glacially slow, and the kitchen does occasionally have a bad night.

○ **Naachghar.** Hotel Yak & Yeti, Durbar Marg. ☎ **248999** or 240520. Reservations recommended. Main dishes Rs170–Rs980 ($2.60–$14.85); Thali plates Rs575–Rs675 ($8.70–$10.20). Daily 7–11:30pm. INDIAN/NEPALI.

Located in the old palace wing of the Yak & Yeti Hotel, Naachghar is one of Kathmandu's most elegant restaurants. The high-ceilinged dining room has a marble floor and classical pillars, while ornate plasterwork and a mural of the signs of the zodiac hint at the tastes of the Rana prime minister who had this palace constructed. A stage at one end is used for the nightly program of Nepali music and dance. Although you can order a *thali* and have a one-plate feast, the tandoori dishes here are the real gems; try the chicken tikka or *paneer* (cheese) tikka and the nan. Accompany this with the *gucchi mattar* (mildly spiced mushrooms and peas). If you still have room—in fact, be sure to save room—try the sikarni, a sweet and spicy yogurt-based dessert.

## INEXPENSIVE

✪ **Mike's Breakfast.** Naxal. ☎ **424303.** Reservations recommended for groups. Breakfast Rs100–Rs300 ($1.50–$4.55); lunch and dinner Rs135–Rs260 ($2.05–$3.95). No credit cards. Daily 7am–9pm. INTERNATIONAL.

For many years Mike's Breakfast has been the most popular breakfast spot in Kathmandu. Local expatriates, middle-class Nepalis, and tourists all appreciate the flower-filled garden, huge portions, bottomless cups of coffee, and classical music on the stereo. I can think of no better way to start a day in Kathmandu. Good breakfast choices are *huevos rancheros* and burritos. For lunch or dinner, the specialty quiches, fried tofu with veggies, or anything Mexican is tasty. The restaurant is housed in a restored European-style minimansion and is a 10-minute walk east of the Royal Palace (located at the top of Durbar Marg). Owner Mike Frame, who hails from Minnesota, now also operates the Northfield Café (see below), located a few doors up the street from the Kathmandu Guest House.

**Nanglo.** Durbar Marg. ☎ **222636.** Reservations recommended for dinner. Vegetable dishes Rs60 (90¢); main dishes Rs95–Rs725 ($1.45–$11). AE, MC, V. Daily 11am–10pm. CHINESE.

The first time I stopped in at Nanglo, I met an older British gentleman who swore that Nanglo served the best Chinese food in Kathmandu and that he would eat nowhere else. Originally just a small restaurant, Nanglo has grown into a veritable dining complex at the south end of Durbar Marg across from the Hotel Sherpa. On the ground floor you'll find a dark and traditional Chinese restaurant with Chinese lanterns and red-and-black decor, which is pleasantly cool on a hot afternoon. The kitchen prepares excellent Cantonese and Mandarin dishes. Try one of the noodle dishes, which feature homemade noodles, or anything with either the ginger-coriander sauce or the Manchurian sauce, which are spicy and tasty. There's a pub in a separate room entered through a door to the left of the Chinese restaurant's door. Behind the pub is a bustling courtyard cafe that extends to a second-floor terrace overlooking Durbar Marg and a bit of the Himalayas. The cafe primarily serves popular continental dishes, all for between Rs60 and Rs175 (90¢ and $2.65).

**Tansen.** Durbar Marg. ☎ **224707.** Reservations recommended for dinner. Main dishes Rs90–Rs375 ($1.35–$5.70). AE, MC, V. Daily 11:30am–10pm. INDIAN.

Under the same management as the ever-popular Nanglo Chinese restaurant across Durbar Marg (see above), Tansen serves very good Indian food at reasonable prices. With copper plates, bowls, and cups, the table settings are as memorable as the meals themselves. You can sit at either Western tables or low Nepali-style tables on pillows on the floor. The white-jacketed waiters offer service that is usually a cut above what you can expect at most Kathmandu restaurants. For an unusual starter, try the *papri chat*—lentil chips in a spicy yogurt sauce. On the whole, sauces here are thick and rich, ideal for sopping up with any of the many interesting breads on the menu.

# THAMEL

For roughly 2 decades, Thamel has been the favored neighborhood of budget travelers. For many of these travelers, a cheap steak is the ultimate meal, especially after traveling in India. Consequently, there are several restaurants in Thamel that are perennial favorites with backpackers. Among these are K.C.'s Restaurant, Helena's, Alice's Restaurant, The Third Eye, and Le Bistro. While the food at these restaurants is certainly cheap, the quality is not necessarily good and service can be lackadaisical.

Cheap breakfasts are the other specialty of Thamel restaurants, and all over the neighborhood you'll see signs for such things as American breakfasts and heavy set breakfasts. These are basically toast-and-egg breakfasts with fried potatoes (not hash browns) and a baked tomato (thanks to the subcontinent's British influence). But don't expect an early breakfast. Nepalis are up and about long before 6am, but tourist restaurants don't seem to be getting into gear until between 7 and 8am.

## MODERATE

✪ **Fire & Ice Pizzeria & Ice Cream.** Thamel. ☎ **250210.** Reservations recommended. Pizzas Rs160–Rs270 ($2.40–$4.10). No credit cards. Daily 11am–10pm. PIZZA.

Extremely popular with both Kathmandu ex-pats and tourists, Fire & Ice is usually hopping, bursting at the seams with Italian music and happy customers. The pizzas, which are small, aren't exactly what you'd expect (more Italian than American), but they are tasty and everyone agrees they're the best in town. In addition to pizzas there are big salads (sterilized, of course) with herb-flavored oil. The cappuccinos here are great, and the wine by the glass isn't as expensive as elsewhere in town. The ice cream is soft serve and the only we've ever had in the whole country. Keep in mind, however, that a lunch or dinner here may be one of your more expensive meals in Kathmandu we paid more to eat here than at some deluxe hotel restaurants. Fire & Ice is located in the "modern" shopping center on Tridevi Marg, the wide street that leads into Thamel from the east.

**Koto Restaurant.** Chhetrapati, Thamel. ☎ **256449.** Also located on Durbar Marg ☎ 226025. Reservations recommended for dinner. Main dishes Rs130–Rs300 ($1.95–$4.55); set menu Rs350 ($5.30). No credit cards. Daily 11am–9pm. JAPANESE.

In the same alley as the Himalayan International Clinic and across from the Gorka Guest House (south of Kathmandu Guest House), you'll find another of Kathmandu's Japanese restaurants. Clean, convenient, and Zen-like, the Koto is frequently full, so be sure to call and make a dinner reservation. Try the miso soup, made with locally prepared miso—it's especially warming on a cold night. Fried tofu in sweetened soy sauce with pickles and rice is a good light meal, as is the Koto bento with soup. A second Koto (actually the original) is located on Durbar Marg near the entrance to the Hotel de l'Annapurna (it's down a dark alleyway and up a flight of stairs).

**Krua Thai Restaurant & Bar.** Thamel. ☎ **414291.** Dishes Rs140–Rs440 ($2.10–$6.65). MC, V. Daily 8am–10pm. THAI.

Located around the corner to the north of Hotel Garuda, this restaurant serves surprisingly authentic Thai food. The food is similar to that served at the popular Yin Yang Restaurant (see below); but the atmosphere is not as elegant, and the prices are a bit higher. The *som tam* (hot-and-spicy green papaya salad), *tom yum* (soup flavored with chili, lime, and lemongrass and loaded with vegetables), and *phad Thai* (savory noodles) are all worth returning for over and over again. The fully stocked bar seems to go hand-in-hand with the overly loud music, but they'll turn it down if you ask. If you didn't get enough while you were trekking, continental fare, of course, is also available.

⊙ **Thamel House.** Thamel Tole. ☎ **410388.** Reservations recommended. Fixed-price dinner Rs550 ($8.35); à la carte Rs50–Rs150 (75¢–$2.25). MC, V. Daily 2–10pm. NEPALI.

Upscale restaurants serving Nepali food in historic buildings are proliferating in Kathmandu, and most have similar interior decors and menus. The Thamel House is not as touristy as some of the other such restaurants, and, if you are staying in Thamel, it is the most convenient and least expensive of the bunch. The restaurant is housed in a 100-year-old brick home (one of Kathmandu's only buildings of this style and vintage that has been restored). As in traditional Nepali homes, shoes are removed before entering the restaurant's dining rooms, and most guests opt to eat at a traditional low table surrounded by pillows. The fixed-price meals, though expensive by Thamel standards, are a bargain when you consider that they are all-you-can-eat and include a tiny clay cup of local rice liquor poured from a pitcher held 3 feet above your table. The set dinner might include rice, bamboo-shoot and vegetable curries, mutton kebabs, wild boar, chicken curry, and pickled vegetables. For dessert, there is rice pudding or *sukarni* (a delicious yogurt dish with cinnamon, nuts, and raisins), and tea or coffee. If all this is too much for you, ask to see the à la carte menu, from which you can order many of the same dishes. Service here is excellent.

## INEXPENSIVE

**La Dolce Vita.** Thamel. ☎ **419612.** Reservations recommended for groups. Main dishes Rs195–Rs215 ($2.95–$3.25); pastas Rs150–190 ($2.25–$2.90). AE, MC, V. Daily 7am–10pm; bar 2–10pm. ITALIAN.

Located on the second and third floors of the building opposite the Kathmandu Guest House entrance, this restaurant is an ode to old films. Dozens of old movie posters (mostly in Italian) decorate the walls, which are painted in a bold mix of black and white and bright red and yellow. The setting alone makes a meal here worthwhile, and the restaurant serves passable Italian meals considering the difficulty of getting ingredients. Try the eggplant baked with cheese and tomato sauce or the *puttanesca* with capers and olives, which also seemed to contain small dried fish from the local market (instead of the traditional anchovies). If it's pizza you want, you're better off going to the nearby Fire & Ice Pizzaria & Ice Cream (see above).

**Mandap Restaurant.** Hotel Mandap, Thamel. ☎ **413321.** Main dishes Rs70–Rs190 ($1.05–$2.90). AE, DC, JCB, MC, V. Daily 7am–10pm. INTERNATIONAL.

A budget traveler's version of the famous (and expensive) Chimney Room at the Hotel Yak & Yeti, Mandap has the same type of high beamed ceiling and shiny copper chimney and has a few similar menu items, which are prepared almost as well as at the more expensive counterpart. Tables are set with linen and fresh flowers, and in one corner there's a small bar. The menu features a good chicken shashlik and a chicken Kiev that comes floating in a sea of mashed potatoes. However, the Indian offerings, such as *malai kofta* and nan, are more reliable. Pizzas and Mexican food are also available, along with a few continental offerings. Stay away from cream-of-anything soup. The patio out front is a very popular spot for breakfast and lunch, and for munching on baked goodies from the Mandap Bakery, which is one of the best in Thamel.

⊙ **New Orleans Café and Blue Note Bar.** Thamel. ☎ **425736.** Meals Rs100–Rs200 ($1.50–$3.05). No credit cards. Daily 6:30am–midnight. INTERNATIONAL.

This place is great all through the day from an early-morning breakfast to a late-night meal or cocktail at the small bar. It's fun to have breakfast in the authentic little temple building that is tucked into the corner of the restaurant's dining patio, while at night the place rocks with the sounds of both local and visiting musicians. There are plenty of good vegetarian dishes including large Greek salads, paneer (a cheese) with spinach, vegetable shashlik, and New Orleans favorites such as jambalaya.

**North Beach Café.** Thamel. ☎ **411991.** Dishes Rs85–Rs250 ($1.30–$3.80). No credit cards. Daily 8am–10pm. INTERNATIONAL/AMERICAN.

Located on the north side of Thamel adjacent to the Hotel Vaishali, this place is a great escape from the hustle and bustle of Thamel. Located in a garden setting on the site of the original Boris's restaurant, this restaurant even has a mural on the back wall from Boris's Jungle Bar. The restaurant is currently owned by an American from San Francisco, and, consequently, there are plenty of American (and vegetarian) dishes on the extensive menu. Good dishes include borscht, giant ravioli, paneer with vegetables, apple-pumpkin soup, and a house specialty, heart-shaped waffles. Dining outside is definitely more appealing than inside, where the large-screen TV is the center of attention.

**Northfield Café & Jesse James Bar.** Thamel. ☎ **424884** or 419530. Breakfast Rs95–Rs180 ($1.45–$2.75); lunch and dinner Rs95–Rs240 ($1.45–$3.65). V. Daily 7am–10pm. AMERICAN/MEXICAN.

Another one of the friendly Mike's restaurants, the Northfield Café is located next door to the Kathmandu Guest House and is popular with Americans. Come here for good Mexican food and breakfasts (which come with bottomless cups of coffee) and attentive service. The garden is somewhat removed from the chaos of Thamel, but the tranquillity is occasionally spoiled by street noise which competes with the classical music. For breakfast, there are burritos as big as your forearm, waffles with fruit and yogurt, and delicious fresh-squeezed orange juice. For lunch and dinner there are chicken enchiladas and bean, cheese, and mushroom quesadillas that are crisp, tasty, and ungreasy. Yummy snacks include nachos (a heaping plate is great with a drink), and Nepali-style spicy chicken nuggets that go by the name of chicken chile boneless. At night, the restaurant's Jesse James bar gets lively, and pizzas are served. If you're homesick for some American food, there's Minnesota-style liver and onions, as well as roast chicken.

**Pumpernickel Bakery & Restaurant.** Thamel. No phone. Sandwiches Rs45–Rs50 (70¢–75¢); breads Rs10–Rs40 (15¢–60¢). No credit cards. Daily 8am–6pm. INTERNATIONAL/BAKERY.

With a large shady garden filled with wicker tables, the Pumpernickel is popular with the kind of folks who frequent European cafes; a large and cluttered bulletin board gives you an idea of how much cross-cultural exchange takes place here. What draws people of all nationalities to the Pumpernickel are the good baked goods, including whole-wheat bread, rolls, bagels, and croissants. The menu is mostly separate lists of the different types of breads and toppings (yak cheese, egg, jam, honey, peanut butter) available. You get to mix and match. I suspect more coffee and tea are consumed here than at any other restaurant in town.

**The Rum Doodle.** Thamel. ☎ **414336.** Soups and salads Rs50–Rs150 (75¢–$2.25); main dishes Rs120–Rs260 ($1.80–$3.95). JCB, MC, V. Daily 10am–10pm. INTERNATIONAL.

Rum Doodle, whose name comes from a parody of old British mountaineering books, has long been the most popular bar in Kathmandu. It's also quite popular for its food. The walls are covered with climbing, kayaking, and mountaineering gear, as well as big cutouts of yeti footprints that have been signed by various mountain-climbing and river expeditions. The menu includes such Kathmandu standards as chicken Kiev, beef stroganoff, and vegetarian lasagne, as well as chicken and fish-and-chips. The steaks and burgers are also popular with trekkers just returned from the hills. In warm weather, you can dine in the garden, and when it's cold, you can sit by the fire in the main dining room.

**Utse.** Jyatha, Thamel. ☎ **228952.** Reservations suggested for groups. Main dishes Rs50–Rs320 (75¢–$4.85). MC, V. Daily 11am–10pm. TIBETAN/INTERNATIONAL.

Utse, located off the lobby of the hotel of the same name, has a homey, Tibetan atmosphere. Long a Thamel favorite, this place stays packed at night, so come early or try to make a reservation. I like the traditional low tables and Tibetan-rug–covered couches, but there are plenty of Western-style tables as well. It's the well-prepared Tibetan dishes that are the main draw here. Dishes worth trying include the kothays (fried dumplings), momos (steamed dumplings), and the thukpa soup. Homemade vegetable-noodle soups are warming and filling. If you give the kitchen 2 hours' notice, they can prepare two special Tibetan dinners: A *gacok* (a dish that's similar to a Mongolian-style hot pot) or *kadug dhayshey* (a combination of about ten dishes, including noodles and dumplings). It takes two to six people to polish off one of these special meals.

**Weizen Bakery & Restaurant.** Thamel. ☎ **260055.** Reservations not necessary. Breakfast Rs60–Rs100 (90¢–$1.50); lunch and dinner Rs60–Rs150 (90¢–$2.25). No credit cards. Daily 7am–11pm. BAKERY/INTERNATIONAL.

Meals other than breakfast are good here, but Weizen is best the first thing in the morning when the aroma of freshly baked breads and cinnamon rolls wafts past your nose. A good budget choice, Weizen is not far from the popular Pumpernickel Bakery and not nearly as crowded, so service is quick and efficient. The well-tended garden provides a relaxing space in which to sit, but we heard that Weizen might be moving to another Thamel location just off the street near the Garuda Hotel, which means it might not have the same sort of comfortable garden as it once did.

**✪ Yin Yang Restaurant.** Thamel. ☎ **425510.** Reservations recommended after 6pm. Dishes Rs120–Rs150 ($1.80–$2.25). AE, DISC, JCB, MC, V. Daily 7am–10pm. THAI.

Located opposite the ever-popular Third Eye (south of the Kathmandu Guest House), Yin Yang serves excellent and authentic Thai food and has great atmosphere. While there is comfortable seating inside the restaurant, the patio out front, shaded by a big tree, is the preferred place to eat. Try the yellow curry, fried tofu, green papaya salad (som tam), and steamed spring rolls. You'll also find a good selection of vegetarian dishes here, and the continental dishes (filet mignon, chicken cordon bleu) are popular, too. You can accompany your meal with a Singha beer, which is about the best beer you can get in Kathmandu. Service is fairly efficient. Yin Yang also has its own bakery and serves breakfast. Stay away from the banana cake; you'll be disappointed.

## THE DURBAR SQUARE AREA

**Festive Fare.** Durbar Square. ☎ **247223.** Reservations not necessary. Main dishes Rs150–Rs350 ($2.25–$5.30); set meal Rs600 ($9.10). MC, V. Daily 10am–10pm. NEPALI/INTERNATIONAL.

Located a couple of floors above the street, this restaurant has wonderful views of Durbar Square, the Taleju Temple, and Swayambunath high on a hill in the distance. Even without the views, Festive Fare would be worth mentioning simply because there are so few dining options in the area. The highlight of the menu is an extensive Nepali set meal that includes basmati rice, herb-fried black lentil curry, chicken curry, grilled mutton, mixed vegetables, a Nepali pickle, and, for desert, sweetened yogurt. There are also less-filling (and less-interesting) meals, including spaghetti, pizza, lasagne, and fried chicken. This restaurant also has the cleanest toilet in the area. You'll find Festive Fare at the north end of the Durbar Square area across from a row of small thangka shops. If you're not hungry, you could just have a bottle of beer or wine or some tea and take in the view.

# KATHMANDU'S EAST SIDE (NEAR PASHUPATINATH, BOUDHANATH & THE AIRPORT)
## EXPENSIVE

**Krishnarpan.** Dwarika's Kathmandu Village Hotel, Battisputali. ☎ **470770** or 473725. Reservations recommended. Set dinners Rs1,255–Rs1,585 ($19–$24). AE, MC, V. Daily 6:30–10pm. NEPALI.

Located in the most architecturally interesting hotel in Kathmandu, this gourmet Nepali restaurant surrounds diners with the exotic atmosphere of old Kathmandu. From the numerous salvaged architectural details to servers in the traditional dress of different Nepali ethnic groups to the old metal platters and dishes on which the meals are served, everything about this restaurant evokes Nepal's cultural heritage. The country's culinary heritage is likewise conjured in the elaborate and very filling meals served here. Be sure to bring a hearty appetite if you plan to have the 12-course feast, which consists of small portions of lots of different dishes. There are also six-course and nine-course meals. You won't find a better introduction to the best of Nepali cooking.

## INEXPENSIVE

**Stupa View Restaurant.** Boudha. ☎ **479044.** Main dishes Rs130–Rs230 ($1.95–$3.50). No credit cards. Daily 8am–9pm. VEGETARIAN/INTERNATIONAL.

This German-run restaurant is one of Kathmandu's best vegetarian restaurants, and it also has one of the best views in the city—it looks directly into the Buddha's eyes on Boudhanath stupa. A perusal of the menu turns up dishes with unusual names such as elephant's feet, rhino's teeth, and buffalo's nightmare. But don't worry, these dishes aren't made with endangered species; they're all meat-free and include brown rice, veggie patties, soy loaf with homemade noodles, seitan steak, and vegetable schnitzel. There's also a daily special.

# KATHMANDU'S WEST SIDE
## EXPENSIVE

✪ **Al Fresco.** Soaltee Crowne Plaza Kathmandu. Tahachal. ☎ **272550.** Reservations recommended for dinner. Pizzas Rs225–Rs300 ($3.40–$4.55); main dishes Rs225–Rs775 ($3.40–$11.75). AE, MC, V. Daily 11am–10:45pm. ITALIAN.

Al Fresco is a fashionable little trattoria and Italian deli that serves the best Italian food in Kathmandu. If you're on a budget, this would be a great place to treat yourself to an excellent meal. The menu is elegant and full of beautiful artwork. The wine and the liqueur lists contain good selections, and the waiters are friendly yet very professional. Among the memorable dishes are wonderfully garlicky crustini, *tortelloni ai funghi* (melt-in-your-mouth tortellini pasta with a few morel mushrooms in a spicy broth), and *zuppa di peperoni 'Fredda'* (a cold and subtly smooth pimento soup garnished with yogurt). The *tartufi di cioccolata* (chocolate truffles with vanilla ice cream and chocolate sauce) is a perfectly decadent way to finish a meal. Although this is not a pizza parlor, the pizza here is as close as you can get to what you'd recognize as pizza in the United States.

✪ **Bukhara.** Soaltee Crowne Plaza Kathmandu. Tahachal. ☎ **272550.** Reservations recommended. Main dishes Rs350–Rs800 ($5.30–$12.10). AE, DC, EU, MC, V. Daily 12:30–2:30pm and 7–11pm hours. INDIAN.

The old favorite Ghar-e-Kabab got some serious competition when Bukhara, part of a Delhi-based upscale restaurant chain, opened at the Soaltee Crowne Plaza. With its exotic northwest frontier decor, this exotic and elegant restaurant specializes in the Moghul cuisine of northern India, with an emphasis on tandoori dishes. If you've never had tandoori prawns, this just might be the place to finally try them (even though they're the most expensive item on the menu). If your budget won't allow prawns, opt for the peshawari kebab, flavored cubes of marinated lamb grilled in the tandoori oven. For accompaniment, don't miss the tandoori potatoes; you'll never be satisfied with mashed potatoes again. Round things out with some of the rich *dal makhani* Bukhara and the tandoori *simla mirch* (a grilled bell pepper stuffed with vegetables, cashews, and sultanas). For dessert, try the saffron-scented *rasmalai.*

**Gurkha Grill.** Soaltee Crowne Plaza Kathmandu. Tahachal. ☎ **272550.** Reservations recommended. Main dishes Rs475–Rs950 ($7.20–$14.40). AE, DC, EU, MC, V. Daily 7–11pm. FRENCH.

If you find yourself craving the sort of special-occasion meal you might have at a restaurant back home, then consider the Gurkha Grill, Kathmandu's best French restaurant. With ingredients flown in from all over the world, this restaurant does its utmost to make you forget that you are half a world away from Paris. While the menu is primarily classic French, the chef does make forays into more nouvelle terrain. A recent menu included, among the appetizers, escargots, caviar, smoked salmon, and camembert wrapped in spinach and served with a walnut sauce. Though the Himalayas are a long way from the sea, lobster flamed with brandy (for a mere $10.30) is still a big hit here. In addition to the many well-prepared meat dishes, there are also such vegetarian creations as morels rolled in cabbage and served in green-pepper and saffron sauce. Round off your meal with a baked Alaska and an imported aperitif, and you'll have a very memorable and relatively economical French dinner.

## PATAN & VICINITY

In addition to the restaurants listed here, there are several other dining options worth noting in and near Patan. The main dining room of the Hotel Himalaya has one of the Kathmandu Valley's finest views of the mountains and serves respectable Indian food. Inside the Patan Museum, you'll find a garden cafe that is operated by the nearby Summit Hotel. Also, at the Summit Hotel, there is a very enjoyable barbecue held each Friday evening starting at 7:30pm. The price is Rs500 ($7.60). Just across the bridge from Patan, in Kathmandu, you'll find the Baber Mahal Revisited shopping and dining arcade, where there are five restaurants. In addition to Chez Caroline Café and Pâtisserie (listed below), you'll find Simply Shutters Bistrot, serving continental fare; Baithak, serving upscale Indian and Nepali meals; Rodeo, an Indian Tex-Mex chain (no kidding!); and K2, serving cocktails and barbecue.

See the map, "Patan Accommodations & Dining," for the location of these establishments.

### EXPENSIVE

✪ **Chez Caroline Café Restaurant and Pâtisserie.** Baber Mahal Revisited. ☎ **263070.** Reservations recommended for Saturday dinner. Rs185–Rs500 ($2.80–$7.60). AE, MC, V. Daily 8:30am–10pm. FRENCH.

With the emphasis on classic French cafe sandwiches, Chez Caroline, a rustic-yet-sophisticated open-air French cafe, works best as a lunch place. However, the daily specials, such as tiger prawns and sole in a white wine sauce, certainly make excellent dinners as well. Sandwiches come with little dollops of interesting salads and are best accompanied by a delicious fresh ginger-lemon soda. Save room for dessert and accept indecision as a necessity of dining here. Lime-basil sorbet, caramel mousse in creme anglaise, and homemade ice cream with caramel sauce are just some of the delicious possibilities. The only problem with Chez Caroline is that there are too many good choices, and you'll likely want to keep coming back so that you can work your way through the menu. You'll find Chez Caroline in the upscale Baber Mahal Revisited shopping and dining arcade near the bridge that connects Kathmandu to Patan.

### INEXPENSIVE

**Café Pagode.** Patan Durbar Square (in front of Bhimsen Temple). ☎ **536629.** Complete meals Rs75–Rs200 ($1.15–$3.05). Daily 9am–9pm. INTERNATIONAL.

If you are spending the day exploring Patan and want to have a view of Durbar Square while you dine, this simple place is a good choice. There is a rooftop dining terrace and a courtyard dining area, as well as a few tables inside. Try the complete Nepali meal (dal bhat), which comes with curried chicken (if you order the nonvegetarian version), two types of curried vegetables, rice, dal, and sweetened yogurt for dessert.

## BHAKTAPUR

There just aren't many places to eat in Bhaktapur, but luckily the available options have great locations.

**Café Nyatapola.** Taumadhi Tole. ☎ **610346.** Light meals Rs85–Rs215 ($1.30–$3.25). No credit cards. Daily 6am–7pm. INTERNATIONAL.

Though the food is unremarkable (the standard international/Chinese/Indian/Nepali menu found in almost all budget restaurants), the setting is superb. Housed inside an old pagoda, Café Nyatapola overlooks the Nyatapola Temple, which is one of the most beautiful temples in Nepal. The cafe building itself has carvings from the *Ramayana* and *Mahabharata* around the outside, and its roof struts are carved with erotic images. Take a seat on the third-floor balcony, and you can observe the activity below while you enjoy your lunch. Watch your head in here; the doorways are low.

---

### Dining with a View

Several of the major hotels in Kathmandu have fine views from one or more of their restaurants, and even many budget hotels have rooftop gardens where you can order a meal through room service. My favorite view is that offered from the Hotel Himalaya's **Chalet,** an Indian restaurant open for lunch and dinner. At the Everest Hotel, there are a couple of rooftop restaurants with excellent views, though at press time, these restaurants were undergoing renovations. The **Explorers Restaurant** at the Hotel Vajra serves lunch and snacks up in the hotel-roof garden, where there is an excellent view of Swayambunath stupa. Over at Boudhanath stupa, there is the **Stupa View Restaurant,** which specializes in European vegetarian meals. In Patan, the **Café Pagode** provides equally memorable views. In Bhaktapur, you can enjoy the views from either **Café de Peacock** or **Nyatapola Café.**

**Cafe de Peacock and Soma Bar.** Dattatreya Square. ☎ **610684.** Main dishes Rs130–Rs220 ($1.95–$3.35). MC. Daily 9am–9pm. INTERNATIONAL.

Bhaktapur seems to have cornered the market on great places to sit above the crowds and soak in the beauties and activities of a medieval Nepali square. If you didn't have lunch at the Café Nyatapola, then by all means dine here. The restaurant has a long balcony set with tables, and inside there is a narrow room with a high ceiling. Both walls and floors are made of brick. The standard please-everyone all-encompassing menu may not be memorable, but the view and general atmosphere certainly are.

# 5

# What to See & Do in the Kathmandu Valley

**D**espite its problems with air pollution and traffic congestion, the Kathmandu Valley is a living museum in which lifestyles long since vanished from the Western world continue. In the older neighborhoods of **Kathmandu, Patan,** and **Bhaktapur**—the valley's three major cities—people still live much as they have for centuries. In these cities of temples and shrines and living gods, worship of Hindu and Buddhist gods and goddesses is an integral and public part of daily life. People still start their days with a trip to the neighborhood temple or shrine, and farmers still carry in produce from their farms on the edge of the city, selling it out of baskets on temple steps and crowded market streets.

Because the Kathmandu Valley is a place where the past comes alive, the valley's greatest attractions are its temples and palaces, markets and fields, narrow lanes and alleys. One of the greatest thrills of a visit to Nepal is to simply wander the back streets of Kathmandu, Patan, and Bhaktapur. Getting lost in any one of these cities can lead to some of the most memorable sights and experiences. So keep your eyes open as you walk the streets—you'll probably find that the simple daily life of Kathmandu's people is as fascinating as any temple, palace, or museum.

Kathmandu, Patan (also known as Lalitpur), and Bhaktapur (also known as Bhadgaon) were all once independent kingdoms. An intense rivalry existed between these cities, and each kingdom's royal family built its own palace on its own temple-filled Durbar Square. (*Durbar* is the Nepali term for "king.") Consequently, today there are three equally beautiful Durbar Squares in the Kathmandu Valley, and each has its own distinct character. Kathmandu's Durbar Square has towering temples but seems to lack cohesion because of the whitewashed European facade of the Gaddi Baithak (built during the Rana period, which began in the mid–19th century). Patan's Durbar Square is compact and very well preserved, with the long facade of the former royal palace (now partly a museum) facing numerous temples that are built in a variety of styles. Bhaktapur's Durbar Square is spacious and open, and still shows signs of the damage done by the massive earthquake that leveled much of the Kathmandu Valley in 1934.

Of the three cities, Kathmandu, the capital of Nepal, has seen the most change in recent years. Old buildings have disappeared at an alarming rate, and the streets are often so congested with cars and people (there are no sidewalks in the older parts of the city) that just walking around is almost impossible. However, the crowds give Kath-

# The Kathmandu Valley

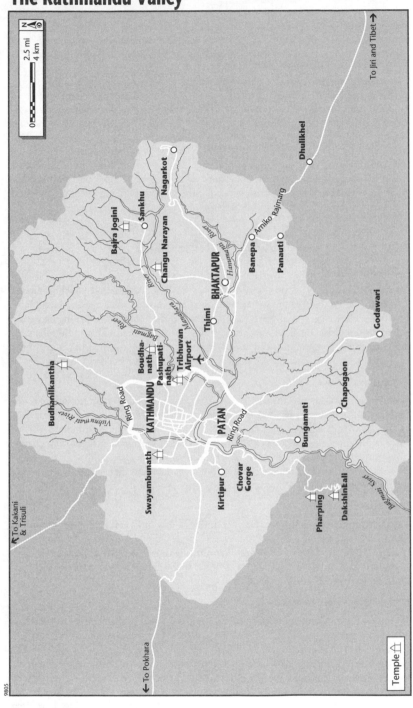

mandu much of its vibrancy, and this city's Durbar Square is always bustling with activity. Patan is best known for its many beautiful temples and its metalworkers. However, it is Bhaktapur that everyone agrees is the most beautiful, medieval, and well preserved of the three cities.

Because the most rewarding part of a visit to the Kathmandu Valley is the opportunity to explore its ancient cities on foot, I have organized this chapter with an emphasis on walking tours. In the sections devoted to each of the valley's three major cities, you will find a walking tour of that city's Durbar Square area and a second walking tour of neighborhoods beyond each Durbar Square. In planning your day's itinerary, keep in mind that the early-morning hours, from dawn until 8 or 9am, are the best times to explore the streets of Kathmandu, Patan, and Bhaktapur. In the hours before the shops open, the streets come alive with produce vendors, and people make their daily visits to the many temples and shrines. Mornings and evenings are good times to visit Swayambunath and Boudhanath.

## SUGGESTED ITINERARIES

### If You Have 1 Day

Start your day as early as you can and head to Swayambunath, where you'll find locals crowding the grounds of the shrine making their morning offerings and circumambulations. Head next to Durbar Square, and spend the rest of the morning exploring the many temples and palaces. In the afternoon, visit Pashupatinath and Boudhanath. The easiest way to see all these sights in 1 day is by booking two half-day tours of the city. Alternatively, you could hire a car, driver, and guide for the day.

### If You Have 2 Days

Spend your first day as outlined above. Start your second day by exploring Kathmandu's old market streets. These markets are liveliest from dawn until about 9 or 10am. After this, head to Bhaktapur, the best preserved of the Kathmandu Valley's three cities. If the skies are clear, continue from Bhaktapur up to Nagarkot for a stunning sunset panorama of the Himalayas. Alternatively, you could skip the early-morning market walk, catch the sunrise from Nagarkot, and then spend the rest of the day in Bhaktapur.

### If You Have 3 Days

See above outline for your first 2 days. On day 3, you might take a 1-hour mountain flight for a close-up view of the Himalayas (that is, if you don't plan to fly into one of the remote airstrips as part of a trek). Later in the day, go to Patan and see this city's Durbar Square and its other beautiful temples. If you are interested in buying a carpet, also visit Patan's Tibetan Refugee Camp.

### If You Have 5 Days or More

If you will be in Kathmandu for more than 3 days, you'll probably want to spend an entire day shopping. This will also allow you to revisit your favorite sights and just wander the streets. A visit to Budhanilkantha to see the Sleeping Vishnu statue is well worthwhile. For those with a taste for the macabre, a trip to Dakshinkali to witness the animal sacrifices is certainly a different sort of holiday experience. The town of Panauti, with its recently restored temple complex, is also worth a visit and makes an interesting combination with a half-day hike to the Namobuddha shrine. I strongly recommend spending one of your last 2 days on a long day hike somewhere in the

Kathmandu Valley. The hikes down from Nagarkot are particularly interesting because they can lead through villages and to different temples.

# 1 Kathmandu

## WALKING TOUR 1
## Kathmandu's Durbar Square Area

**Start:** On New Road at the Visitor Information Center.
**Finish:** At the big bell.
**Time:** Four hours (with museum visit).
**Best Times:** Starting early in the morning or finishing in late afternoon.
**Worst Times:** Tuesday, when Hanuman Dhoka Palace is closed.

*Durbar* is the Nepali term for "king," and it was from the Royal Palace on this square that the kings of Nepal once ruled. Although the current Royal Palace lies elsewhere in the city, the Durbar Square area is still the heart and soul of Kathmandu. Encompassing several squares, Hanuman Dhola Palace, and more than 50 temples and shrines, this area contains one of the most concentrated groupings of historic structures in the valley. Because there is so much to see in this area, it is best to be systematic in your peregrinations. The following are the highlights of the Durbar Square area, but there are dozens of other lesser temples and shrines that you might also find interesting.

From the Visitor Information Center, walk away from the newer cement city and toward the older brick buildings. In a few steps, you will come to:

1. **Basantapur Square.** This wide-open square is across the street from both **Hanuman Dhoka Palace** (the old royal palace) and the **Gaddi Baithak** (a palace built in the European style in the early 20th century). These two palaces abut each other in a striking contrast between Nepali brick architecture and the white-washed neoclassical architecture that was imported from Europe by Rana rulers during the late 19th and early 20th centuries. If it's early in the morning, Basantapur Square may still be empty, but by midmorning, the square will be filled with dozens of vendors selling all manner of Kathmandu curios. If you buy something, remember to bargain hard; these vendors start out asking more for their wares than just about any other vendors in Kathmandu. Leading south from this square is the famous:

2. **Freak Street,** Kathmandu's counterculture hangout back in the 1960s and 1970s. Today, the street still has many small shops and cheap restaurants and lodges. From Freak Street, walk to the far side of Basantapur Square, where you will find the:

3. **Kumari Bahal.** As you enter Durbar Square from New Road, you will see on your left two colorfully painted stone lions guarding the doorway of a three-story brick house that is home to the royal *kumari,* Kathmandu's living goddess (see box on page 116). Built in 1757, this house is a showcase of the wood-carvers' art, for which the Kathmandu Valley has long been renowned. Intricately carved wooden lattice windows cover the building's facade, and on the second floor there are two **peacock windows** that are superior in both workmanship and beauty to the famous Bhaktapur peacock window. On the third floor there are three shallow **latticed balconies,** designed to allow the kumari to watch the

activity in the square without being seen herself. The building's most beautiful window, however, is the central third-floor window, which is gilded and includes two repoussé statues of **Tantric deities.** Also note the *toranas* over every window. These semicircular carved wooden panels each depict different Hindu deities and symbols.

As you step through the low, open door that leads to the building's central courtyard, be sure to notice the **human skulls** carved into the wooden door frame and lintel (also be sure to watch your head). Inside the courtyard there are intricately carved windows even more beautiful than those on the exterior facade. Even the low stone wall that surrounds the sunken courtyard is carved with interesting images. In the middle of the courtyard are a tiny stupa similar to Swayambunath and two *mandalas* symbolizing the universe.

As you leave the house, glance through the yellow gate on the right side of the house. Here you can see parts of the huge chariot that is used to haul the kumari around the city on the few festivals when she is allowed out of the Kumari Bahal. As you leave the Kumari Bahal, you will likely be drawn to the:

4. **Maju Deval (Shiva Mandir),** a towering pagoda that looms above the center of the square. Perched atop a 10-tiered pyramid, the three-roofed pagoda-style Maju Deval, or Shiva Temple, is by far the most impressive temple on the square and is a favorite of people (both tourists and Nepalis) who want to just sit and soak up the passing scene on Durbar Square. Inside this temple is a Shiva lingam, the phallic symbol commonly used to represent Shiva. If your eyesight is good, or if you can strain your neck without falling off the uppermost tier of this temple's base, you will see some of Kathmandu's famous **erotic carvings** on the roof struts. The carvings on the nearby Jagannath temple are, however, much easier to see. At the base of this temple stands a whitewashed shikhara-style temple. This style of stone temple is more common in India than in Nepal.

Directly across the square from the Maju Deval and looking entirely out of place in the otherwise-medieval tableau of Durbar Square, you'll find the whitewashed stucco facade of the:

5. **Gaddi Baithak,** which reflects neoclassical European influences. This palace annex was built in 1908 by one of the ruling Rana prime ministers, whose family had seized power from the royal family in the mid–19th century. The Ranas were well-known for their infatuation with European culture, and they emptied the kingdom's coffers to construct European-style palaces. The building is still used for state functions, and during religious celebrations, the king sometimes observes festivities from a throne that is kept here.

To your left as you face the steps of the Maju Deval is the:

6. **Narayan Mandir,** a three-story pagoda temple atop a six-tiered platform. If you walk around to the far side of the temple, you will see a large and beautiful **stone statue of Garuda,** the half-man, half-bird vehicle upon which the Hindu god Vishnu travels. The presence of Garuda kneeling before this temple indicates that the temple is dedicated to, and contains a statue of, Vishnu. In this case, Vishnu is in his aspect of Narayan, which is the most commonly encountered aspect of Vishnu in Nepal. Unfortunately, the temple is not open to the public, and you will not be able to see the statue inside.

Just behind the stone Garuda statue, Durbar Square abuts a smaller square known as Maru Tole, where vendors sell produce and vibrant marigold garlands to be used as offerings at the nearby Ganesh shrine. Hulking over Maru Tole is the:

# Kathmandu's Durbar Square Area

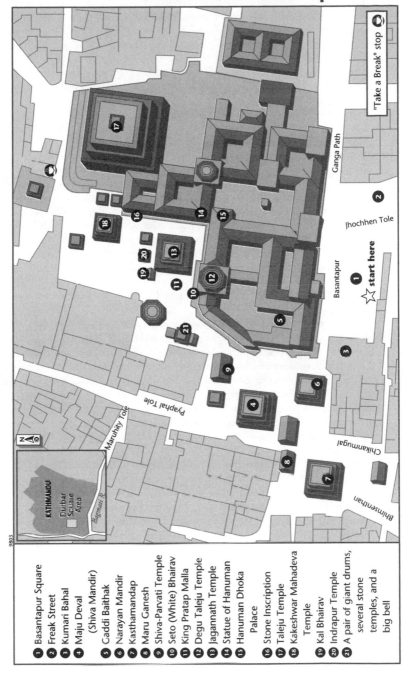

1 Basantapur Square
2 Freak Street
3 Kumari Bahal
4 Maju Deval (Shiva Mandir)
5 Caddi Baithak
6 Narayan Mandir
7 Kasthamandap
8 Maru Ganesh
9 Shiva-Parvati Temple
10 Seto (White) Bhairav
11 King Pratap Malla
12 Degu Taleju Temple
13 Jagannath Temple
14 Statue of Hanuman
15 Hanuman Dhoka Palace
16 Stone Inscription
17 Taleju Temple
18 Kakeshwar Mahadeva Temple
19 Kal Bhairav
20 Indrapur Temple
21 A pair of giant drums, several stone temples, and a big bell

"Take a Break" stop

Ganga Path

Jhochhen Tole

Basantapur

☆ start here

Chikanmugal

Bhimsenthan

Pyaphal Tole

Maruhity Tole

Bagmati R.

KATHMANDU

Durbar Square Area

9803

**7. Kasthamandap,** one of the most unusual buildings in Kathmandu. The Kastha-mandap, meaning "Wooden Pavilion," is an imposing three-story pagoda-style building that legends say was built from a single tree in the 12th century. On each of the four corners of its first floor there is a viewing platform surrounded by low carved wooden railings. In the dark recesses there is a tiny statue of Guru Goraknath, a revered Hindu saint. Today it is a temple of sorts and is frequently used as a gathering spot.

While you're exploring the Kasthamandap, it is impossible to miss the bustle of activity surrounding a closet-sized shrine across the alley that runs behind the old pavilion. This is the:

**8. Maru Ganesh,** also known as the Kathmandu Ganesh or the Ashok Binayak. The gilded roof of this small shrine was erected by King Surendra Bir Bikram Shah Dev in 1874, and to this day all kings come to worship here as part of their coronation ceremony. Ganesh, the most popular of the Hindu gods, is the god of good luck and a bringer of good fortune to new homes and to people going on journeys. Ganesh is also seen as a remover of obstacles and as such is often worshiped (just for good measure) as a preliminary to the worship of other gods and goddesses. People constantly drop by this shrine to leave offerings of food and flowers. Mornings are especially busy. On holidays there are usually two lines of worshipers—one for men and one for women—waiting to get into the tiny room that holds the small statue of Ganesh. The clanging of the temple bell is nearly constant at these times.

With so many pagodas on the Durbar Square, it would be easy to overlook the:

**9. Shiva-Parvati Temple,** an 18th-century house-style temple that stands on the far side of the Maju Deval from the Maru Ganesh. However, two painted statues, the Hindu god Shiva and his consort Parvati, gaze down from a second-floor window. The garish paint jobs allow them to fit right into the colorful scene of the square. The lions guarding the entrance to this temple indicate that the temple houses a goddess, in this case a black stone image of Asta Yogini. The base of the temple and the wide patio in front are popular spots with vendors who set up portable kitchens and cook snacks and tea (I advise staying away from such street foods).

Behind the Shiva-Parvati Temple, Durbar Square is lined with shops selling thangkas and other tourist items. Surprisingly, these shops are in the outside wall of the Hanuman Dhoka Palace. As you round the corner just past these shops, you enter Hanuman Dhoka Square and come to a large lattice screen. If you peer through this screen, you'll see a giant mask of terrifying visage. This is:

**10. Seto (White) Bhairav,** one of the many aspects of Shiva. The gruesome gilded mask with its huge fangs was erected in the late 18th century to protect the royal palace from evil spirits. Today, the mask is associated with an entirely different sort of spirit—home-brewed rice beer (known locally as *chang*). Each year in September, during the festival of Indrajatra, the lattice screen is opened to reveal Seto Bhairav. From a long straw sticking out of the mask's mouth, beer that has been blessed by this god flows into the mouths of eagerly waiting men. To drink this sanctified beer is considered a great blessing.

Above and to the right of the mask is a beautiful three-sided balcony. The wood carving is intricately detailed, and the overall effect is very delicate. Decorating this balcony are gilt repoussé *toranas* (semicircular decorated panels) and *nagas* (protective snakelike animals). Two of the adjacent windows are made of carved ivory and not wood.

Sitting atop a stone pillar and facing Hanuman Dhoka Palace and the mask of Seto Bhairav is a statue of:

11. **King Pratap Malla.** The king, who sits cross-legged atop his pillar, was responsible for the construction of many of Durbar Square's temples and monuments, including the statue of Hanuman and the adjacent stone inscription.

Across from the statue, above the Seto Bhairav mask, rises the:

12. **Degu Taleju Temple.** Because this temple is built atop the roof of the Hanuman Dhoka Palace, it is the tallest temple on Hanuman Dhoka Square.

A few steps away from this statue stands:

13. **Jagannath Temple.** Built in the 17th century, this pagoda is primarily known for its colorfully painted **erotic carvings** on the wooden struts that support the lowest roof—the best in Kathmandu's Durbar Square area. Some say that the erotic carvings were meant to instruct young people. Others contend that the carvings are there to test the powers of concentration of the devout—only inches away from the erotic scenes are beautiful carvings of Hindu deities. The most popular explanation is that the erotic carvings are there to protect the temple from the goddess of lightning, who is quite prudish and shies away from such graphic depictions of sexual union. No temple so decorated has ever been struck by lightning.

Adjacent to the Jagannath Temple, in the far corner of the square, you are likely to spot a bustle of activity surrounding a strange-looking statue atop a short pillar. The focus of all the activity is a larger-than-life:

14. **Statue of Hanuman,** the much-beloved monkey king from the Hindu epic *Ramayana,* which tells the story of Prince Rama and his wife, Sita, who was kidnapped by the evil Ravana. Hanuman, a white monkey, becomes Rama's most loyal ally and helps to rescue Sita. Hanuman has come to symbolize unquestioned loyalty, and that is why his statue guards the gate of the old royal palace. Erected in 1672, the statue stands atop a low pillar and is protected from the sun by an ornate umbrella. Over the years, devout worshipers have covered the figure with a thick layer of orange paste that completely obscures the features of the statue. For the uninformed it is quite curious to see people lining up to leave offerings at the foot of a colorfully cloaked orange blob. It is this statue that gives its name to both the square and the adjacent palace. *Hanuman Dhoka* means "Hanuman Gate" and is a reference to the statue and the adjacent entrance to the old royal palace.

To the right of the Hanuman statue is the entrance to:

15. **Hanuman Dhoka Palace,** the former royal palace, the oldest sections of which were built in the 17th century. However, from that time until early in this century, there were frequent additions. The king no longer lives here (his new palace is at the top of Durbar Marg, Kathmandu's most upscale shopping street), but coronations are still held here. The lavishly decorated Golden Door, beside the statue of Hanuman, is the main entrance to the palace and is flanked by colorfully painted stone lions. Atop one lion sits Shiva and atop the other sits his *shakti* (consort), Parvati. On either side of the door are painted numerous Hindu and Buddhist symbols. Above the door are several statues and bas-reliefs of different gods. Just inside on the left is a stone statue of Narsimha, a half-man, half-lion god, who is shown devouring the evil demon Haranyakashipu.

Today, this sprawling complex contains museums devoted to three Nepali kings and is open to the public every day except Tuesday. Admission is Rs250 ($3.80). For details on the palace's museums, see "Museums & Other Attractions," later in this chapter.

Through the Golden Door is **Nasal Chowk,** the first of 10 courtyards within the palace. This is the largest and most important of the palace's courtyards, for it is here that Nepal's kings are crowned. Rising above the northeast corner of Nasal Chowk is the five-story Pancha Mukhi Hanuman, which has circular roofs and very ornate roof struts. To the left of this tower, mounted atop a pole, is a golden fish, a symbol of the Hindu god Vishnu.

Rising from the four corners of the ornate Lohan Chowk, a smaller courtyard adjacent to the Nasal Chowk, stand four towers that were built in the 18th century by King Prithvi Narayan Shah, who unified Nepal. The towers represent the four cities of the Kathmandu Valley—Kathmandu, Patan, Bhaktapur, and Kirtipur. The **Kathmandu tower,** more properly known as the Basantapur Tower, is the only palace tower that is open to the public.

The stately Kathmandu tower is four stories tall, but because it is built atop the roof of the four-story palace, the top floor is actually eight floors above the ground. Latticed windows look down from every floor and admit only filtered light into the brick-walled interior. Steep stairways lead to the top of the tower, providing an excellent vantage point from which to observe the activity in Basantapur and Durbar Squares. The whole of the Kathmandu Valley spreads out below you with green hills and snowy peaks off in the distance (if you can see through the smog).

Along the wall to the left of the Hanuman statue is a carved:

**16. Stone Inscription.** It is written in 15 different languages and several different alphabets. From the English version of the inscription, you will learn that the stone was erected on January 14, 1664, by King Pratap Malla, who prided himself on his mastery of languages.

Located behind the walls of the northern end of Hanuman Dhoka Palace is the:

**17. Taleju Temple,** which is open only to Hindus, who may visit only once a year (during the Dasain festival). It is by far the largest temple in the Durbar Square area, and it dominates the horizon as you enter from the north. Its three gilded roofs and ornate spire glimmer in the sun, and bells that hang from each of the three roofs can often be heard when the wind blows.

The innermost room of the temple holds a statue of Taleju Bhawani, which was brought from India and is off-limits to everyone but the royal family. The temple is dedicated to Taleju Bhawani, also known as Durga, who is an aspect of Shiva's consort Parvati. Taleju was the tutelary goddess of the Malla kings who ruled Kathmandu from the 14th to the 18th centuries. The current building dates to the mid–16th century, though the temple was founded in the 14th century. Legends say that human sacrifices were once performed here.

☕ **TAKE A BREAK**    Aside from the cheap restaurants on Freak Street, there are few places to eat in the Durbar Square area. However, just off the north end of the square, across the street from the Taleju Temple, you'll find **Festive Fare,** which has a good view from its upper-floor dining rooms. See "Where to Dine" in chapter 4 for details.

After your break, cross back over to the:

**18. Kakeshwar Mahadeva Temple,** an unusual little temple that stands opposite the gate leading into the Taleju temple complex. Erected in 1681, the Kakeshwar Mahadeva Temple incorporates both Nepali and Indian temple architecture. The bottom half of the structure is in the style of a Nepali pagoda, but the top half is a whitewashed stucco shikhara-style building.

A few steps away, in the direction of the Seto Bhairav mask, is a high-relief image of:

**19. Kal Bhairav,** the Lord of Destruction. This fearsome 10-foot-tall stone figure is another of the many aspects of Shiva. Atop his wide-eyed face is a crown decorated with human skulls, and on his back is a human skin. The prostrate figure upon which Kal Bhairav is standing represents human ignorance. It is also said that the prone figure is Kal Bhairav's father-in-law, who insulted Shiva and caused his own daughter, Kal Bhairav's wife, to commit suicide. Kal Bhairav has six arms, and in one of his hands he holds a skull cup that worshipers often toss coins into—and there are always a few boys around to quickly snatch them up.

Erected in the 17th or 18th century, the statue was supposedly used as a lie detector. People suspected of committing a crime would be brought before the statue, made to touch its feet, and then forced to say whether or not they committed the crime. It was believed that if they lied, they would immediately bleed to death. The mere threat of being brought before Kal Bhairav was often enough to elicit a confession.

Directly to the left of the Kal Bhairav statue is the:

**20. Indrapur Temple,** a small temple that would hardly be noteworthy among the other larger and more-impressive temples of the Durbar Square area. However, the offerings brought to this temple will attract your attention. In fact, you'll likely smell the offerings before you see them. The god in this temple requires offerings of billy goats, but unlike at other temples, the goats are not sacrificed. Consequently, the malodorous billies, which are tethered to the posts of the temple's veranda, spend their days bleating and waggling their tongues at passersby, many of whom leave food offerings for the hungry goats. After meeting with these holy offerings, you may never eat goat cheese again.

Across the street from the Kal Bhairav statue are several small temples and shrines, including:

**21. A pair of giant drums, several stone temples, and a big bell.** At the end closest to the police station gates are two giant drums that are played only once a year, during the Dasain festival after a goat and a water buffalo are sacrificed. To the left of the big drums is an unusual octagonal stone temple dedicated to Krishna, who, though quite familiar in the Western world, is rarely worshiped in Nepal. Continuing in the same direction, you come to a temple dedicated to Saraswati, the goddess of learning, and one dedicated to Vishnu. Next stands a large bell that was erected in the 18th century.

Having now seen the major temples, palaces, and shrines of the Durbar Square area, you might want to do a bit of wandering on your own. In Kathmandu, you never know what strange and unexpected sight you might come upon around the next corner or down the next alley.

# WALKING TOUR 2
## The Markets & Temples of Old Kathmandu

**Start:** Hanuman Dhoka Square.
**Finish:** Thamel.
**Time:** Four hours.
**Best Times:** Early in the morning, when the streets are still quiet.

**Worst Times:** Saturday, when the market is particularly crowded.

## The Royal Kumari: Kathmandu's Living Goddess

While the vast majority of Nepals gods and goddesses are carved in stone or cast in metal, there is at least one of flesh and blood. Kathmandu's royal kumari, a young girl who shows her face on only a handful of religious festivals each year, is considered a living goddess. No other figure in Nepal captures the mystery of this isolated Himalayan kingdom better than this dark-eyed little girl.

There are various legends surrounding the installation of the first kumari in Durbar Square's Kumari Bahal, a houselike temple built in 1757. One legend claims that she was installed after King Jaya Prakash Malla exiled a young girl who was said to be possessed by the spirit of the goddess Kumari. This so outraged the king's wife that he brought the young girl back and locked her up in a temple. Another legend holds that the king had sex with a prepubescent girl who later died. To atone for his sins, he enthroned a young girl as a living goddess and worshiped her chastely. Once a year he would take her from her temple and parade her around the city. Yet another legend states that the king, who frequently played dice with the human incarnation of the goddess Taleju (herself an incarnation of Shiva's consort Parvati), angered the goddess by lusting after her. In response to his inappropriate advances, she promised to return only as a chaste virgin.

While some people believe, based on this latter legend, that the kumari is an incarnation of the goddess Taleju, others hold that she is an incarnation of Durga (yet another incarnation of Parvati). Still others claim she is one of the *Asta Matrika,* the eight mother goddesses. Regardless of which goddess she represents, she is highly revered, and several times a year she is paraded through the streets of Kathmandu in a massive wooden chariot. During the festival of Indra Jatra, held in late August or early September, the kumari blesses the king of Nepal by placing the tika mark on his forehead, and for this reason she is known as the royal kumari.

While a walking tour of the Durbar Square area provides an overview of Kathmandu's most important historic buildings, the streets and alleys to the north of Durbar Square provide a glimpse of life in the city today. Here, amid a mix of crumbling old brick buildings and modern, characterless cement structures, you will find the city's busiest markets. Most of these market areas have been providing goods and produce for hundreds of years. Though the best way to experience old Kathmandu is simply to wander off down a few alleys until you are completely lost, this walking tour will guide you past the highlights, many of which are hidden behind walls and tucked down alleys that are easy to overlook, especially when you are staggering under the all-out sensory bombardment of a walk through the streets of Kathmandu. Although there are no street names, per se, in Kathmandu, squares, plazas, and neighborhoods lend their names to general areas. These names are now posted on green street signs at appropriate corners throughout old Kathmandu, and by orienting yourself to these signs and the map in this section, you should be able to keep track of where you are.

Be aware that, as in crowded markets the world over, pickpockets work these streets. If you are carrying any sort of bag, whether it is a purse or daypack, try not to keep anything of value in it, and always keep it in front of you in order to keep an eye on it.

Begin your walk on the north side of Hanuman Dhoka Square (see Walking Tour 1). A wide road lined with modern buildings angles out of the square to the northeast leading to Kathmandu's main market area, which is divided into three

The kumari is not born into goddesshood, nor is it a lifetime position. And despite the fact that the kumari is a Hindu goddess, she is chosen from among the Buddhist Newari goldsmithing caste. The process by which a new kumari is chosen is a grueling and frightening one. First, a number of 4- to 5-year-old girls are chosen as candidates. A candidate must bear 32 specific traits, some of which are freedom from any deformities, black eyes, long slender arms, graceful hands and feet, straight black hair that curls to the right at the bottom, and a beautiful voice. Also, she must never have shed blood prior to her being chosen as a candidate.

The candidates are then subjected to a terrifying test intended to determine which is the real kumari. The girls are locked in a dark room, where men in horrifying masks try to scare them. Freshly severed water buffalo heads are displayed and frightening noises are made. The girl who shows no fear is chosen, since a goddess would have no fear. After the test, an astrologer is called in to determine whether the kumari's horoscope is compatible with the king's. If so, she is enthroned during the Dasain festival.

However, the reign of the kumari is never more than a handful of years. She is considered a living goddess only as long as she never sheds blood, a sign of mortality. Many kumaris have been replaced when they lost a tooth, but often they retain their position until they reach puberty and begin menstruating. After giving up their goddesshood, kumaris are supported with an allowance until they marry, at which time a dowry is provided.

There are actually several kumaris in the Kathmandu Valley, but this one, because she is worshiped by the king, is the most important one. If you are lucky, you may catch a glimpse of her in one of the upstairs windows of the Kumari Bahal, her home on Durbar Square. Be aware that it is forbidden to photograph her.

---

small squares. Head up this street to Indrachowk, the first square, where you will find, on your left just before you enter the square:

1. **A small Ganesh shrine.** This brass shrine is set in the middle of the road, and from the way the brass has been polished and smoothed over the years, it is evident that this shrine is much revered. As you study the shrine, you're likely to see people bend over to touch the shrine and then touch their fingers to their foreheads in order to garner Ganesh's blessings.

Immediately adjacent to this shrine is the:

2. **Akash (Sky) Bhairav Temple,** one of the most colorful and eclectic temples in the city. This house-style temple has a first-floor facade of large green, burgundy, and white tiles set in a checkerboard pattern, while on the balconied second floor stand four rearing bronze griffins that ward off evil spirits. Akash Bhairav, a small silver mask similar to the mask of Seto Bhairav in Hanuman Dhoka Square, gets its name from the way its eyes gaze heavenward. Only Hindus are allowed to enter this temple.

The square that this temple faces is called:

3. **Indrachowk,** which marks the start of the old market quarter of the city. This particular area of the market is devoted to **cloth and carpet merchants,** many of whom display their wares on the terraces of an old pagoda on the north side of the square. The naturally colored shawls, called *pashmina,* are made from the

belly wool of a goat. This wool is similar to cashmere, and the shawls are surprisingly warm. Unfortunately, most of the shawls for sale here are the more-colorful and less-expensive synthetic ones. Don't get ripped off. While here, ask one of the rug merchants to show you a *rari*. These traditional Nepali felt rugs have been overshadowed by the Tibetan rugs that are so readily available, but they have a distinctly different, more rustic appeal.

Across the square from the Akash Bhairav Temple is:

4. **The Bead Bazaar,** where you'll find strands and strands of shiny imported beads hanging in tiny stalls. The vendors, most of whom are Kashmiris, will gladly put together a necklace to your specifications. Strings of beads passed through an ornately worked small gold tube are one of the traditional ornaments worn by married Nepali women.

Continuing into the market on the same road that you took out of Hanuman Dhoka Square, you pass small, old shops selling a variety of goods. Several of these shops are piled high with brass household goods and statuettes of various gods. You soon come to Kel Tole (the next square), which is the site of the:

5. **Seto Machendranath Temple.** This temple is dedicated to a rain god who is particularly popular in the Kathmandu Valley. The temple is through a doorway on the north (left) side of the street just before the square. Outside the entrance are two brass lions and, atop a short pillar, a small statue of Buddha. Inside, there are several statues and chaityas surrounding the main temple. Among the statues of Buddhas and Taras, there is a classical Greek statue of a woman balancing a lamp on her head. This statue was added during the Rana period, when all things European were in vogue among the gentry. The temple itself is incredibly ornate with roofs of gilded copper and a gilded and embossed facade. Once a year, during the **Seto Machendranath Jatra festival,** the temple's statue of Machendra is taken out of its enclosure, bathed, and paraded around the city in a huge chariot. Machendra, who is an aspect of the bodhisattva Avalokiteshwara (also known as Chenrezig in Tibet), is worshiped by Hindus and Buddhists alike.

At the back of this temple's courtyard, which is usually packed with produce vendors and pigeons in the early morning, look for a low doorway. Through this opening lies:

6. **Jana Bahal Temple.** This unremarkable temple sits atop terraces that are usually covered with produce vendors, and surrounding the base of the temple, vendors sell unglazed earthenware. On the lanes around the temple, you will find shops specializing in quilts and cotton-stuffed mattresses. The men in long plaid skirts (called *longis*) leaning against strange-looking single-stringed "musical instruments" are Muslim mattress-stuffing fluffers known as *dhuniya,* and their instrument is called a *dhanu* and *tir* (bow and arrow). They place the bow in a pile of matted cotton and strike it with the arrow, and the action of the string returns the matted cotton to its original fluffy loft.

Head back through the doorway to the Seto Machendranath Temple and from there back out into Kel Tole.

Between Kel Tole and the next square is:

7. **The first house in Kathmandu to have glass windows.** This house is on the left and is recognizable from the bas-relief frieze of soldiers marching across the facade between the first and second floors.

Continuing up the street you'll soon come to:

8. **Asan Tole,** which is the largest of the market squares in this old quarter of Kathmandu and is the heart of the market district. The square is almost always packed with shoppers searching for deals on fruits and vegetables that are displayed in

# In case you want to be welcomed there.

**We're here to see that you're always welcomed at establishments everywhere. That's why millions of people carry the American Express® Card – for peace of mind, confidence, and security, around the world or just around the corner.**

do more

**Cards**

# In case you're running low.

We're here to help with more than 190,000 Express Cash locations around the world. In order to enroll, just call American Express at 1 800 CASH-NOW before you start your vacation.

do more

**Express Cash**

# And in case you'd rather be safe than sorry.

We're here with American Express® Travelers Cheques. They're the safe way to carry money on your vacation, because if they're ever lost or stolen you can get a refund, practically anywhere or anytime. To find the nearest place to buy Travelers Cheques, call 1 800 495-1153. Another way we help you do more.

do more

**Travelers Cheques**

# The Markets & Temples of Old Kathmandu

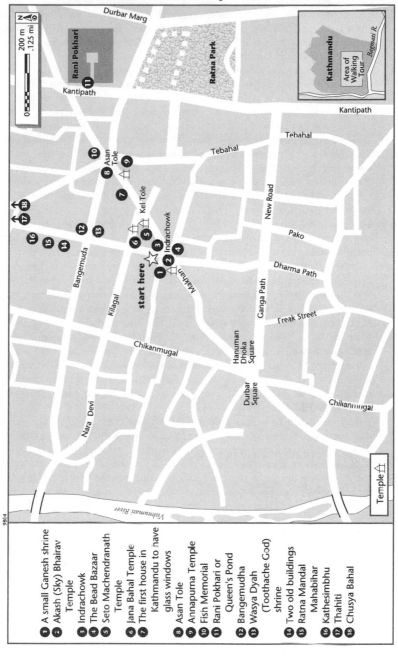

Temple ⛩

1. A small Ganesh shrine
2. Akash (Sky) Bhairav Temple
3. Indrachowk
4. The Bead Bazaar
5. Seto Machendranath Temple
6. Jana Bahal Temple
7. The first house in Kathmandu to have glass windows
8. Asan Tole
9. Annapurna Temple
10. Fish Memorial
11. Rani Pokhari or Queen's Pond
12. Bangemudha
13. Wasya Dyah (Toothache God) shrine
14. Two old buildings
15. Ratna Mandal Mahabihar
16. Kathesimbhu
17. Thahiti
18. Chusya Bahal

baskets or on sheets spread open on the street. There are also several spice stalls around this square. This is a good place to shop for various **Asian spices,** including saffron, cardamom, and the many *masala* spice mixes that are so essential to Nepali and Indian cooking.

On this square, you will find three small temples, the largest of which is the:

9. **Annapurna Temple.** With its three-roofed metal pagoda, this temple is dedicated to the goddess whose name means "Full of Grain." There is no image of Annapurna inside this temple, only a large silver *kialash* (holy water pot). Be sure to notice the two **unusual brass statues** out front. One depicts a fat man, the other a skeleton. Across the square from this temple is a two-story pagoda temple that houses the most elaborate Ganesh statue in the city. The four-armed stone statue wears a silver crown and is surrounded by a gilded frame. In the middle of the square is a small temple dedicated to Narayan, who is an aspect of Vishnu.

In the middle of the square, you'll find what looks like a pothole enclosed by an ornate wrought-iron fence. This is Asan Tole's:

10. **Fish Memorial.** In this shallow hole is an almost-unrecognizable stone carving of a fish that has a very interesting history behind it. This little statue was supposedly placed here to commemorate an event that long ago transpired between an estranged father and son, both of whom were astrologers. In a contest to determine who was the greater astrologer, the two men (not knowing at the time that they were father and son, and who had become teacher and student, with the son in the role of teacher) made predictions about where a fish falling from the sky on a certain rainy day would land. The son's prediction proved correct when the father failed to account for the distance the fish would bounce before coming to a stop. A similar miscalculation had long before caused the father's estrangement from his wife and newborn son, whom he had concluded was not really his son at all. After realizing that he might have miscalculated his son's horoscope, he discovered that his teacher was actually his son and the two were finally reunited.

Six roads radiate from Asan Tole, and if you take the wide road leading almost due east, you will come in another long block to busy Kantipath, across which is a large square pond called the:

11. **Rani Pokhari or Queen's Pond.** In the middle of the pond, connected to the shore by a long bridge, stands a whitewashed Moghul-style temple dedicated to Shiva. The lake is said to be haunted, and the temple is opened only once a year during the October **Tihar festival.** The rest of the year, the lake is locked behind a fence.

From the northwest corner of the lake, cross Kantipath and head back into the market. This is the same street that you followed most of the way from Hanuman Dhoka Square, and you will soon be back at Asan Tole. From Asan Tole, take the street that heads due west, noting the overhanging balconies on the old buildings.

Soon you will come to:

12. **Bangemudha,** a small square, on which stand several small temples. The largest of these is dedicated to Vishnu, which is evident from the stone Garuda statue out front. Unfortunately, this brightly painted temple is set behind a rather ugly fence. One of the square's shikhara-style temples is devoted to Shiva and the other to Saraswati, the goddess of learning. There is also a recently restored brick pagoda temple here.

However, Bangemudha's most interesting shrine lies to the south across the intersection. It is here that you will find the:

**13. Wasya Dyah (Toothache God) shrine,** which must be the strangest shrine in Kathmandu. You may have difficulty recognizing it as a shrine, but the amorphous shape jutting out from a brick wall is a piece of wood into which have been nailed thousands of coins. Nailing a coin on this shrine is supposed to relieve toothache pain. As at other shrines, you may see someone touch this unusual object as they walk past and then touch their own forehead, just in case. Not surprisingly, there are several dentists' offices nearby.

From Bangemudha, walk north and watch on the left side of the street for:

**14. Two old buildings.** Both have ornately carved wooden facades. One building has its entire second floor cantilevered out over the street, while the other has an elaborate wooden balcony. With the narrow streets, three- to four-story buildings, and occasional balconies, the streets of old Kathmandu don't see much sunlight.

Just north of these old houses, watch for the entrance to the:

**15. Ratna Mandal Mahabihar (also known as Nagha Bahal).** Within this small courtyard, you will find several stone statues and chaityas. On the walls of the courtyard are old murals, and over the door of a small temple hangs an interesting gilded torana depicting Garuda.

North of this courtyard, on the same side of the street, you will come to a narrow alley that leads to:

**16. Kathesimbhu,** a 15th-century stupa that, though much smaller than those at Swayambunath or Boudhanath, fills a large courtyard. The sudden sight of the Buddha's eyes staring down an alley between two shopfronts stops many wandering visitors dead in their tracks. Surrounding this whitewashed stupa are dozens of smaller shrines. Kathesimbu is particularly busy with worshipers early in the morning.

Continue up this road and you will come to:

**17. Thahiti,** site of yet another stupa, this time located in the middle of a traffic-filled square. Numerous prayer wheels are set into the low wall protecting this stupa.

If you head east 2 blocks from the north side of this square, you will come to the 17th-century:

**18. Chusya Bahal,** a former monastery that has two stone lions guarding its front door. This building is currently being renovated with the assistance of foreign aid, and when completed should add another significant historic building to the Kathmandu cityscape. Backtracking to Thahiti, you can turn northward and be in the Thamel tourist district within a few minutes.

## KATHMANDU'S MOST IMPORTANT TEMPLES & SHRINES
### ✪ Swayambunath Stupa.

Perched atop a forested hill on the western edge of the Kathmandu Valley, Swayambunath Stupa is the Valley's **most important Buddhist shrine,** and chances are you're already familiar with this historic pilgrimage site (though you may not know it). The sleepy, all-seeing Buddha's eyes that stare out from the top of this hemispherical shrine have become the quintessential symbol of Nepal, and if you weren't familiar with these eyes before you left home, you most certainly have seen plenty of them around Kathmandu.

The earliest record of this stupa's existence dates from a 5th-century stone inscription; however, scholars and archaeologists believe that there was probably a shrine here as far back as 2,000 years ago. Regardless of how old it is, Swayambunath has an ancient feel to it, which is enhanced by approaching it on foot as pilgrims do.

---

## The Origin of Swayambunath
## (or the Story of Kathmandu's First Tourist)

A long time ago, so the story goes, the Kathmandu Valley was a vast lake upon which floated a giant lotus flower glowing with the light of Swayambhu, the primordial, self-born Buddha from whom all creation emanated. The Tibetan god Manjushri heard of the existence of this Buddha and journeyed from Tibet to witness the sight. When he arrived, he could not get a close look at the lotus-flower Buddha because it was too far out on the lake. So Manjushri used his sword to cut a slice out of a mountain on the south side of the lake, draining the lake and creating the Kathmandu Valley. The lotus came to rest on a hill in the western part of the valley, and here Manjushri built a shrine to honor this Buddha. The eerie part of this legend is that researchers have determined that the Kathmandu Valley *was* once a huge lake, but that the lake existed long before people inhabited the area. Chovar Gorge, the gorge that was supposedly cut by Manjushri on the south side of the valley, is a deep, narrow canyon that does indeed look as if it had been cut by a giant sword.

---

The pilgrim's route is a steep stone staircase of more than 300 steps. Some claim that there are 365 steps to the top, but I have never been able to arrive at that number. At the base of the staircase is a large, brightly painted gateway. Leading up to this gate are walls into which are set dozens of copper prayer wheels, inside of which are thousands of Tibetan Buddhist prayers. Buddhists gain a better standing in their next life by saying as many prayers or mantras as possible, and it is believed that when each prayer wheel is spun, all the prayers inside are recited and sent heavenward. Within the gatehouse itself there is a massive prayer wheel nearly 12 feet tall that requires two hands to turn. Filled with thousands of prayers, this wheel strikes a bell each time it makes a complete revolution (perhaps just to make sure someone up there is listening). Be sure to give it a spin before beginning the climb to the top of the hill.

Just inside the gate three large, brightly painted statues of the Buddha sit cross-legged in a meditative pose. In early morning, there are usually Tibetan women doing prostrations in front of these statues. These religious push-ups are another way that Tibetan Buddhists gain better standing in their next life.

Swayambunath is also known as the Monkey Temple, and as you start up the hill, you will likely begin to see the monkeys that lend the stupa this alternate name. The monkeys are Rhesus macaques (*Macaca mulata*), the species often used in medical research and from which the Rh-factor in human blood takes its name. Though cute, these monkeys should be given a wide berth. They can be bad tempered and are carriers of rabies. Should you be bitten by one, wash the wound thoroughly and then see a doctor immediately.

As you climb the stairs, you will pass numerous vendors selling small *mani* stones—stones that have been covered with prayers and serve the same devotional purpose as a prayer wheel. These small stones are strictly tourist trade, but larger mani stones are scattered about the hillside.

If you aren't winded from the climb up, the sudden sight of the stupa and all its shrines and temples will certainly take your breath away. Immediately in front of you as you reach the top of the stairs is a giant *vajra*, the thunderbolt that destroys all ignorance—one of the most important symbols in Tibetan Buddhism. Behind this is the stupa itself, a large hemisphere that looks as if it has been coated with white cake icing. The mysterious eyes of the Buddha gaze out over your head from the gilded cube surmounting the white hemispheric base. Prayer flags, new and old, flutter in the breeze and, as do the mani stones and prayer wheels, send their prayers heavenward on the wind.

Step around to the observation area on the left and take in the hilltop scene before you. Swayambunath Stupa, a white dome crowned with a gilded spire, is one of the two holiest Buddhist shrines in Nepal and is easily seen from all over Kathmandu. The mysterious eyes, painted on all four sides of the stupa's spire, represent the **eyes of the Buddha** and face the four cardinal directions—east, west, north, and south. Between each pair of eyes, where the nose would be, is what looks like a question mark. This is actually the Nepali character for the number 1, which symbolizes unity and the "one" way to reach enlightenment—through the Buddha's teachings. Above this is the third eye, symbolizing the all-seeing wisdom of the Buddha. The upper part of the spire consists of 13 gilded disks tapering up to a gilded umbrella hung with a colorful skirt. The 13 disks represent the **13 steps to enlightenment,** and enlightenment is represented by the umbrella. Between the eyes and the lowest of the 13 disks are four toranas, one for each of the cardinal directions. The toranas each include an image of the Buddha and other important deities.

Facing the steps, which climb the hill from the east, is the first of five ornate shrines set into the base of the stupa. Each shrine, protected by a heavy metal gate, contains one of the Dhyani Buddhas and their consorts. These Buddhas preceded the historic Buddha who was born near the present-day city of Lumbini in the Terai region of Nepal. Each of the Dhyani Buddhas faces one of the cardinal directions, with a fifth, slightly to the left of the east-facing Buddha, representing the Buddha at the center of the compass. Each of the five shrines is surrounded by exquisite gilded copperwork done in the repoussé style of metalworking, for which the Kathmandu Valley is renowned. Between these shrines, facing the subcardinal directions, are shrines containing the consorts of four of the Dhyani Buddhas. Linking the nine shrines is a long wall of prayer wheels and butter lamps.

An odd assortment of temples, shrines, monasteries, and curio shops surrounds the stupa. On the east side of the stupa, flanking the stairs that lead up from the bottom of the hill, are two shikhara-style temples, and on the west are a museum, a *gompa* (monastery prayer room), and a library for Buddhist studies. It is possible to climb the stairs to the gompa and then take a flight of stairs up to the gompa roof, from which there is an excellent view of the stupa with the Kathmandu Valley in the background. From this height, you are looking directly into the eyes of the Buddha. Beneath the gompa is a large open room that is always bustling with people on Saturdays, the only day of the week Nepalis have off from work and school. Women stir pots of stew, boil rice, and fry bread. They are not, however, cooking for themselves. Their meals will be given as offerings to the goddess Hariti Devi, whose temple stands just outside this cooking area.

The Temple of Hariti Devi is a small brick pagoda with a very ornate facade. Hariti is the goddess of smallpox, and though there is no longer any smallpox, her temple is still very popular with both Hindus and Buddhists. On Saturdays, a priest is often on hand to perform *pujas* (religious rituals) for those who have come with special requests. As prayers are said, rice, flowers, and colored powder get thrown every which way. Monkeys, stray dogs, and pigeons fight over grains of rice and the food offerings that have been left at the temple, and there is a general sense of chaos about the premises.

Between the impromptu kitchen area and the stupa there is a shrine dedicated to the goddesses Jamuna and Ganga, who are housed inside an ornate cage surrounded by butter lamps. A flame symbolic of the Adhi Buddha, the primordial Buddha, burns in this shrine. There is also a beautiful bronze statue of a peacock. Behind the Hariti Devi Temple are dozens of small whitewashed chaityas, which are sort of miniature stupas. Surrounding the chaityas are several curio shops, a bas-relief image of a standing Buddha, and the Temple of Agnipur, which symbolizes fire.

The **best time to visit** Swayambunath is early in the morning (before 8 or 9am). It is at this time that local people visit the stupa to say their prayers and make their offerings. By visiting at this time you'll see that Swayambunath is a very active shrine and not just a tourist attraction. During the middle of the day, Swayambunath is often crowded with tourists. There is now a Rs50 (75¢) charge for tourists visiting the stupa.

If you aren't fit enough to climb the stairs to the top of the hill, it's possible to take a taxi up a road on the back side of the hill. You'll still have to climb quite a few stairs before you reach the stupa itself, but not nearly as many as you would if you climbed from the base of the hill. If you arrive by taxi, you will enter the stupa compound from the southwest corner. A taxi from Thamel or Durbar Marg should cost around Rs80 ($1.20).

### ✪ Boudhanath.

Across the city from Swayambunath, on the east side of Kathmandu, stands Boudhanath, the **largest stupa in Nepal.** Similar in appearance to Swayambunath, this whitewashed stupa is also topped with a gilded box on which are painted four pairs of Buddha's eyes, and as at Swayambunath, there are always many devout Buddhists worshiping in various ways around this stupa.

Even more so than Swayambunath, this stupa attracts Tibetans, many of whom are pilgrims who have come to Nepal specifically to visit Boudhanath. These pilgrims, many looking as if they have never seen a city before, circle the stupa in wide-eyed wonder. Often the men wear long braids wrapped around their heads, and the women wear heavy dark cloaks and large chunks of turquoise and coral. Many of these pilgrims carry their own prayer wheels, which they spin incessantly. Others, wearing leather aprons and wooden hand guards, prostrate themselves on the ground with every step they take around the stupa. This form of worship is said to bring great benefits to a person in a future life and also serves as penance for past wrongs.

As at Swayambunath, if you **visit in early morning or late afternoon,** you will be mingling more with Tibetans and Nepalis than with German and French tour groups. Also, in the middle of the day, the whitewashed stupa can be absolutely blinding, whereas in the late afternoon it takes on a warm glow. A taxi from Thamel or Durbar Marg will cost around Rs100 ($1.50).

Legend has it that Boudhanath Stupa was built after an old woman asked the king for enough land to build a shrine to the Buddha. The king agreed to give her only as much land as she could cover with the skin of a water buffalo. The woman cut the buffalo hide into thin strips, and, laying them end to end, formed a large circle that "covered" far more land than the king had intended to donate. Though he had been tricked by the old woman, he agreed, and her buffalo-hide circle became the circumference of the stupa.

With three square tiers surrounding the central circle of the dome, Boudhanath is built in the form of a *mandala,* a symbol of the universe that is often used in Buddhist meditations. The stupa also symbolizes the five elements within its design. The base symbolizes earth; the dome, water; the spire, fire; the crescent atop the spire, light; and the flame shape topping the spire, ether. A low wall set with hundreds of prayer wheels circles the base, and Tibetan pilgrims circling the stupa often spin them.

You enter the stupa grounds through a colorfully painted gateway that leads off the busy bazaar street that runs through the town of Boudha. Once inside the complex, remember to **walk clockwise around the stupa.** Opposite the main gate, on the north side of the stupa, is the entrance to the stupa itself, and just inside the stupa entrance, lamas often set up low tables beneath a tent and perform pujas. You will often hear them ringing their bells and chanting in the hypnotic drone of the Tibetan language. From this antechamber, a wide staircase leads up to the base of the stupa dome, where niches containing images of the Buddha can be seen.

Since the Chinese invaded Tibet in the late 1950s, Boudhanath has become an important center for Tibetan Buddhist studies. There are now numerous monasteries surrounding the stupa, and it is worthwhile to wander the back streets around the stupa peeking in at the various monasteries. You might even be led by the droning of chanting monks to a prayer service in one of the gompas. On the west side of the stupa, you'll find the most readily accessible of the area's many monasteries. The front gate of this gompa opens directly onto the brick lane that surrounds the stupa. Visitors are requested to take off their shoes before entering the main prayer room. Don't miss the huge prayer wheel in a room on the left as you step through the gateway to this gompa. At some of Boudha's monasteries, masked dances are performed by the lamas in February during the Tibetan New Year celebrations.

Over the years, an entire village inhabited primarily by Tibetan immigrants has sprung up around the stupa, and today the stupa is completely encircled by shops, houses, monasteries, and a few guest houses and restaurants. The shops and vendors around the stupa have many interesting items for sale, and their prices are often quite good. Many pilgrims, low on funds, sell off their valuables to local shopkeepers. Consequently, this is a great place to buy old Tibetan artifacts and jewelry. Bargaining with Tibetan shopkeepers is never likely to save you much money, but you can try.

On the north side of the stupa, on the third floor of one of the shophouses is the **Stupa View Restaurant** (see "Dining" in chapter 4 for details), which is a good place for lunch.

A taxi to Boudhanath from Thamel or Durbar Marg should cost around Rs100 ($1.50).

### ✪ Pashupatinath.

On the east side of Kathmandu flows the Bagmati River, which is considered sacred by Nepalis. On the banks of this river stands the Pashupatinath complex, Nepal's **most important Hindu temple.** Dedicated to the god Shiva in his aspect of Pashupati, the Lord of the Animals, this imposing two-story pagoda contains a giant Shiva lingam (phallus) that is the object of much worship. Unfortunately, the temple's surrounding compound is off-limits to non-Hindus and you won't be able to see the lingam, though at the front gate, you do get an unobstructed view of the hind end of a large statue of Nandi the bull, Shiva's vehicle. You should also be able to see the silver and gilded lower-level facade of the temple.

Despite the restriction on non-Hindus, the extensive temple complex is a fascinating place to visit, and the streets leading up to the temple are lined with tiny shops selling brightly colored powders, holy beads, Shiva linga, and offerings to be taken into the temple. However, there is a far more macabre aspect of this temple that proves most fascinating to visitors.

Pashupatinath is the site of numerous cremation *ghats* (platforms), where corpses are cremated atop piles of wood and straw. Though they are the norm in Nepal (as well as throughout India), such open-air, **public cremations** are quite unusual to most

Westerners and have become one of the main tourist attractions in Kathmandu. The ghats are spread out along both sides of the river, with those within the temple precincts reserved for royalty and the wealthy. For the best view of the cremation ghats and Pashupatinath temple, walk down to the river from the parking area on the south side of the temple compound, and cross to the far side of the river on one of the two stone bridges. From either of the bridges or the stone terraces on the far side of the river, you're likely to see cremations in process.

Because Hindus consider it very auspicious to die with their feet in the waters of a holy river, people nearing death are often stretched out on the temple steps. After death (whether the person dies here or elsewhere), cremation takes place on the banks of the river with Hindu priests officiating and male family members participating. The body is piled on a stack of firewood and covered with straw, and during the seemingly haphazard cremation ceremony, the priest throws articles of the deceased person's clothing into the river (the clothing are usually collected a few yards downstream by some enterprising soul). When the cremation is completed, the ashes of the deceased are sprinkled on the waters of the Bagmati River. Any remaining incompletely burned wood is also thrown into the river (and this too is usually quickly retrieved).

If you glance downstream from the main ghats, you may see meager funeral pyres burning on the sandy banks of the river. These are the cremations of poorer people and people of a low caste who are not allowed to be cremated within the temple complex itself.

Looking upstream, you'll see, at a wooded bend in the river, the caves and ramshackle huts of sadhus, **Hindu ascetics,** who can usually be found lounging around amid the Shiva shrines on the terrace opposite the main temple complex. These wandering holy men, who have renounced their former worldly lives to follow a path of self-denial, are followers of Shiva. Often emaciated and frequently wearing little more than a loincloth, these Shaivite sadhus wear their hair in dreadlocks, smear their bodies with ashes, and carry tridents, which are a symbol of Shiva. To help them gain greater spiritual attainment, some sadhus spend their days smoking marijuana and hashish, which for centuries have been a sort of sacrament among the Shaivites.

During the festival of Shivaratri, held each year in either February or March, thousands of pilgrims from all over Nepal and India descend on Pashupatinath. Among these pilgrims there are usually hundreds of sadhus, many of whom display their agility in yoga, while others sit or lie on beds of nails as they meditate or beg for alms. Stories also persist of Pashupatinath sadhus who will, for a sufficient offering, demonstrate their ability to lift weights with their penises.

If you follow the stairs that lead up from the river on the opposite bank from the main temple, you will pass through a shady wood. At the top of the hill are several more temples and buildings occupied by pilgrims. Among these temples and in the trees, you are likely to see troops of monkeys. Though their antics are amusing, give them a wide berth; they are often bad tempered and can carry rabies. If you continue following this path over the hill, you will come to the **Guheshwari Temple,** dedicated to Shiva's consort in the aspect of Kali. This temple is also off-limits to non-Hindus, and though there is very little to see here, it's a pleasant walk.

At the far end of the cremation ghat terrace on the same side of the river as Pashupatinath, you will find a famous seventh-century statue of the Buddha half-buried amid the flagstones. The aging buildings along this stretch of the river are used as a hospice for the destitute.

**Good days to visit** Pashupatinath include the 11th day after a full or new moon, when many local people visit the temple. In August, during the Teej festival, thousands of women visit the temple to bathe in the holy waters of the Bagmati River. Because this ritual is meant to bring a long and happy marriage, many women dress in red saris, which are traditionally worn for wedding ceremonies.

*Warning:* You will probably be approached by very insistent young men offering to be your guide. They are very difficult to shake off once they have attached themselves to you and will go on explaining things about the temple complex whether you are listening or not. They are frequently very helpful, so you might as well let them join you. However, when it comes to paying them (they always say, "Pay what you want"), keep in mind that you can take a 3-hour guided tour of Pashupatinath and a couple of other important sites for around Rs250 ($3.80).

A taxi to Pashupatinath from Thamel or Durgar Marg should cost around Rs80 ($1.20).

## MUSEUMS & OTHER ATTRACTIONS

✪ **The National Museum.** Chhauni, near Swayambunath. ☎ **271478.** Admission Rs50 (75¢); Rs50 (75¢) more if you bring a camera. Wed–Thurs, Sat–Mon 10:30am–4pm (3pm in winter), Fri 10:30am–2:30pm. Closed all national holidays.

Nepal's National Museum contains three separate collections in three buildings. The building on your left as you enter the compound is of the greatest interest to foreign visitors because it houses the country's finest collection of **ancient religious art.** The works on display are primarily sculptural with different rooms devoted to different materials. The first room on the left is full of **stone sculptures** dating as far back as the first century, with the most recent carvings dating to the 13th century. The next room contains **terra-cottas.** It is in the next two rooms, containing **metalwork,** that the skill of past Nepali artists and craftspeople is truly evident. Just to the right as you enter the first metalwork room is a statue of the god Viwarupa with hundreds of arms. Another room contains wood carvings, mostly from the 18th and 19th centuries. Among the interesting pieces here are several **toranas** that you can inspect close up. The last room on the first floor exhibits **thangkas** from the 18th and 19th centuries. Spend a little time examining these paintings so you will know what to look for if you go shopping for a thangka. The second floor has a display on the lost-wax process for casting statues.

---

### Kathmandu's Fruit Bats

From just north of the intersection of Kantipath and Tridevi Marg (on the eastern outskirts of Thamel), the screeching can be heard even over the roar of afternoon traffic. Glancing up, you see what at first seems to be hundreds of quarreling crows. However, as you continue to gawk at all this treetop commotion, you slowly begin to realize that these are not crows but huge bats. For years the trees to the west of the Royal Palace have been the daytime roost of hundreds of fruit bats. During the day, these bats, which have a wingspan of more than 2 feet, hang upside down from nearly every naked tree limb, waking now and then to scratch an itch or bicker with another bat that has moved in too close. Each evening just at dusk, the bats leave their roost (which is then taken over by crows in a sort of time-sharing system) and wing out over the rooftops of Kathmandu for the night. From any hotel roof in Thamel, you can see the large bats as they head out like so many props from a Bella Lugosi movie. Unfortunately, the bat population has been dwindling in recent years, and there is speculation that it is due to air pollution and the incessant roar of traffic below their roost.

At the back of the museum compound is a building filled with Buddhist religious art. This is the newest exhibit at the museum, and it goes a long way toward helping visitors understand the highly complex iconography of Nepal's form of Buddhism. However, currently, the exhibit is not too well organized.

The third building houses a weapons exhibit on the second floor. Among the many old weapons used by various Nepali armies over the years, there is a rare leather cannon captured during a war with Tibet in 1792.

**The Tribhuvan, Mahendra, and Birendra Museums.** Hanuman Dhoka Palace, Hanuman Dhoka Square. ☎ **258034.** Admission Rs250 ($3.80). Feb–Oct Wed–Thurs and Sat–Mon 10:30am–4pm (3pm Nov–Jan), Fri 10:30am–2pm. Closed all national holidays.

These three museums, all housed in the sprawling and historical Hanuman Dhoka Palace, are dedicated to Nepal's last three kings. It was King Tribhuvan who restored power to the Shah family after more than 100 years of rule by Rana prime ministers, and in the Tribhuvan section of the museum, you can see such displays as the king's office, gym, hunting room, and one very enigmatic room simply called Death, which contains the **king's tomb.** Also within this museum is the **royal throne** of Nepal. The Mahendra Museum contains a collection of artifacts that belonged to King Mahendra, who was the father of the current king, Birendra, who also has his own museum here in the old royal palace. Although none of these museums will prove very interesting to most non-Nepali visitors, the old palace is worth seeing if for no other reason than to climb to the top of the Basantapur Tower (see "Walking Tour 1," above, for details). Cameras are prohibited in the museums.

**Kaiser Library.** Ministry of Education, Tridevi Marg. ☎ **411318.** Admission free. Sun–Thurs 10am–5pm, Fri 10am–3pm.

Located on the eastern outskirts of Thamel (across the street from Greenline Tours), this library houses a collection of old and rare books, some of which are more than 1,100 years old. The library is equally interesting for its once-elegant interior and collections of old photographs (many of which are of Rana hunting parties and feature dead tigers and rhinos). Along the same vein as the photos are some sad-looking stuffed animals, including a tiger and the mounted head of a wild buffalo with huge curling horns. With its trees (full of bats, pigeons, and crows) and high wall protecting it from the traffic outside, this place is something of a "natural" escape from the chaos of Thamel.

## 2 Patan, City of Beauty

Once a separate kingdom, **Patan** merged with Kathmandu long ago, and today the two cities are divided only by the Bagmati River. Also known as Lalitpur (City of Beauty), Patan is known for its elaborate and beautiful temples and for its skilled metalworkers, who are the source of most of the cast-metal statues sold throughout the valley. With a population of around 160,000 people, Patan is the second-largest of the valley's three major cities, and it has the largest Buddhist population.

By taxi, it takes 20 or 30 minutes and costs around Rs125 ($1.90) to get to Patan's Durbar Square from either Thamel or Durbar Marg.

### WALKING TOUR 3
### Patan's Durbar Square Area

**Start:** South end of Durbar Square.
**Finish:** South end of Durbar Square.

**Time:** Four hours, including museum visit.
**Best Times:** Saturday, when Nepalis have the day off and visit the temples.
**Worst Times:** Tuesday, when the Patan Museum is closed.

Though Patan is now little more than a district of greater Kathmandu, it was once a separate kingdom, and as such, its kings built their own Durbar Square. Today, because there was little damage during the 1934 earthquake, this is the best preserved of the three Kathmandu Valley Durbar Squares. Most of the buildings on this square date to 16th and 17th centuries, when the Malla kings had made Patan the most important kingdom in the Kathmandu Valley. This square has also benefited greatly from the restoration of part of the old royal palace to serve as the Patan Museum.

The main road from Kathmandu passes through the busy Mangal Bazaar shopping district of Patan before arriving at the southern end of the Durbar Square. Since this is where a taxi is likely to drop you, this is the best place to start a tour of the square. As you face the square, the first building on the right is the former:

1. **Royal Palace.** Though sections of this palace were constructed as early as the 14th century, most of it dates to the 17th century. In the mid–18th century, the palace suffered much damage at the hands of King Prithvi Narayan Shah, who invaded Patan during his campaign to unify Nepal. Taking up nearly the entire east side of Patan's Durbar Square, the palace is a sprawling complex of courtyards and temples. The first of these courtyards is the:

2. **Sundari Chowk.** Guarding this building is an almost-unidentifiable statue of the monkey god Hanuman, which devout worshipers have covered with nearly as much red offering paste as is on the Hanuman in Kathmandu's Durbar Square. The entrance to this ornate courtyard is through a doorway flanked by statues of Ganesh, the elephant-headed god, and Narsimha, the lion-headed god. Through this doorway, you enter a large courtyard. The brick walls of the courtyard are inset with many niches, each of which contains a carved wooden figure of a god. Intricately carved and brightly painted windows and balconies look onto the courtyard, and above the doorways are beautiful wooden toranas.

   In the center of the courtyard is the **Tusha Hiti,** once the royal bath of King Siddhi Narsimha Malla and, with its rich stone carvings of nagas, the most beautiful and elaborate *hiti* (bathing fountain) in Nepal. Positioned along the lip of the bath and set in niches around its walls are more than two dozen 1-foot-tall carved stone statues of various gods and goddesses, including the eight Bhairavs, the eight nagas, and the eight Astha Matrikas. The water spout that once filled this bath depicts Vishnu and his consort Laxmi riding on the back of Garuda and is a masterpiece of repoussé metalwork. At the top of the stone steps that lead into the 5-foot-deep bath, there is an intricate miniature replica of the Krishna Temple that is diagonally across the square from the Sundari Chowk. In front of this miniature temple is a statue of Hanuman, and behind it is a large rectangular slab of stone that is considered very holy. *Note:* Non-Hindus are requested not to touch this stone.

   Next door to the Sundari Chowk, through a doorway carved with intertwined snakes and flanked by two stone lions, is the:

3. **Mul Chowk,** formerly the most important of the palace's three chowks. On the outside walls of this courtyard are attractive roof struts that depict many-armed deities. Inside the courtyard stands the Bidya Mandir, a gilded shrine that looks like a temple finial, and in the northeast corner of this courtyard, there is an

unusual octagonal temple built on the roof of the palace. This is one of the three Taleju temples in the old palace complex. Also here in the Mul Chowk are two large brass repoussé statues of the Hindu goddesses Jamuna (atop a turtle) and Ganga (atop a mythological elephant-headed crocodile called a *makara*). These statues, which date from 1662 and were restored in 1936, flank the entrance to the Taleju Bhawani Temple, which is also known as the small Taleju Temple to distinguish it from the towering Taleju Temple to the north of the courtyard. Surprisingly, this smaller temple is considered much more sacred than the larger temple. The beautiful torana over the entrance to the temple was carved in 1715. Several images from this torana have disappeared, probably due to theft.

On the north side of the Mul Chowk, and towering over Durbar Square, rises the:

**4. Degutale Temple.** Built by King Siddhi Narsimha Malla in 1640, this temple is dedicated to the Malla's tutelary goddess, Taleju, who looks over the Kathmandu Valley. Built atop the three-story palace, the temple has another four stories, which makes it an imposing seven stories tall. Not surprisingly, this temple was completely destroyed by the 1934 earthquake and has been rebuilt. The Taleju Temple is opened to the public only once a year, during the Dasain festival, and then only to Hindus. To the north of the Taleju Temple is the Keshav Narayan Chowk, which is entered through the exquisite:

**5. Sun Dhoka (Golden Gate).** Though it is neither as large nor as ornate as the Golden Gate in Bhaktapur, Patan's Golden Door is certainly a testimony to the wealth of the Malla kings and the skill of Patan's craftspeople. Flanked by two stone lions, the gilded door is crowned by an intricate repoussé torana depicting the Hindu god Shiva and his consort Parvati. Above the doorway is a finely carved triple window. The central panel is gilded, while the two flanking panels are of carved and painted ivory. This doorway now serves as the entrance to the **Patan Museum,** which opened in 1997 after a lengthy restoration of this section of the palace. This is by far the finest museum in the country (see "Other Attractions," below, for details).

☕**TAKE A BREAK**  Not only is there an excellent museum behind the Golden Door, but there also is a very tranquil cafe. This is the only chance you'll get to eat in an old Malla palace, and it shouldn't be missed. The cafe is at the back of the palace amid terraced gardens.

Just north of the Patan Museum, in an area usually packed with vendors selling all kinds of unusual Nepali souvenirs, is the:

**6. Manga Hiti,** the largest public bathing fountain in Patan. Water pours from the carved stone waterspouts, and people can be seen bathing and washing their clothes here throughout the day. At the top of the steps leading into the hiti are a pair of *pathis* (pilgrims' resting pavilions). Across from the Manga Hiti, at the very northern end of the square, stands the:

**7. Bhimsen Temple,** which is dedicated to the demigod Bhimsen, a character from the *Mahabharata* who was said to have been the strongest man who ever lived. Bhimsen is worshiped as a sort of god of commerce and business and is very popular with Patan merchants. The three-story pagoda-style temple was built in 1681 and has been restored three times since then. Deities depicted on the temple's roof struts have many arms and are accompanied by their shaktis; hanging from the front of the temple is a metal ribbon—a symbolic pathway for

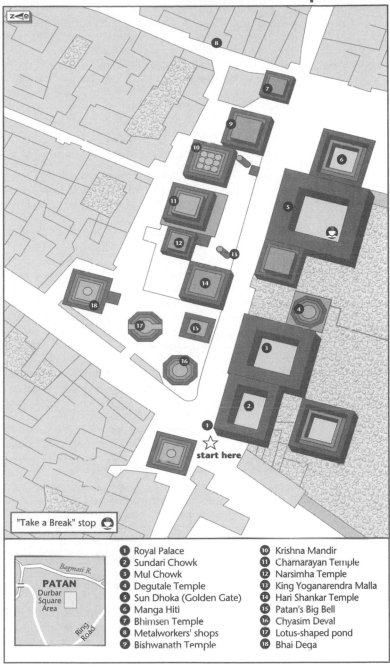

"Take a Break" stop 🍵

PATAN
Durbar
Square
Area

Bagmati R.

Ring Road

1. Royal Palace
2. Sundari Chowk
3. Mul Chowk
4. Degutale Temple
5. Sun Dhoka (Golden Gate)
6. Manga Hiti
7. Bhimsen Temple
8. Metalworkers' shops
9. Bishwanath Temple
10. Krishna Mandir
11. Charnarayan Temple
12. Narsimha Temple
13. King Yoganarendra Malla
14. Hari Shankar Temple
15. Patan's Big Bell
16. Chyasim Deval
17. Lotus-shaped pond
18. Bhai Dega

Bhimsen to descend to earth. Over the doors and windows are ornately carved toranas, and in front, atop a stone pillar, stands a bronze lion. On the front of the temple, on the second floor, there is an elaborate gilded balcony, and on the back there is an equally elaborate ungilded balcony. During the reign of the Rana prime ministers, a marble facade was added to the first floor. To the right and behind the Bhimsen Temple, a lane leads away from the square and is lined with:

**8. Metalworkers' shops.** These shops are packed full of beautifully made small statues of the gods and goddesses that populate the many temples of the Kathmandu Valley. After doing a bit of shopping here, return to the Bhimsen Temple, to the left of which is the:

**9. Bishwanath Temple,** which is dedicated to the god Shiva and is guarded by two large stone elephants. This two-story pagoda-style temple contains a Shiva lingam similar to the one housed in the Vishwanath Temple in Varanasi, India. Roof struts of this temple are carved with erotic images. To the left and behind this temple is the:

**10. ✪ Krishna Mandir.** This is the most ornate of the temples on Durbar Square and is one of the most beautiful temples in Nepal. Dedicated to Krishna and his consort Radha, the temple is constructed from stone and integrates a number of traditional Indian architectural styles. Built in the mid–17th century by King Siddhi Narsimha Malla, the four-story temple sits atop a three-stage plinth. Considered extremely holy, this temple is almost always bustling with reverent worshipers. The uppermost floor is a central shikhara-style tower. Around the second and third floors are profusely decorated pavilions topped with gilded finials. Basrelief friezes around the exterior of the temple on each floor depict scenes from the Hindu epics *Mahabharata and Ramayana.* Unfortunately, it is not possible to get close enough to these friezes to make out any of the details. Kneeling atop a stone pillar in front of this temple is a bronze statue of Garuda erected in the mid–17th century. Though statues of Garuda are usually found outside temples dedicated to Vishnu (since Krishna is an incarnation of Vishnu), this statue is not entirely out of place. Each year on Krishna's birthday, which falls sometime in August or September, a huge crowd gathers here for a nightlong celebration filled with music.

To the left of the Krishna Temple are two temples dedicated to incarnations of Vishnu. The first of these is the:

**11. Charnarayan Temple,** a large pagoda-style temple dedicated to Charnarayan. In front of the temple are a pair of stone lions and two stone guards, Ajaya and Vijaya, traditionally associated with Narayan. The temple may have been built as early as 1565, which would make it the oldest temple on the square. The roof struts of this temple feature erotic carvings. To the left of the Charnarayan Temple is the:

**12. Narsimha Temple,** which is dedicated to the half-man, half-lion incarnation of Vishnu. Built around 1590, this is a simple, shikhara-style structure that is plastered and whitewashed. On either side of the steps are two small stone lions and a pair of deities that includes Garuda, the half-bird, half-man creature upon which Vishnu rides. Directly in front of the Narsimha Temple is a 20-foot-tall stone pillar topped by a gilded bronze statue of:

**13. King Yoganarendra Malla.** The king kneels with his hands clasped together in prayer facing the Taleju Temple that houses the tutelary goddess of the Malla kings. A cobra with its neck flared rears up behind the king, and atop the cobra sits a tiny bird. Erected nearly 300 years ago, the statue is the source of numerous legends. My favorite claims that the king, who was said to be able to converse with gods, never died. He disappeared one night saying he would not die until the little metal bird on his statue flew away. Supposedly, a window of the palace is left open and a door left unlocked each night so that the king will be able to enter his palace should he ever choose to return. To the south of the king is the:

14. **Hari Shankar Temple,** a three-roofed pagoda dedicated to both Shiva and Vishnu. Two kneeling elephants flank the steps leading up to the temple. Around the base of the first floor there are more stone carvings, and above every arch on the first floor there is an ornate torana. The roof struts of this temple differ from others on the square in that they depict not erotic themes but scenes of murder and mayhem. To the left of this temple, raised up on a platform, hangs:

15. **Patan's Big Bell.** Each of the valley's three Durbar Squares contains a similar large bell. However, this one is said to be the first such bell in the valley and was probably erected by King Vishnu Malla in the 18th century. Just to the left of the big bell stands the shikhara-style:

16. **Chyasim Deval,** another Krishna Temple. This octagonal stone temple was constructed in the early 18th century by Yogamati, the daughter of King Yoganarendra Malla. Two stone lions guard the steps of this temple. Behind this temple, in an open area, is a:

17. **Lotus-shaped pond** in the middle of which is a statue of a Rana "queen." The statue and pond were built in 1905 to commemorate the construction of a piped water system in Patan. To the side of this pond is the:

18. **Bhai Dega,** a dumpy little whitewashed shrine that stands atop an overly large platform. This little Shiva temple was erected after the original temple was destroyed by the 1934 earthquake.

## WALKING TOUR 4
## Beyond Patan's Durbar Square

**Start:** North end of Durbar Square.
**Finish:** South end of Durbar Square.
**Time:** Four hours.
**Best Times:** Saturday, when Nepalis have the day off and visit the temples.
**Worst Times:** Tuesday, when the Patan Museum is closed.

While Patan's Durbar Square is an impressive sight, several of the city's most important and impressive temples lie elsewhere. This tour will take you past the Golden Temple, Mahaboudha Temple, and the Rato Machendranath Temple.

Start your walking tour in the northwest corner of Durbar Square, at the Bhimsen Temple. Behind this temple you will find numerous:

1. **Metalsmiths' shops** selling countless Buddhist and Hindu religious statues in all sizes. Many of the bronze, brass, and copper statues have also been painted, much the way statues in Nepali shrines are painted. Quality varies quite a bit among these statues, so it pays to shop around. As you shop, walk down the alley that leads along the right side of the Bhimsen Temple, and when you come to the first intersection, turn right. At the next intersection there is an interesting little:

2. **Ganesh shrine** in which poor Ganesh is almost unrecognizable. If you continue past the Ganesh shrine in the same direction you have been walking, you will see just ahead of you on the left, near the two colorfully painted stone lions, the entrance to the:

**3. ✪ Golden Temple,** which is one of the most ornate temples in the Kathmandu Valley. Also known as the Hiranya Varna Mahavihar and Kwa Bahal, this temple is an active Buddhist monastery, and over the street entrance are several carved stone Buddha statues. Through this first door you enter a tiny courtyard where you will be asked to remove your shoes (and any other leather you happen to be wearing); rubber sandals are provided (which you will appreciate when you see how filthy the temple precincts are). This is also where you must pay the temple's Rs25 (40¢) admission fee.

Through the next doorway, over the top of which are more carved stone figures of various Buddhist deities, stands the **main temple**—nothing about the outer courtyard or entry prepares you for the ornateness of this inner courtyard. When you step through the door, you will be standing on a raised walkway separated from the flagstone courtyard by a low fence of prayer wheels. Two repoussé elephants with riders on their backs flank the inner doorway as it opens onto the main courtyard. Directly in front of the door is a raised mandala surmounted with a large gilded vajra. Behind this Buddhist symbol of the thunderbolt that destroys all ignorance is a small temple dedicated to Swayambu, the primordial Buddha. On the two nearest corners of this temple are metal statues of rearing griffins. On the gilded roof there is an ornate finial consisting of a multitiered miniature umbrella (a traditional Buddhist symbol) held up by the tails of four cobras that stream sinuously down the gilded ribbons hanging from the finial. Unfortunately, this richly decorated little temple only detracts from the nearly completely obscured main temple behind it.

According to tradition, the main temple was built in the 12th century, though the earliest records of its existence date to the early 15th century. With three gilded roofs and a facade covered with embossed and gilded metal and exquisitely detailed repoussé images of various deities, the temple is perhaps the most ornate in Nepal. The main door itself is covered with silver repoussé, and the gilded torana over the door is as beautiful and elaborate as the torana over Bhaktapur's Golden Gate. Above this torana are seven bas-relief images of the Buddha in different poses. Gilded lattice windows flank the entrance to the temple, and numerous gilded metal ribbons stream down from the roof, assuring any god who wishes to visit the temple plenty of paths to follow. Flanking the courtyard, on the corners, are unusual metal statues of monkeys contemplating the jackfruit held in their hands. At the back of the small Swayambunath Temple and facing the main temple are two stone figures and two metal figures, all praying. If you are lucky, you might even catch a glimpse of the statue that is housed in this ornate temple, though worshipers usually crowd the statue's tiny room, obscuring it from view.

The temple is almost always bustling with activity as old women carry offerings of food and flowers to the foot of the main temple and children squeal and shout as they chase each other around the courtyard. The hypnotic drone of chanting Buddhist monks drifts down from a second-floor prayer room. You're likely to see a large turtle or two (released by devout Buddhists hoping to gain merit in their next life) wandering about the courtyard searching for a way out. The daily rice offerings leave the courtyard floor absolutely filthy. Consequently, rats crawl around this temple with obvious impunity, and clouds of flies fill the air.

As you leave this temple (don't forget your shoes), turn left and continue down the same street that brought you here. You will soon come to an open area in which stands:

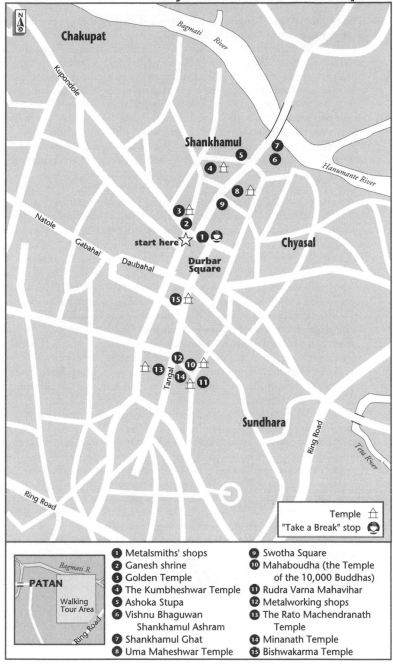

Chakupat

*Bagmati River*

*Kupondole*

Shankhamul

7

5
4 ⛩

*Hanumante River*

8 ⛩

3 ⛩
9

2
*Natole*
start here ⭐ 1 🌀 Chyasal
*Gabahal*
Durbar
*Daubahal* Square

15 ⛩

12 10 ⛩
13 ⛩ 14 ⛩
*Tangal* 11

Sundhara

*Ring Road*

*Tela River*

*Ring Road*

| | |
|---|---|
| Temple | ⛩ |
| "Take a Break" stop | 🌀 |

*Bagmati R.*

PATAN

Walking
Tour Area

*Ring Road*

| | |
|---|---|
| ❶ Metalsmiths' shops | ❾ Swotha Square |
| ❷ Ganesh shrine | ❿ Mahaboudha (the Temple |
| ❸ Golden Temple | of the 10,000 Buddhas) |
| ❹ The Kumbheshwar Temple | ⓫ Rudra Varna Mahavihar |
| ❺ Ashoka Stupa | ⓬ Metalworking shops |
| ❻ Vishnu Bhaguwan | ⓭ The Rato Machendranath |
| Shankhamul Ashram | Temple |
| ❼ Shankhamul Ghat | ⓮ Minanath Temple |
| ❽ Uma Maheshwar Temple | ⓯ Bishwakarma Temple |

4. **The Kumbheshwar Temple,** Patan's oldest temple and one of only three **five-roofed pagodas** in the Kathmandu Valley (the other two are the Nyatapola Temple in Bhaktapur and the circular Panch Mukhi Hanuman Temple in Kathmandu's Hanuman Dhoka Palace). Built in 1392 and set within a compound filled with smaller temples and water tanks, this temple lacks a terraced base and consequently is not as well proportioned as the Nyatapola Temple, but it's beautiful nonetheless. Devout Hindus believe that this temple is the winter residence of the god Shiva, who spends his summers on Mount Kailash, a Tibetan mountain sacred to both Hindus and Buddhists. As you walk through the front gate of the temple, you will be facing the hind end of a statue of Nandi the bull, the animal upon which Shiva is said to travel. Within the compound, there are also many beautiful stone carvings of different gods.

There always seems to be lots of activity here, with children playing in the numerous pools of water, teenage girls rubbing their hands across rows of Shiva linga, and old men and women bathing at the waterspouts of the temple's fountains. North of the main temple, within the large temple compound, is a covered water tank that is said to be filled by a spring originating at holy Gosainkund Lake, which is high in the mountains, an 8-day walk north of Kathmandu.

Within the Kumbeshwar complex, at a small temple to the right of the main temple, you will probably see people lined up to leave offerings. This temple is dedicated to the crane-headed goddess Baglamukhi, who is an incarnation of Shiva's consort Parvati and who is here seen as a flower-bedecked statue beneath a canopy of silver snakes and likewise framed in silver.

During the **festival of Janai Purnima,** held each year in either July or August, pilgrims gather at the temple complex to worship a silver-and-gold Shiva lingam that is erected in the middle of one of the water tanks. During the Kumbeshwar Mela festival, also in August, Hindu shamans known as jhankris gather here to heal the sick by dancing and drumming away the evil spirits.

If you turn right after the Kumbheshwar Temple and then take your first major left, you will come to the:

5. **Ashoka Stupa,** one of four such ancient stupas that were built at the four ancient corners of Patan. Legend has it that the stupas were erected by the Indian emperor Ashoka when he visited the Kathmandu Valley around 250 B.C. You may have seen another of the stupas on your way from Kathmandu; there is one diagonally across the street from the Hotel Narayani. Another of the stupas is southeast of Durbar Square between the bus stop and the Patan Industrial Estate. The fourth is a distance away, on the far side of the Ring Road.

If you continue north from the Ashoka Stupa, you will walk downhill toward the Bagmati River. Watch for a flagstone path angling off to the right toward the river. If you take this fork, you will find the:

6. **Vishnu Bhaguwan Shankhamul Ashram.** Within the courtyard of this aging and unmaintained temple stands a trio of 6-foot-tall stone figures: Ganesh, Garuda, and Hanuman. There are also lions and griffons on the steps of this stone shikhara-style Vishnu temple, and atop a stone pillar that rises from the back of a huge stone turtle is a brass garuda. Exiting the temple compound in the direction of the river will put you on the half-mile-long:

7. **Shankhamul Ghat.** Because the Bagmati River no longer flows past this stone embankment, it is no longer used much for cremations or other religious rituals. However, it still retains a certain grandeur that hints at how powerful Patan was in the days when it was an independent kingdom. From the temple, go left along

the ghat, and at the bridge that crosses the river, climb a flight of stairs and head back up the hill away from the river.

After passing the Ashoka Stupa and Kumbheshwar Temple, you will reach a section of street lined with old brick homes. Along this stretch on the left is the two-story:

**8. Uma Maheshwar Temple,** which houses a stone bas-relief of Shiva and Parvati seated side by side. This carving dates to the Licchavi period, which ended in the 9th century. A little bit farther along this street, you will come to:

**9. Swotha Square,** where you will find three temples. To your immediate left is a temple dedicated to Narayan, an incarnation of Vishnu. In front of the temple is a beautiful stone statue of Garuda. Within this temple is a stone bas-relief of Vishnu, and in the paving stones in front of the temple, there is carving of a snake. Across the square are a three-tiered temple dedicated to Krishna and his consort Radha (this temple was restored in recent years) and a second Krishna temple that was hastily and unattractively rebuilt after the 1934 earthquake. From this square, continue along the road and you will quickly arrive back at Durbar Square.

☕ **TAKE A BREAK**   There aren't too many places in this area that you will want to patronize for more than a bottled drink, but the **Café Pagode,** facing the Bhimsen Temple on Durbar Square (where this tour began), is an exception. If you've worked up a big appetite, try the set Nepali lunch of dal bhat and vegetables. It's an all-you-can-eat affair that will fuel you up for more exhausting touring.

From Café Pagode, walk back to the large road at the south end of Durbar Square and turn left. Continue away from Durbar Square on this street for about 15 minutes until you come to the second major intersection, which has a temple on your immediate right and a bathing fountain across the intersection on the right. Turn right here, and in another 5 minutes, almost at the far end of this narrow street, you will come to:

**10. ✪ Mahaboudha (the Temple of the 10,000 Buddhas).** A Buddhist temple designed in the Indian shikhara architectural style, Mahaboudha takes its name from the thousands of terra-cotta plaques covering it. Each plaque contains an image of the Buddha, and it is said that every brick used in the construction of the temple depicts the Buddha. The bricks used are of an ocher color rather than the usual red so prevalent in the Kathmandu Valley. After the 1934 earthquake destroyed this temple, it was rebuilt. When the reconstruction was completed, enough of the original bricks were left over to build a second, smaller temple, which was then dedicated to Maya Devi, the Buddha's mother. However, the two temples have left the compound very crowded. Because the main temple nearly fills the courtyard in which it stands, visitors must crane their necks to see more than a few feet of the temple's base. *Tip:* Take the flight of steps that leads to the second floor of the building surrounding the courtyard—you'll get a better view.

This neighborhood of Patan is known for the skill of its **craftspeople,** who fashion metal statues of various Buddhist and Hindu deities using the lost-wax method. Within the temple compound and in the narrow alley that leads to the temple, you'll find several small shops selling these religious statues. If you are interested, prices here are usually quite good.

Turn right as you leave this temple, walk to the end of the street, and turn left. Diagonally across the street is the entrance to the:

**11. Rudra Varna Mahavihar,** an inactive 19th-century Buddhist monastery that has in its courtyard an amazing array of interesting metal and stone statuary. Among the metal statues are two European-style lions, a king, two garudas, two Oriental lions atop prostrate elephants, two peacocks, two rearing griffins, two rearing goats, two monkeys contemplating jackfruits, and eight repoussé high-relief icons. There is also a miniature replica of Swayambunath Stupa with a gilded canopy shading it from the sun. Two vajras (dorjes) are mounted atop mandalas.

As you exit this compound, turn left and continue down the street, passing numerous:

**12. Metalworking shops.** You will hear the rhythmic pounding of hammers on copper as you walk along this street, and in the shops you might see metalsmiths making large copper water pots. Other shops are filled with more statues of various Buddhist deities.

At the end of this street, you'll come to the bazaar street that leads south out of Durbar Square. Almost directly across the T intersection with the bazaar street is a lane, which in a few yards, leads to:

**13. The Rato Machendranath Temple,** home for 6 months of each year to one of the most revered gods in the Kathmandu Valley. Completely hidden from the main street, this temple, which is surrounded by a large unkempt garden, is said to date to the early 15th century, though it more likely was built sometime in the late 17th century. Today, the three-story temple has a tile facade on the first floor and a very ornate spire on the peak of the uppermost roof.

Machendra, also known as Avalokiteshwara and Lokeshwar, is the same god as Chenrezig, the patron saint of Tibet, and Hindus consider him to be an aspect of Shiva. As Machendranath, this god is revered as a god of rain in the Kathmandu Valley. The strangely childlike figure of Machendra is made of roughly carved wood that has been painted bright red. The statue is kept in this temple for only half the year; during the other half it resides in the nearby village of Bungamati. Each year in either April or May, during the festival of Machendranath Jatra, the image is taken out of its temple and paraded through the streets of Patan in a huge chariot pulled by devoted worshipers. Once every 12 years, the chariot is pulled all the way to Bungamati, about 3 miles away. This long chariot ride will next be undertaken in the year 2003. To find the temple, walk south on the road that begins to the right of the Sundari Chowk on Durbar Square. Take the first lane you come to on your right, and walk through the gate at the end of the lane.

Return up the little lane that leads to this temple, and almost directly across the main street you will see the:

**14. Minanath Temple,** which is tile-walled and has garishly painted roof struts and numerous copper pots and kitchen utensils nailed to its facade. This two-story temple dates to the 16th century and stands behind a hiti that was built in the 11th century. The deity housed within this temple is associated with Rato Machendra and is also paraded through the city in its own chariot during the festival of Machendranath Jatra.

From the Minanath Temple, walk north in the direction of Durbar Square. A block before reaching the square, turn left down a narrow lane, and you will come to the:

**15. Bishwakarma Temple.** This unusual brick temple is dedicated to the god of coppersmiths and carpenters and consequently has a facade of beaten copper. Retrace your steps up this lane, turn left, and you will shortly be back at the southern end of Durbar Square.

## OTHER ATTRACTIONS

Patan is the site of a Tibetan refugee camp where a large carpet factory turns out hand-knotted wool carpets. You can tour the factory and observe the various stages of the carpet-making process, and then do some carpet shopping of your own. These carpets are among the best buys in Nepal. See "Carpets" in the "Shopping" section, below, for details. Also, before leaving Patan, you may want to drop by the numerous interesting craft shops along Kupondole. See "Gifts & Souvenirs" in the "Shopping" section, below, for details.

✪ **Patan Museum.** Keshav Narayan Chowk, Patan Durbar Square. ☎ **521492.** Admission Rs120 ($1.80). Wed–Mon 10:30am–4:30pm (cafe open until 5:30pm).

Opened in 1997 after a lengthy restoration of the Keshav Narayan Chowk building in Patan's old royal palace, this is now Nepal's finest museum. The building itself dates to 1734 and is entered through the elaborately decorated Sun Dhoka (Golden Gate). The interior of the old palace has been beautifully restored, and dramatic lighting spotlights the exhibits, which cover 13 centuries of Nepali religious art. The well-written explanations of the artwork serve as a superb introduction to Nepal's often-confusing Hindu and Buddhist iconography. Exhibits, which fill the three floors of the old palace, are organized primarily by religion, though there is also a fascinating exhibit on the traditional metalworking techniques of the Kathmandu Valley. Other exhibits include a collection of photos taken in 1899 and an illustrated Hindu Tantric manuscript. If at all possible, make this one of your first stops in Nepal, and you'll have a greater understanding of all that you'll see in your explorations of the country.

**The Central Zoo.** Jawalakhel, Patan. ☎ **521467.** Admission Rs50 (75¢) adults, Rs25 (40¢) children. Tues–Sun 10am–5pm.

About the only reason I can see to ever visit this zoo is to get in a quick elephant ride. Of all the places in Nepal where you can ride an elephant, this is the cheapest at only Rs100 ($1.50) per ride. If you want to take an elephant for a spin around town, you can even hire one for the reasonable fee of Rs1,000 ($15.15) per hour. The zoo itself is an incredibly depressing place, with animals kept in small, dirty, cement-floored cages. One interesting note: The tigers kept here are usually maneaters that were trapped after killing villagers down in the Terai region of the country.

## 3 Bhaktapur, City of Devotees

Built on a hill in the eastern part of the valley and also known as Bhadgaon, ✪ **Bhaktapur** (the name means "City of Devotees") is said to have been built in the shape of a conch shell, a Hindu sacred symbol. Today, however, the city has grown well beyond its original size, and the conch-shell shape is no longer discernible, except perhaps from the air. The city looks impressive when approached from the south, which is where the last stop on the electric bus line is located. From this vantage point, you'll see a wall of faded red brick houses climbing a hillside. The houses seem to be stacked helter-skelter atop one another, but rising from amid this jumble is the perfect symmetry of the five-storied **Nyatapola Temple.** In the distance, framing the city, are the snow-covered peaks of the Himalayas. A 5-minute walk past rice paddies and vegetable gardens brings you to a steep brick road leading up into the dark confines of the city.

The old cities of the Kathmandu Valley are often compared to medieval cities of Europe, and nowhere is this comparison more apt than in Bhaktapur. The entire heart of the city remains virtually unchanged since the 17th century, when many of its most beautiful buildings were erected. In the narrow alleyways that serve as the city's streets, overhanging balconies allow very little sunlight to filter to the ground. Everything seems to be made of brick, wood, or stone. Vegetables and grains hang from the eaves of buildings out of the reach of rats and pigeons.

This cohesive and historic appearance is largely due to the efforts of the German-funded Bhaktapur Development Project (BDP), which has done much to restore and upgrade the city's most interesting buildings. As you wander through the city you will see what appear to be brand-new buildings constructed in the old style. These are the work of the BDP. They have also included indoor plumbing for most of the houses as part of their renovation project. The BDP has also built an official parking area for taxis and tour buses on the north side of the city. If you are dropped here by a taxi, follow the wide brick path up the hill, past the Indrani Temple beneath a gnarled pipal tree, to reach Bhaktapur's Durbar Square.

By taxi, it takes 30 to 45 minutes and costs around Rs300 ($4.55) one way from Kathmandu to Bhaktapur. Buses for Bhaktapur leave regularly from Bagh Bazaar on the east side of the Tundikhel near the clock tower and take 45 minutes to an hour. Electric buses to Bhaktapur leave from the traffic circle beside the national stadium at the southwest corner of the Tundikhel.

To fund further renovation in Bhaktapur, the city now charges visitors a Rs300 ($4.55) admission fee for visiting the old neighborhoods of the city.

## WALKING TOUR 5
### Bhaktapur's Durbar Square

**Start:** Bhaktapur Gate.
**Finish:** Taumadi Square.
**Time:** Four hours, including museum visit.
**Best Times:** Saturday, when Nepalis have the day off and visit the temples.
**Worst Times:** Any day between 10am and 3pm, which is when large tour groups inundate the square.

Large and open, Bhaktapur's Durbar Square, which is closed to vehicular traffic, is a much more peaceful and relaxed place than the Durbar Square in Kathmandu. Bhaktapur also has both a Golden Gate and a museum, as on Patan's Durbar Square, but it does not have the concentration of temples that is found in Patan. In part this is due to the fact that some of the temples destroyed in the 1934 earthquake were never rebuilt. However, Bhaktapur's Durbar Square area more than makes up for this with its Nyatapola Temple, one of the few five-tiered pagoda temples in the valley and by far the most beautiful.

Begin your tour of the square at:

1. **The Bhaktapur Gate,** a large colorfully painted arch that opens onto Durbar Square from the northwest. The gate was built about 300 years ago by King Bupathindra Malla, who was responsible for erecting many of the buildings and works of art on this square. Just outside this gate are a number of small but interesting shrines, while just inside the gate, on the left, is a small gate in a brick wall. Flanking this second gate are:

2. **Four stone statues.** Two large lions are accompanied by smaller statues of the goddess Ugrachandi Durga (on the left) and the god Bhairav (on the right). The statue of Ugrachandi is killing the buffalo-headed demon Mahishasur and has 18 arms. Bhairav, who is an incarnation of Shiva, is shown with 12 arms. These latter two statues, which were commissioned by King Bupathindra Malla, are

some of the finest stone carvings in Nepal. Legend has it that when the artist completed these statues, he had his hands chopped off so that he could not duplicate his work for any other of the valley's kings.

To the right of the gate with Ugrachandi and Bhairav is another gate flanked by:

3. **Four more stone statues.** Again there are two stone lions and two gods. Here the gods are Narsimha (on the right) and Hanuman Bhairav (on the left). Narsimha is shown tearing out the entrails of the demon Haranyakashipu. According to Hindu mythology, this demon had tricked the god Brahma into making him immortal. He could not be killed by man or animal during the day or at night. When he began terrorizing the world, Vishnu manifested himself as the half-man, half-lion Narsimha and killed Haranyakashipu at twilight, which is neither night nor day. These statues guard the entrance to the National Art Gallery (see "Bhaktapur Museums," below, for details).

To the right of the art gallery entrance is the:

4. **Sun Dhoka (Golden Gate).** This masterpiece of metalworking, erected by Ranjit Malla in the mid–18th century, is without doubt the **greatest work of art in Nepal.** Framed in bricks and covered with gilded bronze worked in the repoussé method, the gate includes an amazingly detailed figure of the fearsome goddess Kali at the center of the torana (the fan-shaped panel over the gate). Above Kali is an image of Garuda, in this case shown with the head of a bird rather than a human head. Serpents, nymphs, gods, and monsters cover every inch of the torana and the door frame. Set into either side of the gate are stone inscriptions, and on the curving gilded roof are numerous finials, including some shaped like elephants and winged lions. The gate was designed to be a suitably ornate entrance to the:

5. **Taleju Temple.** The goddess Taleju, whose image is kept within the temple, was the tutelary goddess of the Malla kings and was thus highly revered. Through the gate are several courtyards that contain some excellent wood carvings and colorfully painted struts. In the farthest courtyard is the temple itself, which is the most sacred temple in Bhaktapur and is said to contain the finest works of art in the valley. Unfortunately, this temple is off-limits to non-Hindus, but you should be able to get a peek through the open door, over which is a large and intricate torana. On a pillar directly in front of the Golden Gate is a:

6. **Life-size statue of King Bupathindra Malla.** The king sits cross legged with his hands together as a sign of respect for the goddess Taleju. Though all three of the valley's Durbar Squares have statues of past kings, this is the most elegant and artistic.

Behind this statue rises the:

7. **Batsala Devi Temple,** an ornate stone shikhara-style temple decorated with many excellent stone carvings of gods and goddesses. On a stone plinth attached to this temple is a large bell known as the:

8. **Barking bell,** so named because all the dogs within hearing distance commence barking whenever the bell is rung (or so the story goes). The massive bell, erected by King Ranjit Malla in the early 18th century, is rung during worship of the goddess Taleju in the nearby Taleju Temple. Beside this bell stands the:

9. **Chyaslin Mandapa,** an octagonal pavilion used by kings for viewing processions and meeting with dignitaries and ministers. This pavilion was among the many buildings destroyed by the 1934 earthquake. However, under the auspices of the Bhaktapur Development Program and with a gift from the German government, this unusually graceful structure was completely rebuilt. The reconstruction utilized all the pieces of the original structure that could be salvaged after the earth-

quake, and in addition, a steel infrastructure was incorporated into the design to prevent another earthquake from destroying the pavilion. Around the stone base of the pavilion is an inscription that includes a poem to the eight seasons (thus the eight sides to the building). Roof struts feature lovers embracing affectionately rather than the graphic sexual scenes on many other roof struts around the valley. The second floor of the pavilion is a pleasant place to sit and take in the activity of the square. Across from this pavilion stands the:

10. **Palace of 55 Windows,** which takes its name from the row of ornately carved wooden windows that line the second floor of the palace. Above each of the windows are wooden *tympanas* (similar to toranas) depicting gods, goddesses, and mythological creatures. Behind this ornate facade is the palace's royal audience hall. Though there was a palace on this site as long ago as 1427, this building dates to the early 18th century, when King Bupathindra Malla had the original palace remodeled.

To the right of the Palace of 55 Windows is a large, open square bordered on two sides by an L-shaped building that was once a *dharmasala* (resting place for pilgrims). The first temple on your left as you enter this square is the:

11. **Durga Temple,** a small shikhara-style temple on a five-tiered base. Pairs of carved stone figures, including camels and smiling rhinos, guard the steps leading to the door of this temple. The 1934 earthquake leveled many buildings in Bhaktapur, and behind and to the right of the Durga Temple, you will see the strangest evidence of this quake. Atop a four-tiered pyramid that once must have supported a large and elegant temple stands a:

12. **Shiva Temple,** a whitewashed shikhara-style temple that was erected after the earthquake and is completely out of proportion with the large pyramid upon which it stands. In front of this temple, in the middle of the square, stand two large stone lions.

Return to the main Durbar Square, and behind the Chyaslin Mandapa and the Batsala Devi Temple, you will find the:

13. **Pashupatinath Temple,** a two-story pagoda that is a reproduction of Kathmandu's most important Hindu temple. Erected in the 17th century, this temple is noted for the easily seen erotic carvings on its roof struts.

On the far side of the square from the Palace of 55 Windows, behind the Pashupatinath Temple, follow a shop-lined lane that leads from Durbar Square to Taumadi Square. As you step out of the narrow lane into the square, you will see towering above you on your left the tallest temples in the valley. The:

14. ✪ **Nyatapola Temple** is a magnificent **five-roofed pagoda** standing atop a massive five-tiered pyramid base. Together the roofs and base display exquisite balance and symmetry. Each level of the temple is ornately decorated with colorfully painted roof struts and windows, and hundreds of bells hang from the eaves, tinkling in the wind. Erected in the early 18th century by King Bupathindra Malla, the temple is dedicated to the Tantric goddess Siddhi Laxmi.

On each of the five tiers of the temple's base stand pairs of stone statues that flank the stairs leading to the temple door. These statues have a curious legend associated with them. The two lowermost statues, which are each nearly 8 feet tall, are of a pair of famous wrestlers—Jaya Mal and Patta—who were each supposed to have the strength of 10 men. On the tier above them stand two elephants, which are said to be 10 times stronger than the wrestlers. Above the elephants are two lions, which are believed to be 10 times as strong as elephants. Above the lions are two griffins that are 10 times stronger than lions. Above these

# Bhaktapur's Durbar Square Area

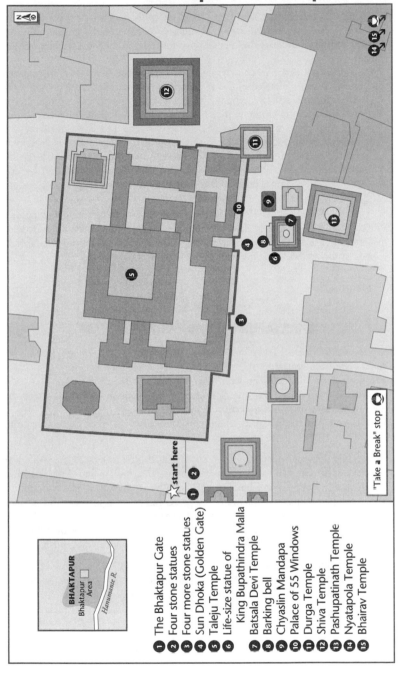

1. The Bhaktapur Gate
2. Four stone statues
3. Four more stone statues
4. Sun Dhoka (Golden Gate)
5. Taleju Temple
6. Life-size statue of King Bupathindra Malla
7. Batsala Devi Temple
8. Barking bell
9. Chyaslin Mandapa
10. Palace of 55 Windows
11. Durga Temple
12. Shiva Temple
13. Pashupatinath Temple
14. Nyatapola Temple
15. Bhairav Temple

start here

"Take a Break" stop

BHAKTAPUR

Bhaktapur Area

Hanumante R.

stand two goddesses, Baghini and Singhini, who are part tiger and part lion, respectively. They are said to be 10 times stronger than the griffins. This progression would indicate that the deity within the temple must be very powerful indeed.

To the right as you face the Nyatapola Temple is the rectangular, three-roofed:

15. **Bhairav Temple.** Erected in the 18th century, the temple was destroyed by the 1934 earthquake and later rebuilt. Though it seems quite plain and uninteresting beside the towering beauty of the Nyatapola Temple, if you look closely you will notice that it has a very ornately decorated facade and is the focus of near-constant worship. The gilded repoussé work of the lower story is kept highly polished by reverent hands rubbing across it. Above the niche into which offerings to Bhairav are thrust are gilded windows similar to the wooden windows that decorate the upper floors of this temple.

☕ **WINDING DOWN**    There is no better way to finish an exploration of the Durbar Square area than at the **Café Nyatapola,** which is housed in a restored pagoda-style pavilion overlooking the Nyatapola Temple. This cafe has one of the best views of any restaurant in the Kathmandu Valley.

# WALKING TOUR 6
## BHAKTAPUR BEYOND DURBAR SQUARE

**Start:** Taumadi Square.
**Finish:** Dattatreya Square.
**Time:** Four hours, including museum visits.
**Best Times:** Early mornings and late afternoons; Saturday, which is the Nepali weekend and when they often worship at the main temples.
**Worst Times:** Any day between 10am and 3pm, which is when large tour groups inundate the city.

Beyond the Durbar Square area lies a city changed little by time. Here you can see more work of the German restoration project, which has even included the restoration of residential buildings. Such buildings are usually overlooked in the name of preserving temples and palaces of national historical value. However, here in Bhaktapur an effort has been made to preserve the town's living history as well. Off the main streets lies a maze of narrow alleys that will never be able to accommodate vehicles any larger than motorcycles, which is partly what makes this city so enjoyable to explore.

Start your tour on Taumadi Square. From here, with your back to the Nyatapola Temple, walk south on a wide (for Bhaktapur) and busy street. As the street heads downhill, watch for a small square on your right. This is the:

1. **Potters' Square.** Here, local potters of all ages busy themselves making simple bowls, water pitchers, and other household containers. Small boys pound the clay at the foot of a shrine, while teenage boys practice spinning the heavy potter's wheels that are made from old tires. Older men shape water jars and yogurt containers with deft fingers. Women wet the gray clay dishes around the square, moving them occasionally to keep them in the sun. The scene is timeless and emphasizes the medieval atmosphere of the city. All the work is done outdoors, and you can watch every step of the process.

# Beyond Bhaktapur's Durbar Square

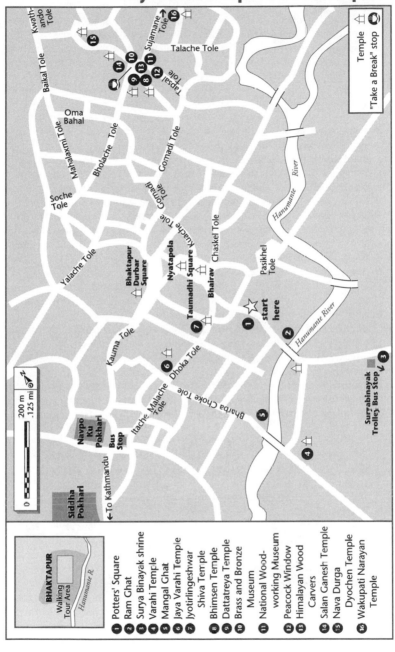

Temple ⛩ 🅘
"Take a Break" stop

**BHAKTAPUR**
Walking
Tour Area

1. Potters' Square
2. Ram Ghat
3. Surya Binayak shrine
4. Varahi Temple
5. Mangal Ghat
6. Jaya Varahi Temple
7. Jyotirlingeshwar Shiva Temple
8. Bhimsen Temple
9. Dattatreya Temple
10. Brass and Bronze Museum
11. National Wood-working Museum
12. Peacock Window
13. Himalayan Wood Carvers
14. Salan Ganesh Temple
15. Nava Durga
16. Dyochen Temple
   Wakupati Narayan Temple

From the Potters' Square, continue downhill on the same street, and you will soon come to the Hanumante River. On your immediate left is:

**2. Ram Ghat,** a sacred site for bathing and cremations. It has a small temple dedicated to Rama, hero of the ancient epic *Ramayana,* but it is not one of the city's more impressive ghats. Continuing south, you cross the river, and after a few minutes' walk, if you turn and look over your shoulder, you get a very impressive view of the city. If you continue for about another half mile (1km) on this road, passing the trolley bus stop en route, you will climb a hill and come to the:

**3. Surya Binayak shrine.** Though hardly impressive to the uninitiated, it is one of the Kathmandu Valley's four most important Ganesh shrines. Parents with a child who is slow in learning how to speak often come to this shrine to ask this Ganesh to intercede on their child's behalf. Return the way you came, and shortly before reaching the bridge over the river, turn left on a dirt road, which, in a minute or two, crosses a paved road. Turn left here to have a look at the:

**4. Varahi Temple,** which is dedicated to a boar-faced goddess said to protect temples and other buildings. As you walk up the hill to this small temple, you'll pass several interesting carved stone statues. Walk back down this hill, cross the bridge, and you will find, on your right, the:

**5. Mangal Ghat,** which has many old shrines and stone carvings. From this ghat, walk uphill on the street that leads up from the bridge. In 3 blocks turn right, on a street that leads back to Taumadi Square. Just ahead on the left is the large:

**6. Jaya Varahi Temple,** which is dedicated to the shakti of Vishnu's incarnation as a boar. The four large, wooden toranas on this temple are particularly impressive, and on the torana of the middle second-floor window, you'll see an image of Jaya Varahi. Continuing along this road, you will come to a square devoted to Shiva. In this square is the:

**7. Jyotirlingeshwar Shiva Temple,** a shikhara-style temple that houses a stone considered a powerful Shiva lingam. The square is filled with interesting little shrines and statues.

Continuing down this lane, you will soon be back at Taumadhi Square. Cross this square, and take the wide road that angles northeast from the far corner of the square. Follow this road for 10 minutes through the main market area of Bhaktapur to Dattatreya Square (also called Tachupal Tole), which is the site of several of Bhaktapur's most important attractions. As you enter the square, you will see on your immediate left the:

**8. Bhimsen Temple.** This temple is dedicated to a demigod, a hero from the epic *Mahabharata,* who is said to watch over business and commerce. Consequently, the Bhimsen Temple is much favored by Bhaktapur businessmen. Facing this small temple is an ornate metal lion atop a stone pillar. At the opposite end of the square stands the:

**9. Dattatreya Temple,** for which the square is named. Built in 1427 and modified in 1458, this temple is the oldest structure on the square. Similar in design to the Kasthamandap in Kathmandu, the Dattatreya Temple is also said to have been constructed from the wood of a single tree. The three-story temple is unique in that it has a separate addition, complete with balcony and finial, built atop its lowest roof. A small face looks down from this little add-on room in the same way that Shiva and Parvati look down from their temple in Kathmandu's Durbar Square. The second and third floors are also surrounded by balconies. The tall stone pillar in front of the temple is crowned with a statue of Garuda, which indicates that this temple is dedicated to the god Vishnu, here in the incarnation of Dattatreya. On both sides of the temple's entrance are statues of the famous wrestlers Jaya Mal and Patta, who are also seen on the steps of the Nyatapola Temple.

Flanking the Dattatreya Temple, on either side of the square, are two museums. On the north side of the square is the:

10. **Brass and Bronze Museum,** which houses a collection of religious statues, as well as traditional household containers and utensils (see "Bhaktpur Museums," below, for details). A visit to this museum provides not only an introduction to Nepali metalworking, but also an opportunity to see the inside of a traditional home. Across the square is the:

11. **National Woodworking Museum,** which is housed in the Pujari Math, a former home for Hindu priests that was built in 1763. Down the alley to the left of the entrance is Bhaktapur's most famous wood carving—an old building that was also once the residence of Hindu priests (see "Bhaktpur Museums," below, for details). As you face this building, you will see an alley on your left. Down this alley, on a wall of the Pujari Math, is Bhaktapur's famous:

12. **Peacock Window,** an exquisite example of local wood-carving skill. This window features a peacock with tail feathers in full display. Nearly three dozen smaller birds are also carved around the window frame, and arabesques, demons, and animals are incorporated into the design. All over Bhaktapur, you'll see for sale, in a wide range of sizes, carved wooden reproductions of this window. If you would like to see wood-carvers at work, walk back around the corner, and beyond the woodworking museum entrance, you'll find the:

13. **Himalayan Wood Carvers,** where local Newari craftspeople keep alive Bhaktapur's ancient art of wood carving. These artisans still carve wood as they have for centuries. A small second-floor showroom displays their work (see "Shopping," below, for details).

**WINDING DOWN**    After this long walk, you'll probably want to stop for some tea or a cold drink before finishing the tour and heading back to Durbar Square. The **Café de Peacock,** overlooking Dattatreya Square, is an excellent place to relax, cool off, and absorb the atmosphere of this medieval square.

If you take the lane that leads north along the right side of the Café de Peacock, you will see on your left, in just a few steps, the:

14. **Salan Ganesh Temple,** a small, attractive temple in front of the little Ganesh *Pokhari* (pond). This temple does not contain a statue or carving but instead houses a natural stone that is said to look like an elephant's head. All over Nepal there are temples and shrines dedicated to such natural likenesses of the gods, and more often than not, it takes a long stretch of the imagination to see anything but a lump of rock in these highly venerated objects. Continue north (uphill) on this lane and you will come to the:

15. **Nava Durga Dyochen Temple,** a houselike temple dedicated to the nine Durgas, Tantric deities that are often worshiped with animal sacrifices. Head south down the street to the left of the temple; in 2 long blocks, take a right, and you will come to the:

16. **Wakupati Narayan Temple,** dedicated to a harvest god that is an incarnation of Vishnu. Several Garuda statues stand in front of the temple. From here, walk west on this road, and you will soon find yourself back in Dattatreya Square, from where you can retrace your steps to Durbar Square. However, before winding your way back in that direction, you might want to explore the smaller side streets to the

west and north of Dattatreya Square. Should you get lost, just ask someone to point to the direction of Durbar Square. You're likely to be escorted by one or more children (who will expect a tip).

# BHAKTAPUR MUSEUMS

All three of the following museums have a single admission price of Rs20 (30¢), plus another Rs20 (30¢) extra if you want to take pictures. Once you have purchased a ticket to one museum, that ticket will get you into the other two museums.

**National Art Gallery.** Durbar Square. ☎ **610004.** Wed–Thurs and Sat–Mon 10:30am–4:30pm, Fri 10:30am–2:30pm. Closed all national holidays.

Partly housed in the Palace of 55 Windows on Durbar Square, this museum is noted for its large collection of Buddhist thangkas. These colorful and intricately detailed paintings on canvas were traditionally rolled up and carried by wandering monks to assist them with meditations and religious services. Also on display are carved stone figures of various Hindu and Buddhist deities that are even more impressive than the thangkas. The sun god at the foot of the stairs leading to the second floor is particularly beautiful. In a large hall on the second floor are cases displaying old illustrated books that record the histories of the kings who once ruled the Kathmandu Valley. In the section of the museum that is within the Palace of 55 Windows, there are the remains of beautiful wall murals that give an indication of how richly ornamented this palace must have been when it was first built.

**Brass and Bronze Museum.** Dattatreya Square. ☎ **610448.** Wed–Mon 10:15am–4:45pm. Closed all national holidays.

Housed in a 15th-century Hindu priests' home across from the Dattatreya Temple, the Brass and Bronze Museum contains examples of Nepal's skillful metalworking history. Many of the pieces in the museum are similar to household utensils still in use today. The *gaagri* (copper water pot) is still used in villages to carry water from the local water tap. The *kala* (ritual offering pot) and *kalasha* (water pitcher) are both seen frequently around temples. In room 2, there is a collection of very ornate oil lamps. One particularly interesting lamp is a replica of the Krishna Temple in Patan.

**National Woodworking Museum.** Dattatreya Square. ☎ **610005.** Wed–Mon 10:30am–4pm. Closed all national holidays.

Located directly across Dattatreya Square from the Brass and Bronze Museum and housed in the 15th-century Pujari Math (another Hindu priests' home), this museum is interesting as much for its collection of wood carvings as for the beautiful woodwork on the exterior of the historic building. Among the displays here are examples of traditional architectural details, including, in one small room, 11 roof struts from a 15th-century temple. When you see a ladder in one of the main display rooms, be sure to glance up into the attic, where you will see the surprisingly cartoon-like figures of Lord Jagannath and one of his siblings. A graceful dancing Nartaki Devi in a glass case wears a quizzical look on her face. In another case there is a very ornate 3-foot-tall carving of the Buddha being tempted by Mara. Also watch for the frightening 17th-century carving of the wrathful Bhairav.

# CHANGU NARAYAN

Perched on a ridge in the eastern part of the Kathmandu Valley, Changu Narayan, a pagoda-style temple dedicated to Vishnu in his incarnation as Narayan, is one of the oldest temples in Nepal, and because it is a bit off the beaten track, it is seldom visited by tourists. You can see the gilded roofs of the temple shining in the sun due north of Bhaktapur. Though you can get to Changu Narayan by a car (a taxi from Bhaktapur will cost around Rs300 [$4.55] for the round-trip), it is much more interesting to walk from Bhaktapur. The walk takes about 2 hours and is easy except for the last steep climb up to the temple. To find the trail, head north from Bhaktapur's Durbar Square and aim for the temple on the ridge. Along the way people will point you in the right direction.

Originally built in the early fourth century during the Licchavi dynasty, Changu Narayan was rebuilt around 1700 after the temple was destroyed by a fire. Though the temple is quite beautiful, especially the repoussé doors and front facade, Changu Narayan is not known for its temple but for the stone statues, bas-relief carvings, and inscriptions that are scattered around the temple courtyard. Facing the entrance to the main temple is a large stone statue of a kneeling Garuda, upon whom Vishnu is said to ride. This statue dates from the 5th century. Behind the statue is an inscription stone from the same century that has provided a great deal of information about the Licchavi period in the Kathmandu Valley's history. Also in front of the temple's main entrance, in an ornate little cage, are small statues of King Bupathindra Malla and his queen.

To the right of the temple entrance, there are several smaller shrines and a platform with only a carved stone atop it. This bas-relief carving, which has had its upper-right corner broken off, depicts two different incarnations of Vishnu. At the bottom of the stone, Vishnu is shown reclining on a bed of snakes, the same pose that is depicted in the large statue of Budhanilkantha (see chapter 6). Above this, a 10-headed standing Vishnu is depicted. The detail in this 5th- or 6th-century stone carving is amazing.

Near the famous double Vishnu is a stone depicting another incarnation of Vishnu—the half-man, half-lion Narsimha. In the northeast corner of the courtyard is an important bas-relief that you might recognize. It depicts Vishnu riding on the back of Garuda and is the model for the image on the back of the Nepali 10-rupee note. All of the stone carvings in the temple courtyard were done between the 5th and 13th century, which makes this one of the single-greatest concentrations of ancient art in Nepal.

## 4  Organized Tours

Basically, two types of organized tours are available in Kathmandu. You can go on a half-day group tour, usually in a van, to various valley sights; or you can hire a car, driver, and guide to show you the sights you are most interested in seeing. The former is, of course, the less-expensive option, though the commentary by the guide may not be too informative.

Virtually every hotel, tour company, and travel agency in Kathmandu can arrange a spot in a **group tour** for you. Most of these companies simply book you onto a Gray Line tour operated by the **Nepal Travel Agency,** Ramshahpath (☎ **430188** or 431013), which offers the best organized city tours available. There are tours to Bhaktapur and Pashupatinath for Rs250 ($3.80); to Patan and Swayambunath for Rs250 ($3.80); to Dakshinkali, Chovar Gorge, and Shesh Narayan Temple for Rs500 ($7.60); to Nagarkot for Rs400 ($6.05); and to Dhulikhel for Rs300 ($4.55). When making a reservation, be sure to ask for the pickup point nearest to your hotel.

**Personal tours** (for two people), including a car, driver, and guide, cost around $25 for half a day and $35 for a full day ($45 to Dakshinkali). The advantage to these tours is that you can stay as long as you like at any sight, though your guide will probably want to hasten you along. **Natraj Tours & Travel,** Ghantaghar, Kamaladi (☎ **222014**

or 222532), offers similar personal city tours. If there are more than three people in your group, the per-person price drops a little bit.

Kathmandu's most interesting organized tours are the daily ✪ **mountain flights** offered by several local airlines. These flights head straight for Mount Everest and fly within 2 miles of the famous peak. Though any travel agency can arrange one of these flights for you (and it's much easier to make bookings through travel agents), try to get a seat on a **Buddha Air** (☎ 977/1-418864) flight. All the seats on planes used by this airline are window seats. Other airlines offering mountain flights include **Gorkha Airlines** (☎ 977/1-487033), and **Necon Air** (☎ 977/1-473860). These 1-hour flights provide a close-up aerial glimpse of the Himalayas, including Mount Everest. The cost is $99 per person, and the flights are offered daily from September to May, weather permitting. Buddha Air also operates sunset flights to Mount Everest, as well as mountain flights all the way to Kanchenunga (the third-highest peak on earth), and flights out of Pokhara that circle Mt. Annapurna.

# 5 Outdoor Activities

**BALLOONING**   One of the most unusual and enjoyable ways to view the Himalayas from Kathmandu is in a ✪ **hot-air balloon** operated by **Balloon Sunrise Nepal** (☎ 424131). Pilot Chris Dewhirst was the first person to fly a hot-air balloon over Mount Everest, though the trips he offers here in the valley aren't quite that exciting. However, because the balloon is able to climb as high as 10,000 feet, you're guaranteed an unforgettable view of the Himalayas. The flights, which last 1 hour, cost $195 per person and must be booked at least 3 days in advance.

**BIRD WATCHING**   Just because Kathmandu is a crowded and congested city doesn't mean there isn't any good ✪ **bird watching** in the area. In fact, more than 500 species have been sighted in this valley. Phulchoki, which, at 9,060 feet, is the highest point on the rim of the Kathmandu Valley, is one of the best birding spots in the country, with sightings of some 265 species. Because there is an elevation difference of more than 4,000 feet between the base of the hill and the summit, a wide range of bird habitats (mostly forested) are present. A trail up this mountain starts near the Godawari Royal Botanical Garden, though it is much easier to take a taxi to the top and then hike down. Be sure to also take a walk around the botanical gardens, where 100 species have been recorded.

Nagarjun Royal Forest, on the north side of the valley, is another good spot to try. For migrant waterfowl, pay a visit to Taudaha, a pond near Chovar Gorge on the road to Dakshinkali.

**GOLFING**   The **Royal Nepal Golf Club** (☎ 472836), reached by the south entrance to Pashupatinath temple, is Kathmandu's only golf course and, to quote a golfing acquaintance in Kathmandu, "is a very dangerous golf course." What makes this course so dangerous is that the tee boxes of different holes sometimes face each other. Consequently, if the person teeing off at the other hole happens to slice, you could wind up with a golf ball in your face. Only in Nepal would golf be an adventure sport! If you're up for this sort of danger, the greens fees are Rs1,250 ($18.95), club rental is Rs250 to Rs500 ($3.80 to $7.60), and a caddie is another Rs100 ($1.50). Avoid Saturdays, because it is the busiest day of the week.

**HIKING**   Whether you're preparing for a trek, can't get enough of the trails after a trek, or if you simply want to do a bit of hiking on a short visit to the Kathmandu Valley, there are plenty of opportunities for hiking. Any trek into the hills that surround the valley will give you a taste of what trekking is all about. There are trails through forests, trails to remote temples, and trails through terraced farmland.

For a long and strenuous forest hike, head north from Thamel on the road to Trishuli Bazaar, through Balaju, to the **Nagarjun Royal Forest Preserve,** which also goes by the name Rani Ban (Queen's Forest). A 3-mile trail leads up through a surprisingly well-preserved and wild-feeling forest to the summit of 6,875-foot Jamacho. The trail climbs roughly 2,500 feet in elevation to a prayer-flag–draped Buddhist stupa that has a commanding view across the Kathmandu Valley.

A similar forest trail also leads to the 9,060-foot summit of **Phulchoki,** the highest peak on the rim of the Kathmandu Valley. This hike, which provides excellent views of the Himalayas, is particularly popular with bird-watchers and, with a 4,000-foot elevation gain, is much more strenuous than the hike up through Nagarjun.

Another good place for a hike is in the **Shivapuri Watershed and Forest Preserve,** which is located north of the Budhanilkantha shrine. It takes about 4 hours to hike to the summit of 8,960-foot Shivapuri. From the summit there are superb views of the Ganesh Himal and Jugal Himal, snow-covered peaks parts of which are seen from the valley floor. There is a Rs250 ($3.80) admission fee for entering this reserve.

A few other valley hikes are outlined elsewhere in this book. See chapter 6 for information on hikes from Nagarkot and Dhulikhel. See "Changu Narayan," in the "Bhaktapur, City of Devotees" section of this chapter, for information on hiking through farmland to one of the valley's most historical temples.

**MOUNTAIN BIKING** Due to dangerous levels of traffic congestion, bicycles are, unfortunately, no longer a safe way to explore Kathmandu. However, out on the rural edges of the Kathmandu Valley, there are quiet roads and wide trails that are ideal for mountain biking. While it's possible to rent a mountain bike in Thamel and head out on your own, you'll do better to book a guided mountain bike tour.

**Himalayan Mountain Bikes** (☎ 977/1-419295 or 977/1-434560; www.bena,com/hmb; e-mail: bike@hmb.wlink.com.np), which has its office adjacent to Pilgrim's Book House in Thamel, offers a half-day exploration of Kathmandu ($14); a full-day downhill ride from ✪ **Nagarkot to Bhaktapur** ($49); a 2-day exploration of the southeast part of the Kathmandu Valley ($99); and a 4-day combination mountain biking and rafting adventure that includes 2 days of Class IV and V whitewater ($159). This company also offers bike tours of as long as 12 days and does trips in Tibet and Bhutan.

**Dawn Till Dusk** (☎ 977/1-418286; fax 977/1-419815; e-mail: dtd@frontier.wlink.com.np), located in the courtyard of the Kathmandu Guest House, offers a 1-day backroads tour ($25), a 2-day Nagarkot ride that includes the climb as well as the descent ($70), and other tours lasting from 3 to 7 days ($110 to $280).

**WHITE-WATER RAFTING** There is no ✪ **white-water rafting** in the Kathmandu Valley, but this is the best place to make your arrangements if you decide to take on the turbulent waters of the Himalayas' many rivers. Most of the trips out of Kathmandu are on the Trishuli (around $80 for a 2-day trip), which is usually run en route to Chitwan National Park, and on the Bhote Kosi (around $80 for a 2-day trip), a heart-pumping stretch of Class IV and V water near the Tibetan border. This is also the starting point for 10- to 12-day trips down the remote Sun Kosi ($375 to $450 for a 10-day trip). Trips to the even-more-remote Karnali in western Nepal also originate here ($400 to $450 for a 12-day trip).

Reliable rafting companies in Kathmandu include **Himalayan Encounters,** Kathmandu Guest House (P.O. Box 2769), Thamel (☎ 977/1-417426; fax 977/1-417133; e-mail: raftnepl@himenco.wlink.com.np); **Equator Expeditions,** Thamel (P.O. Box 8404), Kathmandu (☎ 977/1-424944; fax 977/1-425801; www.equatornepal.

com; e-mail: equator@mos.com.np), which has its office just up the street from the Kathmandu Guest House; **Himalayan River Explorations,** P.O. Box 170, Kathmandu (☎ 977/1-418491), affiliated with Tiger Tops Jungle Lodge and the pioneer river rafting company in Nepal; and **Ultimate Descents,** North Field Cafe, Thamel (☎ 977/ 1-419295; fax 977/1-411933; email: rivers@ultimate.wlink.com.np), which also offers kayak trips and kayaking clinics.

## 6 Shopping

After temple touring, shopping is probably the most popular tourist activity in Kathmandu. The streets of old Kathmandu are literally covered with fascinating souvenirs, works of art, relics, curios, and religious statuary. Street vendors and shopkeepers have set up businesses around virtually every tourist attraction in the Kathmandu Valley, so wherever you go sightseeing, you will be accosted by people trying to sell you all types of trinkets and curios.

### THE SHOPPING SCENE

**BEST BUYS**    Among Kathmandu's best buys are nearly anything made of **wool,** including sweaters, jackets, shawls, handbags, and Tibetan carpets. Silver **jewelry** and **semiprecious stones** such as turquoise, red coral, and lapis lazuli are other good buys. Casual **cotton clothes** for men, women, and children are exceptionally good deals, though most of the ready-made clothes are in styles that look best in Kathmandu or on the beaches of southern Thailand. Metal **religious figurines** in brass, bronze, or copper sell for much less here than they do in the West, though prices can be quite high for those of good quality. **Tea** and **spices** are also good buys and are lightweight and compact, making them great gifts.

**WORST BUYS**    Kathmandu's worst buys are the knock-off outdoors items such as rain jackets, sleeping bags, day packs, and backpacks. Don't be fooled by the name-brand labels (The North Face, Lowe, and Gore-Tex are all popular); these are cheap imitations and many don't last even the length of a trek.

**BARGAINING**    Bargaining is an absolute necessity in Nepal, especially when it comes to tourist souvenirs and curios, and street vendors tend to charge the highest prices. You are expected to bargain for nearly everything in Nepal (Nepalis even try to bargain for the price of bus tickets, though it never works). This said, there are exceptions to the bargaining rule. Tibetan shopkeepers rarely discount their merchandise and will give you the cold shoulder if you try to bargain with them; however, they are low-key and do not pressure you to buy. There are also more and more fixed-price shops showing up around Kathmandu.

Bargaining is most effective when you're buying from street vendors, who regularly quote prices that are as much as four times the going rate for an item. How well dressed you are and whether you are wearing an expensive watch or flaunting an expensive camera will likely determine what a vendor will ask for a particular item. So for the best deals, dress down and keep the watch and camera out of sight.

There are several rules you need to follow in order to play the Nepali shopping game. First and foremost is never pay the asking price for anything without first trying to bargain. As a rule of thumb, offer a third to half of the asking price and work your way up from there. Generally, if you pay more than three-quarters of the asking price, you aren't doing too well.

Second, never ask the price of something unless you are prepared to fend off a ravenous vendor (even looking too long at an item can be a problem). Asking the price of something means you are interested, and a vendor will rarely let you get away without buying whatever it is you asked about. This makes comparison shopping very difficult. However, with a little practice, it can be done. To get away without buying something, you must ignore the vendor as he or she follows you down the street demanding a price from you. This may sound cruel, but there is no other way to deal with Kathmandu's kings and queens of the hard sell. On more-expensive items and in shops, it is much easier to ask prices and not be subjected to merciless demands of "How much you pay?"

Third, look around before buying anything and find out what people are asking for a given item. Prices, and especially quality, vary widely on most tourist souvenirs and clothing. What may seem like a great price may actually be rather high when you realize that the merchandise is of inferior quality.

**HOURS**    Shop hours vary considerably and are rarely as fixed as they are in the West. Street vendors tend to set up around 9am and pack up their wares at dusk. Shops in Thamel open around 9am and usually stay open until 9pm. Shops around tourist attractions such as Swayambunath, Boudhanath, and the Durbar Squares tend to open around 9 or 9:30am (when the first tour buses arrive) and close around 6pm. Upscale shops on Durbar Marg generally open at 10am and close at 6pm. Although most shops are open every day, some in Thamel and along Durbar Marg are closed on Saturday, the Nepali weekend.

**SHIPPING IT HOME**    If at all possible, I recommend that you carry your purchases with you when you leave the country. However, since most people flying out of Kathmandu receive a baggage allotment of only 25 kilograms (55 lb.), it is not always feasible to take all purchases onto the plane as baggage. Should you decide to mail a package home, you can either go to the **Foreign Post Office** on Kantipath beside the main post office and deal with it yourself (a time-consuming and often frustrating process), or pay a shipping company a little bit extra to deal with it for you. We recommend the latter option. Reputable companies include **Speedway Cargo** (call ☎ 410765 or 410595 and get directions; e-mail raju@speedway.mos.com.np); **Muktinath de Cargo** (☎ 417030 or 415378; e-mail: muktinat@vishnu.ccsl.com.np), located in Thamel; and **Kailash Exports** (☎ 258090 or 258969; e-mail: export@ tekhan.mos.com.np). The Kailash Exports office is located in an alley off Thamel Chowk near the United Parcel Service office. Alternatively, you could try **United Parcel Service** (UPS) or **DHL** (call ☎ 222358 or 223222 and get directions). UPS is less expensive than DHL. The Thamel branch of UPS is at Thamel Chowk, second floor (☎ 423300); look for their large sign. The main branch is on Exhibition Road, Kathmandu (☎ 230215).

Air freight generally takes about 7 to 10 days to the United States; sea mail is not recommended. Charges for shipping per kilogram go down as the weight of the package increases. Prices vary with the destination, and service charges vary with the agent. Service charges include paperwork for customs, packing material, and sometimes clearance from the Department of Archeology if the objects seem to be antique. Look for a reputable shipping company rather than the lowest price. Paying the lowest price may mean that you end up having to pay additional shipping charges when you receive your package at home. Also, be sure to ask about insurance for your package.

## SHOPPING AREAS

Though curios and souvenirs can be purchased at virtually every tourist attraction in the Kathmandu Valley, there are areas that are better for certain items. The main shopping areas include the following:

**Bhaktapur**   Known as the wood-carving capital of Nepal, Bhaktapur still produces the carved windows that you have admired in old palaces and temples around the valley. Bhaktapur is also a good place to shop for thangkas (Tibetan Buddhist religious paintings). Around town, you'll see many thangka studios.

**Boudhanath**   This huge Tibetan Buddhist shrine is surrounded by shops selling all types of religious curios, antiques, objets d'art, and goods of Tibetan origin. The vendors and shopkeepers seem to acquire a lot of old Tibetan pieces from pilgrims who have journeyed from Tibet. Consequently, this is a good place to find things you won't see anywhere else in town. I have found that prices here are lower for many items frequently sold by street vendors in Kathmandu.

**Durbar Marg**   On Kathmandu's upscale shopping, restaurant, and hotel street, prices are the highest in town, but the quality is also tops. This is where to head if you are looking for Tibetan antiques or the best that Nepal has to offer in the way of fine cast-metal figures of Tibetan Buddhist and Hindu deities. In recent years, however, this street has begun catering primarily to wealthy Indian tourists, and more and more storefronts are being taken over by jewelry stores, import shoe stores, and other clothing stores that will be of little interest to Western visitors.

**Durbar Square, Basantapur Square, and Freak Street**   This area has a little bit of everything for sale either on the street or in tiny shops in ancient buildings. On Durbar Square itself, there are a couple of antiques shops, and around the edge of Basantapur Square, there are numerous mask sellers. Basantapur Square itself is always filled with dozens of souvenir vendors, who can often be seen giving their wares an instant antique look. Be sure to bargain hard here; vendors have been weaned on tour buses. Freak Street has lots of shops selling cheap fashions and jewelry.

**Indrachowk, Asan Tole, and Kel Tole**   Kathmandu's main market area is a narrow street that runs from Durbar Square to Rani Pokhari, changing names about every block. Along this street you'll find sari shops, bead sellers, produce vendors, shawl and carpet vendors, brass merchants, basket sellers, shops selling fascinating household goods (the uses of which you may only be able to guess at), and much more.

**Pashupatinath**   Most vendors at Pashupatinath, Kathmandu's most important Hindu temple, are in business to sell to Hindu pilgrims, not tourists (though there are a few selling tourist souvenirs). Interesting buys include holy beads and stone Shiva linga. Also keep an eye out for hand-carved wooden blocks that are used for making block-printed fabric.

**Patan**   Known for its metalworkers, Patan is the place to go for cast-metal figures of Buddhist and Hindu deities. All around Patan's Durbar Square and on the narrow streets leading to the Golden Temple are dozens of shops offering quality bronze, brass, and copper figurines at good prices. Between Durbar Square and the Mahaboudha Temple, you also pass many more metalworkers' shops, and within this temple's courtyard are still more such shops.

**Swayambunath**   Lots of little shops around this ancient Buddhist stupa sell Buddhist religious relics and souvenirs. On the steps leading up to the stupa, you'll pass vendors selling mani stones. These are inexpensive and make unique paperweights and jewelry.

**Thamel**   This is the budget traveler's neighborhood and the city's main tourist shopping district. Thamel has a little bit of everything for sale. Of particular interest are Kathmandu fashions (primarily for budget travelers and the 20-something crowd), embroidered T-shirts (given 24 hours, the shops can make any design you want), silver

## Paris, New York, Kathmandu?

While Kathmandu has for many years been a great place to shop for traditional handicrafts, silver jewelry, and funky neohippie clothing, it has not exactly been known for its upscale shopping opportunities. However, with the recent opening of Baber Mahal Revisited, that has changed. This shopping and dining arcade is housed in the restored stables, cow sheds, and outbuildings of the Baber Mahal palace, which was built in 1919 along neoclassical European architectural lines. Patterned after Covent Garden and Boston's Quincy Market, Baber Mahal Revisited consists of five small courtyards that house about 20 interesting shops, including jewelry stores, fashion boutiques, and antiques stores. There are also five restaurants here. **Baber Mahal Revisited (☎ 253337)** is located in the Thapathali neighborhood near the bridge between Kathmandu and Patan.

If, when you packed for your trip to Nepal, you remembered your hiking boots, approach shoes, rock-climbing shoes, and river sandals, but forgot your black leather dress shoes, all is not lost. You can now pick up a pair at Kathmandu's very own Bally shoe store, which is just off Durbar Square in one of the few new buildings in the city to be constructed in the traditional Newari style.

and turquoise jewelry, and books. This is also where you'll find the most trekking supply shops (many of them selling that cheap, counterfeit gear).

# SHOPPING A TO Z
## ANTIQUES

There are dozens of shops along Durbar Marg, in Thamel, at Boudhanath Stupa, and in Patan that sell antiques, near-antiques, and fakes. However, it is illegal to remove any genuine Nepali antiques from Nepal. The government is especially concerned that the country's religious art and antiques do not disappear because, in the past 20 to 30 years, Nepal's cultural and religious possessions have been ravaged by antiques collectors. Active temples all over the country have been plundered, and even a few of the most venerated statues have disappeared. The wholesale theft of religious artwork has gotten so bad that many precious objects are now chained and bolted down.

It is, however, legal to export Tibetan, Bhutanese, Indian, and Ladakhi antiques, all of which show up in Kathmandu shops. Keep in mind, though, that theft of religious antiques is not limited to Nepal. Just because a Tibetan antique is for sale does not mean that it wasn't stolen from a temple in Tibet. Any object that looks even remotely antique, and in fact any religious curio, which includes bells, masks, thangkas, and metal statuettes, need to be cleared with the **Department of Archaeology,** Ram Shah Path (☎ 213701). Clearance usually takes only a few minutes if you do it yourself. Most shops will take care of this for you if you are making a large purchase, but they will probably require a day or two. The process costs only a few rupees per object, and after the object is passed, a wax seal will be affixed to it. When travelers are leaving Nepal, very thorough customs inspections are sometimes conducted. Inspectors are primarily looking for antiques and drugs. Should you have something that could be deemed an antique that doesn't have the archaeology department's wax seal, you will have to leave it in Nepal or take it to get the stamp.

The single-best place to shop for Tibetan antiques is at Boudhanath, where you'll find dozens of small antiques shops selling everything from old jewelry to huge Tibetan lacquered trunks and folding tables. There are also several good Tibetan antiques shops on Durbar Marg, though these tend to charge more than the shops at Boudhanath. Prices are generally quite high, though they are a bit lower than you would pay for the same item in the United States.

**Potala Gallery.** Durbar Marg. ☎ 223375. Sun–Fri 10am–5pm.

Crammed full of Tibetan antiquities, this street-level shop is similar to the nearby Ritual Art Gallery and is a good place to shop for high-quality (and expensive) Tibetan antiques.

**Ritual Art Gallery.** Durbar Marg. ☎ **226409.** Sun–Fri 10am–5pm.

Located about midway down Durbar Marg two flights up from the street, this store specializes in Tibetan ethnographic art and antiquities. There's an excellent collection of old Tibetan carpets and many beautiful iron and gold pieces such as horse stirrups and knives. This shop has long been one of Kathmandu's most respected dealers of Tibetan antiquities.

**Zambala.** Thamel. ☎ **221425.**

Zambala specializes in Bhutanese and Tibetan handicrafts, including ethnic textiles, tribal jewelry, and wooden masks both old and new. Zambala has two shops, one across the street from the Potala Guest House and one around the corner to the east of the Potala Guest House.

## ART

Most art in Nepal is religious in nature, and both Hindu and Buddhist iconography is represented in paintings, metal statues, wood carvings, and terra-cotta figures. Of course, there is good art and there is bad art. To get an idea of what to look for in a thangka or bronze statue, go into a store that appears to sell quality pieces, and ask to see the most expensive piece in the shop. Then ask to see the least expensive comparable piece. If you cannot readily see the differences in quality, ask the proprietor to tell you why one is so expensive and the other is not. Shopkeepers in Kathmandu are usually very friendly and willing to explain their merchandise to you.

### Contemporary Art

**Dangol's Art Gallery.** Hotel Soaltee Rd., Kalamati. ☎ **278345.** Daily 10am–5:30pm.

Artist H. L. Dangol is famous among bird lovers for the illustrations he created for the book *Birds of Nepal.* On display here are both his bird and wildlife paintings and the paintings of his children. You'll find Dangol's opposite the Soaltee Crowne Plaza Kathmandu Hotel.

**Indigo Gallery.** At Mike's Breakfast, Naxal. ☎ **413580.** Daily 8am–5:30pm.

Located on the second floor of the old building at Mike's Breakfast, this gallery sells unique crafts and exhibits the work of both local and international artists.

**The October Gallery.** Hotel Vajra, Bijeswari, Swayambhu. ☎ **271545.** Sun–Fri 5–9pm.

This gallery features works by local and international artists and mounts exhibits of contemporary and traditional Nepali arts.

### Metal Statues

Bronze, copper, and brass statuettes of Hindu and Buddhist deities are among the most beautiful works of art in Nepal. They come in a wide variety of sizes, from tiny figures less than half an inch tall to giant statues weighing hundreds of pounds. There is an equally wide range of quality, so no matter what your budget, you should be able to find something to your liking. Just remember to have it stamped by the Department of Archaeology if it looks even vaguely antique.

These statues are made by the lost-wax process of metalworking. In this process the figure is carved in a piece of wax, which is then covered with clay. The wax is melted, and the cavity is filled with molten metal. After the metal cools, the clay is removed, the figure is cleaned, and fine details are added. You can see metal statues being made in small factories at the **Patan Industrial Estate,** southwest of Patan's Durbar Square on Sat Dobato. These factories also have showrooms, but the prices and selection are not as good as in the shops around Patan's Durbar Square and outside the Mahaboudha Temple in Patan. Shops on Durbar Marg in Kathmandu sell the highest-quality pieces and cost hundreds to thousands of dollars. If you visit the National Museum in Kathmandu, you'll see that many of the statues that are made today are similar in design to metal sculptures created hundreds of years ago.

### Thangkas

Buddhist religious scrolls painted on canvas are very popular with tourists. The scrolls commonly depict Buddhist deities and the Buddhist wheel of life. They may be very simple, depicting a single deity, or they may be incredibly detailed, with hundreds of figures, some painted with single-hair brushes, covering the canvas. There are thangka shops on Durbar Marg and in Thamel, Patan, and Bhaktapur. In many shops, you can see the artists at work. Several thangka shops around Bhaktapur's Durbar Square have open studio areas. If you are interested in comparing contemporary Thangkas with antique ones, visit the National Museum (see "Museums & Other Attractions," in the "Kathmandu" section of this chapter), where old ones are on display.

**Casa Del Art.** Makhan Tole. ☎ **223469.**

Located downstairs from the Festive Fare restaurant, this is one of the better thangka shops in Kathmandu's Durbar Square area. The quality is high and the prices are surprisingly reasonable.

## BOOKS

Kathmandu is a book lover's paradise. In Thamel there are dozens of small bookshops, some of them no larger than a closet, where you can find an astounding array of new and used books from around the world. You'll find books in English, French, German, Italian, Spanish, Japanese, Swedish, Dutch, and other languages.

Most bookshops will buy your used paperbacks, depending on resale value. Also, you can usually return a book to the store where you purchased it and get 50% of the price back. I like to take a stack of unwanted books with me to Kathmandu and swap them for new ones, which I read and return for my 50% rebate.

Though best-sellers and general fiction are the mainstays of the Kathmandu bookshops, the shops also have the largest selection I've ever seen of books on the Himalayas, including titles focusing on Nepal, Tibet, Bhutan, Ladakh, mountain climbing, trekking in the Himalayas, and wildlife. Dozens of picture books are available and, though expensive, are well worth the expense if you didn't shoot any award-winning photos while you were here. There's also one of the world's widest selections of books on religion and esoteric subjects.

**✪ Pilgrims Book House.** Thamel. ☎ **424942.** Daily 8am–10pm.

Located just a few doors up from the Kathmandu Guest House gate, this bookstore specializes in books on Hinduism, Tibetan Buddhism, yoga, Eastern medicine, and spiritual quests. It also has a wide selection of books on other topics and is one of the largest bookstores in Kathmandu. Pilgrims Book House in Patan, opposite the Hotel Himalaya (☎ **521159**) is another large bookstore under the same management.

## CARPETS

Wool carpets are among Nepal's best shopping deals, but it pays to know a bit about the carpets available. The carpets that are a genuine value in Nepal are those known as **Tibetan carpets.** These thick wool carpets, though generally not made in Tibet, are, for the most part, based on Tibetan designs. Traditionally, such hand-knotted carpets have been used as seat and bench cushions and as pony saddles. However, for the tourist trade, these carpets are designed for use on the floor, with the most popular size being roughly 3 feet by 6 feet (1m by 2m).

Carpets generally come in three common grades, based on the number of knots per square inch—60 knot, 80 knot, and 100 knot. The more knots there are, the more time it takes to make the carpet and thus the more expensive the carpet will be. The 60-knot carpets are generally made with a mix of Tibetan and New Zealand wool that has been hand spun on spinning wheels. The 80-knot carpets are usually made with machine-spun yarn from New Zealand (or a mix of New Zealand and Tibetan wool) and are not as durable (or as heavy) as the 60-knot carpets. The 100-knot carpets are the most durable and are usually made either entirely from Tibetan wool or with a higher percentage of Tibetan wool than is usually found in 80-knot carpets. By hand spinning the wool using drop spindles, a tighter, stronger yarn is produced, thus allowing more knots per square inch.

Traditional Tibetan carpets tend to be in rich, dark colors, especially dark blue, deep red, and orange. Old and antique carpets made in Tibet are available at many of the carpet shops around town. These carpets are usually made with a finer grade of wool (supposedly a mix of lamb's wool and silk), producing a very soft, smooth carpet with a bit of shine to it, and they are always in traditional designs that are not to everyone's liking. They often cost two to three times the price of a new made-in-Nepal carpet.

Once you have decided what kind of carpet you'd like to buy, ask yourself the following questions: Is the color uniform throughout the carpet? Occasionally, a different batch of yarn (and consequently a slightly different color) is incorporated into a carpet halfway through production. Are the knots tight? Loose knots are a sign of a poorly made carpet that will not last many years. Is the design straight? On a well-made carpet the design will remain even from one end to the other without developing a slant to it. Is the trimming well defined? The designs in traditional Tibetan carpets are defined by the trimming around the edges of any color change. Also, the surface should be of an even height so that the carpet appears very smooth. Are design details complete and symmetrical? If you don't study a carpet carefully, you won't notice until too late that design details or patterns have not been completed. For example, a flower might not be connected to its stem or a square may be missing a side.

In the Kathmandu Valley, the best place to shop for Tibetan carpets is at the carpet factory adjacent to the **Tibetan Refugee Camp** (☎ 521305) in Jawalakhel, Patan. The factory is open Sunday through Friday from 8am to noon and 1 to 5pm, and a tour here will familiarize you with all the stages of making these carpets, from dying to knotting to trimming. After your tour, you can look through the carpets in the factory's three large showrooms. The designs here range from traditional to contemporary, and there are plenty of carpets to choose from in a wide range of sizes. However, you'll find better prices in the shops just up the street from the camp. Carpet prices at the factory have remained stable for quite a few years now. A 60-knot carpet costs about $80 per square meter; an 80-knot carpet costs around $110 per square meter; and a 100-knot carpet of all Tibetan wool will be $200 per square meter.

**Kashmiri carpets** in silk and cotton are also readily available in Kathmandu, especially in Thamel. These carpets are identified by their finely detailed arabesques and floral motifs. They are thin (less than ¼ in.) with a very rich silky texture and, because they are made with many more knots per square inch than Tibetan carpets, are quite expensive. Common grades of Kashmiri silk carpets include 324, 576, 784, and 1024 knots per square inch. As the knot count increases, the texture of the rug becomes richer and the price goes up. A 2-foot by 3-foot 784-knot rug will cost about $1,100; a 1,024-knot rug of the same size will set you back about $1,950.

Beware of silk carpets that aren't the real thing. Vendors will tell you that they are made of silk, but this isn't always true, as you'll find out when the carpet wears out within a few years. If you're interested in a Kashmiri carpet, stop by **Falcon Arts,** Hotel Pisang Shop No. 8, Thamel (☎ 223778), where the proprietor will gladly explain to you the ins and outs of silk carpets.

## FASHION

One unusual Kathmandu fashion bargain that should not be passed up is the machine-embroidered T-shirt. Though several standard designs are found in every store, shops are more than happy to embroider your own design onto a shirt. They'll even put designs on your clothes for you. It usually takes no more than a day or two to have something custom embroidered.

**Children's Clothing**   Colorful children's clothes in all the popular Kathmandu styles can be found in Thamel and on Freak Street. These clothes are usually 100% cotton or wool and are an exceptional deal if the child you are dressing doesn't mind looking a bit like a hippie. Wool sweaters are one of the better buys for children, as are multi-colored jackets and overalls.

**Men's Clothing**   Attractive all-cotton button-down shirts are available. Wool sweaters, heavy wool coats, and casual jackets are also good buys. Try the shops in Thamel and on Freak Street. If they don't have something in your size, they'll make it up for you overnight. You will undoubtedly have noticed the jaunty little caps the Nepali men wear. These caps, called *topes,* look a bit like fezzes that have been punched in on one side. You'll find topes for sale in the main market near Indrachowk.

**Women's Clothing**   Though the dress shops of Kathmandu aren't as well-known as those in Bangkok, many do good work, and it takes only a day or two to have a pair of pants, skirt, or dress made. Every year, fashions change in Kathmandu, but they do not follow Western trends. Kathmandu fashions are in a world all their own. If your fashion tastes lean toward conservative, you may not find anything you like.

Among the best fashion buys in Kathmandu are sweaters, jackets, and coats. The clothing shops in Thamel have a wide variety of colorful wool sweaters, heavy wool jackets, and cotton coats. Shawls made from pashmina (cashmere) wool, the soft underbelly wool of a mountain goat, are also available. They're wonderfully soft and extremely warm. You'll find stacks of pashmina shawls for sale at tourist shops throughout Kathmandu.

**Chrysalis,** Thamel. No phone. Daily 10am–6pm.

Located upstairs from the Northfield Café, this shop has nice quality casual wear in natural fabrics such as silk and linen. You can also have your clothing custom made.

**Wheels Boutique.** Durbar Marg, ☎ 224554. Sun–Fri 10:30am–6:30pm.

Located on the second floor of a building about halfway down Durbar Marg, Wheels Boutique offers custom-designed women's fashions. Locally made raw silk in rich colors is the primary fabric used for the beautifully tailored blouses, jackets, and coats that are the shop's most popular creations. For custom work, you need to make an appointment.

**Yasmine.** Kasturi Arcade, Durbar Marg. ☎ **227864.** Sun–Fri 11am–6pm.

This shop is located near Wheels Boutique (see above). It also carries high-quality clothing, but the styles are a bit more conservative here. Make an appointment for custom work.

## GIFTS & SOUVENIRS

Gifts and souvenirs are available almost anywhere in Kathmandu. However, the best selections are in Thamel and around Durbar Square. In spots frequented by tourists, vendors will often follow you around trying to sell you trinkets. Be sure to bargain if you decide to buy from one of them.

In recent years Kupondole, the street leading up from the Bagmati Bridge into Patan, has become a center for craft shops that are supported by international aid organizations. Profits go directly back to the craftspeople, who are primarily women. In these shops you'll find not only traditional crafts, but also modern applications of traditional techniques visible in such items as handwoven place mats. Many of these craft items are not available anywhere else in Kathmandu.

**Dhukuti Shop.** Kopundole, Patan. ☎ **535107.** Daily 9am–7pm.

This is another craft shop that serves as an outlet for various development projects. Proceeds from sales of the shop's pillow covers, bedspreads, leather bags, lamps, baskets, place mats, and other items go directly to the craftspeople themselves.

**Mahaguthi.** Durbar Square, Patan. ☎ **534091.** Sun–Fri 10am–5pm. Lazimpat and Kupondole shops open Sat also 10am to 5pm.

Profits from this shop support the Tulasi Mehar Ashram, a refuge and training center for destitute women and children. When you buy here, you know that your money is going directly to the women who produced the handcrafts. Among the attractive, well-made items are beautiful hand-printed note cards, colorful pillow covers, embroidered napkins and place mats, and stylish clothes made from local textiles. There are other Mahaguthi shops on Kupondole in Patan and Lazimpat in Kathmandu.

**Sana Hastakala.** Ga 1/113 Kupondole. ☎ **522628.** Sun–Fri 9:30am–6pm, Sat 10am–5pm.

Located directly across from the Hotel Himalaya, this craft shop is supported by UNICEF and has a wide assortment of interesting and inexpensive items. Specialties include handmade paper, pillow covers, and ceramics.

## JEWELRY

Silver jewelry is another of Nepal's good buys and is sold primarily in shops in Durbar Marg, Thamel, and Freak Street. Much of this jewelry is made with turquoise and coral, as well as a few other semiprecious stones such as malachite, lapis lazuli, and amethyst. All types of bangles and baubles are available, with traditional Tibetan designs predominating. Particularly attractive are bead necklaces, found at many shops in Thamel. Antique Tibetan jewelry is also readily available, though prices are quite steep.

**Marzan.** Baber Mahal Revisited, Thapathali. ☎ **251653**.

For higher-end jewelry than you'll find in Thamel, check out this shop in the Baber Mahal Revisited shopping arcade (see the "Paris, New York, Kathmandu?" box). They carry 18k gold and silver jewelry and also do custom work.

**Sterling Silver Traders.** Thamel. ☎ **271671**.

Located diagonally across from the Potala Guest House, this store has been in business for years and is a reliable source of inexpensive silver jewelry in an eclectic array of designs. The **Sophia Gift House,** a few doors north, is another good place to shop for silver jewelry.

## MARKETS

Kathmandu's main market area is a long, narrow street that cuts diagonally through the old city from Hanuman Dhoka Square to Rani Pokhari (Queen's Pond) on Kantipath near Ratna Park. With each block the market street changes its name, and, in fact, it is better known by the names of the squares through which it passes.

Starting with **Makhan Tole** at the northeast corner of Hanuman Dhoka Square, you pass by shops selling thangkas, clothes for tourists, and saris. At **Indrachowk,** the next square, you will find flower sellers making garlands from marigolds and poinsettia bracts. Married Nepali women traditionally do not wear a wedding ring but wear several strands of shiny beads passing through a gold tube called a *tilhari.* The bead bazaar opposite the tiled temple is where many of these traditional necklaces are made. There are dozens of stalls hung with shimmering strands of beads. You can design your own necklace and have it made up on the spot. At the base of the temple on the north side of this square, sellers of pashmina shawls and felt rugs display their wares in colorful stacks.

As you continue along this road away from Indrachowk, you will pass shops selling carpets, brass and copper pots and household items, baskets, plastic kitchenwares, and saris. Down a side street to the left are numerous shops selling thin mattresses and quilts. The men in long skirts leaning against what seem to be single-stringed musical instruments are stuffing fluffers. Their instruments are used not for music but to fluff up the cotton or kapok stuffing of mattresses that have become matted down.

**Asan Tole,** the next square, is one of Kathmandu's main produce markets, and the crowds can be absolutely daunting. *Be especially careful with your valuables here.* If you happen to be here anytime between November and January, be sure to buy some mandarins. They're the best I've ever tasted. Remember to bargain.

## METAL WORK

Until very recently, Nepali housewares such as pots, pitchers, bowls, glasses, water jars, and oil lamps were made from brass, bronze, and copper and were often ornately decorated. Today, these items are rapidly being replaced by plastic and aluminum products, and as a result, the beautiful old pieces are slowly disappearing. However, shops selling new housewares often receive old pieces in exchange. As you wander the streets of Kathmandu, Bhaktapur, and Patan, keep your eye out for old copper pots in market shops. Though they're heavy, they are quite inexpensive.

**Khukuri House.** Thamel. ☎ **412314**.

Located near the Rum Doodle Restaurant, this gleaming showroom is filled with various styles of authentic *khukuris,* which are the distinctive knives carried by Nepal's famed Gurhka soldiers. This shop is owned by a former Gurkha soldier, and considering the high quality of craftsmanship, prices are extremely reasonable.

**Singing Bowl Centre.** Boudhanath Stupa. ☎ **479801**.

Singing bowls, musical instruments traditionally used for meditation, are made of various metals and when played have a hypnotic vibrating note. There are hundreds to choose from at this shop.

## WOOD CARVINGS

Bhaktapur has been known as the wood-carving center of the Kathmandu Valley for centuries, and this ancient art is continued today by several wood-carving shops in this city. If you have become enamored of the intricately carved wooden lattice windows that decorate the temples and palaces of the valley, you might want to take one home. Small versions of these windows are available and will fit easily in a suitcase or backpack. The scaled-down replica of the famous Bhaktapur peacock window is particularly popular. If you feel this is too ornate for you, perhaps a simple picture or mirror frame will be more to your taste.

**Himalayan Wood Carving Masterpieces.** Dattatreya Square, Bhaktapur. ☎ **610754**.

This shop has its showrooms on the second floor right next door to the National Woodworking Museum. They usually have a few full-size windows on display for those planning an architectural undertaking. A large window can cost as much as $2,500, but a small one can be had for around $400.

## 7  Kathmandu After Dark

Kathmandu has never been known as a late-night town. Locals tend to be early-to-bed-and-early-to-rise types (up and about long before the sun comes up), and most travelers are too jet-lagged to stay up late, are saving their energy for a trek, or are recovering their energy after a trek. The most interesting after-dark activity is simply wandering the streets of old Kathmandu. As you wander the streets at night, listen for traditional Nepali music. In the evenings, impromptu bands often perform at small temples all over the city. This is also a good time to do your shopping since many shops catering to tourists stay open until 9pm. If you're dying to experience video night in Kathmandu, check the restaurants around Thamel. Many show videos, usually pirated, of the latest Hollywood releases. There's also a video theater at the Kathmandu Guest House. Local movie theaters, on the other hand, will likely be of little interest to travelers. They are generally as crowded and dirty as local buses and show almost exclusively Bollywood (Bombay) "masala" movies.

### CULTURAL PROGRAMS

Other than bars, the main nightlife in Kathmandu consists of "cultural programs." These are performances of traditional (and sometimes not-so-traditional) Nepali songs and dances. These programs are staged at numerous restaurants around town, as well as at a handful of theaters. If you're attending a performance at a restaurant, the show will be free of charge, but if you attend one at a theater, you'll have to pay an admission of around Rs300 ($4.55). Restaurants with cultural performances include Naachgar at the Hotel Yak & Yeti, Himalchuli at the Soaltee Crowne Plaza Kathmandu, Bhanchha Ghar, and Bhojan Griha. See "Dining" in chapter 4 for details.

Cultural programs are also staged by the **Everest Cultural Society** (☎ 220676), which has its theater on the grounds of the Hotel de l'Annapurna, and the **New Himalchuli Cultural Group**, B.G. Plaza, Lazimpat (☎ 415280), which has its theater just north of the Hotel Manaslu behind the Peace Zone School.

Another place to check for interesting theater and dance programs is the **Naga Theater** (☎ 272719) at the Hotel Vajra, which is on the road to Swayambunath Stupa. The Hotel Vajra is a regular cultural center with a theater, an art gallery, and a library of books on Eastern subjects. The Naga Theater includes the International Actors' Ensemble Studio 7 and the Institute of Classical Nepalese Performing Arts. They usually give classical Nepali dance performances during the peak tourist seasons. This theater also stages avant-garde theater productions. Admission to dance performances is Rs300 ($4.55).

## THE BAR SCENE

Even in the bustling metropolis of Kathmandu, bars are officially supposed to close at 10pm. However, in bustling Thamel, this rule is generally overlooked, and bars there now stay open until midnight or later. If you aren't staying in Thamel, chances are you'll find a quiet little bar in the lobby of your hotel. All of the major hotels in Kathmandu have bars, and many of these feature live Western (meaning English-language) music several nights a week.

Wandering the streets of Thamel, you'll encounter a dozen or more bars that place an emphasis on loud music and appeal to the young backpacking crowd. Cheap beer and cocktails are the main attraction here, with a large locally brewed beer or mixed drink (made from domestic spirits) usually going for between Rs110 ($1.65) and Rs160 ($2.40). These days there's a brisk business in happy hours, and if you shop around, you can find some good drink deals. Among the more popular Thamel bars are the following:

**Blue Note Bar/New Orleans Café.** Across from Kathmandu Guest House, Thamel. ☎ **425736.**

Though the live and recorded jazz music here might sound familiar, the setting, complete with a traditional temple-style building in a corner of the courtyard, is purely Nepali. Great atmosphere!

**Maya Cocktail Bar.** On an alley near Hotel Excelsior, Thamel. No phone.

With great cocktails and a very long happy hour, this multistory bar is a good place to wind down at the end of the day.

**Maya Pub.** Across from The Third Eye, Thamel. No phone.

This upstairs pub has long been one of the loudest and rowdiest party spots in Thamel.

**Rum Doodle.** 1 block east of Hotel Garuda, Thamel. ☎ **414336.**

With mountaineering and kayaking gear strewn all over the upstairs bar, Rum Doodle has long been Kathmandu's most popular bar. Cutout yeti footprints signed by famous adventurers and mountaineers are plastered on the walls. Grab a stool at the bar, and you may find yourself rubbing shoulders with someone just back from bagging Mount Everest.

**Tom & Jerry's.** Across from Kathmandu Guest House, Thamel. ☎ **228997.**

This upstairs pub has pool tables and something of a British pub atmosphere.

**The Tunnel Club.** Behind Hotel Excelsior, Thamel. ☎ **429943.**

Located just off Thamel's main square, this is a big pool hall and snooker parlor.

**Underground.** Between Tridevi Marg and the main square, Thamel. No phone.

This basement-level bar serves as Thamel's disco, with loud dance music, lots of flashing lights, and hip Nepali men doing their best to score with the foreigners.

## GAMBLING CASINOS

Because gambling casinos are prohibited in India, Kathmandu does a brisk business catering to vacationing Indians interested in doing a bit of wagering. Games played include flush, poker, baccarat, paplu, pontoon, and jackpot, and all play in U.S. dollars or Indian rupees. There are currently four casinos in Kathmandu: **Casino Nepal** at Soaltee Crowne Plaza Kathmandu, Tahachal (☎ **270244** or 271011); **Casino Everest,** Everest Hotel, New Baneswor (☎ **488100**); **Casino Royale,** Hotel Yak &

Yeti, Durbar Marg (☎ 228481 or 410007); and **Casino Anna,** Hotel de l'Annapurna, Durbar Marg (☎ 223479 or 227812). All of these casinos are open 24 hours
a day, and all four offer complimentary transportation.

## Readers Recommend

**Casino Anna**   "This place is straight out of the seventies, and hilariously so, sort
of like the lounge of some St. Louis Holiday Inn, the main difference being the
wacky Indian pop music pumping through the joint. Slot machines are the true
one-armed bandits (no push buttons here!) and hail from the Vegas-McCann Airport (they still bear the McCann Airport/Barbary Coast placards). My husband
played blackjack, which here is played with five decks. Of course, if you're gambling, the waitresses bring you cocktails for free. I noticed a strange lack of women
in this place—very 'boys club' feeling. In Vegas terms, I would class this as an old-
school, downtown-type casino."

**Casino Royale**   "Definitely uptown. The building is an old Rana residence and it
is fab! The gaming area here is *gorgeous:* super-high ceilings, crown molding, gilt all
over the place, beveled mirrors that were imported from Belgium 150 years ago.
There is a plethora of women here—both gambling and employed by the casino
(actually, we even saw *kids* here in this casino). My husband again played blackjack,
and even our dealer was female, but it was a most bizarre session of blackjack
indeed. As at the Casino Anna, it was played with five decks. Unlike in Vegas, however, the dealer did *not* stick at 17. Also, the manner of shuffling was *hilarious:* basically they take all of the cards, smear them across the blackjack table in a manner I
can only compare to playing Go Fish, swirl them around, and then deal. Gambling
purists would have a coronary, but a Vegas card shark could make a killing here—
cards are bent, sticky, tattered at the corners. I could not help but laugh at the
thought of some Vegas pit boss walking around this casino just having seizures!

"There is a whole fleet of fabulously beautiful women in a rainbow array of silk-
satin saris who just wander around making sure people have drinks, answering
questions about how to play the games, and just being very nice and helpful. There
is a fantastic buffet open from 9pm to 1am and free for anyone gambling here—
and it is most decidedly several thousand steps above anything in Vegas. You can
take the salmon, sirloin steaks, Indian food, Nepali food, and spaghetti bolognese
you've loaded on your plate and sit at any of the linen-dressed tables in the buffet
room listening to the most (unintentionally) hilarious Indian pop band playing live
for your dining enjoyment. . . . If you're only going to visit one casino in Nepal, I
would have to say, make it this one. I didn't gamble one spec here and still had a
blast."

—*Erin Culley-LaChapelle, Los Angeles, CA*

# Kathmandu Valley Excursions

**6**

The Kathmandu Valley has for centuries been the cultural heart of Nepal, and scattered across the countryside are innumerable temples and shrines. Among these are several that are worth a visit not only for the priceless works of art they hold, but also for their remote and tranquil locations. So once you have explored Kathmandu, Patan, and Bhaktapur, it is time to head for the distant corners of the valley. In doing so, not only will you visit more of the area's fascinating temples, but you also will finally have a chance to see the countryside—the terraced fields that are so much a part of farming in Nepal. Excursions to such temples as Dakshinkali, Vajra Jogini, and Gokarneshwar offer a chance to escape the congestion of Kathmandu and see what life is like outside the city.

The Kathmandu Valley, due in large part to its rich soil, has also long been Nepal's population center. Dotting the rich agricultural lands are numerous villages and towns, some of which were formerly separate little kingdoms in much the way that Kathmandu, Patan, and Bhaktapur were separate kingdoms. **Kirtipur, Bungamati,** and **Panauti** are among the more interesting valley towns, and excursions to any of them will give you an idea of what Kathmandu looked like until quite recently.

Also found on the outer edges of the Kathmandu Valley are the easiest locations from which to take in extensive panoramas of the Himalayas. While there are views of the mountains from the Kathmandu Valley (when the smog isn't too bad), far better views are to be had from the valley's rim, which stands as much as 3,000 feet higher than the valley floor. From Dhulikhel and Nagarkot, once just quiet villages, it is possible to view almost 200 miles of snow-covered peaks. Sunrises and sunsets from these vantage points are truly remarkable and should not be missed. You can even do a bit of hiking using either of these villages as a base. A day hike along the ridges on the valley's rim will give you an idea of what trekking in Nepal is all about.

## 1 Outlying Temples, Towns & Attractions

### NORTH FROM KATHMANDU: BALAJU & BUDHANILKANTHA

Located a few miles northwest of Kathmandu in the town of Balaju at the foot of Nagarjun Hill, **Balaju Water Gardens** contain a bathing fountain with 22 dragon-headed waterspouts carved from stone. There are also other fountains, fish ponds full of huge carp, and a swimming pool. However, the most interesting feature of the park is its copy of the Sleeping Vishnu statue that is located at Budhanilkantha, a few miles northeast of here. The king of Nepal, who is considered to be an incarnation of the god Vishnu, is forbidden to view the statue at Budhanilkantha, so when it is time to pay respects to Lord Vishnu, the king visits this copy of the statue. The gardens are open daily from 8am to 6pm. Balaju makes an interesting stop before or after a hike through the forests on Nagarjun Hill.

Also nearby (about a 15-min. walk from Thamel) is the small **Mahenpi hill,** which, after Swayambunath, is the second-highest hill in Kathmandu. Located just north of the Vishnumati Bridge, and sacred to both Buddhists and Hindus, this hill is circled daily by the devout, who often sing devotional songs as they walk. The hill is the site of both a Hindu temple and a small Buddhist stupa. It also serves an important role in the repair of Kathmandu temples, many of which are required by tradition to incorporate mud from this hill.

Located north of Kathmandu on an extension of Lazimpat, ✪ **Budhanilkantha** is an unusual 15-foot-long stone statue of the god Vishnu. The statue, which rests in the middle of a small rectangular pond, depicts Vishnu reclining in a bed of snakes. Thought to be between 900 and 1,400 years old, the statue was supposedly found by a farmer plowing his fields. In the sculpture, Vishnu appears quite tranquil, seemingly content to lie atop the giant snakes and gaze up at the sky. As one of the largest sculptures in Nepal, Budhanilkantha is worshiped devoutly, and there are usually people gathered at the statue with offerings of flowers, rice, and colored powders. On special holidays, a priest officiates here, and a small boy carries special offerings from Vishnu's feet, where pilgrims gather, up to his head. The main festivals at Budhanilkantha take place at the beginning and end of the monsoon season. Vishnu is said to sleep during the 4 months of the monsoon.

It is believed that if the king of Nepal ever sets eyes on this statue of Vishnu, he will fall down dead because the king himself is considered an incarnation of Vishnu. However, on Vishnu's two main festival days each year, the king pays his respect by visiting a replica (actually a similar statue) at the Balaju Water Gardens.

A taxi to Budhanilkantha should cost around Rs250 ($3.80) each way, whereas a taxi to Balaju costs only Rs75 ($1.15).

## KIRTIPUR TO DAKSHINKALI

A short distance south of the Ring Road above the campus of Tribhuvan University stands the ancient town of ✪ **Kirtipur.** Built on a hill overlooking the Kathmandu Valley, Kirtipur was once an independent kingdom, and because of its strategic hilltop location, it was the last kingdom conquered by King Prithvi Narayan Shah when he unified Nepal in the late 18th century. Perhaps as a result of Kirtipur's legendary stubbornness, the town has been relatively unaffected by the rapid development that has changed Kathmandu so dramatically in recent years. For this reason, Kirtipur is well worth a visit. The narrow streets are not clogged with smoke-belching trucks, and cement buildings have not yet replaced all of the traditional brick buildings of this Newari town.

The town is most interesting simply as a place to catch a glimpse of traditional Nepali culture. The streets are full of activity, as are the farm fields below the town. Strolling through Kirtipur's narrow lanes, you will come across several small temples. Of particular interest is the three-story **Bagh Bhairav Temple** near the center of town. Nailed to the facade of this temple are a few swords that were once used by the soldiers who fruitlessly defended Kirtipur against the troops of King Prithvi Narayan

Shah. Also in the center of town, on a hill to the east of the Bagh Bharirav Temple, you will find the 30-foot-tall **Chilancho Stupa,** which was built in 1515 and is similar to those at Swayambunath and Boudhanath. Five smaller stupas and several shrines surround this stupa.

Continuing south on the road to Dakshinkali, you come to **Chovar Gorge,** the only outlet for the rivers draining the Kathmandu Valley. A legend holds that this gorge was created when the Tibetan god Manjushri used his sword to slice through the mountains and drain the lake that once filled the Kathmandu Valley. It is easy to believe such a myth when you see the narrow chasm of Chovar Gorge. At the lower mouth of the gorge stands the **Jal Binayak Temple,** a three-tiered pagoda dedicated to the elephant-headed Hindu god Ganesh. Although this temple dates only to the 17th century, there has probably been a temple here since as early as A.D. 600, during the Licchavi period.

South of Chovar Gorge, you come to Pharping, site of the **Sekh Narayan Temple,** which is dedicated to Vishnu, here depicted in his incarnation as the dwarf Vishnu Vikrantha. The temple is tucked into the base of an overhanging cliff, and below it are numerous ponds full of fish, which are considered holy because Vishnu once appeared on earth in the form of a fish. In one of these ponds stands a stone carving of Surya, the sun god, which likely dates to the 13th century. Beside this Hindu temple, there is now a Buddhist monastery.

Above the village of Pharping stands the 17th-century **Vajra Jogini Temple,** which is up a long flight of stairs from the village. A short walk from this temple is the now-much-venerated **Gorakhnath Cave,** said to have been used by a famous Buddhist saint named Gorakh.

Located in a dark wooded valley 12 miles south of Kathmandu is **Dakshinkali,** a shrine dedicated to the terrifying goddess Kali. The image of the goddess is not very big, but Hindus believe it possesses great power. Consequently, every Saturday and Tuesday, thousands of people descend on the shrine to make offerings to the goddess. Though many people bring offerings of fruits, rice, and flowers, Dakshinkali is better known as a place of animal sacrifices, primarily of young male goats and chickens.

Worshipers by the thousands line up for hours in order to have their offerings blessed by the statue of Kali, and the lines of people wind down a hillside and over several bridges. At the shrine itself, total bedlam seems to rule as dozens of people crowd into the confined courtyard in front of the statue. At times it is so crowded that some people just throw offerings of coins in the general direction of the statue and over the heads of the other worshipers.

Those people with offerings of chickens and goats hand them over to a priest, who quickly beheads the animal. The blood is then sprinkled on Kali, and the worshipers depart with their sacrificed animal in hand. The goats and chickens are then usually butchered on the grounds, and the families sit down among the trees to have a picnic with their sacrifice as the main course. All along the road leading down to the temple, vendors sell food and produce to accompany these picnic meals. Most Nepalis can't afford much meat, so a sacrifice is seen as an opportunity to eat well.

These ritual sacrifices, though gruesome, are a very popular tourist excursion, but they are not for the fainthearted (a Jewish friend compared the scene here to a Nazi death camp). Nepalis, on the other hand, see the sacrifices as a cause for celebration and quite often an all-out party. Be prepared for a very bizarre mix of festival and slaughterhouse.

All tour companies in Kathmandu offer Saturday trips to Dakshinkali. These tours usually cost around Rs500 ($7.60) and stop at Chovar Gorge and the Sekh Narayan

Temple in Pharping. Alternatively, you can come here by taxi for around Rs1,000 ($15.15), making the same stops and also stopping in Kirtipur.

## SOUTH OF PATAN: BUNGAMATI, CHAPAGAON & GODAWARI

Heading due south from Patan's Tibetan Refugee Camp at Jawalakhel will bring you to **Bungamati,** a large and prosperous Newari town that was founded in the 16th century and overlooks the Bagmati River. It is here that the Rato Machendranath statue (see "Walking Tour 4—Beyond Patan's Durbar Square," in chapter 5) spends half of every year, and it is to Bungamati that, once every 12 years, this statue is pulled in a massive chariot. Bungamati's **Rato Machendranath Temple** is a shikhara-style temple rather than a pagoda, and it stands on the town's central square. On the northern outskirts of Bungamati is the **Karya Binayak shrine,** one of the Kathmandu Valley's most important Ganesh shrines. The Ganesh of this shrine is actually a natural stone that looks only vaguely like an elephant.

From the southern outskirts of Patan, two other roads lead south. The western road leads to the village of Chapagaon, and the eastern road leads to Godawari Botanical Gardens. To reach these roads, head south from Durbar Square and turn left at the bus park. After passing the Patan Industrial Estate, but before you reach the Ring Road, a fork in the road marks the start of these routes.

**Chapagaon** is a traditional Newari village of brick houses similar to those in Bungamati and Kirtipur. In the center of town is a shrine dedicated to Bhairav. Outside of town, in a grove of trees, stands the **Vajra Varahi Temple,** which is dedicated to a Tantric goddess. The temple was built in the 17th century. If you are traveling on a mountain bike or motorcycle, you may want to continue south from Chapagaon on the rough road that leads to the **Lele Valley.** This route provides additional glimpses of rural Nepali life, and the views back across the valley to the mountains are superb.

Though **Godawari Royal Botanical Gardens** are not well marked nor well cared for, they make a pleasant morning or afternoon excursion if you are exhausted from viewing temples. The focus is on Himalayan and south Asian species of trees, shrubs, and flowers, and an herbarium and orchid house contain many varieties of the Himalayas' more delicate plant species. The gardens are open daily from 10am to 5pm.

Bird-watchers will be interested to learn that the botanical gardens and **Phulchoki,** which rises above the gardens and is the highest point on the rim of the valley, are the best birding spots in the valley. There is a rough road to the top of Phulchoki, and it's possible to have a taxi drop you at the top and then wait for you down at the botanical gardens. It's a long walk down, but the birding is excellent. Start early.

The **best way to visit** Bungamati, Chapagaon, and Godawari is by hiring a taxi for the day (or for half a day). Expect to pay around Rs1,200 ($18.20) to hire a taxi for the whole day. A taxi just to Godawari will cost around Rs600 ($9.10) for the round-trip and a 1-hour wait.

## BEYOND BOUDHA: GOKARNESHWAR & VAJRA JOGINI

Located northeast of Boudhanath Stupa a few miles up the road to Sundarijal (a starting point for treks in the Helambu region), **Gokarneshwar Temple** (also called Gokarna Mahadev Temple) is set on the bank of the Bagmati River at a point where the river has cut a steep-walled little gorge. You'll find the temple on the far side of the village of **Gokarna,** which itself is on the northern edge of the Gokarna Wildlife Reserve. A wide flight of steps leads down to the river from the temple, which is almost a miniature version of Pashupatinath (though far more tranquil). This is one of the most picturesque settings of any temple in the Kathmandu Valley.

# Ten Great Ways to Escape from Kathmandu (Without Leaving Town)

If you spend more than 3 or 4 days in Kathmandu, you might begin to feel trapped by the noise, the congestion, and the inescapable street vendors and beggars. If you reach this point in your visit, here are some suggestions to get away from it all:

1. **The Roof of Your Hotel:** Just about every budget hotel in Thamel has a rooftop garden that allows you to rise above the chaos in the streets.
2. **The Garden of the Kathmandu Guest House:** The streets of Thamel can be a gauntlet of vendors and beggars and blaring car horns, but this garden, on the far side of the lobby, is a true safe haven.
3. **The Lobby and Garden of the Yak & Yeti Hotel:** With a vast expanse of polished granite in the lobby, two swimming pools in the garden, and a European-style palace off to one side, the Yak & Yeti could almost be somewhere in Italy or France.
4. **The Garden of the Hotel Shanker:** This is the largest hotel garden in Kathmandu, and it faces the neoclassical European facade of a hotel that was originally built as a palace for one of the Rana rulers of Kathmandu. Maybe it's not Versailles, but it certainly doesn't feel like Kathmandu.
5. **The Hotel Shangri-la Garden at Lunch:** On a sunny day, the wide lawns ringed by bougainvillea vines are as tranquil a spot as you'll find in Kathmandu.
6. **The Hotel Summit's Friday-Night Barbecue:** With its beautiful gardens, the Hotel Summit is the perfect place for a barbecue.
7. **Mike's Breakfast:** This restaurant, run by an American, is set in the garden of an old European-style mansion and serves bottomless cups of coffee while classical music plays on the stereo.
8. **Godawari Royal Botanical Gardens:** Located far from the madding crowd on the south side of the Kathmandu Valley, this is just about the only place in the whole valley that can pass as a quiet park.
9. **A Good Book:** Sometimes escape lies within the mind and not in the physical world. Retreating into a good book may be the only way to deal with a day of culture shock in Kathmandu.
10. **A Hike Through the Queen's Forest:** Located a quick taxi ride north of Thamel, the Rani Ban (Queen's Forest) is a surprisingly untrammeled spot to be so close to Kathmandu's crowded streets.

The temple lies at the bottom of a short flight of steps that is lined with beautiful stone statues of numerous different gods. Watch for the carving of Parvati, Shiva's consort, who is shown holding a lotus. This statue was carved sometime in the 8th century and is one of the oldest stone carvings in the valley. The pagoda-style temple here is dedicated to Shiva, and inside the temple is a Shiva lingam.

A few miles farther east, you pass through the village of **Sankhu,** which is on the ancient trade route from Kathmandu to Lhasa. Legends assert that the Hindu holy man Shankaracharya was unable to spread the Hindu religion any farther north than here. Beyond Sanhku, you soon come to the end of the road and a stone-paved trail leading up a hill to the three-tiered pagoda-style temple of **Vajra Jogini.** The temple, which dates to the 17th century, is surrounded by sacred forests and is a very tranquil spot. Vajra Jogini is a Tantric goddess and is worshiped by Hindus and Buddhists alike. Intricately carved roof struts represent various deities, and over the main entrance to the temple is a gilded repoussé torana depicting the goddess Vajra Jogini. Outside the temple stand several chaityas, each depicting the four Dhyani Buddhas.

Expect to pay a taxi Rs500 ($7.60) or Rs600 ($9.10) to bring you to both of these temples and back.

## 2 Nagarkot

22 miles (35.4km) E of Kathmandu, 8 miles (12.9km) E of Bhaktapur

Located on the rim of the Kathmandu Valley at an elevation of 7,200 feet, Nagarkot boasts a 200-mile panorama of the Himalayas that extends from Dhaulagiri in the west to beyond Mount Everest in the east. At dawn and dusk, the snow-covered peaks are painted in shades of lavender, rose, pink, orange, and gold. It is a sight not to be missed, though you can never be sure that the mountains will be visible, even in the usually clear winter months. Fog and low clouds often obscure the view, though seeing a single jagged, pink peak suddenly appear can be as thrilling as seeing the whole 200-mile panorama. Since mornings are usually clearer than afternoons, I recommend spending a night up here. Nagarkot isn't much of a village, but there are more than a dozen lodges. Nearly every tour company in Kathmandu offers sunrise or sunset trips to Nagarkot.

### GETTING THERE

**BY TAXI**  Nagarkot is about a 90-minute drive from Kathmandu, and a taxi will cost around Rs1,200 ($18.20) round-trip, including the wait for you to enjoy the sunrise or sunset.

**BY BUS**  To get to Nagarkot, you must first take a bus to Bhaktapur from Kathmandu. Buses leave regularly from Bagh Bazaar on the east side of the Tundikhel near the clock tower. In Bhaktapur, cross the street from the main bus park to catch the Nagarkot bus. These buses leave frequently throughout the day. Total trip time is 2½ to 3 hours. There is also a tourist bus that runs between Thamel and Nagarkot; it takes only 1½ hours and costs Rs100 ($1.50). Tickets can be purchased through travel agencies in Thamel.

**BY MOTORCYCLE**  Nagarkot is also a favorite destination of people renting motorcycles in Kathmandu. If you're an experienced dirt-bike rider and you can rent a motocross-style bike, you can return via the trail to Sankhu.

### WHAT TO SEE & DO

Most of the people coming up here for the **views** simply park themselves on a terrace or prop themselves up in bed at dawn. However, if you want an even better view than the one from your lodge, hike an hour from Nagarkot to the viewing tower that can be seen to the south. From this tower, you can even see Mount Everest, which isn't visible from the lodges at Nagarkot. Ask at your hotel for directions to the viewing tower.

While the top activity at Nagarkot is sitting back and gazing at the long wall of snow-covered peaks that stretches off into the distance, this is also a great place to get an idea of what trekking is all about. Several long **day hikes** are possible from Nagarkot, and destinations include Bhaktapur and the temple complexes such as Sankhu, Changu Narayan, and Vajra Jogini. These hikes can be done as part of your return trip to Kathmandu, as round-trip hikes (though with arduous climbs back up to Nagarkot), or as one-way hikes utilizing buses or a taxi for the return trip to Nagarkot.

The **hike to the Changu Narayan temple** complex and then on to Bhaktapur is a very enjoyable long day hike that works well as a way to return to Kathmandu, or as a hike from which you can easily return to Nagarkot. The route passes through small villages and farmlands that are almost always bustling with activity as the farmers work their fields. To begin this hike, follow the Nagarkot road downhill for about an hour to a saddle on the ridge that leads from Nagarkot to the floor of the valley (Changu Narayan is almost at the end of this ridge). From this point, the trail climbs up through a pine forest, which is part of a reforestation project, for 30 minutes. When you reach the top of this climb, you will once again have good views of the Himalayas. From here, the trail descends gradually along the crest of the ridge, with the gilded roof of Changu Narayan usually visible in the distance. It takes a total of about 2½ hours to reach Changu Narayan from Nagarkot. After visiting the temple (see "Changu Narayan," in the "Bhaktapur, City of Devotees" section of chapter 5 for details), follow the steps down the west side of the hill, cross some pastures, and then descend to the south. Continue on this trail in the direction of Bhaktapur, which you will see to the south. After crossing one deep valley and climbing back out, the trail makes a curve to the east before curving back around to the south. Other than this, it is almost due south to Bhaktapur, which you should be able to reach in under 2 hours. In Bhaktapur, you can get a bus or taxi either to Kathmandu or back to Nagarkot.

Because it is a long and circuitous route by road from Sankhu back to Nagarkot, the **hike to Sankhu** works best as a way of returning to Kathmandu. This route follows a dirt road that heads north past the collection of hotels at the north end of Nagarkot and then begins winding down through the hills, past small villages, to the large valley town of Sankhu. On the outskirts of Sankhu, which is reached in about 3 hours from Nagarkot, you pass an interesting riverside temple. It is also possible to **hike to the Vajra Jogini Temple** instead of Sankhu, by taking a northwesterly fork in the trail at a small village on a treeless saddle about an hour out of Nagarkot.

Nagarkot is also a popular **mountain-biking** destination, and though the ride up here is grueling, the views are wonderful and there isn't a lot of traffic on the road from Bhaktapur to Nagarkot. Best of all, however, is the return trip, which can be done on the wide dirt trail that leads down to Sankhu.

## WHERE TO STAY

✪ **Club Himalaya Nagarkot Resort.** Nagarkot. ☎ **977/1-290883.** Fax 977/1-290868. Reservations in Kathmandu: Thamel (P.O. Box 2769), Kathmandu. ☎ 977/1-413632 or 977/1-418733. Fax 977/1-417133. 42 units. TV TEL. $90 double. AE, MC, V.

There aren't too many "resorts" in Nepal that live up to that name, but this hotel, perched high on a ridgetop and operated by the Kathmandu Guest House, certainly does. With the only indoor swimming pool of any hotel in the country, Club Himalaya is certainly the most luxurious place from which to gaze upon the Himalayas. Next to the pool, there are both a hot tub and a bar. The hotel's dining room is in a semicircular building with walls of glass to take in as much of the mountains as possible, and close at hand you'll always find cards that identify the mountains you're seeing from your table. Guest rooms are large and have balconies and marble bathrooms. If your reason for coming to Nepal is to see the mountains, then consider using this place as your base and making forays to Bhaktapur and Kathmandu. You certainly get more for your money up here. The hotel is even wheelchair accessible.

**❂ The Fort Resort.** Nagarkot. ☎ **977/1-290869.** Fax 977/1-290749. Reservations in Kathmandu: Kantipath (P.O. Box 3004), Kathmandu. ☎ 977/1-254300 or 977/1-257300. Fax 977/1-252177. E-mail: fort@mos.com.np. 33 units. $63 double. AE, MC, V.

Constructed in the style of traditional Newari homes, The Fort combines Nepali architecture with modern conveniences and makes the most of its ridge-top location. The lobby's Tibetan tables and couches covered with colorful pillows give the hotel a very Himalayan flavor that sets this lodge apart from most of the other hotels in Nagarkot. Guest rooms are carpeted and have Tibetan rugs, and most have large windows with a view of the mountains. Watercolors of Nepali scenes and traditional thangka paintings decorate the rooms and halls. The dining room serves good food, and the glass walls let you enjoy the spectacular view at every meal. Hikes and other excursions can be arranged at additional cost.

**❂ Nagarkot Farmhouse Resort.** Nagarkot. ☎ **977/1-228087.** Reservations in Kathmandu: Hotel Vajra (P.O. Box 1084), Kathmandu. ☎ 977/1-272719 or 977/1-271545. Fax 977/1-271695. E-mail: nfh@mos.com.np. 12 units (8 with attached bathroom). $40 double with shared bath, $50 double with private bath. Rates include all meals. AE, MC, V.

Operated by Kathmandu's Hotel Vajra (which is one of the most atmospheric hotels in the valley), this rustic and remote retreat provides a very tranquil escape from Kathmandu. Nagarkot Farmhouse is located a mile or so beyond the other hotels listed here and is down the dirt road that leads from Nagarkot to Sankhu. Because this place is so remote and because it makes a good base for various long day hikes, it's better to spend more than just 1 night here. The farm is in the middle of a reforestation project and an orchard and is surrounded by thousands of apple and peach trees. There are two old mud-and-thatch farmhouses on the property, though the dining hall and buildings that house the guest rooms are newer. The views from here aren't as good as those from other Nagarkot hotels, but the tranquillity more than makes up for it.

**Hotel View Point.** Nagarkot. ☎ **977/1-290870.** Reservations in Kathmandu: Thamel (P.O. Box 1285), Kathmandu. ☎ 977/1-417424. Fax 977/1-417424. 23 units. $20–$30 double. V.

Hotel View Point is the highest hotel in Nagarkot, and you could argue that it has the best views. It's also the best of the budget hotels here. The little brick cottages scattered around the terraced gardens should be your first choice, though they also happen to be the most expensive accommodations. Standard rooms are rather small and basic.

## WHERE TO DINE

Almost everyone who comes to Nagarkot eats at their hotel, but if you want someplace different, try the following restaurant.

**The Tea House.** Nagarkot. ☎ **290880.** Main dishes Rs65–Rs150 ($1–$2.25). MC, V. Daily 5am–6pm. INDIAN.

With a dizzying ridge-top location just above the bus stop, the Tea House takes full advantage of Nagarkot's views. Since there are three patio dining areas, you are almost guaranteed an unforgettable view whether you are here at sunrise, sunset, or noon. Be sure to have some of the special *masala chiya* (spiced tea); it's delicious. On Saturdays there is a lunch buffet for Rs300 ($4.55).

## 3  Dhulikhel & Panauti

19 miles (31km) E of Kathmandu

Located on the rim of the Kathmandu Valley at an elevation of about 5,000 feet, the small town of Dhulikhel is 90 minutes by taxi from Kathmandu (on the highway that leads to the Tibetan border crossing at Kodari). While the view from here is not quite as good as that from Nagarkot, it does manage to take in 130 miles or so of the Himalayas. As at Nagarkot, the sunrise and sunset light shows on the mountains are the big attraction here, though most people are content with the view at any time of day.

In addition to the mountain viewing, area activities include several day hikes, including the walks to Namobuddha Temple and to Panauti. This latter village, with its historic temples, can also be visited by taxi on your way to or from Dhulikhel.

## GETTING THERE

If you are just coming up for sunrise or sunset, a taxi from Kathmandu will cost around Rs1,500 ($22.75) for the round-trip and a wait. If you plan to spend the night, arrange transportation through your lodge. Alternatively, you can get to both Dhulikhel and Panauti on local buses from Kathmandu. These leave from the City Bus Park, on the east side of the Tundikhel. Trip time is 2½ hours. You can also take a bus from Kathmandu to Banepa and then transfer to a Panauti-bound bus.

## WHAT TO SEE & DO
### DHULIKHEL

Just as from Nagarkot, a number of interesting day hikes are possible from Dhulikhel. These provide an opportunity to see the Nepali countryside away from the roads, and they give visitors a feel for trekking.

The easiest **area hike** leads to **Namobuddha** and takes a total of about 5 hours (take water and some food for lunch). The hike is relatively easy and passes through some typical villages before reaching the Buddhist monastery and stupa at Namobuddha. From the center of Dhulikhel, walk around the south side of the hill with the temple on top and climb steeply to a dirt road. Follow this road for a little more than 2 hours. You will be able to see Namobuddha above you. Watch for the trail that climbs up from the road. On the hill above Namobuddha is a famous stone carving depicting a Buddha (there have been many before the historical Buddha) feeding himself to a starving tigress and her cubs. This is from a famous Buddhist tale expressing the great compassion of the Buddha. After lunch, return the way you came, or head down the mountain to the town of Panauti, on the valley floor.

### PANAUTI

The confluence of rivers has traditionally been considered sacred by the Hindus of Nepal. Where two rivers join, you will often find temples and cremation ghats. On the east side of the Kathmandu Valley, close to Dhulikhel and about 4 miles south of the town of Banepa, lies the town of Panauti, which developed centuries ago at the confluence of the Pungamati and Roshi Khola Rivers. Panauti is a Newari town surrounded by rice paddies and forested hills. Many of the town's old brick buildings are still standing, and if you wander through the narrow streets, you will get a sense of how Kathmandu must have looked a short while ago. However, it is Panauti's extensive **temple complex,** which for many years has been undergoing restoration, that makes a visit here so rewarding.

Located at the southeast end of town, at the confluence of the two rivers, the temple complex is centered around the 15th-century **Indreshwar Mahadev Temple,** a three-story pagoda within a walled compound. Records indicate that there was a temple here as long ago as the late 13th century, but whether or not any part of the existing temple dates to that time is uncertain. What is certain is that this temple includes some of the most beautifully carved roof struts of any temple in the Kathmandu Valley. These struts, which date to the 14th century, depict such disparate images as willowy warriors and emaciated hags. The toranas over the temple's doors are also of stunning detail and complexity. Opposite this temple, but within the walled compound, is a house-style temple. Carved wooden statues of several gods stare from the second-floor windows.

Outside this compound stand many more smaller temples and shrines, including a pilgrims' rest house covered with colorful murals on stuccoed brick walls. Another small shrine, built in a sort of Roman-revival style during the reign of the Rana prime ministers, contains stone reliefs depicting Shiva and his consort Parvati, as well as Hanuman, the monkey god. There is also a stone Shiva lingam inside this shrine. As elsewhere in the Kathmandu Valley, the striking contrast of traditional Newari architecture and borrowed European styling verges on the bizarre. Adding further to this mixture of styles is a shrine with a facade of ceramic tiles, many of which draw on classical Greek designs. Inside this shrine is a 5-foot-tall bas-relief stone carving of Vishnu standing on Garuda, his half-man, half-bird vehicle.

Across the Pungamati River from the main temple complex stands the 17th-century **Brahmayani Temple,** a two-story pagoda dedicated to a goddess second in importance only to Indreshwar Mahadev. Within this restored temple are some of the finest examples of traditional Newari religious paintings.

## WHERE TO STAY & DINE

**Dhulikhel Lodge Resort.** Dhulikhel. ☎ **977/11-61494** or 977/11-61114. Reservations in Kathmandu: Kamaladi (P.O. Box 6020), Kathmandu. ☎ 977/1-222389 or 977/1-247663. Fax 977/1-222926. 24 units. $64 double. AE, MC, V.

Located down a dirt road on the west side of town, the Dhulikhel Lodge Resort commands excellent views of the mountains from its vertiginous hillside perch. All the guest rooms face the mountains and have glass walls to capture the maximum view, so you can lay in bed (under the feather comforter and propped against a feather pillow) and enjoy the sunrise. Although this lodge is not very large, there are three separate dining areas—a garden restaurant, a rooftop restaurant, and the main indoor restaurant—all of which have good views. There's also a small bar with a freestanding copper-topped fireplace. There's good bird watching here. Guided hikes and excursions can be arranged.

**✪ Dhulikhel Mountain Resort.** Dhulikhel. ☎ **977/11-61466.** Reservations in Kathmandu: Lazimpat (P.O. Box 3203), Kathmandu. ☎ 977/1-420774 or 977/1-413737. Fax 977/1-420778. 42 units. $78 double. AE, MC, V.

Located just over the rim of the Kathmandu Valley, the Dhulikhel Mountain Resort overlooks the Panchkhal Valley and the eastern Himalayas and was the first such mountain resort in the area. The thatched-roof cottages of the resort are situated on a steep hillside amid colorful gardens. Although the rooms don't have much Nepali character, they are quite large and have picture windows so you can lie in bed and enjoy the sunrise over the Himalayas. While the dining room offers superb views (and good Nepali food), it is the garden terrace that is the preferred spot to dine when the weather is good. There's also a bar with excellent views. The secluded feeling and lush gardens make this a pleasant retreat from Kathmandu. From mid-September to mid-June, the lodge offers guided hikes, daylong rafting trips, and excursions to nearby Panauti and the Tibetan border. Good bird watching.

**Himalayan Horizon.** Dhulikhel. ☎ **977/11-61260.** Fax 977/11-61476. Reservations in Kathmandu: Durbar Marg (P.O. Box 1583), Kathmandu. ☎ 977/1-225092. Fax 977/1-225092. E-mail: bagmati@dmn.wlink.com.np. 28 units. $55–$66 double. AE, MC, V.

Partially built in traditional Newari architectural style, the Himalayan Horizon sits atop a terraced ridge overlooking the mountains. Older rooms, in the traditionally styled building, are cramped, though they do have large windows. The deluxe rooms don't have as much character, but they are much more spacious and have balconies, sunken seating areas, and large windows. If you stay in one of these rooms, you don't even have to get out of bed in the morning to enjoy the sunrise. Both indoor and outdoor dining areas have spectacular views of the Himalayas. There's a small bar and room service available.

# 7

# Pokhara

If Kathmandu is Nepal's cultural and historical center, Pokhara is the country's recreational getaway. This sprawling little city lies in a 2,700-foot-high valley on the shore of **Phewa Lake,** the second-largest lake in Nepal, and it is the starting point for treks into the popular Annapurna region. Serving as backdrop to this subtropical valley is an unequaled Himalayan panorama dominated by **Machhapuchhare** (Fishtail Peak), which, at 22,956 feet (6,997m), is far from the tallest Himalayan peak visible from Pokhara but is as perfect a mountain as you will ever see (think the Matterhorn or the Paramount logo). Rising nearly 4 miles above the valley floor, Machhapuchhare is so impossibly beautiful that it seems artificial. At other times, as you strain your neck to gaze up at this wondrous peak, it appears on the verge of tipping into the valley.

Behind this peak are some of the tallest mountains in the world, including 26,795-foot **Mt. Dhauligiri** and the **Annapurna massif,** which includes two other peaks over 26,000 feet (7,925m) high. It is this view, seen from nearly anywhere in town, that attracts visitors by the droves. Aside from this panorama (and Phewa Lake), Pokhara has little to offer in the way of tourist attractions, but how could you ask for more than one of the most breathtaking views on earth?

The neck can take only so much strain as a result of gazing up at the mountains. After a while a person needs to exercise other parts of the body. **Boating** on Phewa Lake, **bicycling** around the valley, and **hiking** the nearby hills serve just that purpose . . . well, sort of. No matter what activity you pursue in Pokhara, chances are good that a view of the mountains will be the end product of your exertions, unless, of course, you happen to be exploring one of the area's caves.

Because Pokhara is the starting (and ending) point for the most popular treks in Nepal, much of the activity here revolves around planning for or winding down from a trek. Excited trekkers organize their trips on the streets beside the lake, while exhausted hikers, just back from a week or two or three of hiking in the Himalayas, lounge in hotel gardens drinking beer, reading in the sunshine, and, you guessed it, gazing up at the mountains.

Pokhara is such an important **trekking base,** because for centuries it was important as a crossroads trading center. The town's large bazaar has functioned as the end point for pony trains coming down from Tibet with salt and wool to trade for sugar and other commodities traditionally not available in Tibet. Though the trade route up the Kali

Gandaki river valley is still active, trade with Tibet was curtailed in the 1950s after China invaded Tibet. Today, the trekking business is far more important along the old trade routes, but Pokhara is still the region's most important town.

# 1 Orientation

## ARRIVING

**BY PLANE**   Flying is the best way to get to Pokhara. The flight, usually in a small propeller plane, costs $61 each way, takes less than 45 minutes, and provides some spectacular scenery. Airlines flying from Kathmandu to Pokhara include **Buddha Air** (in Kathmandu ☎ 977/1-417802 or 491384, in Pokhara ☎ 977/61-21429); **Cosmic Air** (in Kathmandu ☎ 977/1-246905 or 247485, in Pokhara ☎ 977/61-21846 or 20350); **Gorkha Airline** (in Kathmandu ☎ ?or 435121, in Pokhara ☎ 977/61-25971); **Lumbini Airways** (in Kathmandu ☎ 977/1-483381, in Pokhara ☎ 977/61-25718 or 27233); **Necon Air** (in Kathmandu ☎ 977/1-473860 or 488539, in Pokhara ☎ 977/ 61-23120); **Royal Nepal Airlines** (in Kathmandu ☎ 977/1-226574 or 220757, in Pokhara ☎ 977/61-21021 or 27315); and **Yeti Airways** (in Kathmandu ☎ 977/1421215 or 421147, in Pokhara ☎ 977/61-21720). **Buddha Air** flies the newest planes and for this reason is currently the country's most recommended airline.

The Pokhara Airport is on the east side of town, and there are always taxis waiting to meet the flights. It should cost you between Rs50 (75¢) and Rs100 ($1.50) for a taxi to Damside or Lakeside.

**BY BUS**   Due to the poor condition of the road between Kathmandu and Pokhara, it can take as long as 8 hours (and sometimes more) to cover the 124 miles (200km) by bus. However, this is still how most travelers on a budget get to Pokhara. The buses most commonly used between Kathmandu and Pokhara are the so-called "tourist" buses. These buses, which cost between Rs200 and Rs250 ($3.05 and $3.80), leave Kathmandu from Kantipath, just outside Thamel. Tickets are available in advance through most travel agents in Kathmandu. In Pokhara, these buses use a special "tourist bus" park that is located at Rastra Bank Chowk, about a half mile north of the Damside area. When leaving Pokhara, be sure to book your ticket several days in advance.

For Rs600 ($9.10), you can travel on the Greenline bus, which, with air-conditioning and breakfast served en route, is the most comfortable intercity bus in Nepal. The Greenline office (☎ **977/1-253885**) is just outside Thamel near the corner of Kantipath. In Pokhara, the Greenline office (☎ **977/61-27271**) is at Mustang Chowk, across the street from the airport terminal.

As a last resort, there are the standard buses that leave Kathmandu from the Gongabu Bus Park on Ring Road north of Thamel. These buses, which are very uncomfortable, slow, and usually dangerously overloaded, cost Rs113 ($1.70). These buses use the main Pokhara bus park, little more than a vast potholed and garbage-covered gravel parking lot, which is located on the east side of town (north of the airport). From the bus terminal to either Damside or Lakeside is a 10-minute taxi ride, which should cost between Rs75 ($1.15) and Rs100 ($1.50).

## VISITOR INFORMATION

Pokhara's **tourist office** (☎ **977/61-20028**) is located across the street from the north end of the airport. It's open February 13 to November 16, Sunday to Thursday from 10am to 5pm (until 4pm the rest of the year) and Friday from 10am to 3pm.

However, for the amount of information that can be gained here, this office is not worth the trip. They do, however, give out a map of Pokhara, though better maps can be purchased at any Pokhara bookshop.

The **Department of Immigration** office (☎ **977/61-21167** or 977/61-20028) is located just off the traffic circle at the east end of the Lakeside neighborhood (east of the Hotel Pumori and most of the Hotel Tragopan). This office provides visa extensions, issues trekking permits for the Annapurna region, and collects the Rs1000 ($15.15) Annapurna Conservation Area Project (ACAP) fee, which is collected from everyone planning a trek in this region. There is an ACAP bulletin board here with information about the project. Immigration office hours are Sunday to Thursday from 10am to 5pm (closes at 4pm in the winter season between Nov 17 and Feb 13). Applications are accepted from 10:30am until 1pm only (and until 12:30pm in the winter season). Friday hours are from 10am to 3pm, when applications are accepted only from 10am until noon.

## CITY LAYOUT

Pokhara is a large town that sprawls over a wide area at the edge of the Pokhara Valley. Pokhara proper, which has very little of interest to travelers, is actually a mile or two away from the hotel neighborhoods frequented by foreign tourists. The city is laid out along two roughly parallel main roads that run from the Damside neighborhood in the south to the Seti Gandaki River in the north. From end to end, the town is about 4 miles long but only half a mile wide. At the south (lower) end of the gentle slope upon which the town is built lies Phewa Lake. The lake is surrounded by high hills on the south, west, and north, and by the valley on the east. It is along the lakeshore that you will find all of the town's tourist accommodations, restaurants, and shops. North of Pokhara (between 12 and 20 miles away) are the snow-covered peaks of the Himalayas.

You can get a free map of Pokhara at the visitor center near the airport, or a very basic map of town at any bookshop. However, the Karto Atelier topographic map of Pokhara Town & Valley, available for Rs750 ($11.35) at bookstores around town, is by far the best of the area, and probably far more than you'll need unless you plan to do a bit of exploring on foot or by bicycle.

## NEIGHBORHOODS IN BRIEF

**Lakeside**    Also known as Baidam, Lakeside was once a sleepy village across the rice fields from Pokhara, and as its name implies, it lies on the shore of Phewa Lake. However, this area has seen the bulk of the tourist development over the past decade and has become a real backpackers' Mecca, with both Western and Nepali neohippies making the scene. Sprawling along more than a mile of potholed road, Lakeside is full of budget hotels, cheap restaurants, loud bars, souvenir shops, trekking-company offices, juice stands, momo (stuffed dumplings) stalls, and bike-rental places. There's also a royal palace used by the king when he's in town. Previously known for its greenery and relaxed atmosphere, Lakeside has taken on something of a "Thamel by the Lake" feel with its ugly cement buildings lining the main roads, and taxis, trucks, and buses blaring their horns throughout the day. Still, despite the development, the numerous lakefront garden restaurants here are ideal places to sit and write postcards over a pot of milk tea. Step off the main road and you can be again surrounded by the beauty of rural Nepal.

**Damside**    Located beside a small dam at the southeast end of the lake, Damside (also known as Pardi) is much less of a "scene" than Lakeside and has by far Pokhara's best

# Pokhara

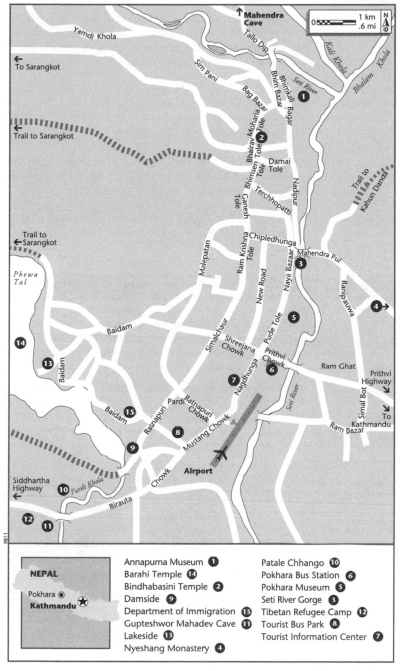

↑ **Mahendra Cave**

Yamdi Khola

← To Sarangkot

Trail to Sarangkot

Tallo Dip

Sim Pani

Bag Bazar

Bhimkali Bagar

Bhim Bazar

Seti River

Kali Khola

Bhalam Khola

Bhairav Moharia Tole

Bhimsen Tole

Damai Tole

Terchhopatti

Ganesh Tole

Nadipur

Trail to Kahun Danda

Trail to ← Sarangkot

*Phewa Tal*

Malepatan

Ram Krishna Tole

Chipledhunga

New Road

Naya Bazaar

Mahendra Pul

Baidam

Simalchaur

Shreejana Chowk

Pude Tole

Prithvi Chowk

Ram Ghat

Ranipauwa

Baidam

Nagdhunga

Seti River

Prithvi Highway

Baidam

Ratnapuri Chowk

Pardi Chowk

Mustang Chowk

Simal Bot

Ram Bazar

To Kathmandu

Ratnapuri Chowk

**Airport**

Siddhartha Highway ←

Pardi Khola

Birauta

NEPAL

Pokhara ◉

**Kathmandu** ★

| | | |
|---|---|---|
| Annapurna Museum ❶ | | Patale Chhango ❿ |
| Barahi Temple ⓮ | | Pokhara Bus Station ❻ |
| Bindhabasini Temple ❷ | | Pokhara Museum ❺ |
| Damside ❾ | | Seti River Gorge ❸ |
| Department of Immigration ⓯ | | Tibetan Refugee Camp ⓬ |
| Gupteshwor Mahadev Cave ⓫ | | Tourist Bus Park ❽ |
| Lakeside ⓭ | | Tourist Information Center ❼ |
| Nyeshang Monastery ❹ | | |

9811

view of the mountains. From several of the budget hotels and from the pair of parks near the dam, the view of the Himalayas reflected in the waters of Phewa Lake is incomparable. However, with most new businesses opting to locate in the Lakeside area, Damside, which was once known for having better hotels than Lakeside, now feels somewhat abandoned. The hotels here seem to cater primarily to young Japanese and Indian tourists, and because the latter tend to visit in the monsoon season, Damside hotels see very little business during peak trekking seasons. The neighborhood's biggest drawback, however, is its lack of decent restaurants, which necessitates taking a taxi or walking a mile or more to Lakeside for dinner every night.

**Pokhara Town**    The main town of Pokhara is long and spread out and begins a mile or two uphill from Lakeside and Damside. The oldest and most interesting parts of town, where you'll find a few old houses and a couple of temples that are worth a visit, are at the northern (uphill) end of town, which is the farthest you can get from Lakeside and still be in Pokhara. This is also where you'll find the Annapurna Regional Museum. The newer business district is at the lower end of town and has nothing to offer except the Pokhara Museum.

## 2 Getting Around

**BY PUBLIC TRANSPORTATION**    The public transportation system in Pokhara is very limited and inconvenient. Battered old buses that frequently break down make a circuit of the town, stopping in Lakeside and Damside before heading up into the main bazaar districts of Pokhara. If you need to use one of these buses, ask at your hotel for the nearest bus stop. A ticket is about Rs5 (8¢).

**BY TAXI**    Taxis in Pokhara are more expensive than in Kathmandu and do not have meters, so you'll have to bargain for the fare. It should cost you between Rs75 ($1.15) and Rs100 ($1.50) from the airport or bus station to Lakeside, a bit less to Damside. Because the bus system is so bad and because Pokhara is so spread out, taxis are the best way to get around town. It costs about Rs1,200 ($18.20) to hire a taxi for the day.

**BY CAR**    There are no self-drive car rentals in Pokhara. However, you can hire a car and driver for the day at nearly any hotel or tour agency (of which there are quite a few in both Damside and Lakeside). The cost is about Rs1,500 ($22.75) per day.

**BY BICYCLE**    A bicycle is the best way of getting around Pokhara, especially for trips around the lake areas. If you want to go up to Pokhara proper, however, it is a long uphill pedal, so rent a mountain bike. Bikes rent for about Rs75 ($1.15) per day. You'll find numerous bicycle-rental stands in Damside and Lakeside. Be sure to check the bell and brakes before riding off.

**BY MOTORCYCLE**    If you have experience riding a motorcycle, you may want to consider renting one while you're in Pokhara. For exploring the more-distant corners of the valley, they can't be beat. They rent for about Rs400 to Rs500 ($6.05 to $7.60) per day plus gas, which is about $2.50 per gallon, and are available at many roadside rental shops in Lakeside.

**ON FOOT**    Pokhara, at least in the Damside and Lakeside areas where visitors usually stay, is a quiet town. There isn't much traffic on the narrow roads, so walking is generally quite pleasant. It will take about 30 minutes to walk between Lakeside and Damside.

# FAST FACTS: Pokhara

**Baby-sitters**    Check with the front desk at your hotel if you need a baby-sitter.

**Business Hours**    See "Fast Facts: Nepal," in chapter 3.

**Car Rentals**    See "Getting Around" in this chapter.

**City Code**    If you are calling Pokhara from elsewhere in Nepal, the city code is **061.** If calling from outside Nepal, drop the 0 and just dial 61.

**Climate**    See "When to Go," in chapter 3.

**Currency Exchange**    In Lakeside and Damside, there are numerous currency-exchange offices, some of which stay open until 9pm or later.

**Dentist**    If you need a dentist, I suggest you go to Kathmandu and contact your embassy for a recommendation.

**Doctor**    If you need medical attention, try to get to Kathmandu and contact your embassy for a recommendation. Otherwise, ask at your hotel.

**Drugstores**    Pharmacies here are called "medical halls" and are generally open from about 7:30am to 7:30pm Sunday through Friday. The **Machhapuchhare Medical Hall** (☎ **24342**) is located across from the Nepal Rastra Bank (south of the Immigration Office) and has a doctor available for consultation from 5 to 6pm daily. The well-stocked **Manish Medical Hall** (☎ **25650**) is located south of the German Bakery.

**Embassies & Consulates**    The nearest embassies and consulates are in Kathmandu (see "Fast Facts: Nepal," in chapter 3).

**Eyeglass Repair**    Your best bet is to head back to Kathmandu before trying to have your glasses repaired or replaced.

**Hospitals**    The **Western Regional Hospital** (☎ **20066**) is on the east side of Pokhara near the Mahendra Pul bridge and is your only option in Pokhara if you need hospitalization. It is even more poorly equipped than the hospitals in Kathmandu. Evacuation to Kathmandu and then to Thailand or Singapore is the recommended procedure if at all possible.

**Information**    See "Visitor Information," above, in this chapter.

**Lost Property**    There is no lost-property office, and going to the police is not likely to produce any results, either. Try posting notices around the restaurants frequented by tourists.

**Luggage Storage**    Almost all hotels offer luggage-storage facilities if you are going off on a trek or to Chitwan and plan to return to the hotel.

**Newspapers/Magazines**    The *International Herald Tribune, USA Today, Newsweek, Time,* and *The Economist* are all readily available at bookshops in the tourist neighborhoods.

**Police**    Dial **20033**.

**Post Office**    The most convenient Pokhara post office is midway between Lakeside and Damside, on the small road that leads northwest from the roundabout with the produce vendors and big shade trees. You'll pass several other government office buildings before reaching the post office. It's open Sunday to Thursday from 10am to 5pm (until 4pm in winter) and Friday from 10am to 3pm. Some bookshops, which sell stamps, also have a postbox which is generally just as reliable as posting at the post office.

**Restrooms**    If you are in need of a restroom, you'll have to find a restaurant or hotel that will allow you to use theirs.

**Safety**    Tourists in Pokhara are sometimes the victims of bag snatchers. Do not be careless with your money, passport, and other valuables. I suggest always carrying tickets, money, and passport in a money belt or neck bag that can be worn under your clothing. Carry only as much cash as you expect to be spending during any foray out of your hotel. Keep this money separate from your money belt so that you don't reveal the location of your valuables to curious eyes. Some hotels will lock your valuables in a safe-deposit box.

**Taxes**    Hotels charge a 10% Value Added Tax, which is levied on top of the 2% Tourism Service Charge and is basically a tax as well.

**Taxis**    See "Getting Around," above, in this chapter.

**Telephone/Fax/E-mail**    Telephone and fax services are offered at many travel companies in the tourist neighborhoods of Pokhara. Services include STD, long-distance calling within Nepal, ISTD, international calls, and collect calling service. Some companies offer Internet services and e-mail for about Rs10 (15¢) per minute, slightly higher than what you'll find in Kathmandu.

## 3  Accommodations

Pokhara has a split personality. Not only does it draw trekkers from autumn through spring, but in the summer monsoon months, it also attracts numerous vacationing Indian families. Trekkers stay at both bottom-end and top-end hotels, whereas Indians tend to patronize hotels in the middle range (say $40 to $80 a night). Unfortunately, the prices at these mid-range hotels are based on the availability of amenities such as TVs, telephones, minibars, and air-conditioning, which for the most part are not usually required by trekkers. Consequently, these Indian-oriented hotels tend to be greatly overpriced for what you get, and are not very good deals. You can get a room that is just as nice for under $30 if you can do without air-conditioning, a TV, and a telephone.

If you're planning a visit in the busy trekking season of October and November and want to stay at one of the more noteworthy hotels, such as the Fish Tail Lodge, Shangri-La Village, or Tiger Tops Pokhara Village, you'd be wise to make reservations at least 6 months in advance. Otherwise, there are now so many hotels in Pokhara that even at the busiest time of year, there are plenty of decent rooms to be had.

Tourist accommodations are generally located in two distinct neighborhoods—Lakeside and Damside—which are separated by about a mile or so. While Lakeside has all the services a traveler could ever need, Damside has by far the better views. Unless you cross to the south side of the lake, Damside is the only place from which you can you see Machhapuchhare reflected in the waters of Phewa Lake.

In low-budget hotels, and even in some of the more-expensive places, you're likely to encounter Asian-style bathrooms. By this I do not mean squat toilets, but showers in the middle of the bathroom with no shower curtain. This concept seems quite bizarre to most Westerners, but in a place where mildew is rampant, a shower curtain would need to be replaced several times a year.

In the listings below, the "Very Expensive" category includes hotels charging more than $150 per night for a double room; the "Expensive" category includes hotels charging between $80 and $150; the "Moderate" category includes hotels charging $40 to $79; and the "Inexpensive" category includes hotels charging less than $40.

# Pokhara Accommodations & Dining

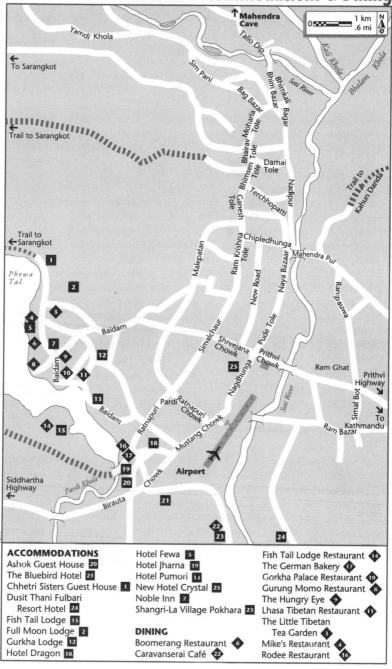

**ACCOMMODATIONS**
Ashok Guest House **20**
The Bluebird Hotel **21**
Chhetri Sisters Guest House **1**
Dusit Thani Fulbari
   Resort Hotel **24**
Fish Tail Lodge **15**
Full Moon Lodge **2**
Gurkha Lodge **12**
Hotel Dragon **18**

Hotel Fewa **5**
Hotel Jharna **19**
Hotel Pumori **15**
New Hotel Crystal **25**
Noble Inn **7**
Shangri-La Village Pokhara **23**

**DINING**
Boomerang Restaurant **6**
Caravanserai Café **22**

Fish Tail Lodge Restaurant **14**
The German Bakery **17**
Gorkha Palace Restaurant **10**
Gurung Momo Restaurant **8**
The Hungry Eye **9**
Lhasa Tibetan Restaurant **11**
The Little Tibetan
   Tea Garden **3**
Mike's Restaurant **4**
Rodee Restaurant **16**

Unless otherwise noted, all rooms have private bathrooms. Remember that it is always possible to bargain at hotels in the lower price categories.

## VERY EXPENSIVE

**Dusit Thani Fulbari Resort Hotel.** P.O. Box 334, Pokhara. ☎ **977/61-23451.** Fax 977/61-23451. E-mail: fulbari@dusit.com. 179 units. A/C MINIBAR TV TEL. $215 double; $400–$1,500 suite. Rates include full breakfast. AE, MC, V.

Located 15 minutes' drive east of the Pokhara airport, the Fulbari, part of a Thai hotel chain, opened in 1998 and is the first and only golf resort in Nepal. The hotel and its nine-hole course are set on the edge of a cliff high above the Seti and Fusre rivers, and while it's a long way to Phewa Lake, the views of the mountains from here are spectacular. From across the garden, the edgeless pool seems to spill into the canyon, further adding to the drama of this hotel's setting. The hotel is unremarkable from the outside, but once you step through the front door, the Nepali architectural references are quite impressive. Across the lobby's wide expanse of marble lies a courtyard with inner walls that were designed to resemble the old courtyards of Kathmandu. Unfortunately, guest rooms, though built to international standards, lack character. The marble bathrooms and balconies are some consolation, but insist on a northside room, because everything else will pale compared to the view out the window.

**Dining/Diversions:** Plenty of dining options, including a Thai restaurant, a poolside Japanese restaurant, and a coffee shop, make up for this hotel's remote location. A library lounge, swim-up bar, beer garden, and lobby bar provide plenty of options for libations, and a planned disco and casino will provide nightlife.

**Amenities:** In addition to the golf course and pool, there are two tennis courts, an extensive fitness center, room service, laundry/dry-cleaning service, currency exchange, travel/trekking desk, and a shopping arcade.

✪ **Tiger Tops Pokhara Village.** In Kathmandu: P.O. Box 242, Kathmandu. ☎ **977/ 1-411225.** Fax 977/1-414075 or 977/1-419126. E-mail: info@tigermountain.com. 20 units. $300 double. Rates include all meals, guided walks, pony rides, use of mountain bikes, and Pokhara transfers.

Affiliated with Chitwan's famed Tiger Tops Lodge, this luxurious and atmospheric little resort opened in late 1998 and is primarily a spot for resting up before or after a trek. The collection of stone-walled, traditionally inspired buildings is perched on a ridge 1,000 feet above the valley and 30 minutes east of Pokhara. The views are outstanding and there is plenty of exploring to be done in the surrounding hills. With hot tubs, a swimming pool, and ridgetop mountain-viewing gazebos, there is really little reason to leave the premises. However, should you wish to get some exercise, plenty of guided activities are included in the rates here. In the main lodge, you'll find an extensive library of Himalayan mountaineering literature, a bar, and a dining room decorated with Nepali artifacts.

## EXPENSIVE

**The Begnas Lake Resort & Villas.** Dundari Danda, Begnas Lake. ☎ **977/61-29330.** E-mail: villas@begnas.mos.com.np. Reservations in Kathmandu: Pratap Bhawan, Kantipath (P.O. Box 3896), Kathmandu. ☎ **977/1-249619** or 977/1-249889. Fax 977/1-249324. E-mail: airborne@begnas.mos.com.np. 28 units. A/C MINIBAR TV TEL. $100 double. MC, V.

If you've come to the Pokhara area searching for a peaceful lakeshore retreat with astounding mountain views, Begnas Lake Resort may be just the place you're looking for. Located 20 minutes east of Pokhara and accessible only by boat, four-wheel-drive vehicle, or hiking trail, this lakeside lodge, which opened in early 1998, is as tranquil a place as you'll find in Nepal—the perfect place to hole up at the end of a trek. The lodge is set into a clearing in the forest on the shore of Begnas Lake, and from here guests can hike around the lake, go boating, or try a little fishing. The two-story stone cottages each house four rooms, all of which have lake and mountain views. Hardwood floors and stone walls give both guest rooms and the dining room and bar a rustic feel.

**The Bluebird Hotel.** Pardi, Pokhara. ☎ **977/61-25480** or 977/61-25481. Fax 977/61-26260. E-mail: hotel@blustar.mos.com.np. 81 units. A/C MINIBAR TV TEL. $150 double; $225 suite. AE, MC, V.

Located on the edge of the Damside neighborhood a short walk from the lake, this large new hotel is something of a homely stepsister to the far-more-elegant Dusit Thani and Shangri-La. However, the views are just about as good, and most of the same amenities are available. If you're looking for a hotel of international standards, this makes a good third choice. While there are great views of the mountains from the lobbies and about half of the rooms, the guest rooms are lacking in Nepali character.

**Dining/Diversions:** There are an atmospheric Tibetan restaurant, a Japanese restaurant, an international dining room that tries to appeal to all tastes, and a cozy, dark bar.

**Amenities:** Outdoor pool, room service, currency exchange, travel/tour desk, laundry/dry-cleaning service.

✪ **Fish Tail Lodge.** P.O. Box 10, Pokhara. ☎ **977/61-20071.** In Kathmandu, contact Hotel de l'Annapurna. Durbar Marg (P.O. Box 140), Kathmandu. ☎ 977/1-221711 or 977/1-225242. Fax 977/1-225236. 62 units. $95–$110 double. AE, JCB, MC, V.

Although this was long the *only* place to stay in Pokhara, the preeminence of this waterfront hotel on Phewa Lake has recently been usurped by the much larger and glitzier Dusit Thani, Shangri-La, and Bluebird. However, for the adventure-minded, Fish Tail Lodge is still the best place to stay in Pokhara. Not only is there an unforgettable view of Machhapuchhare and the Annapurnas, but there's something decidedly offbeat about arriving at your hotel on a raft/ferry made from 55-gallon oil drums. Surrounded by a royal wildlife preserve, Fish Tail Lodge is one of the only hotels on the south side of the lake and is pleasantly removed from the bustle of Pokhara's extensive tourist neighborhoods. Beautiful gardens surround the unusual circular buildings that house the standard guest rooms. These rooms, though small, are attractive and have flagstone floors, brick walls, and wicker furniture. Twin beds and small bathrooms with only showers are the biggest drawbacks of these rooms. Larger, deluxe rooms are more comfortable.

**Dining/Diversions:** The bar and restaurant, which serves decent Indian and continental fare, is housed in a circular building with a curving wall of glass. A cultural program of Nepali music and dance is held nightly.

**Amenities:** Room service, currency exchange, laundry service, travel services, boat rentals.

✪ **Shangri-La Village Pokhara.** Gharipatan (P.O. Box 333), Pokhara. ☎ **977/61-22122** or 977/61-23700. Fax 977/61-21995. E-mail: hosangp@village.mos.com.np. 65 units. A/C MINIBAR TV TEL. $150 double. AE, MC, V.

Located on the southern edge of Pokhara with an expansive view of Machhapuchare and the Annapurnas, the Shangri-La abounds with Nepali character and has a comfortable resort-like air about it. The many interesting architectural and artistic details make this one of the two most culturally evocative hotels in Nepal (Dwarika's in Kathmandu is the other). The hotel's buildings are connected by a thatched-roof walkway, and exterior walls are decorated with murals and bas-relief images inspired by Maithil women's artwork from the lowlands of Nepal. Guest rooms have slate floors, antique furnishings and accent pieces, and large windows and balconies. In the gardens, you'll find a miniature stupa and a Shiva lingam, as well as fish ponds.

**Dining/Diversions:** Perhaps the hotel's only shortcoming is that neither of its two restaurants has much of a view. Reasonable prices at the downstairs restaurant somewhat make up for this. Weekly barbecues in the garden are both a good deal and a pleasant way to spend an evening. The poolside bar is small but relaxing.

**Amenities:** The fan-shaped swimming pool is surrounded by a stone wall and has a great view of the mountains. Other amenities include room service, laundry/dry-cleaning service, currency exchange, a yoga center, an exercise center, and a shopping arcade.

## MODERATE

**Hotel Dragon.** Damside (P.O. Box 15), Pokhara. ☎ **977/61-20391** or 977/61-22630. Fax 977/61-20391. 31 units. A/C TEL. $50 double. No credit cards.

While this hotel has a bit more character than others in the area, its rooms tend to be a bit musty and show their age. It's worth asking to see a few rooms before making a decision. Should you decide to stay, request a substantial discount. Most rooms have large windows, and some have views of Machhapuchhare and the Annapurnas; be sure to ask for a room with a view. The rooftop garden is an excellent place from which to watch the sunrise or sunset; you can even have meals served up there. On the first floor, the hotel's restaurant is decorated to resemble a traditional Tibetan Buddhist gompa (temple).

**Hotel Pumori.** Lakeside, Pokhara. ☎ **977/61-21462.** 20 units. A/C. $60 double. MC, V.

Located near the Fish Tail Lodge, the Hotel Pumori is one of the few economical lodgings in Pokhara that varies from the standard, characterless, concrete-box design. The Pumori's guest rooms are contained in two-single story buildings that resemble primitive bamboo huts set in a rather barren garden. However, inside, the rooms are anything but primitive—they have carpeting, air-conditioning, and attractive block-print bedspreads that give the rooms a bit of Nepali character. Unfortunately, all the rooms are rather dark. The hotel's interesting glass-walled dining room serves Nepali and Indian meals and features a nightly program of Nepali music and dance.

**New Hotel Crystal.** Nagdhunga (P.O. Box 234), Pokhara. ☎ **977/61-20035** or 977/61-20036. Fax 977/61-20234. 89 units. TV TEL. $35–$75 double; $139 suite. AE, DC, JCB, MC, V.

Located directly across the street from the airport, the New Hotel Crystal is an old standby in Pokhara. The garden offers good views of the mountains, but the lake is a 20-minute walk or 5-minute taxi ride away. Rooms in the main wing are much the worse for wear, whereas rooms in the new wing are much more comfortable. The old annex has the cheapest rooms, which are large but quite dreary. The hotel has a restaurant, bar, room service, laundry service, safe-deposit boxes, bicycle rentals, and a travel desk.

## INEXPENSIVE

**Ashok Guest House.** Damside, Pardi, Pokhara. ☎ **977/61-20374.** 10 units (8 with bathroom). $22 double. No credit cards.

With an attractive garden and superb rooftop view of both the lake and the mountains, this is my favorite budget hotel in Pokhara. It's right beside the dam spillway, across from which is a little park with good ○ **bird watching.** The rooms are small and simply furnished but have plaited bamboo walls, carpeting, and some of the best towels in Nepal. There are a small dining room with an extensive menu, and an unusual gazebo in the garden. You can usually get a room here for about half the above rate. At press time a movie theater was under construction next door, which might ruin the atmosphere here entirely.

**Chhetri Sisters Guest House.** Lakeside (P.O. Box 284), Pokhara-6. ☎ **977/61-24066.** Fax 977/61-24066. E-mail: sisters3@cnet.wlink.com.np. 5 units (2 with private bathroom). $3.05 double with shared bathroom, $6.05 double with private bathroom. No credit cards.

Solo women travelers who are looking for someplace to meet other like-minded women should check out this basic little lodge, which is run by three sisters who also operate a trekking company catering primarily to women. The lodge is at the far north end of Lakeside (a rice paddy separates the lodge from the lake) and is particularly quiet. Rooms are fairly large for this price range. Up on the lodge's second floor, there's a simple restaurant with a view of the lake.

**Full Moon Lodge.** Lakeside, Baidam-6, Pokhara. ☎ **977/61-21511.** Fax 977/61-24201. 11 units (5 with private bathroom). $7 double with shared bathroom, $20–$40 double with private bathroom. No credit cards.

Set high on a hill overlooking Phewa Lake and the Lakeside neighborhood, this lodge is not for the out-of-shape. It's 102 steps up from the base of the hill to the guest rooms, and just to reach the 102 steps, you have to walk up a long path. What makes this place so unusual, other than the location, are all the Hindu shrines, both garish and gory, that crowd the lodge's terraced gardens. The rooms with private bathrooms are large and open onto a huge terrace that's great for sunset watching. If you're traveling light, check it out. You'll find the lodge at the north end of Lakeside on the road that leads away from the lake and toward Pokhara proper.

○ **Gurkha Lodge.** Lakeside, Pokhara. ☎ **977/61-20798.** 6 units. $12 double. No credit cards.

Operated by a retired British Gurkha captain and his British wife, this very basic lodge is a collection of traditionally styled stone cottages set in a lush, overgrown, tropical garden. The cottages, which have thatch roofs, are a bit musty despite dehumidifiers, but this can be overlooked if you appreciate a place with Nepali character. This is one of the only budget accommodations left in Pokhara that is not a tasteless concrete box. The gardens are full of birds and butterflies (another plus), and breakfast and light meals are available.

**Hotel Fewa.** Lakeside, Baidam, Pokhara. ☎ **977/61-20151.** E-mail: mike@fewa.mos.com.np. 8 units. $28 double. No credit cards.

Operated by Mike Frame, of Mike's Breakfast fame, this little hotel on the bank of Phewa Lake dates back to 1972 and was one of the first hotels in Pokhara. Set beneath beautiful old shade trees, the hotel is fronted by a popular garden terrace restaurant. Rooms open onto screened verandas and for this reason are a bit dark, but with their unusual platform beds, plaited bamboo floor mats, and Tibetan carpets, they have plenty of character. Boats can be rented right in front of the hotel.

**Hotel Jharna.** P.O. Box 21925, Pardi, Pokhara. ☎ **977/61-21925.** 14 units. $32 double. No credit cards.

Located in the Damside neighborhood, this very basic hotel, popular with Indian and Japanese tourists, offers the best views of any hotel in Pokhara. Not bad for a place where a room with a view can cost as little as $13 (rather than the official rate listed above). The view takes in both the lake and Machhpuchhare and is best from rooms 301 and 305. *Beware:* Some rooms have no views at all and actually look into the windows of another hotel. Should you end up with one of these rooms, you can always head up to the roof. Guest rooms are all carpeted and have large windows.

✪ **Noble Inn.** Lakeside, Pokhara. ☎ **977/61-24926.** Fax 977/61-25261. 12 units (7 with private bathroom). $5 double with shared bathroom, $10 double with attached bathroom. No credit cards.

If you're looking for basic but clean accommodations in the Lakeside area, this lodge should do the trick. Situated on a quiet dead-end street at the north end of Lakeside, this stone-faced cottage is surrounded by a large, neatly manicured garden with mountain views. Guest rooms are relatively large and have big windows and clean bathrooms.

# 4 Dining

While there are dozens of inexpensive restaurants in the Lakeside area, the food scene in Pokhara is not nearly as varied as the one in Kathmandu. For the most part, restaurants here stick to the something-for-everyone menu, and the only real difference from one restaurant to the next is the location and the type of music played on the stereo.

If you're staying in Damside, you'll find your restaurant options very limited, with an emphasis on Indian food for Indian tourists. The German Bakery is good for breakfast and lunch, but at dinner you'll want to head to Lakeside. However, at press time, there were rumors that the K.C. Restaurant, which for years was Damside's most popular eatery, was going to be resurrected in a new building.

## MODERATE

✪ **Caravanserai Café.** Shangri-La Village hotel, Gharipatan. ☎ **22122.** Reservations recommended. Main courses Rs200–Rs400 ($3.05–$6.05). AE, MC, V. 24 hours. INTERNATIONAL.

Stepping into the Shangri-La Village hotel, where this cafe is located, is a bit of a shock. The place feels like an international resort and is a far cry from the tourist neighborhood of Lakeside, but through careful design it still maintains an essence of Nepali character. The emphasis is on Chinese and Indian cuisine, and the succulent chicken tandoori just might be the best in the country (at least as good as the one at Ghar-e-Kabab in Kathmandu). The semicircular restaurant has smart table settings and looks out over the pool and terrace, where, on Friday nights, there is a barbecue buffet for the reasonable price of Rs500 ($7.60). You'll find the Shangri-La Village less than a mile south of the airport and within walking distance of Damside (follow the signs).

✪ **Fish Tail Lodge Restaurant.** Fish Tail Lodge. ☎ **20071.** Reservations recommended. Main courses Rs200–Rs550 ($3.05–$8.35); set meals Rs700 ($10.60). AE, JCB, MC, V. Daily 7–9am, noon–3pm, and 7–9pm. INDIAN/CONTINENTAL.

While the food here is some of the best in Pokhara, so too is the view out the windows, making this restaurant a great place for lunch. The circular room has a glass wall that faces the distant mountains, and most seats have good views. The menu includes plenty of variety (as most Pokhara menus do), including Indonesian and Thai dishes, but you're best off sticking to the Indian dishes. Service is excellent by Nepali standards. In the evening during the busy season, there is usually a buffet that might include unmemorable continental dishes but very tasty Indian offerings.

# INEXPENSIVE

✪ **Boomerang Restaurant & German Bakery.** Lakeside, Baidam. ☎ **22978.** Main courses Rs90–Rs275 ($1.35–$4.15). No credit cards. Daily 6:30am–10pm. INTERNATIONAL.

Of all the waterfront restaurants in Pokhara, Boomerang has the largest garden, the most shade, and, of course, an excellent view of the lake. Big trees, a hammock, and reclining chairs are arranged for relaxation with a specialty coffee such as a whiskey cappuccino. The food? The usual . . . a little bit of this and a little bit of that, and it all tastes about the same. However, the baked goods here are provided by the German Bakery, which has long been a Pokhara favorite. Although designed to appeal to the Aussie market, Boomerang attracts travelers of all nationalities, and they always come back for more. There's even a playground for kids.

**The German Bakery.** Damside, Pardi. ☎ **23175.** Pastries, sandwiches, and light meals. Rs10–Rs135 (15¢–$2.05). No credit cards. Daily 5am–9pm. PASTRIES/SANDWICHES.

Bakeries have long been popular with budget travelers in Nepal, so the Nepalis have had plenty of time to perfect the art of baking. At this very popular Damside hangout, whole-wheat rolls, banana muffins, cinnamon rolls, and apple strudel are the specialties, and they're all done quite well. I like coming here for breakfast, but light meals such as soups or chow mein fill the void later in the day. There's a covered patio with a few tables, but no indoor dining. For entertainment, you can watch the dog chase the cow.

**Gorkha Palace Restaurant and Bar.** Lakeside, Baidam, at the Lakeview Resort. ☎ **21477.** Main courses Rs80–Rs200 ($1.20–$3.05). No credit cards. Daily 6am–9:30pm. INTERNATIONAL/ INDIAN.

Located in a garden setting with thatched-roof covered patios, this is a great place to come for cocktails and an appetizer, as well as for dinner. The classic Nepali snack food "chicken chili boneless," a fiery combination of chicken pieces and onions heavily accented by chilis, makes a tasty starter. For main courses, try the Indian dishes in general—the *malai kofta*, a couple of towering potato dumplings in a savory sauce, and *paneer mahkani*, fried cheese in a spicy gravy, are particularly tasty. The nightly cultural program, consisting of live Nepali music and dancing, is genuinely delightful— authentic and enthusiastic.

**Gurung Momo Restaurant.** Lakeside, Baidam. No phone. Main courses Rs50–Rs150 (75¢–$2.25). Daily 5:30am–10pm. TIBETAN.

This little hole-in-the-wall is located within a group of similar momo stands on the road that leads to the boat launch for Barahi Mandir. Pull up a table out front, ignore the diesel fumes from passing trucks and buses, and dig into some delicious momos. These Tibetan standbys are akin to potstickers and are served either fried or steamed, with a hot sauce or ketchup for dipping. The portions here are generous, and some momos come with a spicy soup. The potato-onion-garlic and spinach-cheese momos are both great.

**The Hungry Eye.** Lakeside, Baidam. ☎ **20908.** Reservations recommended for groups. Main courses Rs100–Rs600 ($1.50–$9.10). AE, MC, V. Daily 6am–10pm. INTERNATIONAL.

Located across from a large old banyan tree and the king's Pokhara palace, The Hungry Eye has for years been one of the most popular restaurants. It has an extensive menu that features the usual Pokhara items: chow mein, lasagne, and various chicken dishes. However, the sizzling steaks and Italian dishes are the most popular items here. The atmosphere is a little more formal than at other Pokhara restaurants (waiters in bow ties), but don't worry, you don't have to dress up (or even be recently washed). Because The Hungry Eye is so large, with a big, bright, and airy covered patio to accommodate the throngs, it's popular with groups. There's a nightly "cultural program," though the performers seem just a little bit bored with their work.

**Lhasa Tibetan Restaurant.** Lakeside, Baidam. ☎ **23066.** Main courses Rs95–Rs450 ($1.45–$6.80). No credit cards. Daily 7am–9:30 or 10pm. TIBETAN.

Located on the Damside end of Lakeside's main drag, this restaurant has a tentlike interior that provides a somewhat exotic atmosphere. *Gyakok,* a traditional Tibetan hot-pot dish that must be ordered in advance, will provide a feast for 3 to 13 people. To accompany this meal, you might want to try some Tibetan butter tea or *tungba,* a traditional fermented millet beer drunk through a straw with a strainer on it. If you're not up for a feast, try the momos or chicken thukpa, both Tibetan specialties. Of course, there are also the ubiquitous Italian and Mexican offerings, tasty if unrecognizable, as well as Indonesian gado gado and good Indian tandoori dishes and nan (unleavened bread).

**۞ Mike's Restaurant.** Lakeside, Baidam, at Hotel Fewa. ☎ **20151.** Main courses Rs140–Rs240 ($2.10–$3.65). No credit cards. Daily 7am–9pm. AMERICAN/INTERNATIONAL.

Set in a pretty garden on a terrace beside Phewa Lake, Mike's is a true oasis and serves the best coffee in town (organic Nepali). Although Mike's is most famous for its huge breakfasts, Mexican and Minnesota-style American food are also served and there are plenty of meat choices, such as filet mignon. Vegetarians will be satisfied with the stir fries, enchiladas, and brown rice. Also worth ordering are the brownie sundaes, fresh juice, and real tequila margaritas. As you sit in your chair listening to mellow classical music, you can gaze out at sailboats drifting by or watch as the waiters use a slingshot to keep crows out of the "rubber" tree that shades the terrace.

**The Little Tibetan Tea Garden.** Lakeside, Baidam. ☎ **24241.** Main courses Rs50–Rs150 (75¢–$2.25). Daily 7am–10pm. TIBETAN/INTERNATIONAL.

Duck into this miniature bamboo jungle to feel worlds away from the hustle and bustle of Lakeside. Offerings are typically international, but the best choices are the Tibetan dishes such as *thenthuk* (broth with dumplings), momos (stuffed dumplings), and potato soups. There's also a good selection of reading materials tucked away here. The Little Tibetan Tea Garden is in north Lakeside, on the road that begins at the lake next to the official campground and leads toward Pokhara proper. To find it, head away from the lake, and a few doors up from the intersection, watch for the bamboo grove on your right.

**Rodee Restaurant.** Damside, Pardi. ☎ **21706.** Main courses Rs90–Rs450 ($1.35–$6.80). No credit cards. Daily 7am–10pm. INTERNATIONAL.

There are few options for dining in Damside, but there *is* the Rodee. Built right on the edge of the lake, this restaurant is little more than a shack, but it has tables in a back terrace that has great sunset views over the lake. The restaurant feels a bit like a stable and the music can be loud (you can bet it will be Tracy Chapman or Bob Marley); but the Indian food is pretty good.

## 5 Attractions

Pokhara isn't exactly a place you visit in order to do something in particular, it's more a place people visit so they can do nothing at all—a hangout. Still, there are some things to see, mostly natural attractions and a few temples, and plenty of outdoor activities to keep you occupied if you tire of sitting and gazing at the astounding views. See the map on page 179 for the location of Pokhara's main attractions.

## POKHARA'S NATURAL ATTRACTIONS

**Mountain Views**    The view of the Himalayas from Pokhara provides one of the world's most awe-inspiring scenery. Nowhere else on earth can you get so close (25 miles) to so many peaks that exceed 22,000 feet while relaxing in a subtropical valley. Starting from the left (west), the mountains are **Dhaulagiri** (26,795 ft.; 8,167m), **Annapurna I** (26,545 ft.; 8,091m); **Machhapuchhare** (22,956 ft.; 6,997m), **Annapurna III** (24,787 ft.; 7,555m), **Annapurna IV** (24,688 ft.; 7,525m), **Annapurna II** (26,041 ft.; 7,937m), and **Lamjung Himal** (22,909 ft.; 6,982m). The sunrise and sunset light shows, when alpenglow paints the peaks in shades of pink, rose, mauve, and lavender, are especially breathtaking.

While most Pokhara hotels have some sort of mountain view, the hotels in the Damside area have a far better view than those in the Lakeside neighborhood. If you aren't staying in Damside, you can enjoy the view from the parks near the dam. From these areas, you'll see not only the peaks, but their reflections in the lake. Another good way to enjoy the mountain views is to rent a boat and paddle out into the middle of the lake. Unfortunately, boats usually can't be rented until long after sunrise.

**Phewa Lake**    Along with the views of the mountains, Phewa Lake is the main reason most people spend time here. While the water is probably too polluted for swimming, sailboats and rowboats can be rented at various places around the lake (See "Outdoor Activities," below for details). For the less active, there are lakeside garden restaurants where you can sit and gaze out across the lake and the forested ridge on the south shore.

**Patale Chhango**    Located south of Damside on the right side of the Siddhartha Highway, the Patale Chhango is one of Nepal's most unusual natural attractions. Known by numerous names, including David's Falls, Devin's Falls, Devil's Falls, and Devi's Falls, this small waterfall disappears into a dark and steamy chasm/cave after coursing through a narrow gorge. There are small natural bridges, strange potholes carved by the river, and beautiful growths of ferns along the steep rock walls. One of the stories surrounding this mysterious little waterfall is that a fellow named David got swept away by the river years ago and was never seen again. The falls are open daily from 7:30am to 5pm, and a Rs5 (7.5¢) admission fee is charged. There are always numerous very-insistent trinket vendors set up outside the entrance to the falls.

**Seti River Gorge**    Best seen from the Mahendra Bridge, midway through the main Pokhara bazaar, this gorge is similar to Patale Chhango. The river has cut a narrow gorge less than 15 feet wide, but the water is nearly 50 feet below the level of the bridge. As you first begin to cross the bridge, you will see nothing but vegetation (and garbage) in the wide valley below you. As you approach the middle of the bridge, you begin to hear the sound of water. Without warning, you are looking down into a dark, mossy gorge.

## MUSEUMS

Currently, there is an international mountaineering museum under construction on the southeast side of Pokhara near the Shangri-La Village hotel. Be sure to see if this museum has been completed when you visit.

**Pokhara Museum.** Pode Tole ☎ **20413.** Admission Rs5 (7.5¢), Rs10 (15¢) extra if you take pictures. May–Sept Wed–Mon 10am–5pm; Oct–Apr 10am–4pm.

---

### The Legend of Phewa Lake

Legend has it that there was once a beautiful town in the valley now filled by the Phewa Lake. When a goddess disguised as an old beggar woman came to the city asking for a little food, none of the city's wealthy residents would give her a bite to eat. At last a poor old couple invited her to share their meager meal. When the goddess finished her meal, she advised the couple to abandon their home and flee to higher ground. Shortly after leaving home, the old couple glanced back to find their city covered with a shining lake. The goddess was Barahi, to whom there is now a temple on the island just off Lakeside.

---

Located north of the airport on the same road that goes past the airport's front gate, this small museum houses exhibits on the different tribal groups living in the Pokhara region, and for this reason it is worth visiting before you head out on a trek. For each ethnic group there is a display of mannequins in traditional dress. Exhibits also show typical homes and village life. There are also displays of musical instruments, old weapons, and old photos. An exhibit on a recently excavated 8,000-year-old village in the Mustang district offers an interesting glimpse into the long history of this region.

✪ **Annapurna Museum (Natural History Museum).** Prithvi Narayan Campus. ☎ **21102.** Admission free. Sun–Thurs 10am–5pm and Fri 10am–3pm (closed for lunch from 12:30–1:30pm).

Located at the north end of Pokhara on the university campus, this small natural history museum, with its poorly stuffed animals and badly painted murals, would hardly be worth mentioning if not for its entomological collection. The large collection of butterflies and moths is a lepidopterist's dream, and even those with only a passing interest in bugs will appreciate this collection. The Annapurna Conservation Area Project also has a very informative display at this museum. Anyone planning a trek should stop by and learn about the effects that trekkers have had on this region.

## TEMPLES, SHRINES & MONASTERIES

**The Barahi Temple**   Located on a small island just offshore from the Lakeside neighborhood, this is one of Pokhara's busiest temples. Dedicated to Barahi, the island temple is sometimes the scene of animal sacrifices, especially on Saturdays, when Nepalis flock to the temple. Boatmen are constantly ferrying people, devout Nepalis and tourists alike, to and from the island for around Rs20 (30¢).

**The Bindhabasini Temple**   Located on top of a small hill at the north end of the old Pokhara bazaar in Mohariya Tole, this small temple is dedicated to the goddess Bhagwati, who is also known as Bindhabasini. Stone steps lead up to the shady hilltop where the shrine is located. Chickens and other domestic animals are sometimes sacrificed to Bindhabasini.

**Nyeshang Monastery**   This modern Buddhist monastery is set on a wooded hilltop a mile or so to the east of the Mahendra Bridge, which is midway through the Pokhara bazaar. Though the monastery itself is not very impressive, there's a nice view. Tall, slender prayer flags flutter from poles beside the main building of the monastery, framing the view of the mountains. Remember to take off your shoes before entering the prayer hall.

**Gupteshwor Mahadev Cave**    Located across the street from Patale Chhango (Devi's Falls), this hot and steamy cave is where the waters of the mysterious waterfall end up. However, for safety reasons, you cannot visit the underground end of the falls. The cave is also the site of a shrine to Shiva. When the cave was discovered a few years back, a natural formation inside the cavern was thought to resemble a Shiva lingam. This natural formation is now the object of much devotion. On a visit to this cave, you're likely to see a priest officiating at the natural Shiva lingam, which is now elaborately decorated and protected inside a fence. Leading up to the cave entrance are numerous handicraft vendors. The cave is open daily from 7am to 5pm and admission is Rs20 (30¢).

Up at the north end of Pokhara, there is another cave, the Mahendra Cave, which is quite large but not very interesting.

## SCENIC FLIGHTS & ORGANIZED TOURS

Though the main attractions in Pokhara—the mountains and the lake—are readily visible from almost anywhere in the valley, you can book a tour that will take you to Pokhara's other main attractions, including important temples and the museums. These tours can be arranged through any travel agency in Lakeside or Damside for Rs200 ($3.05).

For an exhilarating view of Pokhara from the air, contact **Avia Club Nepal** (☎ 977/ 61-25192), which offers scenic flights over the valley in delta-wing ultralight planes. These open-cockpit planes are basically powered hang gliders and are simply the most exciting way to get an aerial view of Pokhara. A 15-minute flight costs $45, a 30-minute flight costs $90, and a 1-hour flight costs $170.

If you haven't got time to do the trek around the Annapurnas, you may still be able to get a close-up glimpse of the mountains on a ✪ **Buddha** airlines mountain flight. These flights had just started up at press time and it was uncertain whether they would continue. Check at a travel agency to find out more about them.

# 6  Outdoor Activities

Most people spending any time in Pokhara tend to be resting up before or after a trek. If, however, you feel like getting some exercise while you're in town, there are plenty of things to do.

**BICYCLING**    Bicycling is the best way to get around in Pokhara, though pedaling all the way to the upper end of Pokhara is exhausting if you don't have a bike with plenty of gears. Multigear mountain bikes rent for Rs75 to Rs100 ($1.15 to $1.50) per day and are readily available in Damside and Lakeside. Just look for a row of bicycles beside the road. You can even rent BMX bikes for kids.

One of the easiest bicycle destinations is Patale Chhango and the adjacent Tibetan Refugee Camp. For a real workout, try pedaling up to the north end of town. It's all initially uphill, but the ride back is a breeze.

For some **dirt-road pedaling,** try heading out from Lakeside along the north shore of Phewa Lake. This potholed road leads all the way to the far end of the lake, through countryside that is reminiscent of the Lakeside of 20 years ago.

For dirt roads and views, try riding south from the airport to Dhungesangu, a natural bridge across the Seti River. The route leads through terraced fields that are slowly being eaten up by the sprawl of Pokhara; but the views back to the north are superb and the natural bridge is fascinating. To get here, take the road just south of the airstrip, pedal east as far as you can, and then turn south. When you come to a small village, about 2 miles from the airport, you'll see a path to your left that leads to the natural bridge. From the bridge, you can look down into the deep, narrow gorge. From here, you can either cross the natural bridge (yes, there's a path across it) and circle back to Pokhara on paved roads or continue south on the dirt road you've been riding on. If you continue south, you will very shortly drop into a deep river valley. A great downhill, but remember that return uphill ride.

If you're interested in a guided bike ride, contact **Himalayan Mountain Bikes,** Lakeside (☎ 977/61-23240), or **Mustang Cycling,** Damside (☎ 977/61-23481).

**BOATING**    Boating on Phewa Lake, whether in a rowboat, sailboat, or kayak, is one of Pokhara's most popular pastimes. You can hire a colorfully painted wooden rowboat for around Rs125 ($1.90) per hour or Rs300 to Rs350 ($4.55 to $5.30) for the whole day if you want to paddle it yourself. If you are feeling lazy, boatmen will gladly paddle you around for an additional Rs30 to Rs40 (45¢ to 60¢) per hour. There are boats available in Damside at the little park adjacent to the Hotel Jharna and in several Lakeside locations, including just past the royal palace (opposite a little island with a temple) and at the north end of Lakeside adjacent to the public campground. The most popular destination for boaters is the island with the temple. There are also small sailboats available for Rs200 ($3.05) per hour at Lakeside's Hotel Fewa. Be careful of the unpredictable winds if you rent a sailboat.

**GOLFING**    Yes, it's even possible to play a round of golf in Pokhara. Out to the east of town, at the Dusit Thani Pulbari Resort, you'll find the nine-hole **Himalayan Golf Course** (☎ 27204), which is set on the edge of a cliff and has absolutely awesome views of the Himalayas. A round of golf costs Rs800 ($12.10) if you aren't a hotel guest, and golf club rentals are another Rs650 ($9.85).

**HIKING**    The Pokhara Valley is surrounded by hills and mountains, and there are numerous opportunities for hiking. Most of the popular hikes are to hills overlooking the valley. If you stop by the tourist office (see "Visitor Information," above, in this chapter) with your Pokhara map in hand, someone there can show you where to find the trails for various valley hikes. Alternatively, splurge on a copy of the Karto Atelier "Pokhara Town & Valley" map available for Rs750 ($11.35) at bookstores around town. This excellent Swiss-made topographic map shows all the major trails in the valley.

**To the Peace Stupa**    Under construction atop the forested 3,800-foot ridge that rises from the south shore of Phewa Lake is a Japanese-financed peace stupa that makes an excellent goal for a day hike. The trail up through this forest preserve begins just below the dam at the southeast end of the lake and climbs 1,000 feet to the ridgetop. A swinging footbridge crosses the narrow river that flows out of the dam, and a trail, which leads up through the forest, begins on the far side of this dam. It takes a couple of hours to hike up to the stupa, and along the way you might see monkeys and will certainly see plenty of birds and butterflies.

As you get closer to the top of the ridge, you'll start to catch views through the trees; when you finally break into the open, amid ridgetop pastures, you will most certainly find yourself breathless both from the hike up and from the scenery. With the lake in the foreground, at the base of a steep forested slope, and Machhapuchhare and the Annapurnas in the background, this is the single-best view in the region. The stupa itself, while large and impressive, can't compete.

An alternative route up here climbs steeply from Fewa Resort, which is on the south shore of the lake and can be reached by boat from Lakeside. There is also a route up here from Patale Chhango (Devi's Falls), though this route, on the south side of the ridge, is hot and generally unshaded.

**To Kahun Danda**  For a somewhat different view of the Pokhara Valley and the Himalayas, try hiking up to the top of Kahun Danda, a 5,000-foot-high hill northeast of town. Plan on about 5 hours to hike to the top and return. In addition to the viewing tower at the summit, there are the ruins of an old fort.

The main trail begins east of the Mahendra Bridge, which is midway up through the Pokhara bazaar area. After crossing the bridge, watch for the telecommunications office, and make a left turn. Follow this road as it winds around (you'll probably have to ask directions), angling generally northeast. You should eventually find the trail, which heads out across the valley before starting to climb the hill. Just keep heading for the viewing tower up at the top, and you should reach the summit in a couple of hours. An alternative route up starts at the Nyeshang Monastery, which is about 1 mile east of the Mahendra Bridge.

**HORSEBACK RIDING**  Small, sturdy ponies have for centuries been used on the trading route between Pokhara and Tibet, and although this route is no longer as important as it once was, there are still plenty of ponies in the area. If you'd like to explore some of the Pokhara Valley from the back of one of these ponies, contact any Pokhara travel agency or **Himalayan Pony Trek** (☎ 977/61-24114), which offers a number of different trips. Prices range from Rs700 to Rs1,300 ($10.60 to $19.70) for a guided half-day ride, between Rs1,150 and Rs2,100 ($17.40 and $31.80) for a full-day ride. Overnight rides are Rs1,500 (22.75) per day.

**WHITE-WATER RAFTING & KAYAKING**  Just as in Kathmandu, there are plenty of ○ **white-water rafting** companies operating out of Pokhara. These companies offer trips on the Kali Gandaki, the Marshyangdi, the Seti, and the Trishuli. The Kali Gandaki has long been the favorite whitewater river in this region, but due to the construction of a new dam, the raftable stretch of the river has been shortened from 5 days to 3. The Seti is considered the warmest and easiest river in the region, a good choice for beginners, whereas the Marshyangdi is the most difficult, with Class IV and V rapids. The Trishuli River starting point is actually closer to Kathmandu than it is to Pokhara, but this Class III–IV river is popular with people heading to Chitwan from Pokhara.

Reliable Pokhara rafting companies include **Himalayan Encounters,** Hallan Chowk, Lakeside (☎ 977/61-21755; fax 977/61-21022); **Ultimate Descents,** Snowland Hotel, Lakeside (☎ 977/61-23240); and **Equator Expeditions,** Lakeside (☎ 977/61-20688), across from the Nirulas Restaurant.

If you'd like to turn your trip to Nepal into an educational expedition, you can learn to kayak while you're here in Pokhara. The **Ganesh Shop,** Lakeside (☎ 977/61-22657), operates 4-day kayaking clinics that start out on Phewa Lake and then continue on the Seti River. These classes cost $145. This shop also rents kayaking equipment.

Any of the small travel agencies around Lakeside or Damside can arrange a rafting trip for you. These trips start at the same place that rafting trips from Kathmandu start. Rates are also comparable. See "The Active Vacation Planner," in chapter 3, for details.

## 7 Shopping

In the plethora of shops selling Nepali, Tibetan, and Kashmiri handicrafts, a couple of shops stand out. In mid-Lakeside, **Dhukuti** (the Association for Craft Producers; ☎ 24802) is a local nonprofit store that benefits disadvantaged craft workers. Dhukuti carries quality Nepali-made crafts, including wool products, leather, and metal work (they also have a shop in Patan; see "Shopping," in chapter 5). **Himalayan Natural Fibres Products** (☎ 21702), located toward the north end of Lakeside, sells items made from hemp by both Nepali and Tibetan artisans from the Tibetan Refugee Camp in Pokhara. A portion of the profits from the sale of these accessories, garments, and blankets benefits the workers.

For an excellent selection of Tibetan and Nepali handicrafts, visit the **Tashiling Tibetan Refugee Camp,** located almost directly across the street from Patale Chhango (Devi's Falls). Here you'll find a lively outdoor souvenir market operated by gregarious Tibetan women who just don't know how to take No for an answer. There's also a carpet showroom adjacent to the camp's carpet factory. At the factory, where large rooms are almost entirely filled with huge wooden looms at which young women sit tying knots, you can view all the stages in making a hand-knotted wool carpet, from dying the wool to trimming the finished carpet with huge shears. While the showroom is open daily from 10am to 6pm, the factory itself is closed on Saturday. There is no charge for looking around the factory, but photography is not permitted.

## 8  Pokhara After Dark

Shops in Pokhara tend to stay open as late as there are tourists out on the streets, and indeed shopping is a major after-dark activity here. However, if you'd rather sit back with a beer or a cocktail and listen to some loud music (sometimes it's even live), try the following.

Currently, **Lakeside's Club Amsterdam Café & Bar,** with a pool table, live music, a great sound system, shiny woodwork everywhere, and a garden overlooking the lake, is *the* place to hang out in Pokhara. It's located on the main street in Lakeside. The **Moondance Pub,** upstairs from Ganesh Kayaking, has a couple of pool tables and is another popular spot.

While shopping and hanging out in bars are the main Pokhara evening entertainments, several restaurants around town put on nightly "cultural programs" that consist of traditional Nepali songs and dancing. In the Lakeside area, there are cultural programs at the Lakeview Resort's **Gorkha Palace Restaurant** (☎ 21477), at **The Hungry Eye** (☎ 20908), and at **Fish Tail Lodge** (☎ 20071). The program at Fish Tail Lodge costs Rs150 ($2.25), whereas at the two restaurants, the program is free if you are eating dinner. The Gorkha Palace show is the best of the lot.

## 9  Easy Excursions from Pokhara

Pokhara also makes a good base for several day and overnight trips in the region. These trips all include a good bit of hiking so are good preparatory excursions if you are getting ready for a trek. If you don't have time for a trek, these day hikes will give you a taste of what trekking is all about.

### SARANGKOT

Sarangkot is a small village perched atop the ridge that rises just to the north of Pokhara's Lakeside neighborhood. From this village, there are superb views both of the Annapurnas and of Phewa Lake and the Pokhara Valley. Because of its proximity to Pokhara, this 5,200-foot hill has long been a popular destination for day hikers looking to do a bit of strenuous hiking. At the top of the hill there are also the remains of an old fortress built by King Prithvi Narayan Shah in the 18th century. It was this king who unified Nepal by conquering the many tiny kingdoms that controlled the Himalayas' valleys.

The hike up to Sarangkot from the base of the hill takes 2 to 3 hours and another 1 to 2 hours to descend, so you need a full day. Better yet, plan to spend the night at the top so you can enjoy the sunset and sunrise views. The main trail, much of which has now been replaced by a paved road, starts near the Bindhabasini Temple at the north end of Pokhara. A sign points the way to Sarangkot. Because much of the route requires hiking along the road, this part of the hike is no longer as enjoyable as it once was. While the road is narrow, scenic, and little traveled, it's still a road, so you might want to skip this part and instead take a taxi to the end of the pavement and start hiking from there. From this point, it is about 45 minutes to Sarangkot. The steep alternative route back to Pokhara descends, mostly on stairs, directly toward the lake, from which you can hike back to Lakeside on a dirt road that parallels the lakeshore.

**GETTING THERE**    A taxi can drive you partway to the top for around Rs400 ($6.05) one way, or Rs500 ($7.60) round-trip. Alternatively, you can rent a motor-cycle and ride up (again, not quite to the top) for Rs400 to Rs500 ($6.05 to $7.60) per day, plus gas.

**WHERE TO STAY**    There are a couple of very basic trekking-style lodges up here that charge Rs100 to Rs250 ($1.50 to $3.80) per person for a room.

## BEGNAS TAL & RUPA TAL
The Pokhara Valley is Nepal's lakes district, and out on the east side of the valley, you'll find two lakes, which are smaller than Phewa Lake but just as scenic. Begnas Tal and Rupa Tal (*tal* means "lake" in Nepali) are far less developed than Pokhara, and the vil-lages along their shores provide glimpses into rural Nepali life.

The best way to see Rupa and Begnas Tals is from the trail atop the ridge that runs between the two lakes. This trail begins in the village where the bus stops. You can also hike around Begnas Lake, and if you have plenty of energy, also hike up into the hills surrounding the lakes. Boats can be rented on Begnas Tal, the larger of the two lakes.

**GETTING THERE**    Buses from Pokhara to Begnas Lake leave from the main Pokhara bus park and cost Rs30 (45¢). The trip takes about an hour. Be sure to ask upon arrival what time buses return to Pokhara.

**WHERE TO STAY**    See Begnas Lake Resort & Villas, under "Where to Stay" in the Pokhara section, above, for information on accommodations.

## GORKHA
Located a little less than halfway to Kathmandu, Gorkha was the seat of power for King Prithvi Narayan Shah, who, in the 18th century, united Nepal by conquering dozens of tiny Himalayan kingdoms, including those of the Kathmandu Valley. The soldiers of Gorkha became so legendary that the British recruited men from this region to serve in the British army. These soldiers are known today as the Gurkhas, some of the most feared soldiers in the world. Today, though there is a good road to Gorkha, the town is rarely visited by tourists.

Though Gorkha is an excellent town for starting a trek into the surrounding hills, its main claim to fame is the **old fort** from which King Prithvi Narayan Shah launched his conquest of Nepal. This fort sits 1,000 feet above the city on a forested hilltop and commands a nearly 360-degree view of the surrounding countryside—an excellent spot from which to conquer everything in sight. There are two routes from town up to the fort—the steep route and the steeper route. Either way, it's going to be a sweaty uphill slog. If you're a fast walker, you can be at the fort in 30 minutes, but 45 min-utes is a better estimate. At the bus turnaround, as you're looking up at the fort, one route will start on your left, and one route will start on your right. The former circles

## Warning

In 1998, Gorkha was one of the centers of the Maoist insurgency in the hill country of central Nepal. Before heading this way, be sure to find out, either by contacting your embassy or by asking locals, whether it is advisable to visit this historic town.

around to the west of town before turning back east on a well-constructed stone stairway. This is the steep route. The steeper route climbs through the center of the town and plows straight up the hillside on a vertiginous stairway. This was the path that visiting vassals were forced to walk when they came to pay respects to their conqueror.

After such a strenuous hike, you'll probably be expecting Camelot, but what you'll actually find is a rather modest brick building that is only loosely a fort. "Palace" might be a better term for the building, but it is a rather humble palace. Newari craftsmen from the Kathmandu Valley were brought in to build the fort, and the similarity to the palaces of the Kathmandu Valley is immediately evident. The building is constructed of red brick with intricately carved latticework windows and is surrounded by several stone-paved terraces.

The fort, which houses a temple to Kali, is also a pilgrimage site. The statue inside this temple is considered so holy and powerful that only priests and the king of Nepal are allowed to view it. Common folks must be content to sacrifice goats and chickens at the front door of the temple, and the steps leading up to the shrine are often stained with fresh blood.

In front of and below the main palace building is a shrine surrounding the cave in which a famous holy man named Gorahknath meditated. It is from this holy man that Gorkha takes its name. Around to the east of the fort are several *stelae*, carved stones that record historical events from Gorkha's heyday.

Down in town there is another palace that is known as the Lower Palace. This building was more of an administrative center and was built around 1750. A parade ground in front of the palace gives the building a very imposing appearance. Look for the peacock windows that are almost identical to the famous peacock window in Bhaktapur.

**GETTING THERE**    To reach Gorkha from Pokhara, you can take a tourist bus as far as the turnoff at Kaireni for Rs200 to Rs250 ($3.05 to $3.80) and then catch a local bus the rest of the way for around Rs15 (25¢). Alternatively, you can catch a regular bus at the main Pokhara bus park for Rs60 (90¢). However, these buses take an hour or so longer to reach the turnoff and are much less comfortable. You can also hire a taxi for the day for Rs2,500 to Rs3,000 ($37.90 to $45.45), or a motorcycle for Rs500 ($7.60) plus gas at Rs40 (60¢) per liter.

## WHERE TO STAY & DINE

**Gorkha Hill Resort.** Laxmi Bazaar, Gorkha. ☎ **977/64-29325.** Reservations in Kathmandu: Kamaladi (P.O. Box 3011), Kathmandu. ☎ **977/1-419798** or 977/1-423128. Fax 977/1-419260. 24 units. $60 double. MC, V.

Located 2½ miles downhill from the town of Gorkha, this small lodge sits on a hill overlooking valleys and mountains and has a good view of Gorkha's old fort. Rooms are comfortable, though simply furnished. Gardens and lawns create a pleasantly relaxing atmosphere for gazing up at snowcapped peaks. If you'd like to get away from the crowds and noise during your trip to Nepal, this is a good choice. Meals are an additional $22 per person per day.

**Hotel Gorkha Bisauni.** Gorkha Bazaar, Gorkha. ☎ **977/64-20107.** 20 units (14 with private bathroom). $1.50–$2.30 double with shared bathroom, $3.05–$9.10 double with private bathroom. No credit cards.

This is the backpacker's first choice in Gorkha, and as you can guess by the prices, the accommodations are Spartan and only marginally clean (slightly better than you might find in a trekkers' lodge on the trail). The restaurant here is your best choice in town, and there's a shady garden. You'll find the lodge back downhill from the bus turnaround.

# 8 The Terai

The Terai, Nepal's lowland area along the Indian border, is primarily an agricultural and industrial region. Its vast flat plains, an extension of the fertile plain created by the Ganges River, are a striking contrast to the jagged peaks that most foreigners associate with Nepal. Until the 1960s, when DDT was used to eradicate malaria-carrying mosquitoes, the Terai was covered with dense forests of hardwoods, primarily *sal* trees. The Tharu people, who have a natural resistance to malaria, were among the few inhabitants of the region. When malarial mosquitoes were brought under control, people from the higher regions of Nepal began migrating to the Terai. Since that time, much of the forest has been cut down for building materials and firewood, and much of the region has come under cultivation.

Fortunately, several areas of the Terai have been set aside as national parks and wildlife preserves, for it is here that Nepal's greatest concentrations of wildlife live. **Tigers, one-horned rhinoceroses, wild elephants, bears, monkeys, deer, antelope, crocodiles,** and many other rare and endangered species make their homes in the Terai. No visit to Nepal is complete without a visit to either ✪ **Royal Chitwan National Park** or **Royal Bardia Wildlife Reserve** to see some of these wild animals in their native habitats.

The Terai was also the birthplace of Prince Siddhartha Gautama, better known as the **Buddha.** What is today the small town of Lumbini was once a garden in the kingdom of Kapilvastu. It was in that garden that the Buddha was born more than 2,500 years ago. Today, Lumbini is one of the world's most important pilgrimage sites, and it is in the process of being developed into a world heritage site.

## 1 Koshi Tappu Wildlife Reserve

310 miles (500km) SE of Kathmandu; 110 miles (178km) E of Royal Chitwan National Park

Located in far eastern Nepal, the Koshi Tappu Wildlife Reserve encompasses an artificial delta on the Sapta Koshi River and covers about 70 square miles (175km²). The wetlands, which compose the majority of this reserve, were created in the early 1960s after the construction of a kilometer-long barrage (diversion dam). The barrage, which lies just north of the Indian border, was built to prevent flooding on the Indian plains to the south. However, one of the side benefits of this flood-control project was the creation of a vast expanse of open water, marshes, mudflats, and lagoons that together attract some 400 species of birds, making this one of the best birding spots in all of Asia. Many species that stop here can be seen nowhere else in Nepal. The best months for birding are October through March, with February and March seeing the highest numbers of waterfowl and shore-birds. During the winter months, when skies are clear, 27,758-foot Mt. Makalu, the fifth-highest peak on earth, dominates the horizon.

The reserve's waters are also known for their populations of **Gangetic dolphins** and fish-eating **gharial crocodiles.** Intermixed with the wetlands are grasslands, farm fields, scrub, and deciduous forests, which together serve as one of the last refuges of the endangered *arna,* the wild **water buffalo.** It was to protect these rare buffaloes that the reserve was created. Other mammals of this reserve include the *nilgai* or **blue bull** (a large antelope), **spotted deer, jackals, fishing cats,** and **leopards.**

## ESSENTIALS

**VISITOR INFORMATION**    The park headquarters are located in the village of Kusaha, 1½ miles (2.6km) north of the Mahendra East-West Highway. Reserve admission (valid for 2 days) is Rs650 ($9.85). However, if you are visiting the park on a package tour, reserve admission will be included with your package. Be sure to bring a flashlight, batteries, sunscreen, insect repellent, sunglasses, a hat, a long-sleeve shirt, and long pants. Clothes should be of neutral colors (avoid white, red, and yellow).

**GETTING THERE**    The nearest airport is at Biratnagar, which has service from Kathmandu on Royal Nepal Airlines, Buddha Air, and Necon Air. The flight takes 45 minutes and round-trip airfare is $140. Buses from Kathmandu to Biratnagar leave from the Gongabu Bus Park on the Ring Road north of Thamel, take 12 hours, and cost Rs298 ($4.50). From Biratnagar to the reserve is another 1- to 1½-hour drive (wildlife camps will pick you up).

## WHAT TO SEE & DO

The best way to see this reserve is by staying at one of the two deluxe tent camps listed below. These camps specialize in ✪ **bird watching,** and daily activities are focused on seeing as many species of birds as possible. Among the rare birds that have been spotted here are Bengal floricans, swamp francolins, red-necked falcons, striated marsh warblers, black-necked storks, greater adjutant storks, lesser adjutant storks, great stone plovers, dusky eagle owls, and Baer's pochards. Guided bird walks in different reserve habitats assure birders that they will add numerous sightings to their life's list.

**Guided hikes, mountain-bike rides, four-wheel-drive excursions,** and even **elephant rides** all provide opportunities for spotting the reserve's wild water buffalo, spotted deer, hog deer, and blue bulls. **Boat excursions** out onto the wide waters of the Sapta Koshi may provide glimpses of Gangetic dolphins, marsh-mugger crocodiles, and gharial crocodiles.

A visit to Koshi Tappu can also be combined with an 8- to 10-day **rafting trip** down the Sun Koshi River or a trek in the Kanchenjunga region.

## WHERE TO STAY

**Aqua Birds Unlimited Camp.** c/o Manaslu Hotel, Lazimpat, Kathmandu. ☎ **977/ 1-429515** or 977/1-413470. Fax 977/1-416516. E-mail: aquabird@ccsl.com.np. 14 tents. 2-night, 3-day package $436 double. AE, MC, V (in Kathmandu only).

Located adjacent to the reserve headquarters overlooking the Kusaha wetlands, this is the newest tent camp at Koshi Tappu. Though not quite as luxurious as the Koshi

Tappu Wildlife Camp (tents don't have attached bathrooms), Aqua Birds offers the same excellent bird-watching opportunities, and it is not unusual to see as many as 100 species of birds in 1 day here. Activities offered include not only bird walks and boat excursions, but elephant rides as well. The thatched-roof dining hall has an excellent view of the marsh, so you won't have to give up birding just because it's mealtime.

**Koshi Tappu Wildlife Camp.** Kamaladi (P.O. Box 536), Kathmandu. ☎ **977/1-247078** or 977/1-247079. Fax 977/1-224237. E-mail: explore@mos.com.np. 12 tents. 2-night, 3-day package $532 double. AE, MC, V (in Kathmandu only). Closed May–Sept.

Located at the northeastern corner of the reserve, this deluxe tented camp was the first such camp at this reserve. Accommodations are in large safari tents that have verandas and attached bathrooms and are pitched under thatched-roof shelters. A large thatched-roof central building serves as dining hall and bar. Guided bird walks are the main activity here (350 species have been seen in the immediate vicinity), but there are also trips by raft out onto the wide waters of the Sapta Koshi. Night drives with spotlights also provide an interesting opportunity for spotting nocturnal wildlife. Mountain bikes are available for exploring the reserve. For those wishing a wilder experience and an excellent chance of seeing Gangetic dolphins and arnas, there is a small camp inside the reserve.

## 2　Royal Chitwan National Park

103 miles (166km) SW of Kathmandu; 127 miles (204km) SE of Pokhara; 93 miles (150km) E of Lumbini

Located along the Indian border in the Terai, Royal Chitwan National Park is Nepal's premier wildlife-viewing area and is one of the few places on earth where you can still see a Bengal tiger in the wild. The park, formerly a royal hunting reserve, covers nearly 400 square miles of dense forest and riverine grasslands and is home to an estimated 100 Bengal tigers and 500 Indian one-horned rhinoceroses. Other wildlife found within the park includes sloth bears, leopards, *gaurs* (Indian bison), several species of deer, wild boars, several species of monkeys, two species of crocodiles, freshwater Gangetic dolphins, and more than 400 species of birds.

Contrary to what you may be led to believe by agents trying to sell you a package trip to the park, Chitwan is neither a jungle nor a rain forest. This area has two very distinct seasons: the wet monsoon season (June through Sept) and the dry winter months. The best time of year to visit the park is March through May, after local villagers have harvested the area's elephant grass, which can grow up to 20 feet tall. With these tall grasses chopped down, it is much easier to spot the park's resident rhinos.

The local Tharu people have traditionally built their homes from various grasses gathered along the many rivers that flow through Royal Chitwan National Park, and each year, usually in January, local villagers are allowed to enter the park for a few weeks to cut as much grass as they want. This grass later forms the walls and roofs of their simple houses. After the grass has been cut, the stubble is set on fire to fertilize the soil, and despite the fires and the hundreds of villagers in the park at this time, January can still be a good time to see wildlife. I've been to Chitwan during harvest season on two occasions and have seen many rhinos, deer, monkeys, and even a tiger.

## ESSENTIALS

**VISITOR INFORMATION**　Although the park headquarters are in Kasara, there is also a visitor center and museum in Sauraha. Park admission for 2 days is Rs650 ($9.85). Be sure to bring a flashlight, batteries, sunscreen, insect repellent, sunglasses,

# Royal Chitwan National Park

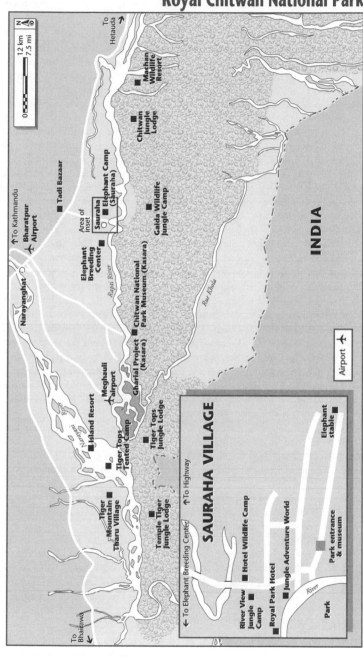

N

0  12 km
0  7.5 mi

To Hetauda

Machan Wildlife Resort

Chitwan Jungle Lodge

Tadi Bazaar

Elephant Camp (Sauraha)

To Kathmandu

Bharatpur Airport

Area of inset

Sauraha

Galda Wildlife Camp

Elephant Breeding Center

Narayanghat

Rapti River

Chitwan National Park Museum (Kasara)

INDIA

Rue Khola

Gharial Project (Kasara)

Meghauli Airport

Island Resort

Narayani River

Tiger Tops Tented Camp

Tiger Tops Jungle Lodge

Airport ✈

To Highway

Tiger Mountain Tharu Village

Temple Tiger Jungle Lodge

To Bhairawa

To Elephant Breeding Center

## SAURAHA VILLAGE

Elephant stable

Hotel Wildlife Camp

Jungle Adventure World

Park entrance & museum

River View Jungle Camp

Royal Park Hotel

River

Park

203

a hat, a long-sleeve shirt, and long pants. Clothing should be in neutral colors (not white, red, and yellow).

**GETTING THERE/DEPARTING**  There are **two airports** in the Chitwan area, Meghauli and Bharatpur, with service from Kathmandu. Meghauli airport is used primarily by Tiger Tops and Temple Tiger, and a round-trip ticket from Kathmandu is $144. The Bharatpur airport is used primarily by Gaida Wildlife Camp, Chitwan Jungle Lodge, and Machan Wildlife Resort, and a round-trip ticket costs $110. Either flight takes about 25 minutes. Airlines flying to these airports include Gorkha Airlines, Lumbini Airways, Royal Nepal Airlines, Cosmic Air, and Yeti Airways (Meghauli).

If you are headed to one of the many lodges in the village of Sauraha and if your budget allows you to travel only by bus, your best bet is to book a seat on one of the tourist buses, which run from both Kathmandu and Pokhara. These buses take slightly less time than the regular **bus** and are a bit more comfortable. The fare is Rs140 ($2.10) one-way. Tickets are available at hotels and travel agencies in either city.

The Sauraha tourist bus park is at a ford in a small river 6 kilometers south of Tadi Bazaar and the main road. From here, most visitors transfer in battered Land Rovers and the like, although the bus park is close enough that you can hike if your pack isn't too heavy. Regular buses stop right on the main road, in Tadi Bazaar.

If you want to travel by regular bus (and, trust me, you really don't), plan on at least a 10-hour ride from either Kathmandu or Pokhara, with a probable bus change in Bharatpur or Narayanghar. Be sure to tell the driver of the second bus that you want to get off at Tadi Bazaar. Buses leave Kathmandu from the Gongabu Bus Park on the Ring Road north of Thamel. Buses also leave daily from the main bus terminal in Pokhara. The bus from Kathmandu to Narayanghat, just a few miles from Tadi Bazaar, costs around Rs81 ($1.25). From Pokhara, you'll pay about the same.

When you get off the bus, whether it is a tourist bus or a regular bus, you will immediately be assaulted by touts screaming at you and grabbing your bags. If you are on a prepaid package tour, there will be a representative of your lodge waiting to pick you up; just wave your travel voucher at the touts, and they'll leave you alone. If, however, you don't have a reservation, you're fair game.

If you can fight off the touts, try to find a Jeep going to the lodge you have chosen. If your preferred lodge does not have a Jeep meeting the bus, you'll have to negotiate passage on another Jeep for Rs30 (45¢). No doubt a tout will climb into the vehicle with you and convince you that you should have a look at his excellent and hygienic lodge.

If you're coming to Chitwan on a package tour, you will almost certainly be given the option of traveling by car. The round-trip by car will cost between $60 and $100, but if you're going to spend $100, you might as well fly.

If you are on a package trip, your departure arrangements will be taken care of; otherwise, you will need to arrange with your lodge to transport you to the tourist bus park, Tadi Bazaar (for regular buses), or the Bharatpur airport. Be sure to let the lodge staff know a day in advance so they can arrange for a jeep. If traveling to Pokhara, Kathmandu, or India by regular bus, you will need to change in Bharatpur.

## WHAT TO SEE & DO

Most visitors to Royal Chitwan National Park are on a package tour that includes an elephant ride, a canoe trip, a jungle hike, a bird walk, a trip to the elephant breeding center, and a Tharu cultural performance. However, if you are on a budget and want to choose from among these activities, the following information should help you to make your selections. No matter which activities you choose, please remember that many of the animals that live in this park are very dangerous. You visit at your own risk.

You can arrange any of the tours below with various guide outfits located in Sauraha. Also in Sauraha, beside the ticket kiosk for the park, you'll find a small museum with information on Chitwan's wildlife and the Tharu people. There's also a gift shop here.

**Elephant Rides**   The very first thing you should do is get your name on the list for an elephant ride (or elephant safari, as it's called). The best and safest vantage point for viewing rhinos is from the back of an elephant, and this elevation also makes it easier to spot other wildlife. Even if you don't see any wild animals (and some people don't), riding through the forest on the back of an elephant is great fun. A 1-hour ride inside the park costs Rs650 ($9.85) per person, and a 2- to 2½-hour ride outside the park in one of Sauraha's community forests costs Rs550 ($8.35) per person. You are just about as likely to see rhinos outside the park as you are to see them inside.

**Bird Walks**   Chitwan is well-known for its abundant and varied bird life, and no visit to the park is complete without doing a bit of bird watching, even if you aren't a birder. It's hard not to get interested in this region's birds when there are wild peacocks in the trees. Guided bird walks usually head along the river and then return through the small forest that surrounds the park offices in Sauraha. A 4-hour bird walk costs Rs300 ($4.55) per person.

Binoculars can be rented for Rs10 (15¢) per hour or Rs80 ($1.20) per day in Sauraha at the Bird Education Society, which is located near the village's main intersection. A Chitwan birding checklist is also available for Rs100 ($1.50).

**Dugout Canoe Trip**   A ride in one of the Terai's long (and tippy) dugout canoes is an experience not to be missed. You're likely to see lots of kingfishers and other birds, and, if you're lucky, you might even see a few marsh-mugger crocodiles sunning themselves on the river banks. This species of crocodile is known as a man-eater throughout India and Nepal and is best given a wide berth. For some strange reason, the dugouts always seem to feel more tippy when there are crocodiles around. Currently, canoe rides are offered in conjunction with a visit to the elephant breeding center for Rs500 ($7.60) per person. These canoe rides last only about 30 minutes.

**Elephant Breeding Center**   An hour's walk (or a 20-min. bike ride) from Sauraha, there is a government elephant breeding center where the adorable baby elephants are the big attraction. At any given time, there are usually three baby elephants under a year old at the camp. This breeding center was established in 1975 to provide elephants that could be trained to carry people on the ever popular rides here at Chitwan. Keep in mind that while the baby elephants are incredibly cute, they are also amazingly strong and can be very aggressive. Beware of their trunks, which they sometimes use to smack unsuspecting visitors. Admission to the breeding center is Rs15 (20¢), though most people now visit as part of a canoe-ride excursion. If you want to visit on your own, take the side road that leads out of Sauraha from Hotel Jungle Camp.

There is also an elephant camp in Sauraha, though this one is simply where the park's elephants are stabled when they aren't carrying visitors into the park. Here you can often watch men making elephant power pills (dietary supplements) by filling a grass cup with rice and sugar and then shaping the cup into a ball.

**Jungle Drives**   During the dry winter months, when it's possible to drive a Jeep across the Rapti River, jungle drives deep into the national park are offered. These drives are not likely to turn up much wildlife, since the truck's engine generally scares away everything in the area, but the trip's final destination, the gharial breeding center, is interesting. Gharials are a type of fish-eating crocodile with a long, thin snout that gives them a supercilious appearance. Many years ago, floods swept away much of the region's gharials, so this center was set up to help restore the population to its previous levels. You can see baby gharials that look like they belong in terrariums and 12-foot-long adults that look like dinosaurs. A 4-hour jungle drive costs around Rs500 ($7.60) per person.

**Jungle Walks**  If you are in good physical shape and don't mind being exposed to a little danger, a 4- to 5-hour walk through the park with a trained naturalist/guide is one of the best ways to see wildlife up close. You may, however, have to spend some time up in a tree if you get *too* close to a rhino. These lumbering behemoths have poor eyesight, and to protect themselves they will charge almost anything that moves. Should one charge at you, the best thing to do is climb a tree. If there is no tree, run in a curve and throw down some article of clothing; this will usually distract a rhino. On a walk through the park, you are likely to see rhinos, deer, wild boars, monkeys, and crocodiles. A full-day hike will cost around Rs350 ($5.30) per person.

**Bike Rides**  Another possible activity in the area is a guided bike ride. These rides sometimes turn up wildlife and usually stop at a nearby Tharu village. One of the destinations for these rides is a forested, marshy area known as 20,000 Lakes, which is home to many species of birds not usually seen around Sauraha. Rhinos, deer, and sloth bears are also sometimes spotted in this little-visited area, which is a good place to get away from the crowds of tourists around Sauraha. Four-hour guided bike rides cost around Rs350 ($5.30). If you'd just like to do a little exploring on your own, or want to ride to the Elephant Breeding Center, you can rent a bike in Sauraha for Rs100 ($1.50) a day.

**Cultural Programs**  Package tours to Chitwan always include a "cultural program" put on by a local dance troupe. These programs include various traditional dances, and a dance using short sticks that are beaten together by the dancers. Whether these programs are traditional or not, they're mildly entertaining and are about the only nightlife there is in these parts. The programs always culminate with a bit of audience participation.

## WHERE TO STAY
Most people who come to Chitwan are on 2- to 4-day package tours that include transportation, accommodations, all meals, park entrance fees, and activities. This applies to people staying at lodges inside or outside the park. The main difference between staying inside or outside the park is that should you choose to stay inside the park, you'll have much more of a wilderness experience (though you'll pay considerably more for this feeling of being deep in the wilds of Nepal).

Outside the park, prices are generally much lower (sometimes only a few dollars), and accommodations are much more basic (sometimes a tiny mud-walled, thatched-roof hut with shared bathroom). In fact, the village of Sauraha, on the northern edge of the park, has dozens of cheap lodges catering to backpack travelers. All lodges, whether located inside or outside the park, include the same basic excursions (though inside the park, you'll likely spend much more time on elephants), and your chances of seeing rhinos and tigers (usually the main objective of anyone coming here) are generally the same no matter where you stay. As elsewhere in Nepal, the newest lodges and hotels are usually the best because maintenance is rarely a priority at such places and within a few years they generally become quite run down.

While most people staying at lodges within the park arrive by plane and those staying in Sauraha arrive by bus, it is also possible (and quite popular) to spend 2 (or even 3) days white-water rafting en route to Chitwan.

One more thing you should know is that the rates listed here are *published* rates. In actuality, Chitwan lodges almost never charge these prices, not even in the high seasons. It is not unusual to walk into a lodge office in Kathmandu and immediately be offered a 30% discount; always ask for a discount. Also, keep in mind that if you're planning to stay at one of the cheaper lodges in Sauraha, you might save a bit of money by just showing up instead of booking the room in advance. On the other hand, if you show up without a reservation, you will have to deal with the touts (not a pleasant way to begin your "jungle adventure").

## IN THE PARK

Whether it's to create the appropriate atmosphere or to save on fuel costs, lodges within the park do not have electricity in the rooms. Instead, you are provided with a kerosene lantern each evening at sunset. These lodges do, however, provide hot showers, heating the water either with firewood or with solar panels. The one thing electricity is used for at most lodges is slide shows on the natural history of the national park. These slide shows usually alternate with Tharu "cultural programs" (see "What to See & Do," above). Also, should you have your kids along, you'll be glad to know that children under 12 usually get a 50% discount off the rates.

### Very Expensive

**Chitwan Jungle Lodge.** Durbar Marg (P.O. Box 1281), Kathmandu. ☎ 977/1-228458 or 977/1-228918. Fax 977/1-228349. E-mail: wildlife@resort.wlink.com.np. 32 units. 2-night, 3-day package $400 double (transfers extra). MC, V.

Located just inside the eastern end of the park, which is within the least-visited part that is easily accessible, this lodge is built close to the south bank of the Rapti River. Accommodations are in traditional Tharu-style huts with grass-and-mud walls and thatched roofs. These huts are built around a sunny garden where guests can lounge in the sun when they aren't busy viewing wildlife. As one of the most economical lodges inside the park, this is just about your best bet if you want to feel as though you're truly out in the jungle. However, you may not get in as much elephant riding here as you will at some of the more expensive jungle lodges inside the park.

**Gaida Wildlife Camp.** Durbar Marg (P.O. Box 2056), Kathmandu. ☎ 977/1-220940 or 977/1-227425. Fax 977/1-227292. E-mail: gaida@mos.com.np. 30 units at lodge, 12 tents at camp. 2-night, 3-day package (1 night at camp) $424 double; 2-night, 3-day package (both nights at lodge) $470 double (transfers extra). MC, V.

While Gaida's main lodge is located just outside the village of Sauraha on a tiny piece of the park on the north bank of the Rapti, the lodge's jungle camp is deep inside the park at the base of the Churia Hills. For this reason, should you decide to stay here, it is definitely worth opting for a package that includes a night at the tented camp. The tented camp will be especially appealing to avid bird-watchers, who will see many more species of birds than can be seen around the main lodge. Though the location is remote, you'll be staying in safari tents that actually have attached bathrooms, so you won't be lacking for creature comforts. The tented camp is, however, open only from October through May.

**✪ Machan Wildlife Resort.** Durbar Marg (P.O. Box 78), Kathmandu. ☎ 977/1-245401 or 977/1-245402. Fax 977/1-240681. E-mail: wildlife@machan.mos.com.np. 36 units. 2-night, 3-day package $450 double (transfers extra). AE, MC, V.

This is the easternmost lodge in the park, and it takes its name from the viewing blinds (*machans*) that have traditionally been used for spotting wildlife in this region. Machan stands out from other Chitwan lodges because of its rock-lined swimming pool (which was made by widening a stream that flows across the property). Rooms are in vaguely chalet-styled duplexes that are not as rustic as rooms at other lodges but are quite comfortable. Rooms have two sleeping areas (including an upstairs loft that's great for kids), large windows, Tharu-inspired murals, and decks on which you can sit and listen to the forest or do a bit of bird watching. Though there is no electricity in the rooms, kerosene lanterns and hot showers are provided. There's also a well-stocked library containing books and films on wildlife, ecology, and culture of the Indian subcontinent.

**Temple Tiger Jungle Lodge.** Kamaladi (P.O. Box 3968), Kathmandu. ☎ **977/1-225780** or 977/1-227559. Fax 977/1-220178. E-mail: temtig@mos.com.np. 32 units, 10 tents. 2-night, 3-day package $838 double (transfers extra). AE, MC, V.

Reaching this lodge is an adventure in itself. Whether you travel from Kathmandu by car or plane, you will transfer to a dugout canoe to cross the Narayani River, and once on the far shore, you will be met by an elephant (or a Land Rover) that will take you to the lodge. Packages here include plenty of elephant rides, which means you'll have lots of opportunities to safely observe some of the park's larger and more dangerous wildlife. Also, because this lodge is close to the Narayani River, there are good opportunities for seeing crocodiles and Gangetic dolphins. Accommodations are in either safari tents or rustic thatched-roof cabins raised up on stilts. These cabins are not very big, but with all the scheduled activities here, you won't be spending much time in your room. The camp's location 80 feet above the grasslands along the Narayani River makes it an excellent vantage point for observing rhinos, especially in January and February when the tall grasses have just been cut by local villagers.

**✪ Tiger Tops Jungle Lodge/Tiger Tops Tented Camp/Tiger Mountain Tharu Village.** P.O. Box 242, Kathmandu. ☎ **977/1-411225.** Fax 977/1-414075. E-mail: info@tigermountain.com. 27 units at Jungle Lodge, 12 tents at Tented Camp, 12 units at Tharu Village. 2-night, 3-day package $440 double at Tharu Village, $680 double at Tented Camp, $840–$1,240 double at Tiger Tops Jungle Lodge (transfers extra). AE, MC, V.

Tiger Tops is the oldest jungle lodge in Royal Chitwan National Park, and it remains the most expensive and best run. Accommodations at the Jungle Lodge are in buildings constructed on stilts and made from local materials. Plaited bamboo walls and a thatch roof provide a rustic atmosphere, while the rooms are comfortably furnished. Programs here include lots of elephant riding and are generally very well run; the staff is very knowledgeable. Tiger Tops Jungle Lodge is also the site of an annual elephant polo competition usually attended by a few celebrities.

The tented camp is in a picturesque valley 3 miles east of the main lodge. Tents are roomy, with two twin beds and a table. Because this camp is deeper into the park, where fewer people venture, wildlife is often easier to spot. Though the accommodations at Tiger Mountain Tharu Village, designed to resemble a traditional Tharu village longhouse, are the least expensive, they have the most Nepali character. The lodge is, however, outside the park, though close to the Narayani River. While there is good wildlife viewing nearby, more leisurely pursuits such as swimming and horseback riding are the preferred activities here. Elephant rides are offered in the summer months only. This is more a place to relax than a place to experience wildlife.

## OUTSIDE THE PARK
### Moderate

**Hotel Wildlife Camp.** Thamel (P.O. Box 2525), Kathmandu. ☎ **977/1-251384.** In Sauraha ☎ 977/56-60008 or 977/56-29363. Fax 977/56-60235. 14 units. 2-night, 3-day package $110–$130 double. AE, MC, V (in Kathmandu only).

Located in the village of Sauraha, Hotel Wildlife Camp is just a short walk from the park entrance and is situated beside a rice paddy. The lodge consists of a collection of new brick buildings, and rooms are carpeted and comfortable. Though there aren't many trees on the grounds, the gardens are still attractive. There is a circular thatch-roofed dining hall in the middle of the compound. The staff is friendly and the lodge even has its own resident elephant, on which guests can explore the nearby community forest.

**Jungle Adventure World.** Heritage Plaza, 3rd floor, Kamaladi (P.O. Box 2561), Kathmandu. ☎ **977/1-248390** or 977/1-224310. Fax 977/1-221309. In Sauraha ☎ 977/56-29364. 10 units. 2-night, 3-day package $140 double. MC, V (in Kathmandu only).

Located in a shady spot overlooking the Rapti River (and the beach bars that have sprung up along the river in recent years), this lodge consists of a collection of odd little cabins that look like half-timbered cottages. Though they would seem more at home in the Cotswolds, these cabins are comfortable and have porches, fans, carpeting, and tiled bathrooms. The trees that shade the garden even have identification tags, in case you happen to have botanical inclinations. Both the park's museum and the ferry across the river to the park are located just outside the lodge's driveway, which makes this a very convenient choice among the budget properties.

**River View Jungle Camp.** Thamel (P.O. Box 5801), Kathmandu. ☎ **977/1-425970.** Fax 977/1-418075. In Sauraha ☎ 977/56-60164. Fax 977/56-60235. 10 units (5 with shared bathrooms). 2-night, 3-day package $110–$150 double with shared bathroom, $130–$170 double with private bathroom. MC, V (in Kathmandu only).

Although the view of the river isn't much to speak of, this lodge is conveniently located on tree-shaded grounds. The rooms with private bathrooms are definitely the way to go. These rooms are built of brick, are carpeted, and have large porches with chairs. The rooms with shared bathrooms are built in traditional Tharu style with grass-and-mud walls and are rather musty.

✪ **Royal Park Hotel.** Bhagwan Bahal, Thamel (P.O. Box 8964), Kathmandu. ☎ **977/1-412987.** Fax 977/1-253020. In Sauraha ☎ 977/56-29361. 29 units. 2-night, 3-day package $264 double. No credit cards.

Set on the banks of the Rapti River amid a spacious, well-manicured garden, the Royal Park Hotel is a joint Nepali-German project and is the best of the Sauraha lodges. Flagstone walkways lead to the guest rooms, which are housed in several buildings. The rooms are all large and have brick floors, high ceilings, and attractive bathrooms with slate or marble floors. You won't find nicer rooms even at the most expensive Chitwan jungle lodges. There's a large dining hall with screen walls and brick-and-flagstone floors. In the garden, you'll find an open-air bar and a few shaded tables where you can watch for rhinos as you sip your cocktail.

## 3 Lumbini

176 miles (284km) W of Kathmandu; 125 miles (201km) S of Pokhara; 13 miles (21km) W of Bhairawa

More than 2,500 years ago, Prince Siddhartha Gautama, who would later become the Buddha, was born at Lumbini, in what is now Nepal. At the time of his birth, Lumbini was part of the kingdom of Kapilvastu, which had its capital 17 miles west on the site of modern Tilaurakot. Today, Lumbini is just a small town, but it is very important as a Buddhist pilgrimage site. Emperor Ashoka of India, one of the earliest pilgrims to visit Lumbini, erected an inscribed stone pillar here in 249 B.C. When this pillar was discovered late in the 19th century, it helped archaeologists to uncover many other ruins in the area.

## GETTING THERE/LEAVING

The nearest **airport** is at Bhairawa, which has service from Kathmandu on Necon Air, Lumbini Airways, Royal Nepal Airlines, and Buddha Air. Flights take 45 minutes and cost $144 round-trip.

**Buses** from Kathmandu to Bhairawa take 8 to 12 hours, cost Rs155 ($2.35), and leave from the Gongabu Bus Park on the Ring Road north of Thamel. Buses from Pokhara take 8 to 10 hours, cost Rs130 to Rs175 ($1.95 to $2.65), and leave from the main Pokhara Bus Park.

From Bhairawa, hourly local buses costing Rs12 (18¢) cover the 13 miles to Lumbini in about 45 minutes. It's also possible to hire a taxi for Rs600 ($9.10), or a three-wheeled taxi called a tempo for Rs300 ($4.55).

Buses back to Kathmandu and Pokhara leave from the main bus terminal in Bhairawa early in the morning. It is best to buy your ticket at the bus terminal the night before departing.

## WHAT TO SEE & DO

In recent years, Lumbini, under the auspices of the Lumbini Development Project, has been undergoing development as a major **Buddhist pilgrimage site,** and new monasteries, shrines, and hotels have been constructed. Among these is the Myanmar Stupa, which is built in the style of the famous Shwedagon Stupa in Yangon, Mynamar (Rangoon, Burma). Currently under construction are a Vietnamese monastery, a Chinese monastery and pagoda, a Thai monastery, three Korean monasteries, a Japanese peace pagoda and monastery, and even an American park.

Lumbini's main attraction, however, remains the **Sacred Garden,** which encompasses the site where Siddhartha Gautama is said to have been born. For many years the main focus of this site was the Maya Devi Temple, which was dedicated to the Buddha's mother, and a large banyan tree growing out of the temple. However, a recent archaeological excavation, with the objective of determining whether this truly was the spot where the Buddha was born, has resulted in the removal of the Maya Devi temple. The controversial excavation of this temple was in part brought about by its continued deterioration, which was caused by the banyan tree that had long been growing on it. During the excavation, an engraved stone proclaiming this to be the site of the Buddha's birth was discovered beneath the temple.

The pillar erected here in 249 B.C. by Emperor Ashoka, a Buddhist ruler of ancient India, can also be seen nearby. Just south of this pillar is the pond where Maya Devi is said to have taken a bath before giving birth.

The easiest way to visit Lumbini is on a **guided tour** offered by **Kanjiroba Travels & Tours,** Thamel (P.O. Box 11480), Kathmandu (☎ 977/1-227882); full-day tours of Lumbini and other nearby archaeological sites of Buddhist significance are offered. Tours cost $20. This company also arranges complete 3-day package tours for $75 to $150 per person.

## WHERE TO STAY

**Hotel Himalaya Inn.** New Road, Siddhartha Nagar-7 (Bhairawa). ☎ **977/71-20347.** 24 units. $25 double. No credit cards.

This is a very basic hotel, but if you can't afford to stay at the Lumbini Hokke or Hotel Nirvana, this is your next-best choice. The rooms are Spartan, but they do have fans. Be sure to have some mosquito coils with you since the window screens aren't always in such good shape. About half of the rooms have Asian squat toilets, and these are actually preferable to the rooms with Western toilets.

**Hotel Nirvana.** Paklihawa Road (P.O. Box 24), Siddhartha Nagar, Lumbini ☎ **977/ 71-20837** or 977/71-20516. Fax 977/71-21262. In Kathmandu: Teku (P.O. Box 1904), Kathmandu. ☎ 977/1-225370 or 977/1-247422. Fax 977/1-270048. E-mail: nirva@ccsl.com.np. 42 units. A/C MINIBAR TV TEL. $105 double; $150 suite. AE, MC, V.

At press time, this was the newest hotel in Lumbini; it also seemed to be catering primarily to Japanese pilgrims. While the guest rooms are standard Western-style rooms, the hotel boasts a large Japanese-style bathhouse. Attractive gardens surround the hotel. The hotel has a restaurant serving Nepali, Chinese, Indian, and continental meals, and there is also a bar for those post-pilgrimage cocktails. Amenities include 24-hour room service, laundry service, money exchange, and safe-deposit boxes.

**Lumbini Hokke Hotel.** Lumbini Sacred Garden, Lumbini. ☎ **977/71-80236** or 977/ 71-80136. Fax 977/71-80126. 27 units. $120 double. AE, JCB, MC, V.

Built and managed by the Japanese primarily for Japanese Buddhist pilgrims, the Lumbini Hokke has some of the best rooms in Nepal. Twenty of these rooms are done in Japanese style with tatami floors and sliding shoji screens between the bedroom and sitting area. For a room such as this, you would probably have to spend a small fortune in Japan. Among the amenities here are a pilgrim's gift shop, Japanese bathhouse, meditation room, and large dining room. It's too bad that such comfortable accommodations are so far off the main tourist routes.

## 4 Royal Bardia National Park

370 miles (597km) NW of Kathmandu; 290 miles (468km) NW of Royal Chitwan National Park

Located in western Nepal, Royal Bardia National Park covers 372 square miles (968km²) and is the largest undisturbed natural area in the Terai. As such, it offers unequaled wildlife-viewing opportunities. A mix of deciduous and riverine forests, savannahs, and grasslands, the park is home to Bengal tigers, Indian one-horned rhinoceroses, wild Asian elephants, black buck antelope, swamp deer, and more than 350 species of birds. Marsh-mugger and gharial crocodiles, as well as rare Gangetic dolphins, can also be seen here.

While many of these same animals can be seen in the more popular Royal Chitwan National Park, which is only half as far away from Kathmandu, Bardia sees far fewer visitors each year and thus provides a greater sense of adventure for visitors. The lower numbers of park visitors also mean that your chances of seeing a tiger are somewhat better than at Chitwan (I recently met a couple who saw a tiger here within an hour of their arrival at the park). Bardia is also one of the only places in Nepal where you are likely to see wild elephants (the same people who saw the tiger were also chased by a wild elephant while exploring the park on a domestic elephant). If you have the extra time and/or additional budget, a trip to Bardia is likely to be more rewarding, satisfying, and memorable than a trip to Chitwan. Keep in mind, however, that unless you stay at the Tiger Tops Tented Camp, a visit to Bardia is not entirely a wilderness experience. All the lodges serving the park (and there are still just a handful) are located in a Tharu village just outside the park boundary.

## ESSENTIALS

**VISITOR INFORMATION**   The park headquarters are located in the village of Thakurdwara, 8 miles (13km) down a gravel road from the village of Ambassa. Park admission (valid for 2 days) is Rs650 ($9.85). However, if you are visiting the park on a package tour, park admission will be included with your package. Be sure to bring a flashlight, batteries, sunscreen, insect repellent, sunglasses, a hat, a long-sleeve shirt, and long pants. Clothes should be of neutral colors (avoid white, red, and yellow).

**GETTING THERE**   The nearest **airport** is at Nepalgunj, which has service from Kathmandu on Royal Nepal Airlines, Buddha Air, and Necon Air. The flight takes an hour, and round-trip airfare is $198. **Buses** from Kathmandu to Nepalgunj leave from the Gongabu Bus Park on the Ring Road north of Thamel, take 12 hours, and cost Rs293 ($4.45).

From Nepalgunj, it is another 1½ to 2½ hours to the village of Thakurdwara, site of the park's lodges. Most lodges will pick you up in Nepalgunj, either at the airport or at the bus terminal. Be sure to find out if the transfer service is included in your package price.

## WHAT TO SEE & DO

Most people coming to Bardia do so on a prearranged package tour that includes lodging, meals, and various activities. If you stay at one of the inexpensive lodges here, you will do a lot of exploring of the park on foot. However, a Jeep safari and an elephant ride are usually also part of the standard package. If you choose to stay at Tiger Tops Karnali Lodge, you will be doing much more exploring from the back of an elephant.

Most people come to Bardia because this is the most likely place in Nepal to spot a **Bengal tiger** (the park was created specifically to provide a habitat for tigers). The tigers thrive on the park's abundant prey, including black buck antelope, blue bull antelope, and rare swamp deer. This is also the best place in the country to spot wild Asian elephants.

Until 1986, there were no Indian one-horned rhinos in Bardia (they had long before been killed off), but in that year rhinos from Chitwan were transplanted here to create a second population (in case disease should ever strike the Chitwan herd). This project has been very successful, and rhinos continue to be transplanted from the ever-growing herd at Chitwan. These, combined with the rhinos born at Bardia, have created a substantial herd. However, there are still far fewer animals in Bardia than in Chitwan, so you stand less of a chance of seeing a rhino here than you do at Chitwan.

The Geruwa River, a tributary of the Karnali, forms the western border of the national park, and a **boat ride** down this river is an essential part of any visit to Bardia. From the water, you are likely to spot marsh-mugger and long-nosed gharial crocodiles, as well as rare Gangetic dolphins, which also have long snouts similar to those of the gharials.

A boat trip also provides an opportunity for bird watching, as do walks through the forest and along the park's waterways. With more than 350 species of birds having been sighted within the park, Bardia is considered one of Nepal's best birding spots. Among the rare species here are Bengal floricans, lesser floricans, and sarus cranes.

A visit to the village of **Thakurdwara** offers a glimpse into the lives of the Terai's native Tharu people, who have lived in these lowlands for centuries. Their mud-and-grass–walled huts are well adapted to this humid region, where grasses grow as high as an elephant's eye.

## WHERE TO STAY

**Forest Hideaway Hotel & Cottages.** Royal Bardia National Park, Thakurdwara. ☎ **977/ 84-29716.** E-mail: hideaway@silkroad.mos.com.np. 3-night, 4-day package $280 double. No credit cards.

This is probably the best of the budget "jungle lodges" that have sprung up in Thakurdwara in recent years. Built in the traditional Tharu style with mud-walled, thatched-roof huts, this lodge is operated by a Scots-Nepali couple. Programs here are patterned after the ones offered at the budget lodges outside Chitwan National Park and include forest hikes, bird walks, and elephant rides. However, the emphasis is on long hikes.

**Rhino Lodge Bardia.** Thamel, Kathmandu. ☎ **977/1-416918** or 977/1-416300. Fax 977/1-417146. E-mail: rhinotvl@ccsl.com.np. In Thakurdwara ☎ 977/84-29720. 15 units (3 with shared bathroom). 3-night, 4-day package $340 double. AE, MC, V.

Under the same management as the Rhino Lodge in Sauraha (outside Royal Chitwan National Park), this lodge is situated 5 minutes outside the park. Though accommodations, in cement duplexes with corrugated metal roofs, lack the regional style of Forest Hideaway, they are moderately comfortable, and the surrounding gardens somewhat make up for the buildings' shortcomings. Activities available here are virtually identical to those offered at Forest Hideaway. However, a rafting trip on the Karnali to see Gangetic dolphins is available for an additional $25 per person.

✪ **Tiger Tops Karnali Lodge & Tented Camp.** P.O. Box 242, Kathmandu. ☎ **977/ 1-411225.** Fax 977/1-414075. E-mail: info@tigermountain.com.; 12 tents. 3-night, 4-day package $720–$1,020 double. AE, MC, V.

Under the same management as the famous Tiger Tops Jungle Lodge in Royal Chitwan National Park, this lodge, a 5-minute walk from the village of Thakurdwara, is by far the top operation at Bardia. Accommodations are in buildings designed to resemble traditional Tharu village longhouses, and though there are mud walls (with Tharu murals) and straw mats on the floors, the rooms are impeccably clean. This lodge is far more expensive than any other in the area; but the service is excellent and there are always plenty of naturalists/guides on hand to answer questions about the park and its wildlife. Activities here center around elephant rides into the park to search for tigers, wild elephants, and one-horned rhinos. Guides always accompany these excursions. There are also boat trips on the Karnali River to look for gharial and marsh-mugger crocodiles and Gangetic dolphins. The lodge also operates a deluxe tented camp (the only accommodation actually inside the park), and a night spent at this camp should be part of any Tiger Tops Bardia visit.

# 9 Planning a Trek

The Himalayas are the highest mountains on earth, and among their peaks and valleys wind thousands of miles of trails—the human highways of the Himalayas. For centuries the people of Nepal, Tibet, and India have traveled these trails as farmers, traders, and pilgrims. Today, thousands of foreigners from around the world are also walking these trails, discovering the countless wonders of the Himalayas.

If you are one of those people who for years has longed to climb the Himalayan peaks, this chapter will provide the basic information for planning your trek in Nepal. Should you book at home or in Nepal? How do you get a trekking permit? When should you go? What should you pack? Should you carry your own backpack or hire a porter? These are some of the questions that this chapter will answer.

Here you'll also find the names of some good Nepali trekking companies. However, if you'd rather make your trek arrangements before you leave home, see the adventure-travel companies listed in chapter 3.

Keep in mind that a trek can be anything from an easy walk of just a few days to a months-long expedition, and that a trek of any length requires a great deal of advance planning. At least 6 months to a year before your trip, you must get your immunizations and start getting in shape if you're planning a long and strenuous trek. You should also make an airline reservation at least 6 months in advance. If you opt for a fully catered camping trek operated by a foreign adventure-travel company, you'll also want to see about making a tour reservation at least 6 months in advance. Choosing the right trek and the right mode of trekking is also of primary importance. What are your interests—people, mountains, birds, wildlife? This chapter will address these issues and help you to prepare for one of the most memorable experiences of your life.

## 1 What Is Trekking?

Trekking is simply another name for hiking. The term, which is from Afrikaans and originally meant a journey by ox cart across South Africa, was first applied to hiking in Nepal in the early 1960s by retired Ghurka Col. Jimmy Roberts. Roberts, who was the first person to take paying clients on guided hikes in Nepal, patterned his treks after early Nepal mountaineering expeditions. His trips had basically everything the big expeditions had—guides, Sherpa porters, cooks, and kitchen boys. Clients didn't scale the peaks; but they came close and that was what they wanted. Today, camping treks are still done the way Col. Roberts pioneered them.

However, unlike in the early 1960s, there are now hundreds of lodges scattered along Nepal's many miles of trails, and trekkers have the option of hiking from lodge to lodge either on their own or with a porter and a guide, or even just a porter. This style of trekking is called teahouse trekking, from the teahouses (*bhattis*) that first served as lodges for adventurous trekkers (mostly hippies) who headed off into the hills on their own in the late 1960s and early 1970s. The original teahouses were very simple affairs that had traditionally catered to Nepali traders and porters. Today, there are still such simple places along some trekking routes, but the lodges frequented by trekkers are, for the most part, much more elaborate, with large dining rooms, terraces, gardens, private rooms, and sometimes even indoor plumbing.

For most first-time visitors, the chance to view the Himalayas, the highest mountains on earth, is the primary reason for trekking. Imagine hiking at elevations above 13,000 feet (almost as high as the highest mountains in North America) and gazing up at mountain peaks that are another 13,000 feet higher. This is a powerful draw. Although trekking is basically backpacking, it's quite different from backpacking as North Americans know it.

Trekking, by and large, is not a wilderness experience but rather a cultural experience. Nepal is an ethnic mosaic, and a trek is not just an opportunity to gaze at snow-covered peaks, it is a chance to observe the lifestyles of the different peoples who have inhabited these mountains for centuries. There are lowland Hindu farmers of the Brahmin and Chhetri castes, proud Gurungs whose villages have supplied the Gurkha regiments for decades, Thakali innkeepers whose families have catered to travelers for centuries, and high-country Sherpas who have made a name for themselves as superior mountaineers. Each ethnic group has its own cultural identity and is distinguished by its clothing, farming practices, architectural styles, and religious beliefs. Of course, there are beautiful mountains to look at here (and there's no denying that they are impressive), but it is the cultural diversity that makes Nepal unique. And though you may come for the mountains, it is the people that are likely to leave the greatest impression on you.

This cultural diversity is in part due to Nepal's varied landscape. From the subtropical valleys of the middle hills to the alpine meadows of the high Himalayas to the desert-like conditions of the trans-Himalayan regions, Nepal boasts an amazing range of natural habitats. Humans, plants, and animals have all evolved and adapted to these conditions. On south-facing slopes, terraced fields stair-step up mountainsides, allowing farmers to grow barley, rice, wheat, and millet. In moist, shaded valleys, bamboo forests thrive and ferns proliferate. On more-open, cloud-swept hillsides, rhododendrons grow into trees and color the mountains with their spring blossoms. In the upper elevations, blue sheep and Himalayan tahrs (a type of mountain goat) graze in alpine meadows dotted with tiny gentians. In the rainy shadows to the north of the Hima-layas, a barren landscape of thorny scrub and ground-hugging plants belies the fertility of fields watered by extensive networks of irrigation canals. A trek of only a week can take in all of these habitats, providing a journey through a myriad of landscapes. This is what trekking in Nepal really means—exploring the country's culture, geography, and wildlife amid the highest mountains on earth.

## 2 Choosing Your Trekking Style

After you've decided to trek in Nepal, you'll need to decide what type of trek is best for you, and whether to make the arrangements from home or once you're in Nepal.

## The Himalayan Explorers Club

Founded in 1995 and patterned after the famous South American Explorers Club, the Himalayan Explorers Club is an excellent source of up-to-date information on trekking in Nepal. Club headquarters is in the United States, and there is a clubhouse in Kathmandu as well. The club serves as a source for books and maps on Nepal and also maintains trek reports furnished by members. For more information, contact the **Himalayan Explorers Club,** P.O. Box 3665, Boulder, CO 80307 (☎ **303/494-9656;** fax 303/494-8822; www.abwam.com/himexp/; e-mail: himexp@aol.com). Basic membership is $30 per year.

There are basically two styles of trekking: lodge-to-lodge (teahouse) treks and camping treks. Teahouse treks can be done on your own and are the most economical. On a teahouse trek you'll stay in rustic lodges used primarily by independent trekkers. By carrying your own pack, you can get by on less than $10 a day. Hire a guide or porter, and you might spend $16 to $20 a day.

**Teahouse treks** can be booked through a trekking company. On an organized teahouse trek, you will essentially hire a guide and a porter to walk with you from village to village. You'll be paying more than if you had done the teahouse trek on your own, but less than if you had opted for a camping trek. The only real benefit of doing an organized teahouse trek is that you don't have to worry about the planning or preparations, such as hiring guides and porters, or deciding on the route and where to stay. The only organized lodge-to-lodge treks I can wholeheartedly recommend are those run by **Ker & Downey Nepal** (☎ **800/324-9081** or 713/744-5244), which operates its own system of deluxe lodges in the foothills north of Pokhara (see chapter 3 for details).

An organized **camping trek,** on the other hand (whether arranged in Nepal or in your home country), includes a large entourage that will have a guide (often a Sherpa), porters, cooks, and kitchen boys. These treks are patterned after the first mountaineering expeditions in Nepal. Today, a camping trek includes the same basic support personnel as a major mountaineering expedition, though generally on a smaller scale. For this reason, camping treks are the most expensive. Because they are basically self-sufficient, they aren't restricted to staying near villages, but on the more popular routes, these groups almost always use lodge gardens as their campgrounds (this seems to defeat the purpose of going on a camping trek). More-remote and less-traveled routes provide a truer glimpse of life in the hills and also give you a greater feeling of adventure because you see fewer trekkers. If you decide that a camping trek is for you, consider one that shuns the more-popular routes in favor of more-remote trails.

When and how to book your trek is another important question to answer early on. If you have more money than time, or if you want everything arranged before you leave, you'll probably want to book your trek through an agency in your own country (see the list of adventure-travel companies in chapter 3). By booking your trek this way, all you'll need to do is show up in good health with your bag. Rates vary widely: A teahouse (lodge-to-lodge) trek booked through a smaller company goes for as little as $60 per person per day, and a trek into Mustang, which requires a $700 trekking permit, costs $200 or more per day.

On the other hand, if you have more time than money, consider booking your trek after you arrive in Nepal, or working directly with a Nepali trekking company (see the list below). With this method, trekking rates can be as low as $40 a day for a teahouse trek, or up to $100 a day for an organized group trek with porters, guides, and cooks.

## INDEPENDENT TREKS

If you're an experienced traveler and backpacker, you may want to hit the trail on your own. This is by far the cheapest option, and there are several ways to do it. Sure, you can bring your tent and camp stove and carry your own food, just like you would back home, but in Nepal there's really no need to lug all that gear along. A big part of the trekking experience is staying in lodges run by Nepalis. By doing so, you not only get to carry less stuff in your backpack, but also get to interact more with the Nepalis, while at the same time contributing directly to the local economy.

### GUIDES, PORTERS & DOING IT ON YOUR OWN

**With a Porter and Guide**    Even if you are not going on a group trek, you can have a traditional experience by hiring a porter and a guide. The porter carries your pack, and the guide shows the way, acts as interpreter, and explains things along the trail. Though it costs a bit more, this arrangement can be very beneficial. Not only are you free from the burden of carrying a pack, but you also learn more about Nepal, and your porter and guide have someone to talk to besides you. This may sound strange, and it's less important if you're traveling with a companion; but if you're on your own, it can be tiresome trying to communicate with just a smattering of English and Nepali.

**With Only a Guide**    Trails can be difficult to follow even with the best guidebook. Trails change with every monsoon, and more hotels are built every year. Therefore, it is worth having a guide who is familiar with the year-to-year changes, or who can ask locals about trail conditions and directions. I once trekked without a guide and was forced to spend Christmas Eve in a half-constructed building when, in a thick fog, I missed a village that was slightly off the trail. In the clear skies of dawn, I saw, less than a quarter of a mile away, a newly opened trekkers' lodge to which a guide could have directed me.

Traditionally, trekking and mountaineering guides have been Sherpas, who come from the high elevations of the Solu-Khumbu region near Mount Everest. Their knowledge of the mountains has made them legendary, and the term *Sherpa* is often used interchangeably with *guide*. However, not all guides are Sherpas.

Guides who speak English well are always more expensive than those who do not, and it is sometimes possible to hire what is called a porter-guide. A porter-guide will carry your pack and keep you on the right trail, but he usually speaks only a few words of English. A porter-guide costs more than a porter but less than a guide.

### Readers Recommend

"I wanted to share a recommendation for a trekking guide/porter who has been with me on two treks. His name is Ram Nepali and he lives in Pokhara. He speaks English very well, he knows his way around the Himalayas like his own back yard and always has a positive attitude. On a recent trek he carried two packs when one woman got sick and couldn't carry her pack. He's friendly and knows people in many villages around the Annapurnas. He is reliable and honest, and best of all he has an email address so you can make arrangements ahead of time. For anyone doing a trek starting in Pokhara, I think Ram would be a great help. His email address is globenet@cnet.wlink.com.np."    —*Jon Kaplan, Berkeley, CA*

Daily rates for hiring a guide range from about $10 to $20, which may or may not include the guide's room and board along the trail. Most smaller trekking companies will quote you a rate that does not include food and lodging. In this case, you can expect to pay an additional $5 or $6 per day for your guide's room and board. A porter-guide can usually be hired for around $6 to $10 per day. Larger trekking companies that deal primarily with groups may not be willing to arrange a guide for you, but guides can easily be hired at the smaller companies around Thamel and in Pokhara. It is not advisable to hire someone off the street, though many people do so and don't usually have problems.

**With Only a Porter**   If you need to cut costs, you may want to head out with only a porter. A porter will carry your pack for $5 to $6 a day (plus room and board) but rarely speaks English. Though porters are not expected to inquire about trail conditions or lead the way, they will often perform this duty simply to avoid getting lost. Porters are inexpensive, and by carrying your pack, they make it much easier for you to walk up and down steep mountain trails.

Your porter is likely to travel faster than you, even though he's carrying your pack. It's a good idea to carry the items you'll need during the day, such as a water bottle, first-aid kit, and camera, in a day pack that you carry yourself. Before setting out in the morning, you should make it clear where you plan to stop next, whether it is for tea or lunch or for the day. That way your porter will know where to stop and won't get too far ahead of you. At other times, your porter may lag behind you, especially if you are a particularly fast walker. If this is the case, bear in mind that your porter may have had only tea for breakfast and will want to stop for lunch around 10am, which is the traditional Nepali time for the midday meal.

Though I have not met anyone who has had anything stolen by a porter, it does happen. The best way to avoid this is to hire your porter through an established and trustworthy trekking agency. I have listed the names of a few companies (see "Trekking Companies in Nepal," in this chapter), but you can also ask around once you reach Kathmandu. People who have just returned from a trek may be able to recommend the company they used.

If you plan to trek in the winter months or at very high elevations, it is your responsibility to provide your porter with adequate shoes, jacket, sleeping bag, sunglasses, and other sundries. Your responsibilities should be clarified before leaving Kathmandu or Pokhara. With the exception of Namche Bazaar near Mount Everest, there are few places on any trail where you can rent or buy appropriate gear for your porter.

**On Your Own**   It is no longer a good idea to trek alone. In the past few years, crime on the trail has been increasing. Each year a few trekkers are murdered or disappear, and others are robbed. Individuals should either trek with companions or hire a porter or guide. People seeking trekking partners often put up notices on the bulletin boards around Thamel in Kathmandu. The bulletin board at the Kathmandu Environmental Education Project (KEEP) office is a good place to check. This is also an excellent place to learn more about altitude sickness and about how to lessen your impact on the environment and culture of Nepal. Even if you don't need to find a trekking companion, it's a good idea to stop in.

## TREKKING LODGES (TEAHOUSES)

When the first independent trekkers began exploring the hills of Nepal, they took their meals and slept in tea stalls or teahouses called bhattis. Today, the term "teahouse trek" is still commonly used, though the teahouses have graduated to full-scale lodges and hotels on the more popular trails. In the past few years most lodges have offered private double rooms, and some now have rooms with private bathrooms (with Western sit-down toilets). However, you may still encounter smaller and older lodges that have only dormitory rooms.

In the busy October-November trekking season, you will find that lodges get very crowded. It is often necessary to stop by 2 or 3pm in order to get a room. However, if you don't stop until later in the day, you won't be turned away—you'll just have to sleep wherever there is space available, which will usually be on a mat on a bench in the dining room.

Whereas traditional bhattis usually serve only tea, dal bhat, and chang (rice beer) or rakshi (rice or millet liquor) and cater primarily to porters and traveling Nepalis, newer lodges are built specifically for trekkers. The menus at trekking lodges are amazingly extensive, listing Nepali, Indian, Chinese, English, American, Italian, Swiss, German, and even Mexican meals. However, despite what you order, it tends to taste pretty much like everything else on the menu since the ingredients used are basically the same. To give the cook plenty of time, try to order well in advance of when you want to eat (order breakfast before you go to sleep and dinner in the early afternoon, specifying when you would like to have it served). I have seen trekkers become irate and abusive when it took several hours for their meal to arrive. This sort of behavior won't get you your meal any faster, and it gives Nepalis a bad impression of trekkers. You can speed meal preparation by having everyone in your group order the same items. This will avoid the time-consuming process of preparing several different meals on a stove that has only two or three burners.

Staying in lodges has some drawbacks. Rooms are sometimes directly above the kitchen, and smoke from open cooking fires may drift upstairs. If another room isn't available, the only thing you can do is stay in the kitchen or dining room until your host family puts out the fire and goes to bed. In a crowded lodge it can often take hours for everyone's meals to be prepared, and orders are sometimes mixed up. *Please be patient and understanding.* The meals at the lodges are often prepared by older men or women who speak little or no English and must rely on their children or grandchildren for translations of orders. Occasionally, cooks get sick. If this happens, food may not be available, or young and inexperienced children may assume the task of cooking.

Luckily, most trekkers are so tired at night that they never hear a thing once they fall asleep. But with coughing, crying babies, crowing roosters, family arguments, drunken porters, and the inescapable Radio Nepal broadcasts, a good night's sleep can sometimes be hard to come by. Think of these disturbances as part of the cultural experience of a teahouse trek. Occasionally, you may stumble upon a village celebration or a family gathering that will likely go on all night with much drinking and noise. If this happens, the best thing you can do is join the party. No doubt you'll have one of the most memorable experiences of your trek.

## ORGANIZED TREKS

This type of trekking is what most people think of when they hear the term "trekking"—tents, porters, and hot tea brought to you in your tent each morning. For people unfamiliar with independent adventure travel, booking an organized trek before leaving home may be the best way to ensure that you have the experience you are dreaming of. For information on booking an organized trek through an international adventure-travel company in your home country, see "The Active Vacation Planner," in chapter 3. Alternatively, you can book your trek through a Nepali company either before or after you arrive in Nepal. You can often save quite a bit of money by booking this way. Again, you'll need to decide whether you want to do a camping or a teahouse trek.

## TREKKING COMPANIES IN NEPAL

There are hundreds of small trekking companies operating out of Kathmandu and Pokhara, many of which are used by international adventure-travel companies. By bypassing the international adventure-travel company and going directly to the trekking company in Nepal, you can usually save quite a bit of money. You'll still have to make your own hotel arrangements for when you're not trekking, but with this book in hand, that won't be a problem. Also, most Nepali trekking companies are now on the Internet, so you can make your arrangements and reservations as easily as you could with a company located in your home country.

When arranging a trek through a Nepali company, keep in mind that it is almost always cheaper per person if you have four or more people in your group. Some companies will not organize treks for fewer than four people, but most will make arrangements for as few as two people (sometimes even one person). Some Nepali companies also have preset departure dates that individuals can sign on for. Treks in the Annapurna region and north of Kathmandu in Helambu and Langtang are usually less expensive than treks in other areas. The price quote from a Nepali trekking company for a camping trek usually includes the guide, porters, cooks, tent, sleeping bag, mattress, kitchen equipment, food, transportation to and from the trailhead, trekking permits and visa extensions, Annapurna Conservation Area Project or national park entrance fees, and porter insurance. Be sure to always verify what is included in the price.

The following are some of the more reliable trekking companies in Nepal.

### In Kathmandu

**Asian Trekking,** Tridevi Marg (P.O. Box 3022), Thamel, Kathmandu (☎ 977/ 1-424249; fax 977/1-411878; www.asian-trekking.com; e-mail: asianadv@mos.com.np). Sherpa-owned Asian Trekking not only offers a wide range of treks, but also arranges rafting and jungle safaris and has its own chain of trekking lodges in the Everest region. Most treks cost between $60 and $80 per person per day.

**Eco Trek,** Thamel (P.O. Box 6438), Kathmandu (☎ 977/1-424112; fax 977/ 1-413118; e-mail: jyoti@ecotrek.wlink.com.np). This was one of the first trekking companies in Nepal to promote its treks as being environmentally responsible. From $30 to $100 per person per day.

**Ganesh Himal Trekking,** Thamel (P.O. Box 3854), Kathmandu (☎ 977/ 1-416282; fax 977/1-424360). Ganesh Himal Trekking has long been one of Kathmandu's better economy companies and offers budget-minded treks throughout the country. From $30 to $40 per person per day.

**Himalayan Encounters,** Kathmandu Guest House (P.O. Box 2769), Thamel, Kathmandu (☎ 977/1-417426; fax 977/1-417133; raftnepl@himenco.wlink. com.np). Known for its white-water rafting trips, they also offer short treks out of Pokhara to areas not normally traveled by independent trekkers. $40 to $50 per day.

**Karnali Excursions,** Thamel (P.O. Box 4583), Kathmandu. (☎ 977/1-430383; fax 977/1-410853; e-mail: excel@wlink.com.np). This small company specializes in treks in far-western Nepal and also organizes treks across the border to Mount Kailash in Tibet. If you want to trek someplace where you'll see fewer people, contact this company. Camping and teahouse treks. From $40 to $60 per person per day.

**Mountain Travel,** Tiger Mountain, Lazimpat (P.O. Box 170), Kathmandu (☎ 977/ 1-411225; fax 977/1-414075). The oldest trekking company in Nepal; founder Col.

---

### Avoiding the Crowds

The single-biggest drawback of teahouse trekking (or a camping trek on the more popular trails) is that everyone follows the same routes, and consequently, during the peak season (Oct and Nov), trails along the Annapurna circuit and in the Everest region are so crowded that it can feel like rush hour on the Santa Monica Freeway or the Long Island Expressway. If you want to see as few teahouse trekkers as possible, I suggest that you come in either the winter or the monsoon season. However, you'll have to deal with the cold and snow, and with leaches and landslides during the monsoon. For some people, these are small prices to pay for more solitude on the trail. You can also avoid the peak-season crowds by doing the more costly organized camping trek. While not all camping treks shun the main trails, there are plenty that do. Choose a trek off the beaten path, and you may think your group is the first exploratory expedition into these mountains.

---

Jimmy Roberts originated the term *trekking* for this type of mountain hiking. Caters primarily to groups who make reservations through foreign agents, though it's possible to arrange a trek directly. Clients have included Mick Jagger, Prince Charles, and Sir Edmund Hillary. $75 to $130 per day.

#### In Pokhara

**Mountain Way Trekking,** Nepal Rastra Bank Chowk (P.O. Box 59), Pokhara (☎ 977/61-20316; fax 977/61-21240; e-mail: mountway@trekkin.mos.com.np). This small company has long been one of Pokhara's more reliable outfits, and it offers both camping and teahouse treks. Most treks range from $60 to $75 per person per day.

**3 Sisters Adventure Trekking,** Lakeside (P.O. Box 284), Khahare, Pokhara-6. (☎ & fax 977/61-24066; e-mail: sisters3@cnet.wlink.com.np). Operated by three Nepali sisters who go by the names of Lucky, Dicky, and Nicky, this small company caters almost exclusively to women and uses primarily women guides and porters. From $25 to $40 per person per day.

## 3 When to Trek

Because Nepal is subject to monsoon rains from June through mid-October, the trekking season is effectively limited to October through May. However, the favored time is the 6-week period immediately following the monsoon (between mid-Oct and the end of Nov). During this time, the skies are usually clear for most of the day, there is rarely any rain or snow, and temperatures are warm by day and cool at night. At lower elevations it can even be too hot for vigorous exercise, and trekking at low elevations can be quite unpleasant. The rains don't usually let up until sometime around the 15th to the 20th of October, so the very best time to arrive is around October 20th. Because this is the busiest season of the year, expect long lines for trekking permits and throngs of other trekkers on the more popular trails.

From the end of November through the end of January, the weather is cold and clear with temperatures going below freezing at night at altitudes above 3,000 or 4,000 feet. During the day, however, the cool temperatures make trekking very pleasant. You can expect 1 or 2 days of rain or snow sometime during this period. Fewer people trek in this season because of the weather; permit lines are shorter and the trails are less crowded. This is the best time to trek if you want to avoid the crowds and still see the mountains, but allow for some snow days and bring plenty of warm clothes.

By the end of January, the weather begins to warm up again, making February and March the next-most-popular trekking months. The sky is clear most of the time, though haze begins to obscure the views of the mountains. By April and May it is very hot in the lower elevations, and the haze often obscures the mountains entirely.

## 4 Physical Preparations, Health & Insurance

Physical preparation is the single-best way to get more enjoyment out of your trek. The better shape you're in, the easier the trek will be. However, even people in the best physical condition sometimes get ill on the trail, and anyone can get altitude sickness.

I'd like to share another piece of advice: Don't spend too much time in Kathmandu before trekking. Kathmandu has a bad reputation for giving people gastrointestinal and respiratory problems. The sooner you get on the trail, the better your chances of remaining healthy for the trek. Even the most physically fit person can become too weak to trek after a several-day bout with diarrhea or a bad chest cold.

### PHYSICAL PREPARATION

While almost anyone can go trekking (even someone who is out of shape), hiking in the Himalayas requires a lot of physical exertion, sometimes at altitudes higher than you are used to. You'll enjoy your trek more if you are physically prepared. The best way to do this is to begin or maintain a regular program of aerobic exercise several times a week. This will develop the cardiovascular system and give you more stamina. However, trekking in the Himalayas presents challenges for which a simple exercise regimen cannot prepare you. On several of the most popular treks, there are ascents and descents of 2,000 to 6,000 feet at a time. This is usually on trails that have been made into seemingly endless stairways by the locals who prefer a steep, but direct, route rather than an indirect one with switchbacks. Legs, especially knees, take a real beating on these unrelenting stairways. The best way to prepare yourself for these trails is to find a tall building and walk up and down the fire-escape stairs with a loaded backpack (a Stairmaster won't help you prepare for the downhills). However, this only simulates the difficulty of trails in Nepal. Remember: You will be climbing the stairs at elevations that are likely to deprive you of your normal oxygen intake, which causes additional fatigue.

### STAYING HEALTHY
#### ALTITUDE SICKNESS

Anyone (even those in top shape) can develop altitude sickness. To learn more about this potentially fatal sickness, see "Health, Insurance & Other Concerns," in chapter 3. Better yet, stop by **The Himalayan Rescue Association (HRA),** Jyatha, Thamel (P.O. Box 4944), Kathmandu (☎ **977/1-262746;** e-mail: hra@aidpost.mos.com.np), located south of Tridevi Marg on the eastern edge of Thamel in Kathmandu. The goal of this organization is to reduce the number of casualties among trekkers and mountain climbers in Nepal. The HRA disseminates information on altitude sickness and also maintains two health and rescue posts—one at Pheriche on the way to Everest Base Camp and the other in Manang at the foot of Thorong Pass. At the Kathmandu office, you'll also find a bulletin board that is used by independent trekkers looking for trekking companions. There are also log books filled with detailed descriptions of treks written by people who have stopped by the HRA office.

## HYGIENE

It is especially important to make every attempt to maintain personal hygiene on the trail. Unfortunately, you will not find much in the way of facilities. Toilets are often tiny outhouses with a hole in the ground and can be pretty disgusting.

If you are staying in a village off the beaten track, there might not be a toilet in the entire village. The best thing to do in this case is to locate the communal toilet area on the edge of the village and use it before sunrise or after sunset, which is what Nepalis do. If you'll be trekking off the normal routes, carry a trowel and bury your feces. Organized group treks will have a latrine tent set up somewhere near camp.

Washing your hands before eating is one of the best things you can do to avoid diarrhea, but water is not always available. (Sometimes water is available only from a stream or a communal spigot.) It's a good idea to carry sterilizing hand gel or moist towelettes to clean your hands when water is not available for washing. Though solar hot showers are more commonplace than they were a few years ago, you'll probably have to go longer than you would care to without bathing. Many places still use wood fires to heat water for trekkers; thus, taking a shower contributes to the deforestation of Nepal. If you can stand to be dirty for longer than usual, you'll help to preserve Nepal's natural environment. Try to hold out for a solar shower, or tough it out and take a cold shower. If you absolutely must have a hot shower in a place using firewood, a small bucket of water is probably all you'll get (you'll be surprised how far you can make a little hot water go), and you will be charged for it. Several of the treks pass by natural hot springs, which are the ideal way to clean up while trekking. Just remember not to use soap in the bathing pools themselves.

You will need to wash socks and clothes while on the trail. This should be done at a village water spigot, which is where Nepalis usually do their washing. It's a good idea to always keep a set of dry clothes that you will wear only in the evening. The clothes you wear while walking will probably get sweaty and will become quite cold when you stop exerting yourself.

## WATER

Never drink untreated water. It's that simple. All water, whether from a village water tap, stream, or spring, should be considered unsafe to drink. Though this is not always the case, taking chances while trekking can lead to extreme complications. Even though you treat your water, you will not necessarily know whether the tea that you're served is safe to drink. It's often questionable whether tea has been boiled long enough to kill the bacteria or protozoa that might be present, but this is an unavoidable risk of trekking. You should always carry a water bottle and a means of treating water, such as iodine or a two-stage (iodizing) filter. See "Health, Insurance & Other Concerns," in chapter 3, for details on treating water.

Because it is easy to become dehydrated when trekking at higher elevations, even if you are not exercising heavily, it is important to drink plenty of fluids above 9,000 feet. Making frequent stops for tea is one of the best ways to avoid dehydration, and it will also prevent you from overexerting yourself. Drink enough fluids to maintain a normal output of urine. If you do feel that you're dehydrated, it is a good idea to mix rehydration salts (electrolyte powder) into your water bottle, especially if you have been sweating a lot.

## FIRST-AID KIT

Your first-aid kit is one of the most important pieces of equipment in your pack. On the trail you often will be several days' walk from the nearest clinic and even farther from the nearest hospital or doctor. You need to be prepared for a wide variety of possible illnesses and accidents. You may think that your first-aid kit is excessively large, but over the years, I have used almost every item I carry. Stock your first-aid kit with enough of the following supplies and medications for two people. You can also buy prepackaged kits from many outdoors stores.

- Thermometer
- Scissors—for cutting bandages and tape
- Tweezers—for removing splinters and the like
- Needle and thread—for stitching wounds
- Finger splint—for broken fingers
- Temporary wire-mesh splint—for larger broken bones
- 4 butterfly bandages—to be used instead of stitches
- 1 roll of surgical tape—for taping down gauze pads and cotton bandages
- 3 small gauze pads—for covering wounds and infected eyes
- 3 large gauze pads—for covering larger wounds
- 2 rolls of cotton bandages—for dressing large wounds
- 1 triangular bandage—for a sling
- 20 adhesive bandages in an assortment of sizes—for protecting cuts
- 1 dropper bottle of antiseptic such as iodine—for sterilizing cuts; best purchased at home because those sold in Nepal tend to leak
- 1 Ace bandage (elastic bandage)—for sprains, strains, and twists, especially of the knee
- 1 package Moleskin—used to prevent blisters; not available in Nepal
- 1 package Second Skin—used to protect blisters after they form; not available in Nepal
- 1 temporary dental filling kit—can help protect a chipped tooth (rocks frequently show up in dal bhat) or temporarily replace a lost filling

**Medications**    The medications listed below are just a recommendation of what to include in your first-aid kit. Consult your doctor for any necessary prescriptions, dosages, and warnings. For further advice on immunizations and medications, contact the nearest International Health Care office in your area.

- Acetaminophen—for fever, aches, and pain. Unlike aspirin, this drug will not reduce swelling or inflammation. Sold as Paracetamol in Nepal.
- Antibiotics (Ciprofloxacin or Norfloxacin)—useful in treating a variety of bacterial infections, including diarrhea, urinary-tract infections, bronchitis, inner-ear infections, sinusitis, strep throat, and skin infections. Septra (Bactrim), widely used in the United States, is ineffective in Nepal due to bacterial resistance.
- Antidiarrheal or antimotility drug—will stop diarrhea but will not treat its cause. Antidiarrheal agents should *not* be taken if food poisoning is suspected.
- Antihistamine and nasal decongestant—used for treating symptoms of colds and hay fever.
- Antiprotozoal drug—treats giardiasis and amoebas. Flagyl is most common in the United States; Tiniba is prescribed in Nepal.
- Anti-itch cream—used to stop the itching of mosquito, flea, and bedbug bites.
- Aspirin—for aches, pain, fever, cold symptoms, inflammation, and swelling.
- Diamox (acetazolamide)—to relieve minor symptoms (headaches, nausea, insomnia) of altitude sickness. This is not a cure, and signs of acute mountain sickness should not be ignored.
- Eardrops—for treatment of outer ear-canal infections.
- Eyedrops—to treat bacterial eye infections (conjunctivitis), which are very common in Nepal.

- Hydrocortisone cream—used to stop itching caused by rashes and insect bites.
- Mycostatin—for treatment of vaginal yeast infections. Yeast infections frequently develop after a course of strong antibiotics.
- Pepto-Bismol tablets—your first line of defense against upset stomach and diarrhea. Pepto-Bismol is not sold in Nepal.
- Rehydration salts—oral rehydration salts (electrolyte powder) should be added to a quart or liter of treated water and drunk by those suffering from severe diarrhea. Oral rehydration salts are sold as Jeevan Jal in Nepal and are very inexpensive. In the United States they are available at outdoor-equipment and sporting-goods stores.
- Sore-throat lozenges—sore throats are a fact of life in Nepal, where the winds kick up a lot of dust. Trekkers, especially in the winter months, often have chronic sore throats from the dust.
- Sunscreen—despite the cool temperatures you are likely to encounter during the prime trekking seasons, Nepal is a subtropical country, which means that the sun is probably stronger than at home. At higher elevations, the sun is particularly intense. If you keep your arms and legs covered, you will need only enough sunscreen to keep your face and hands protected.

## EVACUATION INSURANCE & HELICOPTER RESCUES

While trekking, you may be many days' walk from the nearest medical facility or doctor. In the case of an emergency, it is possible to be evacuated by helicopter. A helicopter evacuation usually costs between $600 and $1,400 per hour, and a rescue operation will usually take 2 to 3 hours. Consequently, you can expect to pay as much as $1,200 to $4,200 for a helicopter rescue, and before the helicopter will take off, there must be proof of your ability to pay. Neither a trekking agency nor your embassy nor the Nepali government will pay the bill. If you happen to be carrying enough cash, you won't have a problem, but most people don't carry this much money while trekking. The best solution is to buy travel-assistance insurance that provides evacuation coverage. This type of insurance is not readily available in Nepal, so it's very important to get it before leaving home. Before you are allowed to participate in a group trek, you will probably have to show proof that you have purchased evacuation insurance. Adventure-travel companies outside Nepal will be able to arrange the insurance for you. If you are traveling on your own, let your embassy know that you're going trekking and that you have evacuation insurance. See "Health, Insurance & Other Concerns," in chapter 3, for a list of insurance companies that provide evacuation insurance.

If you or someone in your party needs to be evacuated by helicopter, this is the procedure you must follow. First, locate the nearest two-way radio, telegraph, or telephone, and contact Kathmandu. You will need to relay the following information to your embassy or trekking agent: injured person's name, passport number, location, nature of emergency, whether a medical team needs to be on board the helicopter, and identification of the person supplying the information to the authorities in Kathmandu. Before the helicopter will leave Kathmandu, your trekking agent or embassy must guarantee payment for the rescue.

Members of the American Alpine Club receive, as part of club membership, evacuation insurance in an amount that is usually sufficient to cover a helicopter rescue. This insurance is in effect only when you are on the trail. For information on membership, contact the **American Alpine Club,** 710 Tenth St., Suite 100, Golden, CO

80401 (☎ **303/384-0110;** fax 303/384-0111; www.americanalpineclub.org; e-mail: getinfo@americanalpineclub.org).

# 5  What to Pack

The key to staying comfortable on a trek is layering. Temperatures can vary 30° or 40° between night and midday, so you need to be prepared with a variety of clothing. During the day, you'll generate a lot of heat by walking, especially if you're carrying a pack. Even in November, shorts and a T-shirt are adequate attire in the middle of the day, but at night, you'll need thermal underwear, wool socks, a sweater or fleece jacket, and a down jacket. In December or January, layering is especially important. You might start the day wearing long pants, a sweater, and a down jacket, but within a couple of hours of hiking uphill, you might need only a T-shirt and shorts. By lunchtime, you may need to put the sweater and sometimes the jacket back on. At the end of the day, it's important to have a dry set of layers to change into, including a thermal underwear top and bottom. Layering, however, is necessary only at higher elevations and during the winter (late Nov to early Feb). In October and early November, you probably won't need so much warm clothing, but it's still a good idea to bring it along.

## CLOTHING & ACCESSORIES

**First Aid Kit**   See "First-Aid Kit," on page 223.

**Boots**   The single-most-important item for trekking is a good pair of hiking boots. To avoid blisters while trekking, your boots should be thoroughly broken in before you leave. Since you can easily walk 150 miles or more on a 2-week trek, it is crucial that your boots are sturdy, rugged, and well made so that they will stand up to the strain of steep trails. Good ankle support is crucial; a twisted ankle can ruin a trek. Although a wide assortment of hiking boots, both new and used, is now available in Kathmandu, it is much better to buy your boots before you arrive so that they can be broken in.

**Sneakers**   It's smart to carry some sort of lightweight athletic shoe for use at night, because your boots are likely to be quite damp with sweat after a day of hiking (unless you have Gore-Tex boots). Also, should your hiking boots give you blisters or give out on you entirely, you can hike in your athletic shoes. A nylon walking shoe with a sole that provides good traction is the best choice.

**Socks**   Good boots should be accompanied by appropriate socks. Polypropylene sock liners and wool outer socks are still the best combination for keeping your feet dry and free from blisters. I like to carry three pairs of each type of sock. I keep one pair of wool socks for changing into at night, and alternate between the other two pairs during the day. Wool socks take a long time to dry. Try to put them near the cooking fire after washing them.

**Down Jacket**   Though it can be hot in Kathmandu in October and November, higher up in the mountains, it's likely to be below freezing at night. Down jackets are the best choice because they offer warmth without a lot of weight. (Down jackets can be rented in Kathmandu.) Some people prefer fiber-filled jackets because, although they are heavier than down, they provide warmth even when wet. You're not likely to have much rain during the normal trekking seasons.

**Wool Sweater or Synthetic Fleece Jacket**   Despite its weight, wool is still one of the best materials to have on a trek. It will keep you warm even if it's wet. The wool sweaters sold in Kathmandu, though pretty, are neither tightly woven enough nor durable enough for life on the trail. In the past few years, synthetic fleece jackets have surpassed wool sweaters in popularity. These jackets offer the same benefits of wool, and they dry faster.

**Shorts**    Men (and women who don't mind being stared at) will want a sturdy pair of walking shorts. Even in late November, long pants can be too hot during the day. By wearing your shorts while you hike, you can keep your long pants dry for the evening.

**Long Skirt**    Though a skirt may seem like strange hiking attire to most Western women accustomed to hiking in shorts, in Nepal, where exposing more than an ankle is frowned upon, it's a good choice. You'll find that you get much more respect if you keep your legs (and shoulders) covered. However, if you choose to wear shorts, no one will treat you with disrespect, though your cultural interactions may become limited. A spacious, midcalf-length skirt provides room for long strides and is useful when relieving oneself by the side of the trail if privacy is impossible to find.

**Wool or Fleece Pants**    If you're hiking in December or January, wool or synthetic fleece pants are a good idea, especially above 9,000 feet, where nights and early mornings are cold.

**Loose Cotton or Nylon Pants**    Pants that you can pull on over shorts make it easy to change back and forth while you're on the trail. Pants that you convert into shorts by zipping off the legs are very popular. With these you get two articles of clothing in one and reduce weight in your pack.

**Down Pants**    Down pants, which can be rented in Kathmandu, are really necessary only if you're planning to spend several days above 12,000 feet in midwinter. At other times of the year and at lower elevations, they are simply too hot.

**Thermal Underwear**    Thermal underwear is a necessity at night from November through January, and at higher elevations even during the day. Above Jomosoml, strong winds can cut right through a single layer of pants or through a shirt and sweater.

**Rain Gear**    Though you are not likely to encounter more than 1 or 2 days of rain while trekking (if any at all), it's still a good idea to be prepared. A simple plastic or coated nylon poncho that can be worn over your pack is the best choice, since it keeps your pack dry and won't cause you to sweat excessively in warm weather. A waterproof, breathable jacket and pants, however, are more versatile and will probably keep you drier.

**Wool or Fleece Hat**    A balaclava or ski hat is invaluable after dark at higher elevations. Good wool hats with earflaps are available in Kathmandu. A sun hat, to keep the glare out of the eyes, is also a good idea. If you're hiking up the windy Kali Gandaki River (the Jomosom trek), make sure your hat has a cord to keep it from blowing off.

**Gloves or Mittens**    Wool gloves or mittens are necessary at night at high elevations and in the winter. Since you won't be using your fingers for much, mittens are the better choice. A combination of glove liners and either wool mittens or ski gloves is the best choice for high-elevation winter treks.

**Sunglasses**    If you expect to be crossing any snowy areas, sunglasses are essential to prevent snow blindness. Sunglasses also come in handy during dust storms, which are frequent around Manang and Jomosom.

**Sleeping Bag**    A down- or a fiber-filled bag rated to 20° is the best bet. If you're trekking in the Everest region or anywhere else above 11,000 feet in December or January, a 0° bag is a good idea.

**Backpack or Duffel Bag**   If you're carrying your own load, you'll need a comfortable backpack. Hundreds of models are available in several basic styles. A well-designed travel pack that can be converted into a suitcase for airplane travel works well for trips to Nepal. External-frame packs are difficult to get into crowded buses; internal-frame packs work better. If you're going on a group trek, a large duffel bag is all you'll need since your bag will probably be crammed into a porter's basket.

**Day Pack**   A small pack is essential if you're trekking with a porter. Keep your water bottle, camera, snacks, rain gear, and some warm clothing in your day pack.

**Flashlight**   A good flashlight is an absolute necessity when trekking. The power, in villages that have electricity, is usually on for only a few hours each night. The best choice is a headlamp, which is available at most outdoor-equipment stores. These lights leave your hands free for reading and, more importantly, balancing yourself in dirty outhouses. Only large flashlights requiring heavy D-cell batteries are available in Nepal, but they can be found almost anywhere. Be sure to bring spare batteries (and carry out the used ones).

**Water Bottle**   A 1-quart (liter) water bottle is a must while trekking. Never drink water that has not been treated. Carry either a two-stage (iodizing) filter or a small bottle of iodine, or ask for boiled water at your lodge. The latter, however, uses precious firewood and is not necessarily safe because you don't know whether the water was boiled for a sufficient amount of time. You take the same risk when drinking tea on the trail, but unfortunately, it's unavoidable.

**Playing Cards**   Card playing is very popular on the trail, especially when cold weather keeps people indoors for most of the day.

## MAPS

A map seems like an obvious item for a trek, but most trails in Nepal are so well marked, and the main routes so evident, that maps aren't that necessary. And if you've hired a guide, you shouldn't need a map at all. Also, many of the maps of the trekking routes are full of errors, making them more confusing than they are useful. This said, it's still a good idea to have a map.

A variety of maps are available at bookshops in Kathmandu and Pokhara. The best are the German Schneider maps, but they are expensive and hard to find. The next best are the Italian-designed Nepa Maps, which cost anywhere from Rs200 ($3.05) to Rs600 ($9.10), depending on the area covered. You can find these maps at most bookstores in Kathmandu and Pokhara. The most inexpensive maps are those produced by Mandala Maps. These maps are not very detailed, but they'll give you an idea of what to expect each day and may help you to identify peaks.

In the United States, one of the best sources of Nepal maps is **Omni Resources,** 1004 S. Mebane St. (P.O. Box 2096), Burlington, NC 27216-2096 (☎ **800/ 742-2677** or 336/227-8300; fax 336/227-3748; www.omnimap.com; e-mail: custserv@ omnimap.\com).

## MONEY

Although there are banks in a few of the villages on the main trekking routes (Namche Bazaar, Jomosom, Tatopani), plan to carry enough money for your entire trek if you're trekking independently. Don't count on banks to be open when you need cash. If you are staying in local lodges, plan on spending around $10 per day. Carry more money if you like to have a beer or two at the end of the day, and if you are paying for a porter's or guide's meals and lodging. Small change is hard to come by on the trail, so carry plenty. I usually get the bulk of my money in 50- and 100-rupee notes, plus several hundred rupees in smaller bills.

If you're on a group trek where everything is catered, you won't need much money. However, you will be passing through villages that sell soft drinks, beer, and domestic liquors—carry some change to make these purchases. In Helambu, in Namche Bazaar, and all along the Jomosom trek, you're likely to encounter traders with goods for sale or trade. Prices on the trail are not necessarily any better than they are in Kathmandu, and most of the items for sale have actually been hauled up from Kathmandu. These traders occasionally have unusual and rare pieces from Tibet or from Nepali mountain villages, and they are sometimes bargains.

# 6 Trekking Permits & Other Fees

Securing a trekking permit can be an aggravating and frustrating experience if you're arranging your own trek. Be prepared. (The outfitter will take care of the permit if you're going on an organized trek.) Because permit applications are accepted in the morning and permits are issued in the afternoon, you'll need the better part of a day to get the permit. If you are heading to the Annapurna region, you'll find that it's a bit easier to get a trekking permit in Pokhara.

To apply for a trekking permit, you'll need your passport and two extra passport-size photos of yourself. If you forgot to bring extra photos with you, go to one of the photo shops in Thamel or, in Pokhara, down the street from the Department of Immigration. If you can, pick up the permit application forms a day ahead, and fill them out at your leisure (you can often get copies at trekking companies in Thamel).

After filling out a trekking-permit request form and the trekking permit itself, you must stand in line (this is the ordeal). Make sure you are in the correct line; some of the lines are for visa extensions and some are for trekking permits. If you filled out forms in advance, you might even get to go to the head of the line.

## DEPARTMENT OF IMMIGRATION OFFICES

**In Kathmandu**    The Department of Immigration office is at No. 10 Baneswor, Prabha Kanhaiya Complex (☎ **977/1-494273** or 977/1-494337), on the east side of Kathmandu on the road that runs between the Everest Hotel and the International Convention Center (take a taxi). In Kathmandu, trekking-permit applications are accepted Sunday through Thursday from 10am to 1pm and on Friday from 10am to noon. Permits can then be picked up Sunday through Thursday from 4 to 5pm and on Friday from 2 to 3pm. You pick up your permit on the same day that you apply. If it's during the busy trekking season of October and November, you can expect the line to form at least 2 hours before the Department of Immigration office opens.

**In Pokhara**    The Department of Immigration office (☎ **977/61-21167** or 977/ 61-20028), is located just off the traffic circle at the end of the Lakeside neighborhood (east of the Hotel Pumori and west of the Hotel Tragopan). Trekking-permit applications are accepted Sunday through Thursday from 10:30am to 1pm (12:30pm between mid-Nov and mid-Feb) and Friday from 10am to noon. Permits are then issued.

## TREKKING-PERMIT FEES

Trekking-permit fees vary by area, with the most popular routes (those favored by independent trekkers) having the lowest fees. You have to pay for an entire week, so even if you are going for only 10 days, tell them you are going for 14, just in case something happens or you decide to extend your trek. For the more popular trekking routes (Annapurna region, Everest region, and Langtang/Gosainkund/Helambu), the fees are $5 per week for the first 4 weeks and $10 per week thereafter. For the Mustang and upper Dolpo region, fees are $700 for the first 10 days and $70 per day after that. In the Manaslu region, fees are $90 per week from September through November and $75 per week from December through August. In the Humla region, the fees are $90 for the first week and $15 per day after that. In the Kanchenjunga and lower Dolpo areas, fees are $10 per week for the first 4 weeks and $20 per week thereafter.

If you will be trekking beyond the length of your visa, you will have to get a visa extension in addition to your trekking permit. Visa extensions cost $1 per day and are also issued by the Department of Immigration.

## OTHER FEES

In addition to a trekking-permit fee, you'll also have to pay a national-park entrance fee if you are headed into the Everest or Langtang regions. Admission to either Sagermatha National Park (Everest region) or Langtang National Park is Rs650 ($9.85). Currently, fees are payable at the National Park Entry Fee Counter in the Sanchayakosh Building on Tridevi Marg, which is on the wide street that leads into Thamel from the east. However, now that the Department of Immigration has moved across town, this office may also move. Ask at the Department of Immigration when you get your trekking permit.

If you are heading into the Annapurna region, you will have to pay a Rs1,000 ($15.15) Annapurna Conservation Area Project (ACAP) entry fee. This fee is used to promote conservation and to build rubbish pits, water systems, schools, trails, bridges, and public outhouses in the villages of the Annapurna region. ACAP also sets food and lodging rates in the region and operates lodge-management training courses for Nepalis. The goal of ACAP is partly to standardize trekking accommodations so that trekkers will know what to expect from lodges along the trail. To this end, ACAP in recent years closed down several small lodges on the route to the Annapurna Sanctuary so that the trail would not become one long string of lodges. On this route there are now collections of lodges at roughly 2-hour intervals beyond Chhomrong, which helps to maintain some feeling of wilderness. ACAP maintains information centers in Pokhara at the Natural History Museum and in the Gurung village of Ghandruk. The ACAP fee is paid at the same place that national-park entry fees are paid.

You may also be able to pay both national-park and ACAP fees at the Department of Immigration and at park entries, but be sure to ask when you get your trekking permit.

## 7  Minimizing Your Impaact on the Environment & the People

## SOCIALLY RESPONSIBLE TREKKING

There's just no getting around the fact that trekking has had a profound effect on Nepal—just ask the kid wearing the *Titanic* T-shirt or the old man in the Chicago Bulls baseball hat. Villages that once depended primarily on farming now focus their energy on catering to trekkers. Plastic water bottles float in remote mountain streams, and children greet trekkers with cries of "one rupee, one rupee" (and sometimes throw rocks if you don't give in to their demands). Perhaps the single-most-important thing to remember when trekking in Nepal is to tread lightly. Think about the trekkers who will come after you. Of course, you can't be expected to leave your modern high-tech

## Packing in Nepal for a Trek

If you decide after arriving in Kathmandu that you want to go trekking (or find that you have forgotten your sleeping bag or down jacket), don't worry. You can rent all kinds of gear, including sleeping bags, jackets, and other essentials, at shops around Thamel in Kathmandu and in the Lakeside neighborhood in Pokhara. Most rental items such as down sleeping bags and jackets are available for between Rs30 and Rs60 (45¢ and 90¢) per item per day. You will also have to leave a deposit of between $45 and $100 per item. Other items to pick up before hitting the trail are toilet paper, oral rehydration salts, and iodine.

camping accessories and conveniences at home, but try not to leave behind your modern garbage on the trail. There are a number of ways that you can be socially and environmentally responsible during your visit to Nepal. Do what you can to reduce the use of firewood (shower less often, eat local foods, dress warmly instead of sitting by a fire), and you will help to preserve the forests of the Himalayas. Respecting local customs, packing out nonbiodegradable garbage (especially batteries), and refraining from buying bottled water and beers will all help minimize your physical impact on the Himalayas.

Before heading out on a trek, or before even booking a trek (if you are arranging a catered trek after your arrival), you should stop by the **Kathmandu Environmental Education Project (KEEP)**, Thamel Mall Building Complex, Jyatha (P.O. Box 9178), Thamel (☎ **977/1-259275** or 977/1-259567; fax 977/1-411533; e-mail: tour@keep.wlink.com.np), which is located south of Tridevi Marg near the Hotel Utse. Here you can find out the names of the most environmentally conscious trekking companies, learn about the impact trekking is having on Nepal's environment, and pick up some tips on how to minimize your impact on the environment and culture. You can also pick up a copy of *Trekking Gently in the Himalaya,* a booklet on trekking responsibly and reducing your impact on the environment. You can also learn about altitude sickness, register with your embassy, and read other trekkers' comments about various treks.

In the past few years trekking companies have begun offering environmentally conscious treks. These include treks to plant trees as part of reforestation projects and to pick up garbage left by previous mountaineering and trekking expeditions. However, it is important to take care of the sensitive Himalayan environment on any trek. The most salient thing to remember is that deforestation is one of the greatest problems facing Nepal today. Each year during the monsoon, vast amounts of soil wash away from deforested hillsides, causing landslides, destroying villages, and eliminating productive cropland. The large numbers of trekkers in Nepal have played a big part in deforestation in recent years. On most trekking routes, food is prepared primarily over wood fires, as are tea and bath water. If at all possible, try to patronize lodges that use kerosene for cooking (in some areas, use of kerosene is mandatory).

Don't litter on the trails, and in villages try to be sure that there is some sort of garbage pit for biodegradable garbage. All nonbiodegradable garbage should be carried out, especially batteries, which are becoming an insidious form of toxic pollution throughout the hills. If there are no toilet facilities where you are staying, burn your toilet paper or store it in a plastic bag until you can dispose of it in a garbage pit. Don't use soap or shampoo in lakes, streams, or hot springs. Instead, take a bucket or pail and rinse the soap off away from the water source.

In recent years the biggest pollutants along the trekking routes are beer and soda bottles and plastic water bottles. Although there is a deposit on soda bottles, which means there is an incentive to pack them out, there is no deposit on beer bottles. Consequently, these have been piling up at such an alarming rate that in 1998, glass bottles were banned from Sagarmatha National Park, which encompasses the trails and villages in the Mount Everest region. In the Annapurna region, the Annapurna Conservation Area Project has set its sights on banning bottled water, which is sold in plastic bottles. The empty bottles either litter the villages or are burned, sending the stench of burning plastic drifting across the hills. You can do your part to solve these problems by not purchasing bottled drinks of any sort. Purify your own water and stick to the tea, coffee, and hot lemonade (a popular drink along the trekking routes). Consider bringing along your own drink powders for flavoring your water.

## TIPPING

Guides, porters, and other trek personnel have traditionally been tipped at the end of treks. In the past, well-funded mountaineering expeditions have been very lavish in their tips because they didn't want to pay to ship unneeded gear back home. Sleeping bags, hiking boots, down jackets, and the like became tips, and consequently, trekkers often think they must tip in an equally lavish fashion. This is not so. A standard tip is 1 day's wages for each week of service. Alternatively, warm clothes (particularly sweaters and good socks) that you no longer need also make appropriate tips. If you have room in your bag for unwanted warm clothes, bring them to Nepal and hand them out as tips.

## BEGGING

Begging has, unfortunately, become a fact of life along Nepal's more popular trekking routes. It is done primarily by small children who greet you with cries of "Hello, one pen. Hello, one rupee. Hello, *mithai* (sweet)." This behavior is a direct result of previous trekkers passing out gifts indiscriminately along the trail. The damage has already been done, and an entire generation has grown up expecting rich foreigners to give them whatever they demand. Please do not encourage begging by passing out candies, pens, balloons, or other gifts.

# The Trekking Routes 10

Imagine walking for 3 to 6 hours every day for a week or two or three. In this amount of time, you might cover 150 miles and climb the Elevation Loss:Now imagine strolling for a few hours a day for 4 or 5 days. This, too, is what it means to trek. Trekking can be a long and arduous journey or it can be a relatively easy walk in the hills. The route descriptions in this chapter cover the most popular teahouse treks and should help you decide which one is right for you. The routes will also get you from point A to point B and back again.

We have broken the descriptions into days, reflecting the distance we traveled at our normal pace (some days are a bit long due to the lack of suitable lodgings at an easy stopping point). Your trekking pace may vary from ours but probably not by much. Some trekkers prefer to get up at dawn, toss down a cup of tea, and hit the trail, making use of as much sunlight as possible. If you are such a person, you're likely to find that you can hike farther than is suggested each day. However, by hiking quickly, you may miss one of the most important reasons for going on a trek—to slow down from the hurried pace of life back home.

If you are going on an organized trek, you may find that you do not follow any of the treks described here. More and more trekking agencies are trying to take groups to less-traveled areas. However, if you are going on a group trek that has selected one of the more popular trails, the route descriptions here will give you a sense of what to expect. Compare your trek itinerary to mine to get an idea of what you will be covering each day.

Perhaps the most important information to note in these descriptions are the **elevations.** A trek that sounds easy at first may include a 6,000-foot (1,829m) ascent in 1½ days (the Jomosom trek) or three ascents and descents of 3,000 to 5,000 feet (914m to 1,524m) over 3 days (the trek to Namche Bazaar from Jiri). It is always a good idea to prepare yourself mentally for such difficult days. Also, some treks ascend to elevations where **altitude sickness** is a very real danger. Many people have died over the years in Nepal because they ignored signs of altitude sickness. Pay attention to the elevations and make sure you spend the required numbers of days acclimatizing at high elevation.

# 1  Solu-Khumbu & the Everest Region Treks

For many trekkers, nothing else will do but to trek as close to Mount Everest as possible. For this reason, the trails above Lukla (the nearest regularly used airstrip to Everest) are among the most crowded in Nepal during October and November. If Everest is your goal, reconcile yourself to crowds. There are several ways that you can trek through the Solu-Khumbu region, depending on the amount of time you have available for your trek.

If you have **28 to 30 days** to spare, you can trek from Jiri to Kala Pattar or Gokyo Ri for a close-up view of Mount Everest and then hike back out. Add another 5 days to this schedule if you want to visit both Kala Pattar and Gokyo Ri. Keep in mind that in the first few days of the trek this route climbs and descends three major ridges before beginning the steady climb up the valley of the Dudh Kosi to Namche Bazaar. This is a grueling section of the trail, but it will get you in shape for trekking higher up and will allow you to trek through interesting and attractive villages, terraced fields, pastures, meadows, and different types of forests. The first part (week) of this hike now sees relatively few trekkers due to the popularity of flights to and from Lukla. There aren't many views of the high peaks until you reach Namche Bazaar, so be psychologically prepared for a week of anticipation.

Alternatively, you can hike in and then fly out of Lukla (or vice versa) and save yourself 5 to 10 days of trekking. Unfortunately, flying out of Lukla is often a problem due to bad weather, and you have to have both patience and a flexible schedule if you opt for this choice. Flying in to Lukla and then hiking out allows you to avoid problems with getting on a departing flight, but you then end up hiking through the low country with few mountain views and lots of ups and downs after you've been up there in the thin air and shimmering peaks. With nothing to look forward to at the end of your trek, hiking out can be a rather tedious experience. This itinerary will take **18 to 20 days.**

These days, most people skip the trail between Jiri and Lukla entirely and instead fly in and out of Lukla. By doing this, you can trek up to Kala Pattar for a view of Everest and be back in Kathmandu in 15 days. The main drawback of this option is that you're stuck with the crowds for your entire trek. You also don't get the physical-conditioning benefits of hiking in for a week, and you have a higher risk of developing altitude sickness because you will be starting your trek at 9,200 feet (2,804m). By flying in, you also bypass a week's worth of interesting villages that provide a broader look at Nepali hill life than do the few villages beyond Lukla.

Beyond Namche Bazaar (1½ days from Lukla), the trek continues at high elevations where altitude sickness is a very real danger. For a close-up view of Mount Everest, it is necessary to climb as high as 17,000 or 18,000 feet (5,181m or 5,486m). Many

## Trekking Tip

Every year at the end of the monsoon season, thousands of adventurers descend upon Nepal from all over the world. They set off for the hills with trekking guidebooks in hand only to find that the trail they are supposed to take no longer exists. Landslides are a constant problem, and frequently they cause trails to be rerouted. Flooding washes away bridges and makes it impossible (or at least very difficult) to cross rivers. These unforeseen problems are inherent in any trek. Please keep this in mind and ask locals about trail conditions as you follow the route descriptions in this chapter.

# Solu-Khumbu Trekking Routes

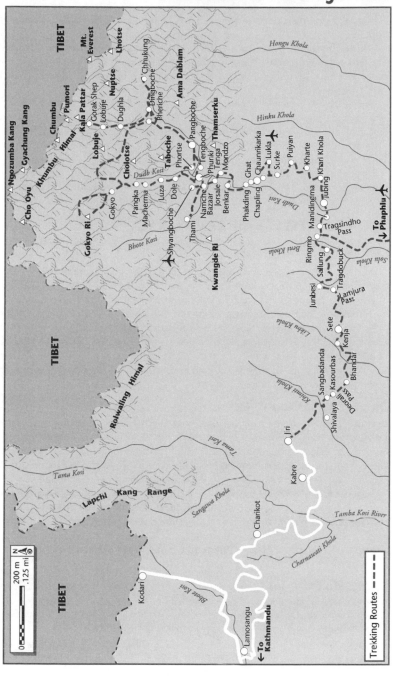

trekkers abandon their quest to see Everest close up because they cannot handle the altitude.

Whichever way you do choose to visit this region, you'll have a very rewarding trek. The terrain and vegetation change dramatically between Jiri and the glaciated regions in the immediate vicinity of Mount Everest, and the high peaks beyond Namche Bazaar are spectacular.

One of the most popular times to visit this region is during November, when the **Mani Rimdu festival** is held at Tengboche Monastery (a day's walk from Namche Bazaar). During this festival, the monastery's Buddhist monks don colorful masks and elaborate costumes and perform various religious dances in the monastery courtyard. There is a similar festival at the monastery in Thami each May.

One more word of advice: Don't make Everest Base Camp your ultimate goal unless you have a very good reason. Despite the name, you cannot see Mount Everest from here, and you won't be allowed to wander among the tents of the expeditions.

## LUKLA TO EVEREST BASE CAMP & KALA PATTAR
Number of Days: 15. TOTAL ELEVATION GAIN: 11,159–12,128 ft. (3,401–3,697m). TOTAL ELEVATION LOSS: 9,989–10,058 ft. (3,014–3,066m).

As of 1998, helicopters other than genuine charters had been prohibited at Lukla. In the years previous to this prohibition, choppers had become the favored means of getting to Lukla because they were able to fly in worse weather than planes could. With numerous helicopter companies operating out of Kathmandu, expect the prohibition to be lifted in upcoming years, and if it is, helicopters are the better way to get here. Currently, you'll have to fly in a fixed-wing plane with Royal Nepal Airlines (RNAC), Lumbini Airways, or Yeti Airways. Airfare is $83 each way. The steeply angled airstrip at Lukla provides one of the most hair-raising landings in the world, a memorable beginning to a trek.

### DAY 1: KATHMANDU TO LUKLA
Because of the airstrip and the frequent passenger backups caused by bad weather, **Lukla** (9,200 ft.; 2,804m) is a very lively place. There are dozens of lodges, hotels, teahouses, and shops catering to the thousands of trekkers who pass through here annually. Despite the many accommodations, Lukla can be crowded. Because the altitude here is about as high as you should fly into if you want to avoid suffering from altitude sickness, it is advisable to spend the rest of the day here acclimatizing. The best way to acclimatize is to do a bit of walking, preferably above the village. If you want to hire a guide, a porter, or both, ask at your lodge. Avoid dealing with any touts that might approach you as you get off the plane. The **Himalaya Lodge** just above the airstrip is popular. However, if you aren't quite ready to give up private bathrooms, you could stay at the very pricey **Sagarmatha Resort.**

### DAY 2: LUKLA TO JORSALE
Lukla to Chapling: 45 minutes; Chapling to Ghat: 45 minutes; Ghat to Phakding: 1 hour; Phakding to Benkar: 1¼ hours; Benkar to Mondzo: 1 hour; Mondzo to Jorsale: 1 hour. ELEVATION GAIN: 700 ft. (213m). ELEVATION LOSS: 800 ft. (244m).

The trail from Lukla begins at the far end of the village from the airstrip and leads gradually downhill to **Chapling** (8,767 ft.; 2,672m). This section of the trail is mostly without shade, so it's a good idea to start while it's still cool. As in Lukla, there are views down into the valley of the Dudh Kosi. Several hundred feet below, you can see the village of Chaunrikarka. Shortly before reaching Chapling, the trail up from Jiri joins the trail from Lukla.

# Detail of Solu-Khumbu Trekking Routes

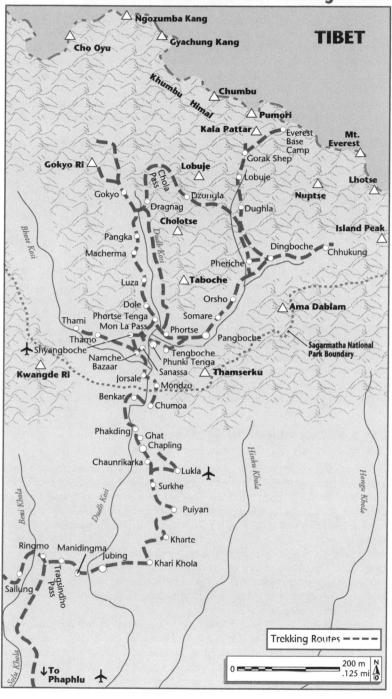

Beyond Chapling, the trail crosses a tributary stream and descends to **Ghat.** Keep to the east bank, climbing, descending, and climbing again before reaching **Phakding** (8,600 ft.; 2,621m). Cross over the Dudh Kosi to the west bank and continue north to the village of **Benkar** (8,850 ft.; 2,697m). Beyond Benkar, you cross back to the east bank of the river and climb to **Chumoa.** The trail continues climbing, then descends to a stream and climbs to **Mondzo** (9,300 ft.; 2,835m). There are several lodges in each of these villages, but I suggest moving on to Jorsale. Sagarmatha National Park has its entrance here in Mondzo, and you will have to show your park permit (purchased in Kathmandu) and sign the register.

Because the trek now leads through a national park, all trekking groups are prohibited from cooking with firewood; consequently, kerosene must be carried. There is a kerosene depot in Namche Bazaar and Lukla, and containers for kerosene can also be purchased. This rule does not, however, apply to lodges catering to trekkers. Many lodges still use wood to cook and heat water for showers. Though a few lodges have begun using kerosene (and even propane) stoves, these are still the exception. If you ask a few lodge owners whether they use kerosene and if you express an interest in staying at a lodge that does use kerosene, maybe things will begin to change. Using kerosene may add a little bit to the cost of a meal, but saving the forests of the Himalayas is well worth the expense.

Beyond the park entrance, the trail descends a stone stairway, crosses back to the west bank of the river, and continues to **Jorsale** (9,100 ft.; 2,774m). There are quite a few lodges here, and I suggest staying for the night. Though it is possible to reach Namche Bazaar on the same day, it is still a very steep 3-hour hike away. It is better to make this climb in the morning when you are rested and full of energy.

You will probably encounter yak caravans all along the trail from Lukla. These caravans are a constant source of danger. Yaks can be bad tempered, so always be prepared for a nudge from one. Keep to the uphill side when passing these slow-moving beasts to avoid being pushed or accidentally knocked off the trail. Luckily, this steep section of trail is not very long.

## DAY 3: JORSALE TO NAMCHE BAZAAR
Jorsale to Namche Bazaar: 2½ to 3 hours. ELEVATION GAIN: 2,200 ft. (671m).

From Jorsale, the trail crosses the river on the long suspension bridge and then follows a flat trail upriver for 20 minutes or so. The path then climbs above the valley floor to one of the highest suspension bridges I have ever seen in Nepal. From there the trail continues climbing steeply through the forest to a teahouse with a partially obscured view of Mount Everest. This is a steep climb, and the teahouse is a welcome resting spot.

Beyond the teahouse, take the right fork, which leads into Namche Bazaar through an area that is used as a market on Saturdays. In addition to this short day of hiking, you'll need to spend at least 1 full day (preferably 2) acclimatizing in Namche Bazaar before continuing to higher elevations. Find a lodge and spend the afternoon exploring the village or relaxing in the sun.

**Namche Bazaar** (11,300 ft.; 3,444m) is the largest village and the administrative center of the Khumbu region. Situated in a horseshoe-shaped valley high above the Bhote Kosi and surrounded by steep hills, it faces the impressive north face of Kwangde peak (20,285 ft.; 6,183m). There are a police checkpoint, a bank where it is possible to change money, and a post office here. A small hydroelectric project provides electricity at night. There are also dozens of lodges and hotels here. **The Khumbu Lodge** and the **Himalayan Lodge** are among the best in town. The village shops sell an amazing variety of imported foods—the leftovers of international mountaineering

## Because It Is There

"Because it is there."

George Mallory's reply to the question of why he wanted to climb Mt. Everest ranks right up there with Neil Armstrong's words on setting foot on the moon. However, unlike Armstrong, Mallory never made it back down to where the air isn't so thin. When Mallory disappeared into the clouds near the summit of Everest on June 8, 1924, he left the world with one of the great unanswered questions of the 20th century. Did he and teammate Andrew Irvine make it to the summit or not? If they did reach the summit, then they, and not Sir Edmund Hillary and Tenzing Norgay Sherpa, would have been the first to the summit of the highest peak on earth.

In May, 1999, the world came just a little closer to solving this mystery when Mallory's body was discovered on a narrow ledge at 27,000 feet. The body was found by a mountaineering expedition that had come to Everest specifically to search for the bodies of Mallory and Irvine. At press time, searchers were still trying to locate the camera that Mallory carried with him on his summit attempt. Should this camera be found, it could prove once and for all whether Mallory was or was not the first to summit Mt. Everest.

expeditions. You can also buy hand-knitted wool sweaters, socks, and gloves and rent down jackets and sleeping bags. The Sagarmatha National Park headquarters and visitor center are above the police checkpoint on the hill to the east of the village. This hill has a spectacular view up the valley to Mount Everest and all its surrounding peaks. Sunrises and sunsets from this ridge are worth all the grueling days it takes to get here.

### DAYS 4 & 5: ALTITUDE ACCLIMATIZATION DAYS

**DAY HIKES FROM NAMCHE BAZAAR**    The best way to acclimatize is to hike to higher elevation and then return to Namche Bazaar for the night. There are a few day hikes (and overnighters) possible from Namche Bazaar.

**Shyangboche Airstrip Area**    One of the most interesting day hikes is the climb up the hill north of town to the Shyangboche airstrip area. From the east end of this little-used airstrip, a trail leads to the Hotel Everest View, a deluxe hotel built by the Japanese in the 1970s. The long, low stone and glass building is so incredibly out of place in this remote landscape that it's fascinating. Stop by for a very expensive pot of tea, and enjoy the view of Everest from the dining room or terrace. For more information on the hotel, contact ✪ **Hotel Everest View,** Durbar Marg (P.O. Box 1694), Kathmandu (☎ **977/1-224854;** fax 977/1-227289). Rates are around $320 per night for a double (with meals included).

**Thami**    You start this day hike by walking west toward the village of Thami. In Thamo, 1½ hours out of Namche Bazaar, climb the steep slope to a small gompa built by the English-speaking lama who helped found Kopan monastery in Boudha. This gompa is frequently used as a retreat for Western Buddhists who come from all over the world to get away from it all. The Sherpa caretakers of the gompa are always happy to have guests, and even the Westerners staying here may be willing to talk with you about Buddhism if you are interested.

From Thamo, continue up the valley to **Thami,** which you should reach in about 2 hours. After exploring Thami, you can visit the monastery outside of the village before heading back to Namche Bazaar.

## DAY 6: NAMCHE BAZAAR TO TENGBOCHE

Namche Bazaar to Sanassa: 1 hour; Sanassa to Phunki Tenga: 1 hour; Phunki Tenga to Teng-boche: 2 hours. ELEVATION GAIN: 2,519ft. (768m). ELEVATION LOSS: 1,140ft. (347m).

The route to Kala Pattar is by far the most popular trail originating in Namche Bazaar. If this is the route you intend to follow, climb the hill to the park headquarters, where the trail levels off. The Dudh Kosi is far below, and the view from here is spectacular, with Thamserku (21,675 ft.; 6,607m) directly across the valley, Kwangde to the south across the Bhote Kosi valley, and Everest (29,028 ft.; 8,848m), Nuptse (25,845 ft.; 7,878m), Ama Dablam (22,488 ft.; 6,854m), Cholotse (21,125 ft.; 6,439m), and Khumbila (18,900 ft.; 5,761m) all ahead of you up the valley. Keep your eyes open for pheasants along this stretch of trail.

The wide path descends slowly through steep pastures. Within 1¼ hours you pass **Sanassa** and the trail up to Khumjung, a large Sherpa village in a desolate valley. Con-tinue descending on the main trail, entering a forest, to reach the Dudh Kosi and the village of **Phunki Tenga** (10,660 ft.; 3,249m) with its water-driven mills and prayer wheels. There are a few lodges here. Cross the river and climb steeply through a dense forest.

**Tengboche** (12,679 ft.; 3,865m), the largest monastery in Khumbu, perches on the saddle of a ridge and commands an outstanding panorama with peaks in every direction. The monastery is especially beautiful with Ama Dablam rising up behind it. This is one of the most memorable sights anywhere in Nepal. Tengboche monastery is the site of the annual Mani Rimdu festival, held at the November full moon. During the fes-tival, monks wearing masks and colorful costumes act out traditional dances in the courtyard of the monastery. It is an amazing sight, though it is always very crowded with trekkers. Stay at the excellent **Tengboche Trekkers Lodge** or the **Gompa Lodge,** which is operated by Tengboche's monks. If you are camping, you will be asked to pay a small charge for pitching your tent on monastery land. While in Tengboche, you can visit the **Sherpa Cultural Center,** a small museum with infor-mative displays about the Sherpa people. It's in a building behind the gompa. Because the monastery has banned hunting in the vicinity, you may see pheasants, musk deer, Himalayan *tahr* (mountain goats), or jungle cats along the nearby trails.

## DAY 7: TENGBOCHE TO PHERICHE

Tengboche to Pangboche: 2 hours; Pangboche to Pheriche: 2 hours. ELEVATION GAIN: 1,221 ft. (372m).

Descend a steep trail through a damp rhododendron forest to the village of Deboche, which has two lodges, a long mani wall (a wall of stones that has had prayers carved onto it), and a nunnery. Continue descending through the rhododendrons until you cross the Imja Khola (12,400 ft.; 3,780m). Across the river you have an excellent view of Ama Dablam as you begin climbing past chortens (small stupa-like shrines) and mani walls. Remember to always keep mani walls and chortens on your right side as you pass them. It is considered disrespectful to have your left side to one of these structures.

At a fork in the trail, keep to the right to reach lower **Pangboche** (12,800 ft.; 3,901m). The left fork climbs to Pangboche Monastery and upper Pangboche village, which once claimed to have the partial remains of a yeti. Unfortunately, in 1991, these relics were stolen from the monastery and were never recovered. Upper Pangboche is the more interesting section of the village and is surrounded by large cedar trees. If you decide to stay the night, try the **Pangboche Gompa Lodge** or, in lower Pangboche, the **Ama Dablang Lodge** or the **Shiri Dewa Lodge.**

On the far side of the lower village, cross a stream and ascend through terraced fields, eventually climbing above the treeline. The trail proceeds up a gentle slope and passes the small village of Somare, where there are some teahouses. Beyond Somare, the trail flattens a bit and passes a lodge at Orsho.

Beyond Orsho there is a fork in the trail. The right fork leads to Dingboche, but you should take the left fork. Climb a ridge before descending to the wooden bridge that crosses the stream flowing from Khumbu Glacier. **Pheriche** (13,900 ft.; 4,237 m) is about 10 minutes beyond the stream. There are many small lodges in Pheriche. There is also a **Trekkers' Aid Post** staffed by Western physicians and sponsored by the Himalayan Rescue Association. If you have not yet familiarized yourself with the symptoms of altitude sickness, it is a good idea to stop by this post and learn more about this potentially fatal illness.

## DAY 8: PHERICHE: ACCLIMATIZATION DAY

It is necessary to spend a day in Pheriche acclimatizing. Try to take a day hike up to a higher elevation and then return to Pheriche for the night. If you hike to a higher altitude from here, you are likely to be rewarded with amazing views of the peaks.

## DAY 9: PHERICHE TO LOBUJE

Pheriche to Dughla: 2 hours; Dughla to Lobuje: 2 hours. ELEVATION GAIN: 2,370 ft. (692m).

From Pheriche head up the valley to Phulong Karpo, a grassy pasture used for grazing yaks in the summer. The mound of rocks in front of you is the terminal moraine of **Khumbu Glacier.** The trail climbs up and over the moraine and down to a stream that flows from beneath the glacier. Cross the stream and ascend to **Dughla** (15,100 ft.; 4,602 m), which has several lodges. Not far beyond Dughla there is a collection of memorials to Sherpas and climbers who have died scaling nearby peaks. At this point the trail descends a little and then levels off and continues up the valley to **Lobuje** (16,170 ft.; 4,929 m), which most people agree is an absolute dump. Lobuje is very crowded during the prime trekking seasons, so it is a good idea to arrive as early as possible. Although there are several lodges here (the **National Park Lodge** is the best), they are always crowded, and food is expensive. Nights are very cold, contributing to the general atmosphere of misery that hangs over this spot. The altitude makes it difficult for most people to sleep, and a lack of toilet facilities results in an inordinate number of people coming down with gastrointestinal problems in the upper reaches of this trek.

## DAY 10: LOBUJE TO GORAK SHEP & KALA PATTAR

Lobuje to Gorak Shep: 2½ hours; Gorak Shep to Kala Pattar: 1½ hours; Gorak Shep to Everest base camp and back: 6 hours; Gorak Shep to Lobuje: 2 hours. ELEVATION GAIN: 2,020 ft. (616m) to Kala Pattar.

The final destination of most trekkers following this route is not Everest Base Camp, but rather a small peak called Kala Pattar (Black Rock). Kala Patter rises above the collection of huts at **Gorak Shep** (17,000 ft.; 5,182 m) and provides an unforgettable panorama dominated by the south face of Mount Everest. There are a few simple lodges at Gorak Shep, but they are so utterly basic that you're better off doing a day hike to the summit of Kala Pattar from Lobuje. This will also allow you to avoid spending a night almost 1,000 feet (305 m) higher than Lobuje. However, if the weather isn't clear when you reach Gorak Shep, you'll probably want to spend the night and climb Kala Pattar in the early morning, when the peaks are more likely to be visible. If you do plan to make it a day trip from Lobuje, start as early as possible.

To reach Gorak Shep and Kala Pattar, continue up the valley from Lobuje along a level path with Khumbu Glacier to your right. The trail climbs a moraine, from which there is a view of Gorak Shep (a sandy, flat area with a frozen lake) and Kala Pattar. Descend the moraine to the sandy flats, and skirt the lake to reach the few huts at **Gorak Shep.** If you're spending the night in Gorak Shep, you probably won't want to do much more than sit around for the afternoon; it's very likely that you'll be feeling the effects of the elevation at this point.

From Gorak Shep, it is about a 1½-hour steep climb to the top of ✪ **Kala Pattar** (18,190 ft.; 5,544m). At the top you have not only a stunning view of Everest, but a 360-degree panorama of peaks including Nuptse, Ama Dablam, Kantenga, Thamserku, Tawetse, Pumo Ri, and Changtse. Once you've taken in the view, hustle back down to Lobuje and be thankful that you'll soon be getting back to where the air is a bit thicker.

From Gorak Shep, the route to Everest base camp follows the Khumbu Glacier. It's a 3-hour hike up and another 3 hours back, and once you get there, there isn't much to see other than a lot of tents and a lot of garbage. Mount Everest is not visible from base camp, so unless you absolutely must see this famous spot, your time and energy are better spent climbing Kala Pattar, from where there is a superb view of Everest's south face.

If you plan to hike to Everest Base Camp or if bad weather or lack of energy forces you to spend the night in Gorak Shep, add a day to this itinerary.

## DAY 11: LOBUJE TO PANGBOCHE

Lobuje to Dingboche: 4 hours; Dingboche to Chhukung and back: 5½ hours; Dingboche to Pangboche: 2 hours. ELEVATION LOSS: 3,370 ft. (1,027m).

Rather than retrace your steps from Lobuje down, you can take an alternate route that follows a high trail down the east side of the valley to **Dingboche** (14,432 ft.; 4,400m). The Dingboche trail leaves the main trail at the bridge below Dughla and climbs up the hill to the north side of the valley. There are a couple of lodges in Dingboche; try the **Snow Lion Lodge.**

If you have a day to spare, it's worthwhile to continue up the valley of the Imja Khola to the yak pastures at **Chhukung** (15,525 ft.; 4,732m). Several lodges operate here during the main trekking seasons. Explorations in this valley will give you close-up views of Ama Dablam from the north, providing a much different perspective than from elsewhere on this trek. There are also good views of other peaks, including Cholatse, Taboche, Kongde, and Numbur. This is the route taken by expeditions headed for Island Peak, one of Nepal's most popular trekking peaks.

From **Dingboche,** descend steadily to cross the Khumbu Khola on a wooden bridge. From there, climb steeply to meet the Pangboche-Pheriche trail. This trail soon brings you into upper **Pangboche,** which makes a good stopping point for the night (see Day 7 for lodge recommendations in this area).

## DAY 12: PANGBOCHE TO NAMCHE BAZAAR

Pangboche to Phortse: 2 hours; Phortse to Phortse Tenga: 1 hour; Phortse Tenga to Namche Bazaar: 3½ hours. Pangboche to Tengboche: 2 hours; Tengboche to Namche Bazaar: 4 hours. Via Phortse: ELEVATION GAIN: 1250 ft. (381m). ELEVATION LOSS: 2,750 ft. (838m). Via Tengboche: ELEVATION GAIN: 1,419 ft. (432m). ELEVATION LOSS: 2,919 ft. (890m).

From upper Pangboche, you can return to Namche Bazaar either by way of Phortse or by way of Tengboche. To return via Phortse, climb up out of the village, contouring across the steep, south-facing valley wall to the village of Phortse. From Phortse, descend to the Dudh Kosi and then climb a little bit to Phortse Tenga. Here you meet the trail to Gokyo. Turn south and climb to the Mon La (a 13,000 ft [3,965m] pass), and continue to Namche Bazaar.

To return via Tengboche, descend from upper Pangboche to the Imja Khola, cross the river, and climb through Deboche to the monastery and lodges at Tengboche. From here, descend to Phunki Tenga, cross the Dudh Kosi, and climb steeply to meet the trail from Gokyo.

## DAYS 13–14: NAMCHE BAZAAR TO LUKLA
ELEVATION GAIN: 800 ft. (244m). ELEVATION LOSS: 2,900 ft. (844m).

Though it is possible to hike from ✪ **Namche Bazaar to Lukla** in 1 long day, the journey is better split into 2 short days. **Phakding** makes a good stopping point on the day you leave Namche Bazaar. The next day, you can reach Lukla by lunchtime. Remember: You need to reconfirm your return plane reservation to Kathmandu before 4pm the day before departing.

## DAY 15: LUKLA TO KATHMANDU
Be aware that several days of bad weather can cause a human logjam of trekkers waiting to catch flights out. Planes don't fly if there are too many clouds, because, as they say, the clouds in Nepal have rocks in them. Waiting in Lukla for a flight is not a pleasant pastime. There is little to do but sit around hoping that your name will be called. Many people spend their time drinking beer or local home brew. The combination of alcohol and elevation often leads to violent outbursts from people who *absolutely must* be on the next flight out. If you are trekking in the Everest region and intend to fly out of Lukla, be sure to give yourself a buffer by allowing at least a week between flying out of Lukla and departing from Kathmandu. This will give you time to hike out if necessary. There are also airstrips at Tumlingtar, about 4 days from Kharte, and Phaphlu, 4 hours south of Ringmo. You may be able to get a flight out of either of these places, though whether it will get you back to Kathmandu faster than if you walked all the way back to Jiri and caught the bus is questionable.

You can be back in Kathmandu on Day 15 if: You are very lucky and have a confirmed return ticket out of Lukla, you arrive early enough the previous day to reconfirm your ticket, and good weather prevails. Unfortunately, even people with reconfirmed tickets sometimes get bumped from flights. Instead of flying out, you can hike from Lukla back to Jiri in 6 days. A description of the route from Lukla to Jiri is provided below.

# NAMCHE BAZAAR TO GOKYO
Number of Days: 12–13. TOTAL ELEVATION GAIN: 8,790 ft. (2679m). TOTAL ELEVATION: LOSS 8,790 ft. (2679m).

The following is a route description of the trek to Gokyo. This trek can be done in addition to or instead of the trek to Kala Pattar and Everest Base Camp. There are several picturesque lakes along this route, including **Gokyo Lake.** It takes 2 fewer days to get a spectacular view of Everest than it would to reach Kala Pattar, which makes this route a good choice if you are short on time but still want to see Everest up close. If you fly into Lukla you can reach Gokyo and be back in Lukla in **12 to 13 days.** If you choose to visit both Gokyo and Kala Pattar, plan on **20 to 21 days.** To reach Namche Bazaar from Lukla, follow Days 2 and 3 of the Lukla to Kala Pattar trek described above.

This route has come to be known as "the valley of death" because of the many trekkers who develop (and ignore) symptoms of altitude sickness as they trek up to Gokyo. It is very easy to gain too much elevation too quickly on this route, so be particularly watchful for signs of altitude sickness in both yourself and the other members of your trekking party. Do not even think about continuing up to Gokyo from Namche Bazaar until you have spent at least 2 and preferably 3 days acclimatizing. You may want to try one of the day hikes from Namche Bazaar described in the Kala Pattar section in the Lukla to Everest Base Camp & Kala Pattar trek.

## DAY 1: NAMCHE BAZAAR TO DOLE

Namche Bazaar to Sanassa: 1¼ hours; Sanassa to Mon Pass: 2 hours; Mon Pass to Phortse Tenga: 45 minutes; Phortse Tenga to Dole: 2 hours. ELEVATION GAIN: 3,150 ft. (960m). ELEVATION LOSS: 1,050 ft. (320m).

There are two routes out of Namche Bazaar to Phortse Tenga, the small village from which you begin the steep climb up to Gokyo. You can climb the steep hill directly behind Namche Bazaar to Shyangboche airstrip and continue from there, through fields and forests of dwarfed pines, to Khumjung, a large Sherpa village in a wide gray valley (at least, outside of the monsoon season it's gray). The trail then joins the main route below Khumjung.

Alternatively, you can reach Phortse Tenga by starting the route from Namche Bazaar to Tengboche described in Day 6 of the Kala Pattar trek. Climb to the national park headquarters and head north up the valley. This trail, which passes through open pastures, is much easier than the trail through Shyangboche. After about 1¼ hours, you will come to **Sanassa,** where there are several lodges and teahouses. The trail divides here, with the lower trail leading to Tengboche and Kala Pattar and the upper trail leading toward Gokyo. Watch for musk deer and danphe pheasants (the national bird) in the vicinity of Sanassa. From here the trail leads up to the **Mon Pass** (13,000 ft.; 3,962m) and then descends steeply to **Phortse Tenga** (11,950 ft.; 3,642m), where there are a couple of very basic lodges. I don't recommend staying here unless it's too late in the day to continue for another 2 hours to Dole. From Phortse Tenga, the trail stays on the west side of the valley and climbs through dense forest to the yak pastures and stone huts at Gyele (13,150 ft.; 4,008m) and on to **Dole** (13,400 ft.; 4,084m). The lodges here, including the **Yeti Lodge,** have good views across the valley. Because the elevation gain from Namche Bazaar to Dole is a bit more than is recommended for a single day at this altitude, watch for symptoms of altitude sickness. If you or anyone in your party experiences difficulties with the altitude (headaches, loss of appetite, dizziness, nausea), it may be wise to take an acclimatization day in Dole.

## DAY 2: DOLE TO MACHERMA

Dole to Luza: 1½ hours; Luza to Macherma: 30 minutes. ELEVATION GAIN: 1,250 ft. (381m).

For acclimatization reasons, this is a very short day. At Dole, the forest ends and the trail becomes easier and more gradual. Above Dole, you enter high pastures in a narrow valley and the huts of **Lhabarma** (14,200 ft.; 4,328m). Here the trail levels off for a while before climbing gradually again. Just past **Luza** (14,400 ft.; 4,389m) the trail tops a low ridge from which you can see **Macherma** (14,650 ft.; 4,465m) across a side valley. Of the several lodges in Macherma, try the **Himalayan Lodge.**

## DAY 3: MACHERMA TO GOKYO

Macherma to Pangka: 30 minutes; Pangka to first lake: 1½ hours; first lake to Gokyo: 1¼ hours. ELEVATION GAIN: 924 ft. (282m).

Climb from Macherma to crest a ridge. The view from this ridge is quite good, with Cho Oyu (26,750 ft.; 8,153m) ahead of you and Kangtenga (22,226 ft.; 6,774m) behind you. Across the valley to your right are Cholotse (21,125 ft.; 6,439m) and

Taboche (21,460 ft.; 6,541m). From this ridge the trail descends to Pangka (14,689 ft.; 4,477m), which has one lodge. Looming ahead of you is the terminal moraine of Ngozumba Glacier.

Continue descending from Pangka to a stream flowing down the west side of the valley. Cross the stream and climb up the steep, rocky moraine to the source of the stream, a small glacial lake at 15,350 feet (4,679m). This is the first of five lakes that often take on a startling shade of blue, which is in brilliant contrast to the gray and brown of the surrounding hills. Continue past this lake; in less than an hour, you'll reach a second lake. Continue up the valley to Dudh Pokhari, the third lake. Passing a mani wall, you arrive in **Gokyo** (15,574 ft.; 4,747m). There are numerous lodges in Gokyo. The most comfortable is the Gokyo **Resort Lodge,** which has a sun room.

## DAY 4: GOKYO

Gokyo to Gokyo Ri: 2 hours. ELEVATION GAIN: 2,416 ft. (736m).

Though the view from **Gokyo** is spectacular enough, you may want to climb just a bit higher for a truly memorable view. There are two choices. The most popular mountain-viewing spot is the top of Gokyo Ri (17,990 ft.; 5,483m), the peak that rises above Gokyo and Dudh Pokhari. The summit of this peak can be reached in about 2 hours. (Though the skies are usually clearer in the morning, you might want to give your body time to acclimatize and wait until afternoon to climb above Gokyo.) You can also hike up the valley to the fourth or fifth lake; the views are good above these lakes. From any of these locations, you will be treated to breathtaking views of Cho Oyu, Everest, Nuptse, Lhotse, Makalu, and many other peaks. Below, in the valley, are the shimmering turquoise lakes and the convoluted gray bulk of Ngozumba Glacier. Remember to take it easy as you climb these peaks.

If you're bothered a little by the altitude, give yourself an extra day to acclimatize before attempting Gokyo Ri. If you're feeling fine, consider sticking around for another day or two to explore this high-altitude region.

## DAYS 5–6: GOKYO TO NAMCHE BAZAAR

Gokyo to Phortse Tenga: 1 day; Phortse Tenga to Namche Bazaar: 1 day. ELEVATION GAIN: 1, 050 ft. (320m). ELEVATION LOSS: 5,324 ft. (1,623m).

Since you will be descending and won't have to worry about altitude sickness, you will make much better time on the return to Namche Bazaar. You should be able to reach Phortse Tenga in 1 day from Gokyo. The next day you should be able to reach Namche Bazaar with no trouble. Alternatively, you can hike down the east side of the Dudh Kosi valley and stop your first night in Phortse, which is across the valley from the much smaller Phortse Tenga. The lodging situation in Phortse is much better than that in Phortse Tenga. Try the **Namaste Lodge.** From Phortse you can return to Namche Bazaar by dropping down to the Dudh Kosi and climbing up to Phortse Tenga to rejoin the route you followed up to Gokyo.

Another alternative, if you have an extra day to spare, is to proceed from Phortse to Tengboche and from Tengboche back to Namche Bazaar. This route follows the trail out of Phortse at the upper end of the village near the gompa, and goes toward Pangboche (see Day 12: Pangboche to Namche Bazaar, above) before branching off and descending precipitously down a shadeless slope to the Imja Khola. Use caution on this section of the trail: it is steep and covered with loose rock, and a slip could be fatal. It takes less than an hour to reach the valley floor from Phortse. From the river, the trail climbs even more abruptly than it descended, though luckily it is through a cool, moist forest. Tengboche is about an hour from the river.

---
**Reminder** ─────────────────────────────────

During the course of your treks, you will see **mani walls** (walls of stones that have had prayers carved onto them) and **chortens** (small stupa-like shrines). Remember to keep these mani walls and chortens on your right side as you pass them. It is considered disrespectful to have your left side to one of these structures.

---

## LOBUJE TO GOKYO VIA PHORTSE
### DAY 1: LOBUJE TO PHORTSE

Lobuje to Pheriche: 3 hours; Pheriche to Pangboche: 1 hour; Pangboche to Phortse: 2 hours. ELEVATION LOSS: 3,582 ft. (1,093m).

If you have plenty of time and want to see as much of this region as possible, you may want to climb both Kala Pattar and Gokyo Ri. There are a couple of options for linking up the Kala Pattar trek and the Gokyo trek. The easier route is to head back down the valley from Lobuje through **Pheriche** to upper **Pangboche.** From upper Pangboche, follow the trail that contours high above the Imja Khola. Do not take the trail that leads down to the river, because it will take you to Tengboche. About 2 hours from Pangboche, the trail rounds a ridge into the valley of the Dudh Kosi and reaches the spread-out village of **Phortse** (12,588 ft.; 3,840m), where many of the homes are surrounded by walled fields. There are several lodges here.

### DAY 2: PHORTSE TO MACHERMA

Phortse to Phortse Tenga: 1 hour; Phortse Tenga to Dole: 2 hours; Dole to Macherma: 2 hours. ELEVATION GAIN: 2,700 ft. (820m). ELEVATION LOSS: 638 ft. (194m).

From Phortse there are two possible routes: the east valley route and the west valley route. The east valley route, which is on the same side of the valley as Phortse, is rarely used by trekkers and consequently has few lodges and may sometimes be difficult to follow. However, if you are doing this route in reverse, you can make good time descending the east valley route. You should be able to walk from Gokyo to Phortse in a day.

The west valley route, though it entails descending to the Dudh Kosi and then climbing the far side to regain lost elevation, is preferable. It takes 45 minutes down to the river and another 10 minutes up to Phortse Tenga and the main trail from Namche Bazaar to Gokyo. From this point on, there are lodges and teahouses every hour or two. You can probably reach Macherma on the same day. See above for a description of the route from Macherma to Gokyo.

## LOBUJE TO GOKYO VIA THE CHO LA (PASS)
### DAY 1: LOBUJE TO DZONGLA

Lobuje to Dzongla: 3 hours. ELEVATION LOSS: 291 ft. (89m).

During the main trekking season, it's possible to cross the 17,377-foot (5,297m) Cho La. However, this strenuous route, which can require the use of an ice ax, crampons, and a rope, is difficult to follow. I recommend trying it only if you have a guide and previous experience crossing glaciers or snow.

From Lobuje, return down the main valley toward Dughla for 30 minutes, and watch for a trail that contours around a ridge and heads up the valley to the northwest. Below this trail you will see Tshola Lake. Continue up this valley to the yak-herding huts and basic lodge at **Dzongla** (15,879 ft.; 4,840m). The views from here are stupendous.

### DAY 2: DZONGLA TO GOKYO

Dzongla to Cho La: 3 hours; Cho La to Gokyo: 4 hours. ELEVATION GAIN: 1,972 ft. (601m).
ELEVATION LOSS: 2,277 ft. (694m).

From Dzongla, the trail ascends a bit and then descends before starting the climb up
to the pass. The trail, which is not very distinct, heads in the general direction of a
glacier, passing to the east of the glacier for a while before actually crossing the glacier
itself. For much of the year, crampons and an ice axe are essential for crossing the
glacier. The crossing is quite steep at the beginning but then levels out as you approach
the **Cho La** (17,377 ft.; 5,297m).

Dropping down from the pass, you cross snow at first and then reach a slope of
loose rocks. Footing can be precarious through this section. After descending the pass,
you cross a lateral moraine; keep to the right as you go. The trail follows a valley down
to Dragnag, where there is a very basic lodge operating during the main trekking
seasons.

From Dragnag (15,100 ft.; 4,604m), the trail leads across the Ngozumba Glacier
and winds around quite a bit. Each year, many trekkers get lost on this section of trail.
It is primarily this stretch that requires a guide. Crossing the lateral moraine, you reach
the main trail from Namche Bazaar to Gokyo, just below the second of the Gokyo
lakes.

# JIRI TO NAMCHE BAZAAR
## DAY 1: KATHMANDU TO JIRI

**Jiri** (6,250 ft.; 1,905m), the trailhead for hiking into the Everest region, is an unap-
pealing little town with a wide main street lined with shops, teahouses, and lodges. It
is an 8- to 12-hour bus ride from Kathmandu to Jiri, depending on whether you get
on the express bus. Buses leave from the Gongabu Bus Park on Ring Road north of
Thamel, and the fare is Rs143 ($2.15). This bus is usually so crowded that many
people ride on the roof, and pickpocketing and theft of, or from, backpacks have
become all too common. Take all possible precautions and never let your backpack out
of your sight. Your best bet is to buy two tickets and place your backpack in the seat
next to you. Also, landslides during the monsoon often wash out sections of the road,
adding hours to the journey and making it a real adventure. You can also hire a taxi to
drive you to Jiri for around Rs6,000 ($90.90).

The best lodges in Jiri are the **Hotel Gaurihimal, Cherdung Lodge,** and the **Hotel
Jirel Gabila.**

### DAY 2: JIRI TO SHIVALAYA

Jiri to Shivalaya: 3½ hours. INITIAL ELEVATION GAIN: 1,625 ft. (495m). ELEVATION LOSS:
1,975 ft. (602m).

The trail starts at the eastern end of the main road into Jiri and begins ascending
immediately. It is about 1½ hours through a scrubby rhododendron forest to the crest
of this first ridge (7,875 ft.; 2,400m). From this ridge, which is topped by a small
cairn, the trail drops quickly to a bridge over the Yelung Khola. After crossing this first
small river, the trail crosses the larger Khimti Khola and enters the village of **Shivalaya**
(5,900 ft.; 1,798m). If you'd rather skip this first steep climb, there is an alternative
trail that follows the Jiri Khola downstream to the confluence with the Khimti Khola.
The trail then heads up the Khimti Khola, through the village of Those, to Shivalaya.
A road is being built to a hydroelectric project on the Khimti Khola, and when this
road is completed, the start of this trek may change a bit.

Although it is possible to continue from Shivalaya, you won't reach the next village of any size, Bhandar, for 5½ hours, which makes for a grueling first day.

## DAY 3: SHIVALAYA TO BHANDAR

Shivalaya to Sangbadanda: 2 hours; Sangbadanda to Deorali Pass: 2 hours; Deorali Pass to Bhandar: 1 hour. ELEVATION GAIN: 3,000 ft. (914m). ELEVATION LOSS: 1,700 ft. (518m).

From Shivalaya, the trail begins climbing again, this time quite steeply. **Sangbadanda** (7,200 ft.; 2,195m) is reached in about 2 hours. Here the trail forks. Take the right fork, which goes through the small village of **Kasourbas;** you'll reach **Deorali Pass** (8,900 ft.; 2,713m) in about 2 hours. At first the trail climbs gradually, but after leveling off for a while, it climbs steeply through a forest to Deorali Pass. There are several lodges at this windy pass, which makes a good lunch stop. Since it is only another hour downhill to Bhandar, you might want to consider making a side trip up to the cheese factory at Thodung, which is another 1½ hours and 1,250 feet (381m) above the pass. Take the trail leading north up the ridge. There are also several large mani walls at this pass, an indication that you are now in Sherpa country. The trail descends the far side of this ridge, cutting across the ridge toward the village of Bhandar, which can be seen from the pass. Just below the pass, the trail forks. Take the left fork and continue descending steadily toward Bhandar.

**Bhandar** (7,200 ft.; 2,195m) is a picturesque Sherpa village in a wide valley. The path, almost a road, passes two large chortens before entering the village itself. A chorten is a Buddhist shrine similar to the huge stupas in Kathmandu. It incorporates the same elements and symbols as a stupa, only on a much smaller scale. Beside the chortens, there's a gompa, which you are welcome to visit if it's unlocked when you pass by. In Bhandar, there are several lodges, which will be welcomed after this long and exhausting day. Try the **Ang Dawa Lodge,** which makes its own pasta.

## DAY 4: BHANDAR TO SETE

Bhandar to Kenja: 3 hours; Kenja to Sete: 3 hours. ELEVATION GAIN: 2,020 ft. (616m). ELEVATION LOSS: 3,261 ft. (944m).

From Bhandar, the trail continues across the wide valley and enters a dark and damp forest. The trail then drops steeply through a luxuriant forest full of ferns and mosses. Long ribbons of water cascade down the opposite wall of the narrow valley the trail passes through. At the bottom of this valley, the trail crosses to the opposite side of the stream and heads north up the valley of the Likhu Khola, a much larger river. Continue up the west bank of the Likhu Khola to the bridge (5,180 ft.; 1,579m), and cross to the east bank. The trail continues on this bank to the village of **Kenja** (5,350 ft.; 1,631m), where there are several lodges. You should eat a big lunch with lots of carbohydrates before continuing the day's trek. If you have any mending to be done, local tailors, who set up their hand-cranked sewing machines along the trail, will fix you right up.

From Kenja it is a long, steady, and steep climb up to the Lamjura Pass. Luckily, you reach the village of **Sete** (8,441 ft.; 2,573m), which is below the pass, in about 3 hours, which makes it a good place to stop for the night. There are several lodges in Sete and a good view down into the valley of the Kenja Khola. Sunsets can be spectacular here even though you can't see any snow-clad peaks.

## DAY 5: SETE TO JUNBESI

Sete to teahouses: 2 hours; teahouses to Lamjura Pass: 2 hours; Lamjura Pass to Tragdobuck: 2 hours; Tragdobuck to Junbesi: 1 hour. ELEVATION GAIN: 3,139 ft. (957m). ELEVATION LOSS: 2,805 ft. (855m).

Before leaving Sete, be sure to fill all your water bottles. Little, if any, water is available between here and the far side of the Lamjura Pass. From Sete, the trail continues climbing steadily toward the pass. At first you walk through an oak forest, but as you gain more elevation, the vegetation changes to fir trees and eventually to rhododendron. About 2 hours above Sete, there are teahouses where you should have lunch. At a mani wall 2½ to 3 hours from Sete, take the left fork. You will reach the **Lamjura Pass** (11,580 ft.; 3,530m) about 4 hours after leaving Sete. The forests leading up to this pass are quite magical. The trunks of the rhododendrons below the pass are often covered with moss almost a foot thick, which gives you some idea of how often this pass is covered with clouds. At the pass itself there is an amazing jumble of sticks and stones that have been assembled into several cairns and festooned with prayer flags and marigolds. These are offerings left by travelers as they've crossed this spot that is just a bit closer to the gods.

From the pass it is a steep and slippery descent through a damp forest. However, as the trail leaves the forest, it becomes much less steep and enters a green pasture crisscrossed with wooden fences. The trail leaves the forest and passes through hills covered with meadows. Before reaching the village of **Tragdobuck** (9,400 ft.; 2,865m), the trail passes under an impressive outcropping of rock. In Tragdobuck there are two huge boulders, both of which have been carved with Buddhist prayers. The trail continues across the meadows until it rounds a notch in the ridge and reveals the village of Junbesi ahead and below. The snow-covered mountain you see above Junbesi is Numbur (22,825 ft.; 6,957m). Its Sherpa name means God of Solu (Solu, which is inhabited by Sherpas, is the lower part of the region known as Solu Khumbu).

From the notch it is about an hour to **Junbesi** (8,775 ft.; 2,675m), a very attractive Sherpa village, where you will find a monastery above the village on the trail from Tragdobuck and an older monastery in the middle of town. There are several large lodges in Junbesi (some even have satellite TV!), so you might want to check them all out before making a choice. The **Junbesi Guest House** is popular, and the **Ang Chopa Lodge** even has a "penthouse" room complete with skylights. You'll also find a good bakery in Junbesi.

## DAY 6: JUNBESI TO MANIDINGMA

Junbesi to Sallung: 2½ hours; Sallung to Ringmo: 2 hours; Ringmo to Tragsindho Pass: 1 hour; Tragsindho Pass to Tragsindho: 20 minutes; Tragsindho to Manidingma: 1½ hours. ELEVATION GAIN: 2,600 ft. (793m). ELEVATION LOSS: 3,775 ft. (1,150m).

To reach the onward trail, head south out of Junbesi past several stone chortens. Just after crossing the river on a wooden bridge, the trail forks. The right fork goes to Phaphlu, which has a hospital and an airstrip; the left fork continues toward Khumbu and the Everest region. This trail climbs through different types of forest. Near the top of the ridge, the forest gives way to open pastures, and at the crest (10,000 ft.; 3,048m) you get your first glimpse of Everest (called Sagarmatha by the Nepalis and Chomolungma by the Tibetans). The trail then descends through forest, again heading northeast up a wide valley. In 2 hours you reach **Sallung** (9,750 ft.; 2,972m), where there are several lodges. The trail continues descending to the Beni Khola (8,700 ft.; 2,652m), crosses the river, and then climbs to the village of **Ringmo** (9,200 ft.; 2,804m). Be sure to stop here for apple pie or apple cider from the large orchard.

An alternative route from Junbesi to Ringmo leads 1½ hours up the valley from Junbesi to the large **Thubten Chholing Gompa,** which is home to nearly 200 Buddhist monks and nuns. This monastery is well worth a visit. From here, it's possible to take a little-used trail up and over the ridge to the east of the monastery, joining the main trail from Junbesi just before the village of Ringmo. It should take 3 or 4 hours to cross this way.

At Ringmo, the trail widens, but it is still a steep climb up to **Tragsindho Pass** (10,075 ft.; 3,071m), which is marked by a large chorten, mani walls, prayer flags, and several lodges.

Descending from the pass, you reach the village of **Tragsindho** in about 20 minutes. There are more lodges and a large Buddhist monastery here. It is an hour's descent through lush forest alive with birds to the village of **Manidingma** (7,600 ft.; 2,316m), also known as Nuntala, which has quite a few lodges.

## DAY 7: MANIDINGMA TO KHARTE

Manidingma to Dudh Kosi: ½ hour; Dudh Kosi to Jubing: 1 hour; Jubing to Khari Khola: 2 hours; Khari Khola to Kharte: 1½ hours. ELEVATION GAIN: 2,635 ft. (803m). ELEVATION LOSS: 2,700 ft. (823m).

Continue descending through forests to the valley of the **Dudh Kosi** (Milk River), which gets its name from the pale blue color of its water and from its many rapids. This large river flows south from the glaciers of Khumbu. Cross the river on a suspension bridge (4,900 ft.; 1,494m) and head north to the village of **Jubing.** The trail passes through the terraced fields surrounding this village. Jubing is inhabited by people of the Rai ethnic group, who are found primarily in eastern Nepal. You may notice that the houses look different from Sherpa homes and are often decorated with garlands of marigolds. The trail continues north up the valley of the Dudh Kosi to the village of **Khari Khola.** There are several good lodges here, so if you are ready for an afternoon of rest, make this a short day. If you are full of energy and want to continue, walk through Khari Khola, cross the bridge, and begin climbing to the villages of **Bupsa** and **Kharte** (7,535 ft.; 2,300m), which you can see from Khari Khola. There are several large lodges in Bupsa and a few smaller ones in Kharte.

## DAY 8: KHARTE TO CHAUNRIKARKA

Kharte to Puiyan: 2 hours; Puiyan to Surkhe: 2½ hours; Surkhe to Chaunrikarka: 2 hours. ELEVATION GAIN: 2,915 ft. (898m). ELEVATION LOSS: 1,750 ft. (533m).

From Kharte, continue climbing through forest with the river far below you in a steep-walled valley. The trail reaches the top of a ridge at about 10,000 feet (3,048m) before descending through the canyon of a tributary. Use extreme caution on the trail through this canyon. It is often icy and at times is very narrow with a steep drop-off. At the head of the canyon, you cross a landslide area that can be unstable in the first weeks after the end of the monsoon. After crossing this stream, it is a short walk with a gentle slope to **Puiyan** (9,300 ft.; 2,835m), where you'll find numerous lodges. The trail continues climbing to another ridge (9,650 ft.; 2,941m) beyond which it is possible to see Lukla and its airstrip. You may even get to see a plane make the hair-raising landing on this postage-stamp field.

The trail descends through shady forest to another tributary of the Dudh Kosi. In the little valley beside this stream is the village of **Surkhe,** which has a couple of lodges. The trail climbs steeply out of Surkhe to a junction with a trail to Lukla. If you are hoping to fly back to Kathmandu, it is worthwhile to hike up to Lukla and put your name on the waiting list for the day you want to return. Remember, getting on a flight out of Lukla can take days of waiting, so leave yourself plenty of time. After passing this junction, the trail continues climbing steeply on a path blasted out of the mountainside. The trail then crosses a rocky pasture strewn with giant boulders, several of which have been turned into finished-looking caves. These caves are used by porters as resting and camping spots on their way to the Saturday market in Namche Bazaar. **Chaunrikarka** (8,700 ft.; 2,652m) is shortly beyond these caves. There are several lodges here.

### DAY 9: CHAUNRIKARKA TO JORSALE

Chaunrikarka to Chapling: 45 minutes. ELEVATION GAIN: 400 ft. (122m).

Leaving Chaunrikarka, you pass several mani walls and a large chorten, and the trail passes through attractive fields. At the top of a low ridge, this trail joins with the trail from Lukla. Be prepared to suddenly find yourself in the company of dozens and possibly hundreds of trekkers. The trail up to Namche Bazaar from here becomes a human highway, with trekkers and porters often blocking the trail as they stop to rest. The village of **Chapling** is just below this ridge.

Start with Day 2 of the "Lukla to Everest Base Camp Kala Pattar Route" description above to continue this trek onward toward Namche Bazaar. You should be able to reach Mondzo or Jorsale on this day.

## 2 The Annapurna Circuit

Though the Pokhara-to-Jomosom half of this trek is much more popular than the entire **18- to 20-day** route, the **Annapurna Circuit,** a huge loop covering more than 150 miles, is still one of the more popular treks in Nepal. Offering amazing variations in topography, vegetation, and culture, the trek around the Annapurna massif is fascinating from beginning to end. Starting in the subtropical Pokhara Valley, the trek climbs to the arid valley of Manang, which is in the rain shadow of the Himalayas. Crossing over the Thorong La (pass) at 17,770 feet (5,416m), the route descends to Muktinath, a pilgrimage site sacred to both Buddhists and Hindus, where a sacred flame burns on bare rock (a natural gas leak). On either side of the pass are several fascinating villages built of flat-roofed mud-and-stone houses and populated by people akin to Tibetans. These villages offer anyone who has never been to Tibet a chance to see what village life is like across the border. Descending from Jomosom, the trail passes through villages inhabited by various ethnic groups, giving the trekker a chance to observe different Nepali lifestyles. In and near Tatopani, there are hot springs that can provide a welcome hot bath after 2 weeks on the trail. Above Tatopani at Poon Hill, there is one last opportunity for great mountain views, though the views from the Manang Valley and from around Jomosom are far more spectacular.

Much of this trek's popularity is due to the fact that there are plenty of lodges along the entire route, which makes carrying a tent and food unnecessary. Lodges vary from bamboo-walled huts to three-story stone chalets. The food available on this trek is also quite good, especially on the Jomosom side. Hardly a day goes by without apple pie. The major drawbacks of the trek are, of course, the crowds of trekkers and the Thorong La. Many people have died trying to cross this high pass. You must be watchful for signs of altitude sickness in yourself and your companions, porters, and guides. If you become ill, *do not* attempt to cross the pass, and descend immediately to a lower elevation.

During the main trekking season, thousands of trekkers take to the trail here, and you are likely to see as many trekkers as Nepalis. If you're expecting to be the only foreigner on the trail, this is not the trek for you. You can, however, avoid some of the crowds by not doing this trek in October or November. The large number of trekkers descending on the region has brought about some changes that detract from the trekking experience. Lodges along the Jomosom trek have lost much of their unique Nepali character; many now even have satellite TVs. So if you're expecting an escape from civilization, these modern "conveniences" may be an unwelcome surprise.

There are several ways to start this trek. Most people take a bus to Dumre, from either Kathmandu (6 hr.) or Pokhara (2 hr.), and then take a truck to Besi Sahar. I don't recommend this route, because the trucks and buses that operate between Dumre and Besi Sahar are notorious for breaking down and crashing. These trucks take at least 4 hours and usually much longer. If you start the day from Pokhara (2,898 ft.; 884m), you can usually be in Besi Sahar by nightfall, but if you start from Kathmandu, you will probably have to spend the night in Dumre (not a pleasant prospect).

The route I describe below lets you avoid the long bus ride to Besi Sahar and instead start with a short bus or taxi ride from Pokhara to Begnas Lake. This route takes a day or two longer and joins the main route about 1½ hours' walk up the valley from Besi Sahar.

If you are unable to cross the Thorong La, you can fly back to Pokhara from Hongde (below Manang). Royal Nepal Airlines flies here 5 days a week, and airfare is $50 each way. If you only wanted to hike the Manang side of the Annapurna Circuit, you could plan to fly out of this airstrip. Or you could fly in and then hike out, but the airstrip is above 10,000 feet, which makes your risk of developing altitude sickness quite high.

## DAY 1: POKHARA TO KARPUTAR

Pokhara to Sisuwa: 1 hour; Sisuwa to Sakra Bhanjyang: 3 hours; Sakra Bhanjyang to Karputar: 2 hours. ELEVATION LOSS: 1,298 ft. (396m) from Sisuwa to Karputar.

The main advantages of following this route are that you spend only 1 hour on a bus (or even less in a taxi) before beginning your trek, and you avoid the hair-raising truck/bus ride from Dumre to Besi Sahar. From the main bus park in Pokhara, take a bus to the village of **Sisuwa** between Begnas Tal and Rupa Tal, two lakes to the east of Pokhara. Sisuwa is the end of the line, and the bus usually stops right at the beginning of the trail, which leads uphill from the collection of shops at the east end of the village. The trail climbs moderately up a ridge, from the top of which there are views of both Rupa Tal and Begnas Tal, with the Annapurna Himal reflected in the waters of Begnas Tal.

The trail descends the ridge at the far end of Rupa Tal and heads up the terraced river valley to the village of **Tarbensi,** where there is a teahouse. From Tarbensi, the trail ascends gradually to the east through a narrow, rocky valley and then climbs steeply and steadily through forest to a pass at **Sakra Bhanjyang,** where there are more teahouses. The trail then descends very steeply, still in forest, on an eroded trail paved with stone steps. Leaving the forest, you continue descending gradually across a rocky, dry riverbed, eventually crossing the shallow river itself. The trail then enters the forest again and descends through the beautiful **Achari Bhanjyang,** a village of stucco and thatch houses that are painted orange and white, with black trim. Shady pastures surrounding the village give it a very idyllic atmosphere. After reaching the valley floor, the trail cuts across rice paddies to **Bagwa Bazaar** and a long suspension bridge across the Madi Khola. Just across this bridge, the trail enters the village of **Karputar** (1,600 ft.; 488m), which is shaded by several large pipal trees. Karputar has a large stone lodge just before the suspension bridge and a couple of very basic teahouses right in town.

## DAY 2: KARPUTAR TO BAGLUNGPANI

Karputar to Phedi: 3 hours; Phedi to Nalma: 1½ hours; Nalma to Baglungpani: 3 hours. ELEVATION GAIN: 3,765 ft. (1,132m).

Get an early start because it is a long day to Baglungpani. From Karputar, head northeast up the wide valley of the Midim Khola to **Laxmi Bazaar.** From Laxmi Bazaar, the trail leads to **Shyauli Bazaar,** where there are a few teahouses. The valley here is below

# The Annapurna Region Trekking Routes

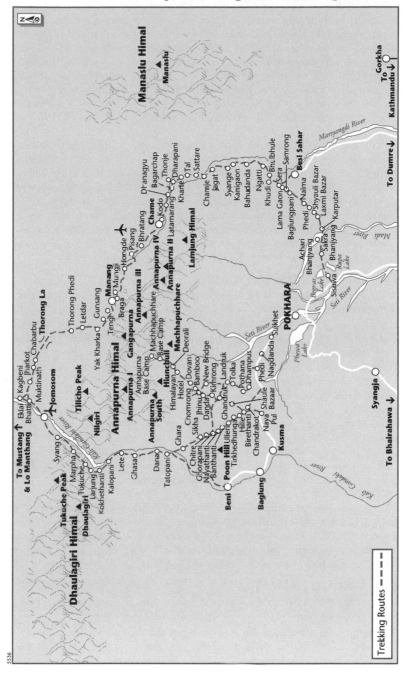

1,600 feet (488m), which makes it lower and hotter than Pokhara. Be prepared to sweat profusely all day. Beyond Shyauli Bazaar, the trail enters the woods again and winds up and down the steep walls of the narrowing valley. At times the trail is very steep. In the dry season, when the river is low, it is possible to walk up the riverbed. On the high route, you will cross a suspension bridge and come to a teahouse perched high above the valley floor. If you have walked up the riverbed, you must climb to the teahouse when you see the suspension bridge. This teahouse is called **Phedi,** which means "foot of the hill." From here it is nearly 4,000 feet (1,219m) up to Baglungpani.

From the teahouse, you begin climbing in earnest up a steep forest trail. When you finally reach the ridge crest, the trail becomes much less steep and crosses terraced fields to the village of **Nalma.** This picturesque Gurung village is scattered along the crest of the ridge and has several teahouses. If you're tired and don't feel like walking the remaining 3 hours to Baglungpani, consider staying here for the night. From Nalma, the trail climbs steeply up a stone stairway. This ridge trail climbs and levels off three times before descending through a damp forest and then ascending to **Baglungpani** (5,315 ft.; 1,620m), a small village on a saddle. There are several small lodges here. Sunsets and sunrises from Baglungpani are stunning.

## DAY 3: BAGLUNGPANI TO NGATTI

Baglungpani to Lama Gaon: 1½ hours; Lama Gaon to Khudi: 1 hour; Khudi to Bhul Bhule: 1 hour; Bhul Bhule to Ngatti: 1 hour. ELEVATION GAIN: 585 ft. (178m). ELEVATION LOSS: 3,015 ft. (919m).

The trail descends steeply from Baglungpani through forests full of birds. Slightly more than halfway to the valley floor, you come to the village of **Samrong.** From here the trail descends toward the river with **Lama Gaon** village on both sides. At the far end of the suspension bridge across the river, the trail drops down a large boulder and continues east along the riverbank. The trail then angles away from the river, crosses through terraced fields, and passes Sera village. Beyond Sera, you enter the wide valley of the Marsyangdi River, which you can see below you. The trail continues descending gradually until you come to the Khudi Khola, a tributary of the Marsyangdi on the far side of which is the village of **Khudi** (2,300 ft.; 701m). There are several lodges here, and the road through Besi Sahar is being extended to this point as well. From Khudi you have a view up the Marsyangdi valley to Ngadi Chuli (25,820 ft.; 7,870m) and Manaslu (26,755 ft.; 8,155m). The trail continues up the west bank of the Marsyangdi, passing Khudi's school in about 10 minutes. You pass through two small villages and then cross the Marsyangdi on a suspension bridge. On the east bank is **Bhulbhule** (2,700 ft.; 823m). The trail continues up the east bank past an impressive waterfall and through a wide expanse of terraced fields to **Ngatti** (2,885 ft.; 880m). There are several lodges in both Ngatti and Bhulbhule.

## DAY 4: NGATTI TO JAGAT

Ngatti to Bahudanda: 2 hours; Bahudanda to Syange: 2 hours; Syange to Jagat: 1½ hours. ELEVATION GAIN: 1,920 ft. (585m). ELEVATION LOSS: 575 ft. (175m).

The path crosses a stream at the edge of Ngatti and continues across terraced fields before crossing the Ngatti Khola, a major tributary of the Marsyangdi. After crossing the bridge, the trail winds around a hill before starting a steady climb up through the village of Lampata. Beyond Lampata, the trail becomes steeper and very dusty before finally reaching **Bahudanda** (4,300 ft.; 1,311m) at the top of the hill. There are several lodges here, as well as a police checkpoint. After the hot, sweaty climb up to the top, the shade of Bahudanda is a welcome spot for a rest.

The trail out of the village passes a bamboo grove before descending rapidly on an eroded path worn into soft rock (muddy in the fall, dusty in the winter). After 15 minutes the trail levels off, crosses a stream, and contours through terraces. The valley narrows above Bahudanda, and its walls become very steep. Down below you can see the milky, turquoise waters of the Marsyangdi, which is fed by the glaciers of the Annapurna Himal. The trail crosses a steep mountainside, where it is actually cut into the rock, and then enters **Kanigaon** (3,870 ft.; 1,180m). The trail then winds along the steep valley walls before descending rapidly to a suspension bridge over the Marsyangdi. On the far side of the bridge, wedged between the river and a cliff, is the narrow village of **Syange** (3,725 ft.; 1,135m). There are several lodges here.

From Syange the trail climbs toward Jagat on the steep walls of the now-very-narrow canyon. Much of this trail is carved out of cliff walls with steep drop-offs. In places, water and stone stairs make the trail even more nerve-racking. Eventually, the trail begins to descend again, almost as steeply as it climbed. **Jagat** (4,230 ft.; 1,289m), with huge boulders strewn about its environs and its dark houses built of rock, looks like a Stone Age village. The village's precarious perch on a jutting cliff high above the river only adds to the prehistoric atmosphere. There is a large lodge on the far side of the village, and a couple of smaller, less-appealing ones right in the middle of the village.

## DAY 5: JAGAT TO DHARAPANI

Jagat to Chamje: 1¼ hours; Chamje to Tal: 2 hours; Tal to Dharapani: 2 hours. ELEVATION GAIN: 2,064 ft. (631m).

The trail descends steeply from Jagat almost to the river before ascending an equally steep path. The opposite bank is almost a sheer cliff, with several long ribbon-like waterfalls streaming down its face. After this next climb, the trail levels off before reaching **Chamje** (4,700 ft.; 1,433m). Chamje, like Jagat, is situated precariously high above the river on a steep mountainside. There are several lodges here. After Chamje the trail descends again and crosses the Marsyangdi on a long suspension bridge (4,625 ft.; 1,410m). Again the trail climbs on a very steep path with drop-offs. You'll pass through the village of **Sattare** and continue climbing steeply. Looking down into the valley, you'll see that the river is no longer visible, though it can still be heard. Above Sattare, the river flows under the giant boulders of a landslide that once blocked the valley and formed a lake.

The Nepali word for lake is *tal*, which not coincidentally is the name of the village you soon come to on the wide, flat valley that was once the lake bed. It is a beautiful sight as you top a hill and see the village of **Tal** and the valley below you. Adding to the beauty of the setting are waters that stream down the cliffs above the wide, flat plain. It is an easy walk into the village, which consists of colorfully painted wooden houses, many of which have balconies. There are several lodges here. As you leave the village, you pass by a beautiful waterfall with a large white chorten and prayer flags at its base. If you're lucky, you might even see a rainbow in the waterfall.

Beyond Tal, the trail continues up the wide, flat valley, skirts a cliff, and then crosses over to the west bank of the Marsyangdi. Once across the river, the trail begins to climb again quite steeply in places and is often blasted out of rock. The trail crosses the Marsyangdi again at Kharte. Just below Dharapani, you cross back over the river on a suspension bridge. On the west bank once again, you soon come to **Dharapani** (6,294 ft.; 1,920m), a dark and rather dismal village overlooking the confluence of the Dudh Khola and the Marsyangdi. There are several lodges here, as well as a police checkpoint. **Thonje,** about 10 minutes below Dharapani and across a bridge, is well worth a visit. It's a fascinating little village built almost entirely of stone. You'll see many mani walls and chortens here.

## DAY 6: DHARAPANI TO CHAME

Dharapani to Bagarchap: 30 minutes; Bagarchap to Dhanagyu: 1½ hours; Dhanagyu to Koto: 3 hours; Kodo to Chame: 30 minutes. ELEVATION GAIN: 2,606 ft. (793m).

At Dharapani, the Marsyangdi, which has been flowing from the north, makes a wide bend to the west. As you round this bend, you'll see Annapurna II (26,035 ft.; 7,935m) far ahead of you. You soon come to **Bagarchap** (7,100 ft.; 2,164m), a sunny village that was devastated by a landslide in 1995. There are several lodges here, most of which were built after the landslide occurred. Above the village is a Buddhist monastery of the Nyingmapa sect. Beyond Bagarchap, the trail enters a thick rhododendron forest, where you might see gray langurs, a long-tailed monkey that frequents the higher elevations. The trail passes the small village of **Dhanagyu,** which has several lodges but which is almost always cold and dark due to its location on the north side of a steep ridge.

Beyond Dhanagyu the trail crosses a bridge in front of a powerful waterfall, beyond which the trail becomes a steep stone stairway that is almost always wet or icy be especially careful. The trail continues through enchanting forests for several hours, passing through the village of **Latamarang,** where there are several lodges. From the rhododendron forest of the lower elevations, you climb to forests of fir and pine. Finally, the forest gives way to a flat cultivated area, and you enter the village of **Koto,** where there is a police checkpoint. Entering the forest again, the trail climbs gradually to **Chame** (8,900 ft.; 2,713m), a government administrative center with many offices, lodges, and shops. The better lodging choices are across the river close to a small hot spring that is used by locals as a combination laundry and public bath. There is an excellent view of Manaslu back down the valley to the east.

## DAY 7: CHAME TO PISANG

Chame to Bhratang: 2½ hours; Bhratang to Pisang: 2½ hours. ELEVATION GAIN: 1,550 ft. (472m).

After crossing the river in Chame, the trail leads through an older section of the village and then traverses cultivated fields and apple orchards past a few houses and a lodge. The far side of the valley becomes a very steep wall as you hike through forests toward **Bhratang** (9,575 ft.; 2,918m). The old village of Bhratang, which is on the south bank of the river, was, until the 1970s, populated by Tibetan Khampas (an ethnic group renowned as warriors). New Bhratang consists mostly of a collection of lodges at the foot of a sheer cliff. Just beyond these lodges, the trail is blasted out of a vertical rock wall with the river several hundred feet below a challenging bit of trail if you suffer from vertigo.

After this vertiginous section, the trail climbs through a rocky, and often icy, forest to a bridge over the Marsyangdi. As you approach this bridge, you begin to see, above you on your right, the awesome rock slope of the Paungda Danda, which rises nearly 5,000 feet (1,524m) and curves from south to west. High on this rock face, you can even see a tiny shrine. This marks the beginning of the glaciated reaches of the Marsyangdi Valley.

Continue climbing through the quiet forest until the trail crests a hill and descends slightly into a wide valley with meadows scattered among the trees. Ahead of you, on a brown hillside on the opposite side of the river, you see the stone houses and prayer flags of upper **Pisang** (10,800 ft.; 3,292m) and soon reach lower Pisang (10,450 ft.; 3,185m), on this side of the river. Lower Pisang is surrounded by barren, rocky hills and has a long wall of prayer wheels as you enter the village. The people of the Manang region (known as Manangis) are closely related to the Tibetans, with whom they share a similar architectural style. The homes are all tiny stone fortresses with flat roofs for storing fodder and for sunning on in the cold winter months. A trip up the steep slope to upper Pisang affords a glimpse of a fascinating Manangi mountain village. The lodges in lower Pisang are better than those in upper Pisang, so there is no reason to make the steep climb up the hill with your backpack on. If you cross the bridge in Pisang and follow the stream that leads upstream, you will reach, in about 20 minutes, an unbelievably beautiful mountain lake. The waters of the lake are turquoise and reflect Annapurna II. Don't miss this little excursion.

## DAY 8: PISANG TO MANANG

Pisang to Hongde: 2 hours; Hongde to Manang: 2 hours. ELEVATION GAIN: 1,150 ft. (351m).

Keeping to the south bank of the Marsyangdi River, cross a tributary stream as you leave lower Pisang. Pass a mani wall and several small chortens, and then enter the forest again. The trail climbs steeply to the top of a ridge bedecked with many prayer flags. From this ridge a rugged panorama spreads before you with Tilicho Peak (23,400 ft.; 7,132m) at the far end of the valley. This is the Manang Valley, and directly below you is the Manang airstrip, which is served by Royal Nepal Airlines. There are flights 5 days a week. Airfare is $50 each way.

The trail descends to the flat valley, passing the airstrip and a few lodges at **Hongde** (10,800 ft.; 3,292m). There is also a police checkpoint here. Beyond the airstrip, at a wide valley opening up to the south, there is a mountaineering school.

The landscape here is very barren, with rocky, brown mountains rising all around. In the monsoon months, however, the valley is green with barley fields. Cross the Marsyangdi to the tiny village of **Mungji** (11,425 ft.; 3,482m). Ahead of you on the right, you can see, on an eroded brown hillside, the village of **Braga** (11,500 ft.; 3,505m). The homes of this village are built one on top of the other, with the roof of one serving as the front yard of the one above. Steep paths wind up through the village to a large old gompa, and above the gompa are the eroded rocky pinnacles that line both sides of the windswept Manang Valley. There are several good lodges in Braga, including the **Hotel Buddha,** making this a pleasant alternative to staying in Manang. Just past Braga there are several chortens and a prayer wall with many carved slates depicting various Buddhist deities. Crossing a barren and rocky stretch, you come to a small stream, where there are small water-driven flour mills. Cross the stream and climb the hill trail to enter **Manang** (11,600 ft.; 3,536m). The **Hotel Yak** and the **Annapurna Lodge** are two of the better choices in Manang.

An alternative route from Pisang to Manang stays on the north bank of the Marsyangdi, passes the beautiful lake mentioned above, and climbs to the two fascinating little villages of Ghyaru and Ngawal. Not only are these two villages among the most interesting in the valley, but the view to the south just can't be beat.

## DAY 9: ACCLIMATIZATION DAY IN MANANG

Because of the elevation that you will gain in the next 2 days, it is necessary to spend at least 1 full day acclimatizing in Manang. The best way to do this is to hike to a higher elevation and then return to Manang on the same day. Though the view across the valley to the Annapurna Himal is spectacular, you can get an even better view by hiking up the ridge to the north of Manang. From this ridge, you can see (from east to west) Annapurna II (26,035 ft.; 7,935m), Annapurna IV (24,685 ft.; 7,524m), Annapurna III (24,787 ft.; 7,555m), Gangapurna (24,450 ft.; 7,452m), and Tilicho Peak (23,400 ft.; 7,132m). From this point you should also be able to walk back down the valley to a large red gompa on a ridge between Manang and Braga. You probably saw this building as you walked up the valley from Braga on the previous day. Another good day hike would be to continue up the main trail to Tengi (12,000 ft.; 3,658m), the last permanent village before the ascent of Thorong La.

Manang itself is a fascinating place to explore. Perched on the edge of a high ridge overlooking a glacial lake and the Gangapurna icefall, the village is a maze of narrow alleyways, some of which actually go under houses. Each home is a multilevel compound with a stable on the first floor, living quarters on the second floor, and storage on the roof or the third floor. The villagers are primarily farmers and goat herders. Each afternoon the children herd the goats back into the village, and the tinkling of bells and bleating of goats fill the air. There is a small gompa toward the west end of the village. It's usually locked, but you should be able to see the murals on the exterior walls of the gompa's porch.

In Manang you will also find the **Trekkers' Aid Post** of the Himalayan Rescue Association. If you have any questions about altitude sickness or should you begin suffering from it as you climb higher, you can get information and help from the doctors here.

## DAY 10: MANANG TO YAK KHARKA

Manang to Yak Karka: 3 hours. ELEVATION GAIN: 1,940 ft. (582m).

From Manang, the trail climbs through **Tengi** (12,000 feet; 3,660 meters), beyond which there are only summer villages used by herders who bring their flocks up to the high pastures. Above Tengi, the trail leaves the valley of the Marsyangdi and turns northwest up the Jarsang Khola. In the village of **Gunsang** (12,890 feet; 3,900 meters) there are several lodges. After Gunsang, the next lodges are at **Yak Kharka** (13,540 feet; 4,100 meters), a spot that was formerly nothing more than a yak pasture.

## DAY 11: YAK KHARKA TO LETDAR

Yak Kharka to Lattar: 1¼ hours. ELEVATION GAIN: 235 ft. (71m).

From Yak Kharka, the trail climbs steadily to a wide alluvial plain at **Letdar** (13,775 feet; 4,200 meters), where there are several simple lodges. Although this seems like a very short day, remember the elevation gain.

## DAY 12: LETDAR TO THORONG PHEDI

Lattar to Phedi: 2½ hours. Phedi to Phedi High Camp: 1¼ hours. ELEVATION GAIN: 690 ft. (207m).

From Lattar, climb a ridge and then descend and cross the Jarsang Khola. The trail then climbs on the west bank of the river before crossing back to the east bank. The trail then climbs to the flat area called **Thorong Phedi** (14,465 feet; 4,410 meters).

This is the last inhabited outpost before crossing over the Thorong La, and the two lodges here are often very crowded. However, the accommodations are relatively luxurious. Rooms with private bathrooms are available, and the menu includes fresh pasta. There's even a satellite phone (and you can pay for calls with a Mastercard or Visa). From Phedi, which translates as "Foot of the Hill," it is a long steady climb to Thorong La.

If you are fully acclimatized and want to your day going over the pass, you can climb a bit higher to the more primitive lodge at Phedi High Camp.

## DAY 13: THORONG PHEDI TO MUKTINATH

Phedi to Thorong La: 4 hours; Thorong La to Chabarbu: 3 hours; Chabarbu to Muktinath: 1 hour. ELEVATION GAIN: 3,299 ft. (1,006m). ELEVATION LOSS: 5,289 ft. (1,612m).

Do not attempt to continue over Thorong La if the weather is bad. It is very easy to lose the trail in snow. This will be a long day, and fresh, unbroken snow can make it impossible to reach Muktinath before nightfall. Even when there isn't any snow, the strong winds blowing over the pass make every footstep difficult. After Phedi, the trail immediately begins switchbacking up a steep hill. For the next several hours, the trail climbs and descends several moraines and hills before beginning a steady but gradual climb up to the pass. The many false passes will make you think the true pass is never going to appear. **Thorong La** (17,764 ft.; 5,414m) is marked by a chorten, several cairns, and prayer flags.

The descent of more than 5,000 feet (1,524m) is gradual at first, but after an hour, it becomes steeper and crosses a scree slope and a steep cliff. Be very careful through this section if there is snow on the ground. Below this steep section is the lone stone lodge at **Chabarbu** (13,450 ft.; 4,100m). As you descend, you can see Dhaulagiri (26,790 ft.; 8,166m) to the southwest down the Kali Gandaki Valley. From Chabarbu to Muktinath, the descent is much more gradual. Crossing two streams near Chabarbu, you descend gradually across grassy slopes to **Muktinath** (12,475 ft.; 3,802m). In Ranipowa, just below Muktinath, there are numerous lodges and a police checkpoint. Try the **Hotel Muktinath,** the **Himalaya Hotel,** or the **North Pole Lodge.** Jharkot, another hour down the trail, is actually a much more pleasant place to stop for the night, but most people are so beat and so glad to be over Thorong La that they're content with Ranipauwa.

### DAYS 14–21: MUKTINATH TO POKHARA

Because Muktinath is the uppermost destination of the Jomosom trek, the route onward from here, including a description of Muktinath itself, is covered in "The Jomosom Trek" section, below. Trekking from Muktinath down the Kali Gandaki to Pokhara takes 6 to 8 days, depending on which route you follow. Because you will be descending for most of the trip, your trekking times will probably be shorter than those listed for the uphill journey.

## 3 The Jomosom Trek

Spectacular views of Annapurna, Dhaulagiri, and Machhapuchhare, combined with natural and cultural diversity, make the ✪ **Jomosom Trek** by far the most popular trek in Nepal. The trail passes through picturesque villages inhabited by different ethnic groups, and climbs from lush lowland forests to the arid wastelands of the upper Kali Gandaki, which is similar in many ways to the Tibetan Plateau. Except for 1 long day of climbing at the beginning, this trip is relatively easy and never ascends above 13,000 feet (3,962m), so most people will not experience altitude sickness. The lodges along this route are among the most luxurious (relatively speaking) of any trekking route in the country, which also adds to the enjoyment of the trek. For all of these reasons, this route, during the peak October-November trekking season, is positively overrun with trekkers. Expect human traffic jams and problems getting a room if you stop any later than 2pm. However, the large numbers of trekkers are generally a problem only if your expectation was to get away from it all and have a wilderness experience. If this is what you expected, do not hike this route in October or November. Try the winter or the monsoon seasons, or skip it entirely. Better yet, put aside your desire for solitude, and enjoy what is the finest trek in Nepal.

Although we describe this trek from Naya Pul up to Jomosom and Muktinath, it is also possible to fly in to Jomosom and then trek back down to Naya Pul (after visiting Muktinath). If you plan to fly one direction anyway, you should definitely fly in and hike out you'll have more downhill trekking this way. Also, you avoid the potential problem of getting stranded in Jomosom due to bad weather. Airlines that fly between Pokhara and Jomosom include **Cosmic, Lumbini, Royal Nepal Airlines,** and **Yeti.** These flights cost $55 one-way and are in very small planes, so make your reservation as soon as you can. Try to get a seat on the right side of the plane for a better view of the Himalayas.

## DAY 1: POKHARA TO ULLERI

Pokhara to Naya Pul: 1–3 hours; Naya Pul to Birethanti: 30 minutes; Birethanti to Hille: 2½ hours; Hille to Ulleri: 2½ hours. ELEVATION GAIN: 3,300 ft. (1,006m) from Naya Pul to Ulleri.

This first day is a long one, so try to get an early start. From Pokhara, you can take a taxi or bus to the trailhead of Naya Pul. A bus to Naya Pul costs Rs26 (40¢), and a taxi can cost anywhere from Rs500 to Rs700 ($7.60 to $10.60). It takes an hour by taxi or 2 to 3 hours by bus to reach this trailhead. Naya Pul is a classic Nepali trailhead boomtown. Actually, it's not really a town at all, but rather an untidy collection of roadside stalls that spill down a steep slope to the decrepit bridge that marks the start of this trek. Ironically, Naya Pul means "new bridge," yet this bridge is in worse condition than any other bridge on this entire trek (barring one or two that have been washed away by landslides).

From here it is a 30-minute walk up a flat trail to **Birethanti** (3,500 ft.; 1,067m), which is at the confluence of the Modi Khola and the Bhurungdi Khola. Birethanti is a very attractive and prosperous-looking village with a wide stone-paved trail and several comfortable lodges. The first lodge on the left as you enter the village has a terrace overlooking the river and the bridge. This terrace is an excellent place to have lunch. If for some reason you need a place to stay in Birethanti, check out the **Lakshmi Lodge** (straight ahead from the bridge), which, at Rs800 ($12.10) per night, is expensive by trekking standards but is among the most attractively decorated lodges you'll find anywhere in Nepal.

From Birethanti, the trail climbs northwest up the valley of the Bhurungdi Khola, passing a waterfall just as you leave the village. Stay on the north bank of the river. During the dry season the trail may be in the riverbed, whereas in the wetter months it is likely to climb high on the slope above the river. Pass through the small villages of Ramghai and Sudame, beyond which the trail becomes wider and easier to follow. Crossing terraced fields, you enter the village of **Hille** (5,000 ft.; 1,524m), where there are a few lodges. Continuing through Hille, you reach **Tirkhedhunga** (5,175 ft.; 1,577m), where there are a couple more lodges, in another 20 minutes.

Beyond Tirkhedhunga, the trail crosses first a stream and then the Bhurungdi Khola. Here begins the climb up the infamous **Ulleri staircase,** a switchbacking stairway of stone steps that climbs 1,600 feet (488m) up a south-facing slope without shade. At the top of this stairway is **Ulleri** (6,800 ft.; 2,073m), an attractive Magar village with slate-roofed houses and several good lodges. From Ulleri you can see Annapurna South (23,680 ft.; 7,218m) and Hiunchuli (21,130 ft.; 6,440m).

## DAY 2: ULLERI TO GHORAPANI

Ulleri to Nayathanti: 2 hours; Nayathanti to Ghorapani Pass: 1½ hours; Ghorapani Pass to Poon Hill: 1 hour. ELEVATION GAIN: 2,700 ft. (823m), plus 975 ft. (297m) gain and loss to climb Poon Hill.

By climbing to Ulleri on your first day, you break up the long climb to Ghorapani, which is the goal of the second day. Above Ulleri, you leave the terraced hillsides for oak forest. In the middle of this forest is the tiny village of **Banthanti,** where you'll find several teahouses. Above Banthanti, you enter a dense forest that is almost perpetually enshrouded in clouds. Mosses and ferns grow on the twisted, gnarled branches of huge old rhododendron trees. This trail is almost always muddy or snowy or both, so watch your step. Continue climbing to the village of **Nayathanti,** which has several lodges. Ascend through forest to the village of **Ghorapani** (9,365 ft.;

2,854m), which is just 10 minutes below **Ghorapani Pass** (9,500 ft.; 2,896m). At the pass itself there are about 20 lodges that, with their sheet-metal siding, are among the ugliest lodges of this entire trek. The **Super View Lodge** and the **Hotel Snowland** are about the best choices here.

Rising above Ghorapani is the reason for all the lodges (and trekkers) at this particular spot: **Poon Hill** (10,475 ft.; 3,193m). The sunrises and sunsets from this hill are some of the highlights of this trek. It is about an hour from Ghorapani Pass to the top of Poon Hill. From west to east, the view encompasses Dhaulagiri (26,790 ft.; 8,166m), Tukuche (22,700 ft.; 6,919m), Nilgiri (22,765 ft.; 6,939m), Annapurna I (26,540 ft.; 8,089m), Annapurna South (23,680 ft.; 7,218m), Hiunchuli (21,130 ft.; 6,440m), Tarke Kang (23,595 ft.; 7,192m), and Machhapuchhare (22,942 ft.; 6,993m).

All the hotels at Ghorapani Pass are recent constructions. There was no village here until trekkers began traveling this route in large numbers. Since the opening of all these lodges, the deforestation of Ghorapani Pass has been rapid. The massive old rhododendrons that make this area so beautiful are disappearing at an alarming rate. In order to reduce your impact on this area, please don't demand a large fire to sit by at night, and wait until you get to the hot springs at Tatopani for a hot bath (or use a solar shower). These two simple measures will do much to ensure the future beauty of this pass.

## DAY 3: GHORAPANI TO TATOPANI

Ghorapani to Sikha: 2½ hours; Sikha to Tatopani: 3½ hours. ELEVATION LOSS: 5,465 ft. (1,666m).

From Ghorapani, the trail descends 5,465 feet (1,666m)—all of the elevation gained climbing up from Birethanti. It's this 5,465-foot ascent and 5,465-foot descent that many inexperienced and out-of-shape trekkers find so difficult and discouraging. Many trekkers make it as far as Tatopani and give up on the trek altogether. By breaking the ascent to Ghorapani into 2 days, it's much easier to descend all the way to Tatopani in 1 day. However, if you climb to Poon Hill from Ghorapani Pass for sunrise, you will be adding almost 1,000 feet (305m) of extra climbing and descending, which means you might want to split up the descent as well.

From Ghorapani Pass, a steep, muddy (often icy) trail descends through rhododendron forests that are home to gray langurs. Lower down, the forest changes to oak trees before terraced fields take over above the village of **Chitre** (7,600 ft.; 2,316m). In Chitre there are numerous lodges and a good view of Dhaulagiri. Try the **New Dhaulagiri Lodge** or the **Namaste Lodge.** Continue descending through extensively terraced hillsides, crossing a landslide area, to **Sikha** (6,300 ft.; 1,920m), a Magar village with picturesque slate-roofed houses and several lodges. There is a fantastic view of Dhaulagiri from here. From Sikha, the trail descends more gradually, crossing another landslide area before reaching **Ghara** (5,800 ft.; 1,768m), where there are more lodges. Beyond Ghara, the trail climbs slightly up a rocky slope to a teahouse and then begins descending again. From this teahouse, the trail descends 1,600 feet, (488m) mostly on a stone stairway. The trail finally bottoms out at the confluence of the Ghara Khola and the Kali Gandaki, where there is an Annapurna Conservation Area Project (ACAP) checkpoint. This is also the junction with the trail to Beni and Baglung. Head upstream here and cross a suspension bridge over the Ghar Khola. A little farther, the trail crosses the Kali Gandaki on another suspension bridge.

There may be a new trail between this bridge and Tatopani by the time you arrive. In September 1998, a massive landslide broke loose from the slope on the opposite bank of the river. The landslide completely blocked the Kali Gandaki River, slammed into the river bank, and destroyed the trail. A temporary trail, which climbed steeply 400 feet (122m) up to get around a cliff and then dropped 500 feet down into Tatopani, was built soon after the landslide, but there were plans to create a more permanent route in the future. Parts of Tatopani were flooded by the temporary lake that formed behind the natural dam created by the landslide.

**Tatopani** (3,900 ft.; 1,189m) means "hot water" in Nepali, and there are indeed hot springs here. Consequently, Tatopani is a favorite resting spot for both trekkers and Nepalis. The main hot springs are just below the center of the village and were almost completely inundated with silt when the lake formed behind the landslide. They may have been restored by the time you arrive, but don't get your hopes too high. Because of their location beside the river, these springs have been repeatedly damaged by floods, and even when they're in the best condition, they are usually dirty and not very appealing. However, if you desperately need a hot bath, you may want to try soaking here. There are also several more hot springs along the trail to Beni and Baglung. You'll see lots of signs advertising lodges near these other hot springs. Remember, nudity is not acceptable in any of the hot springs.

There are lots of lodges in Tatopani, and some even have satellite TV (you just can't escape from CNN). A specialty of the lodges here is evening happy hour, with cheap beers and free popcorn. The **Dhaulagiri Lodge** and the **Trekkers Lodge,** both with attractive gardens, are the top choices here. Be sure to show your trekking permit at the police checkpoint just south of the village.

## DAY 4: TATOPANI TO GHASA

Tatopani to Dana: 2 hours; Dana to Kabre: 2 hours; Kabre to Ghasa: 2 hours. ELEVATION GAIN: 2,900 ft. (884m).

From Tatopani, head up the west bank of the Kali Gandaki on a trail that ascends gradually. The surrounding mountains give the false impression that you're quite high up, but near the village of Jhartare, you pass through orange groves, indicating the low elevation here. In the winter months there are always people selling oranges along this stretch of trail. It's a good idea to stock up for the higher altitudes. After passing the Miristi Khola, a large river flowing into the Kali Gandaki on the opposite bank, you pass through a small tunnel. After two small villages you cross a stream and enter **Dana** (4,700 ft.; 1,433m), a long village surrounded by orange groves. Dana has several lodges. Shortly before reaching Dana, you pass a suspension bridge across the Kali Gandaki, but you should stay on the west bank. In the upper section of Dana, be sure to notice the old three-story homes with their ornately carved wooden windows.

Continuing up the valley, you climb steadily and pass a beautiful waterfall, at the base of which is the Waterfall Lodge and the village of Rupse Chhara, which not coincidentally means "beautiful waterfall." Continuing, you soon cross a wooden bridge over a narrow gorge of the Kali Gandaki River. Above this bridge, the trail passes through **Kopchepani** (5,575 ft.; 1,699m) and then traverses rocky cliffs on a wide trail that is cut into the cliff face in places. The trail then recrosses the Kali Gandaki, this time on a suspension bridge. From the bridge, the trail climbs to **Ghasa** (6,800 ft.; 2,073m), a large Thakali village that is divided into three distinct sections. In the lower section, try the **Eagle Nest Guest House;** in the upper section, try the **New Florida Guest House** or **Dhaulagiri Guest House.**

## DAY 5: GHASA TO TUKUCHE

Ghasa to Kalopani: 3 hours; Kalopani to Larjung: 3 hours; Larjung to Tukuche: 1½ hours. ELEVATION GAIN: 1,700 ft. (518m).

Above Ghasa, the trail climbs steadily through forests with a view of a massive land-slide on the far side of the Kali Gandaki. When the wind blows, clouds of dust billow up from the landslide. Cross a stream and then pass through Kaiku. Continue climbing, through an area prone to landslides that can be seen on either side of the Kali Gandaki, and cross the Lete Khola; a couple of teahouses are located here. Climb a bit more to reach the spread-out village of **Lete** (7,800 ft.; 2,377m), where there are several lodges. Do not cross the river on the suspension bridge you see here. Right before reaching Lete, you begin to have an excellent view of (from west to east) Dhaulagiri, Nilgiri, and Annapurna I.

Beyond Lete, the trail ascends very gradually through pine forests as the valley becomes wide and flat. It takes about 30 minutes to get to **Kalopani** (8,300 ft.; 2,530m). In Kalopani, the **See You Lodge** and **Kalopani Guest House** are both good choices. The huge Pine Forest Lodge, an American-funded training center for Nepalis going into the tourism industry, is a bizarre and expensive place that lacks the family atmosphere of other lodges on this trek.

Just past Kalopani, you pass between Dhaulagiri (26,790 ft.; 8,166m) and Anna-purna I (26,540 ft.; 8,089m), two of the tallest mountains on earth. It is nearly 3½ miles from the riverbed at Kalopani to the top of Annapurna I. The Kali Gandaki Valley, between Dhaulagiri and Annapurna I, is said to be the deepest river valley on earth.

Just past Kalopani, cross to the east bank of the Kali Gandaki on a suspension bridge. The trail climbs up above the river through dry pine forests interspersed with pastures before descending again to the wide valley floor at Kokhethanti, where there are several lodges. Depending on the time of year, continue up the rocky riverbed, or on the high route through the forests to a suspension bridge that takes you back to the west bank of the Kali Gandaki. Continuing up the valley from this bridge, you have the option of following the trail up a tributary valley to another bridge or taking a shortcut across this tributary's alluvial plane and icy braided streams. Instead of removing your boots to cross the streams, it's probably easier to just walk the extra dis-tance to the bridge. On the far side of this river is **Larjung** (8,400 ft.; 2,560m), where there are mani walls and a gompa, signs that you are now in a region inhabited by Buddhists. There are several lodges in Larjung; try the **Larjung Lodge.**

The village of Khobang just beyond Larjung is architecturally similar, with the trail winding through the village in a narrow, often-covered alley. As the trail leaves Khobang, it also leaves the riverbed and climbs slightly through terraced hillsides to the Thakali village of **Tukuche** (8,500 ft.; 2,591m). This large village was once an important trading center. Tibetan traders would come down the Kali Gandaki (also known as the Thak Khola above this point) with salt and wool, and exchange it for rice and barley from Nepal. When the salt trade was stopped in 1959, Tukuche began to decline in regional importance. When trekking became popular, the Thakali people, who dominated the salt trade in Nepal, turned to operating lodges, which they now do very successfully up and down the Kali Gandaki. There are several very com-fortable lodges in Tukuche, most of which are in old homes that were built on the profits of the salt trade. Houses in this region are traditionally built with central court-yards to block the fierce winds that blow down the Kali Gandaki. In the winter, when it is sunny but cold and windy, a courtyard can be very cozy, while outside the wind chill makes it very uncomfortable. As you wander through the village, admire the carved and brightly painted wooden balconies. Try the **Tukche Guest House** or the **Himali Hotel.**

## DAY 6: TUKUCHE TO KAGBENI

Tukuche to Marpha: 1½ hours; Marpha to Jomosom: 2 hours; Jomosom to Kagbeni: 3 hours.
ELEVATION GAIN: 700 ft. (214m).

As you leave Tukuche, the trail passes through the last bits of juniper forest. Ahead lie the barren upper reaches of the Kali Gandaki, where annual rainfall is less than 10 inches. This is the high desert, and thorny shrubs begin to dominate the vegetation. However, before reaching Marpha, you cross terraced and irrigated fields, which are part of an agricultural project. There are apple and apricot groves in this area, and up and down the valley you will find apple pie on lodge menus, and dried apples in the shops. You'll also find lots of apple brandy, which comes from a government distillery here in Marpha. The distillery is surrounded by apple orchards and is worth a visit.

Passing several whitewashed mani walls, you enter the handsome village of **Marpha** (8,750 ft.; 2,667m), where the flat-roofed houses stairstep up a steep hillside. While most villages along the trekking route have had muddy streets strewn with garbage, Marpha has a system of stone-covered canals that act as a sewer system, giving the village a very tidy appearance. You enter and exit the village through gateway chortens known as *kanis*. On the inside walls and ceiling of the kanis are paintings of various Buddhist deities. There is also a large, modern gompa in Marpha that is set at the top of a long, impressive, and out-of-place flight of cement stairs. You're likely to encounter Tibetan traders near Marpha. They live across the river in Chhairo and come over to sell curios to the trekkers. These vendors are often willing to trade for anything you want to get rid of, but prices are not always better than in Kathmandu, which is where most of their wares come from (not Tibet). High on the hillside above Marpha is a brightly painted large rock that is topped with prayer flags.

If you have time to spare, Marpha is actually a much nicer place to stay than Jomosom. The **Paradise Guest House** and the **Dhaulagiri Guest House** are good choices here.

From Marpha you can take a shortcut up the rocky riverbed during the dry season, or you can follow the main trail through the small village of Syang. Either route will soon bring you to **Jomosom** (8,900 ft.; 2,713m), the largest village on this trek and the district headquarters. You first come to the newer end of town, which is the site of the airstrip and several upscale lodges (several of which have rooms with private bathrooms). Also at this end of town is the very interesting **Mustang Eco-Museum,** which has lots of information on the history of the Mustang region. Beyond the airstrip are a police checkpoint and some houses on the west bank of the Kali Gandaki.

Two wooden bridges cross the river to old Jomosom, which has more lodges (including one that Jimi Hendrix reputedly once stayed in), a bank, a post office, and an army base. The view from Jomosom is dominated by Nilgiri (23,160 ft.; 7,059m), which towers above the south side of the valley. To the left of Nilgiri is Tilicho (23,400 ft.; 7,132m), and down at the west end of the valley is Dhaulagiri. Though there are plenty of good lodges here serving some of the best food on the trek, Jomosom lacks the traditional character of other villages on this route. The **Xanadu Himalayan Pension, Hotel Nilgiri View, Hotel Snowland,** and **Rita Guest House** are among the better lodges here.

If the winds aren't blowing, it is an easy, though rocky, hike up the valley, and I recommend continuing to **Kagbeni.** However, the winds in this valley can sometimes be ferocious, making it almost impossible to be outside in the afternoon. You'll be walking in the middle of a dry riverbed and will be exposed to the wind. Luckily, the winds blow up the valley toward Kagbeni, so even if you set out on a windy day, you'll have the wind at your back.

The trail leaves from the north end of old Jomosom and follows the east bank, sometimes in the riverbed, sometimes on a trail cut into the rock high above the river, to the cluster of lodges at **Eklai Bhatti.** Here the trail forks. The right fork climbs up a rocky slope and continues to Muktinath. Take the left fork, which follows the riverbed to **Kagbeni** (9,200 ft.; 2,804m), a fascinating warren of mud-and-stone houses piled one on top of the other. Narrow alleyways wander through the village, sometimes under houses, sometimes across their roofs. In the middle of the village are the ruins of an old fortress that guarded the two valleys above this point. There is also a large, though decrepit, gompa in Kagbeni.

Across the Kali Gandaki and on the steep hillside above the village are numerous **caves** once used by Buddhist hermits. Up the Kali Gandaki from Kagbeni lies the Upper Mustang region, which is a restricted area. Trekking permits for this area cost $700 and are good for 10 days (see "Trekking-Permit Fees" in chapter 9). The **Royal Guest House** and the **Shangrila Lodge** are two of the better choices here.

## DAY 7: KAGBENI TO MUKTINATH

Kagbeni to Jharkot: 3½ hours; Jharkot to Muktinath: 1 hour. ELEVATION GAIN: 3,275 ft. (998m).

To continue up to the pilgrimage site of Muktinath, cross back over the stream you crossed just outside Kagbeni, and turn southeast up the valley. This trail climbs a barren hillside to meet the direct trail from Jomosom to Muktinath in 1 hour. Across the valley you can see more caves and the ruins of an ancient fortress village. In another hour, you will pass a large grove of trees at the village of Khingar. Climb across terraces to enter **Jharkot** (11,440 ft.; 3,487m), where there are more fortress ruins. Jharkot sits atop a small hill, and around the flanks of the village, you're likely to see the yak-cow crossbreeds used as draft and pack animals in this region. These animals are shaggy and stocky but have a better temperament than a purebred yak. They are used both for producing milk and as pack and draft animals.

Jharkot is very similar in architecture and design to Kagbeni, though due to its hilltop location it gets far more sun and feels a bit more prosperous than Kagbeni. A large red cube-shaped gompa dominates the Jharkot skyline. Try the **Hotel Sonam** or the **Hotel New Plaza.**

From Jharkot, the trail continues climbing past more trees and across terraced fields to **Ranipowa.** In Ranipowa, there are numerous lodges and a police checkpoint. However, because Ranipowa is little more than a collection of trekkers' lodges, Jharkot is a much more appealing place to stay. If you really want to stay up here, try the **Hotel Muktinath,** the **Himalaya Hotel,** or the **North Pole Lodge.**

A few minutes beyond Ranipowa, in a glade of trees, are the shrines of Muktinath. **Muktinath** (12,475 ft.; 3,802m) is one of the most important pilgrimage sites in Nepal and is visited by both Buddhists and Hindus. Within the main temple here are the sacred flames that were mentioned 2,000 years ago in the Indian epic *Mahabharata.* These flames, caused by natural gas leaks, burn on rock and earth. If you give a small donation, the keeper will gladly open the temple and show you the flames, which are hidden behind curtains. There are also 108 waterspouts, most of them shaped like cows' heads, through which flow holy waters. Because one of the temples is dedicated to the Hindu god Vishnu, and because Buddha is considered an incarnation of Vishnu, the shrine is sacred to both Hindus and Buddhists. Over the years, devout pilgrims have planted thousands of trees, and Muktinath is now something of an oasis in the barren hills. The annual pilgrimage and festival takes place during the full moon of late August or early September.

If you want to visit Muktinath but don't look forward to the hike up, you can rent a pony for around Rs500 ($7.60) in Kagbeni and ride up. Just don't do this if you are suffering from symptoms of altitude sickness. You can also hire a pony to take you to Jomosom for the same price. Look for signs around the villages for lodges that rent ponies, or ask the proprietor at your lodge to give you a recommendation.

## DAYS 8–15: MUKTINATH BACK TO POKHARA

If you are in a hurry to get back to Pokhara or you need to catch a plane in Jomosom, you can bypass Kagbeni and go directly from Muktinath, via Jharkot and Eklai Bhatti, to Jomosom. This direct trail continues past the junction with the trail from Jharkot to Kagbeni, descending a long slope to the floor of the Kali Gandaki valley at Eklai Bhatti. You should leave Muktinath as early in the morning as possible to avoid the winds, which usually pick up around 11am and will now be in your face rather than at your back. Unless you are planning to fly out of Jomosom, I suggest continuing on to Marpha. It takes about 3 hours to get from Muktinath to Jomosom.

A number of options are available for the return trip from Jomosom to Pokhara. If you don't have much time and you have the cash handy, you can fly back to Pokhara. The flight takes only 45 minutes and costs $55. Another choice is to retrace your steps as far as Tatopani, and instead of making the grueling climb up to Ghorapani and back down the other side, you can follow the Kali Gandaki to Beni or Baglung. There are regular buses from Baglung and irregular transport (buses or trucks) from Beni back to Pokhara. You might even find a taxi or two waiting around Baglung if you feel like splurging. It's a long day's walk to Beni, but along the way there are several nice lodges, so you might want to break this into a 2-day hike. In Beni, try the **Hotel Yeti,** or stop an hour outside of Beni in Galeswore at the **Riverside Guest House,** which has rooms with attached bathrooms.

If you are full of energy and feel up to making the climb to Ghorapani and down the other side in only 2 days, you can get back to Pokhara in 6 days, rather than the 7 days it took to reach Muktinath. An alternative route worth considering is to leave the main route at Ghorapani and take the trail to Ghandruk, a large Gurung village on the main route to the Annapurna Sanctuary. If you want to extend your trek, you can then continue up to the sanctuary (see "Annapurna Sanctuary," below). If you return to Pokhara through Ghandruk, you can go by way of Birethanti to Naya Pul or by way of Landruk and Dhampus to Phedi. From either Naya Pul or Phedi, you can get a bus or taxi back to Pokhara (see "Annapurna Sanctuary," below).

## ✪ GHORAPANI TO GHANDRUK

Ghorapani Pass to Deorali: 1½ hours; Deorali to Banthanti: 1 hour; Banthanti to Tadapani: 1 hour; Tadapani to Ghandruk: 3 hours. ELEVATION GAIN: 1,780 ft. (543m). ELEVATION LOSS: 4,240 ft. (1,292m).

It is a long day's walk from Ghorapani to Ghandruk with several steep ascents and descents, but the trail passes through beautiful dense forests unlike any other you will have seen while trekking in this region. There are waterfalls and clear-running streams and, yes, several lodges where you can stay if you want to break up the hike into 2 days. *Do not attempt this hike on your own.* Always go in a group and stay close together. In the past there have been attacks and robberies along this trail but almost always of lone trekkers.

From Ghorapani Pass, head due east along the top of the ridge, past the school and into the forest. There are many trails heading in this direction, but eventually they all begin climbing up through the forest. In an hour you'll come out on a grassy hilltop at 10,300 feet (3,139m). The view from this point is superb and virtually identical to that from Poon Hill, so if you are planning on heading this way anyway, skip Poon Hill, get an early start, and catch sunrise from here instead. You'll even be able to see the crowds over on Poon Hill.

The trail reenters the forest and climbs a bit more before beginning a descent to several lodges at **Deorali** (10,100 ft.; 3,078m). Signs at this little clearing in the forest advertise the view from nearby Gurung Hill (yet another hill) as being every bit as good as those from Poon Hill, making this an alternative overnight spot for anyone seeking memorable mountain views. Here at Deorali, you meet a trail from Chitre, a shortcut if you are coming from Tatopani and headed to Ghandruk or the Annapurna Sanctuary. Taking this shortcut eliminates the climb to Ghorapani.

From Deorali, the trail descends steeply to **Banthanti** (8,720 ft.; 2,658m), a collection of lodges at the base of some limestone cliffs. The setting is enchanting, making this a great spot for lunch. From here, the trail continues descending briefly, then climbs steeply for a while before descending again to 8,250 feet (2,515m). From here it is a steady climb up to **Tadapani** (8,840 ft.; 2,694m), a collection of lodges that is a popular overnight spot because of its excellent views of Machhapuchhare, Hiunchuli, and Annapurna South. Keep an eye out for langurs around here.

Two trails leave Tadapani. The longer route goes directly to Chomrong by way of Kyumnu for anyone pressed for time and headed to the Annapurna Sanctuary. The other trail makes a long, steady descent to Ghandruk, passing the lodges at Bhaisi Khark in about 45 minutes. After another 1½ hours, you'll come to a fork in the trail marked by a large sign showing the many lodges in Ghandruk. Take the right fork at this point. From here it is another 30 minutes to **Ghandruk** (6,750 ft.; 2,057m), which you enter from the upper end of town. If you want to stay in the old part of town, take a left fork steeply downhill when you come to a dense cluster of houses.

## 4  Annapurna Sanctuary

Because of the amazing scenery in the **Annapurna Sanctuary**, this trek has become one of the most popular in Nepal. The sanctuary is a huge amphitheater surrounded by 10 peaks that are more than 20,000 feet (6,100m) tall, including Annapurna I, Annapurna South, Annapurna III, and Machhapuchhare. While there are no villages between Chomrong and the sanctuary, there are collections of lodges about every 2 hours. However, many of these lodges are open only during the peak seasons of October to November and February to March. During December and January, innkeepers move back down to Chomrong because of heavy snows. In the spring, frequent avalanches close down the sanctuary and make trekking very dangerous. In the winter months, if it has been raining at low elevations, you can be sure that snow has been building on the slopes above the trail into the sanctuary and that avalanches are likely to follow. Be sure to ask anyone you meet coming from the opposite direction about trail conditions. This is a remote area a day or two beyond the last village and is as close to a wilderness experience as you are likely to find on a trek in Nepal. Look for Himalayan tahrs on the slopes above the sanctuary, especially to the north of Machhapuchhare Base Camp.

As part of the Annapurna Conservation Area Project, there is a kerosene depot at Chomrong village (though it is not always available), which is between the large village of Ghandruk and the sanctuary itself. If you are doing your own cooking, you should stop at the depot and secure enough kerosene for your trip into the sanctuary. The use of firewood is prohibited beyond Chomrong, and all lodges are required to use kerosene for cooking. Consequently, the price of meals goes up considerably beyond here, making this one of the most expensive teahouse treks you can do. Expect to pay around Rs800 ($12.10) per day beyond Chomrong. The numbers of trekkers on this route have had a heavy toll, worsening deforestation and increasing the amounts of trailside garbage along the trail to the sanctuary. It was in part due to the abuse of this pristine area that ACAP was founded. In recent years, ACAP has standardized lodges along this route and, in order to limit deforestation and provide a more wilderness experience, has closed lodges that had sprung up between the groupings of lodges that are spaced at 2-hour intervals.

Pokhara is the starting point for this trek, and you should allow at least **10 or 11 days** and preferably **2 weeks** to allow for avalanches interrupting your trek.

## DAY 1: POKHARA TO LANDRUK

Pokhara to Phedi: 30 minutes; Phedi to Dhampus: 1½ hours; Dhampus to Pothana: 1½ hours; Pothana to Tolka: 1½ hours; Tolka to Landruk: 1½ hours. ELEVATION GAIN: 3,350 ft. (1,021m). ELEVATION LOSS: 1,450 ft. (442m).

Take a taxi from Pokhara to the trailhead at Phedi for around Rs300 ($4.55). The ride takes about 30 minutes. **Phedi** (3,700 ft.; 1,128m), which means "Bottom of the Hill," is at the foot of a moderately steep trail that climbs through scrubby forest to the ridge-top village of **Dhampus** (5,700 ft.; 1,737m). This 2,000-foot (610m) climb is a tough way to start a trek, but after you reach Dhampus, the trail becomes easier. There are excellent views of Machhapuchhare and Annapurna from along the trail near Dhampus. **Ker & Downey's Basanta Lodge** is the nicest lodge in the village, but because this lodge caters primarily to organized teahouse treks, you usually have to have a reservation (contact Ker & Downey's in Kathmandu for reservations; see chapter 4). From Dhampus, the trail climbs slowly as it contours around a forested ridge with only a few simple teahouses. Just below the crest of this ridge is the village of **Pothana,** where there are several lodges with glassed-in rooftop dining rooms that make the most of the mountain views.

From Pothana, where there is a great view of Machhapuchhare, the trail first climbs a bit and then, after cresting the ridge, descends very steeply. You will pass the hamlet of Beri Kharka and reach the small village of **Tolka** (5,900 ft.; 1,798m), where there are more lodges with rooftop dining rooms. The trail continues descending through the forest and, after leveling off at Medigala, enters **Landruk** (5,600 ft.; 1,707m), a fairly large village with lots of unremarkable lodges. Try the **Maya Guest House.** If you don't mind having a slightly longer walk tomorrow, you'd do better to stay in Tolka. The large village across the valley from Landruk is Ghandruk.

## DAY 2: LANDRUK TO CHOMRONG

Landruk to New Bridge: 1½ hours; New Bridge to Jhinu Danda: 1½ hours; Jhinu Danda to Chomrong: 1½ hours. ELEVATION GAIN: 2,280 ft. (695m). ELEVATION LOSS: 500 ft. (152m).

From Landruk, there are two possible routes. If you take the trail that descends steeply from Landruk to the floor of the Modi Khola Valley, you will be headed for Ghandruk, the largest village in the area. The trail is a steep 1,000-foot (305m) descent followed by an equally steep 2,000-foot (610m) ascent. To avoid this grueling stretch of trail, I suggest you take an alternative route that descends slowly to the valley floor. To follow this route, do not drop down the steep trail that leads to Ghandruk, but instead keep to the right on what is a relatively level trail leading out of Landruk. This trail, which descends at a much gentler angle, leads up the valley of the Modi Khola on the east bank. The trail finally crosses the river at a spot known as **New Bridge** or Himal Kyu (5,100 ft.; 1,554m). There are several lodges at the bridge.

From here the trail climbs steeply to **Jhinu Danda** (5,800 ft.; 1,768m), where there are at least six large lodges. A 30-minute walk from Jhinu Danda will bring you to a very relaxing hot spring on the banks of the Modi Khola; unfortunately, it is a steep climb back up to the lodges after bathing. From Jhinu Danda, the trail continues climbing steeply, and without shade, to a few lodges on the shoulder of a ridge at 7,240 feet (2,207m). These lodges mark the junction with the trail to Ghandruk. Turn right on this trail, and you soon reach the first of the lodges in upper **Chomrong** (7,380 ft.; 2,249m). Although the actual village of Chomrong lies some 800 feet (244m) lower, the views are better up here, and most trekkers choose to stay at one of these upper lodges. The lodges here boast flagstone terraces, gardens, solar showers, and sun rooms. Try the **Chomrong Guest House, Excellent View Lodge, Kalpana Guest House,** or the ever-popular **Moonlight Lodge.** They can also claim one of the best views in the region, one that takes in Machhapuchhare, Annapurna South, and Hiunchuli.

From upper Chomrong, the trail descends on a steep stone staircase, passing lots of lodges, to the village itself. The upper lodges have much better views and consequently are very popular with trekkers on their way up to the sanctuary. However, people heading down often stay in lower Chomrong rather than face the seemingly endless staircase that climbs to the lodges in upper Chomrong. The **Captain's Lodge** and the **Annapurna Guest House** are the best choices in the village itself. *Note:* There are no more villages beyond this point, so before continuing, find out whether lodges in the sanctuary are open.

## DAY 3: CHOMRONG TO DOVAN

Chomrong to Sinuwa: 1½ hours; Sinuwa to Khuldi Ghar: 1 hour; Khuldi Ghar to Bamboo: 30 minutes; Bamboo to Dovan: 1 hour. ELEVATION GAIN: 2,420 ft. (695m). ELEVATION LOSS: 1,620 ft. (494m).

This is a short and fairly easy day. From Chomrong, the trail descends and crosses the Chomrong Khola (6,180 ft.; 1,884m), a tributary of the Modi Khola, before beginning the long climb to Khuldi Ghar. As you cross the bridge, look downstream and you'll see the tiny micro-hydroelectric project that supplies electricity to Chomrong. The entire generating system isn't much bigger than a refrigerator.

From the bridge, you climb up the steep slope of this tributary valley and, at about 7,000 feet (2,134m), come to the large Sherpa Guest House and contour around a ridge into the main valley of the Modi Khola. From here it is almost an hour more to the lodges at **Sinuwa** (7,720 ft.; 2353m). The trail continues climbing (though with lots of ups and downs) to **Khuldi Ghar** (8,020 ft.; 2,444m), where there is an ACAP checkpoint. Part of this section of trail is paved with tight-fitting paving stones and even has a gutter. From here, the trail descends very steeply, sometimes along rock outcroppings that have had steps set into them. At the bottom of this steep stretch, you'll find the collection of lodges known as **Bamboo** (7,600 ft.; 2,316m). This makes a good lunch spot.

Beyond Bamboo, the trail continues through dense, damp forest to the lodges at **Dovan** (8,180 ft.; 2,493m). These lodges all have large slate patios. Although it will likely still be early in the day, you should probably stop here for the night. From here on up, you have to stop early in the day if you want to be assured of getting a room. However, if you continue and the next lodges don't have any rooms left, they'll always let you sleep on a foam pad in the dining room.

## DAY 4: DOVAN TO DEORALI

Dovan to Himalayan Hotel: 1½ hours; Himalayan Hotel to Deorali: 1½ hours. ELEVATION GAIN: 2,160 ft. (659m).

Dovan is little more than a clearing in the forest, and as you leave the collection of lodges, on a stretch of trail that can be extremely slippery, you enter a forest of giant rhododendrons. These are not the shrubs you have in your garden at home, but trees with trunks several feet in diameter. Due to the lack of sunshine and the clouds that often roll up the valley around noon, this section of trail is almost always cool and damp. The valley is extremely steep-walled at this point and, because of its north-south orientation, gets little sunlight but plenty of rain. Streamers of water plunge hundreds of feet down the opposite valley wall and can occasionally be glimpsed through breaks in the forest. At one such break there is a small shrine and a memorial to a trekker who died near here several years ago. Directly behind this shrine, there is a new trail that was constructed in 1998 to bypass a stretch of the old trail that was prone to avalanches and landslides. This trail climbs steeply up through the forest before making a more gradual ascent to the collection of lodges called **Himalayan Hotel** (9,300 ft.; 2,835m). These lodges, with their large patios, are much sunnier and drier than the lodges of Dovan and Bamboo.

Tree roots and mud make the footing treacherous on many stretches of the trail between Dovan and Himalayan Hotel. However, beyond Himalayan Hotel, you climb above the forest and get back on dry trail again, this time in scrubby grasslands. A steep climb brings you to **Hinko Cave** (9,900 ft.; 3,018m), an overhanging cliff where for many years there was a very basic lodge. From the cave, you can see the lodges at Deorali situated below and up the valley. The trail descends a bit and crosses an avalanche chute (you may be walking on mud-covered ice) before climbing up to the lodges at **Deorali** (10,340 ft.; 3,152m). Most people can feel the effects of the elevation by the time they reach Deorali—it's a good idea to stop early and make this an acclimatization day. It is possible to reach Annapurna Base Camp on this day, but because it's at 13,300 feet (4,054m), you would be risking altitude sickness.

## DAY 5: DEORALI TO ANNAPURNA BASE CAMP

Deorali to Machhapuchhare Base Camp: 1½ hours; Machhapuchhare Base Camp to Anna-purna Base Camp: 2 hours. ELEVATION GAIN: 2,960 ft. (902m).

The trail from Deorali first climbs up and then descends to the bed of the Modi Khola with good views of Machhapuchhare to the east and Gangapurna to the north. Between Deorali and Machhapuchhare Base Camp, you pass through the natural gateway to the sanctuary. This gateway is formed by Machhapuchhare on the east and Hiunchuli on the west as they pinch the Modi Khola into a steep-walled valley. This is another avalanche area and the trail is sometimes obliterated—so be careful. If you lose the trail, just continue following the riverbed. **Machhapuchhare Base Camp** (11,800 ft.; 3,597m), more commonly referred to as MBC, is on a gently sloping grassy hillside scattered with gigantic boulders and is about 1½ hours beyond Deorali. There are five lodges here and an excellent view of Machhapuchhare, Annapurna III, Fang, and Annapurna South. From here the trail leads almost due west at the base of the north slope of Hiunchuli. To the north of the trail are South Annapurna Glacier and the moraine formed by this impressive glacier. Look for Himalayan tahrs on the slopes to the north of Machhapuchhare Base Camp. Many people choose to stay here for the night to avoid risking altitude sickness. If you do stay here, hike up to Anna-purna Base Camp before sunrise the next morning so you can catch the dawn light on the peaks that surround the sanctuary.

From MBC, it is about 2 hours to **Annapurna Base Camp** (13,300 ft.; 4,054m), which is most often referred to simply as ABC. The 360-degree panorama from here is one of the most spectacular sights in all of Nepal and includes (starting on the south side and moving clockwise) Hiunchuli (21,130 ft.; 6,440m), Annapurna South (23,680 ft.; 7,218m), Fang (25,089 ft.; 7,647m), Annapurna I (26,545 ft.; 8,091m), Annapurna III (24,787 ft.; 7,555m), and Machhapuchhare (22,942 ft.; 6,993m). ABC got its name when it was used in 1970 as base camp for famed mountaineer Chris Bonnington's ascent of Annapurna I. Bonnington scaled the nearly vertical south face of Annapurna I, which is the massive peak you see to the northwest of Annapurna Base Camp. Three peaks within the sanctuary—Tharpu Chuli (Tent Peak, 18,580 ft.; 5,663m), Singu Chuli (Fluted Peak, 21,315 ft.; 6,497m), and Hiunchuli—are designated trekking peaks, which you can climb if you have the proper permits. All three require the proper equipment and extensive mountaineering skills.

ABC lies at the foot of the Annapurna Glacier's lateral moraine, and if you hike up to the top of the moraine, you will see the gray, rock-strewn bulk of this glacier far below. The rumble of rock and ice slides coming off Annapurna South frequently break the silence of the sanctuary. Park yourself on the lip of the moraine west of the lodges, and, with patience, you may see one of these thunderous slides. Closer at hand, there are unusual alpine plants that grow here, including a tiny gentian that is often still in bloom in early November.

Of the four lodges at ABC, the **Paradise Garden Hotel,** though it has no garden and is hardly a paradise, is the best. Expect the lodges up here to be crowded and food to be relatively expensive. These two factors are enough to prevent most people from spending more than a day or two in the sanctuary.

## DAY 6: EXPLORING ANNAPURNA SANCTUARY

If it is not too cold and windy, you may want to spend a day exploring the sanctuary. One favorite excursion is the hike up the hill directly south of the lodges. As you climb this hill, known as Rakshi Peak, the views get better and better. Alternatively, for a longer hike, you can follow the trail down to the Annapurna Glacier and hike across to the north side of the valley. Because Annapurna Sanctuary is above 12,000 feet (3,658m), it is very important to be alert for symptoms of altitude sickness. You will almost certainly be short of breath and find exercising much more difficult than at lower elevations.

## DAY 7: ANNAPURNA BASE CAMP TO BAMBOO

Annapurna Base Camp to Deorali: 3 hours; Deorali to Bamboo: 3 hours. ELEVATION LOSS: 5,700 ft. (1,737m).

Before heading back down, be sure that there is no danger of avalanches. (Lodge owners are usually aware of the level of avalanche danger, but note that the possibility of an avalanche is highest after a recent snowfall.) The route back is the same as the route up, but you can expect to make better time going out since it is mostly downhill.

## DAY 8: BAMBOO TO CHOMRONG

Bamboo to Sinuwa: 2 hours; Sinuwa to Chomrong: 1½ hours. ELEVATION GAIN: 1,620 ft. (494m). ELEVATION LOSS: 1,840 ft. (561m).

Although you have to make two long ascents and two long descents, it is possible to reach Ghandruk in 1 long day from Bamboo. However, you'd be wiser to take a short day and spend the afternoon resting in Chomrong. The views just don't get any better than this for the rest of the trek.

## DAY 9: CHOMRONG TO GHANDRUK

Chomrong to Kimrong: 2½ hours; Kimrong to Kimrong Pass: 1½ hours; Kimrong Pass to Ghandruk: 1 hour. ELEVATION GAIN: 2,170 ft. (661m). ELEVATION LOSS: 1,540 ft. (469m).

I suggest that rather than retracing your steps from Chomrong to the road, you return by way of Ghandruk. From Chomrong, the trail climbs a bit to a spur ridge (7,240 ft.; 2,207m) that looks down on Jhinu Danda and the lodge near the hot springs (the way you came up). Be sure to glance back over your shoulders for one last close-up glimpse of Machhapuchhare, Hiunchuli, and Annapurna South. From here, take the trail to the right and contour up the valley of the Kimrong Khola. This stretch of trail is fairly level for a while and offers easy walking. Parts of the trail are in forest, but most of it is through terraced millet fields and is open to the warmth of the sun, a welcome change from the cold and damp of the Modi Khola. Along this stretch of trail, you will find the junction with the route from Ghorapani (by way of Tadapani). For a description of this route, which links the Annapurna Circuit or Jomosom trek with the Annapurna Sanctuary trek, see the end of "The Jomosom Trek," earlier in this chapter.

Above the village of **Kimrong** (6,000 ft.; 1,829m), the trail suddenly drops in short, steep switchbacks to the village, which itself is 200 feet (61m) or so above the river. There is a shortcut that descends steeply to a teahouse on the banks of the river, but it is worthwhile to take the longer route through the village. On the opposite bank of the river, the trail follows a stream through terraced fields before entering a rather open forest. It is a steep climb up to the **Kimrong Pass** (7,340 ft.; 2,237m), but luckily it is in the shade and does not take too long. At the pass, there are a few lodges. You can see Ghandruk below you, across a sparsely wooded hillside. The trail descends quickly and then contours through open rock-strewn fields to **Ghandruk** (6,750 ft.; 2,057m).

Ghandruk, a Gurung village, has grown large and prosperous on the pensions of retired Gurkha soldiers. The village is broken up into three sections, and coming from Chomrong, you first reach the oldest section of town, where two- and three-story stone houses with slate roofs and flagstone terraces are crammed tightly together in a maze of narrow paved alleys. Passing through this section of the village, you will come to a smaller grouping of old homes, a few of which have been opened up to the public as museums and teahouses serving traditional Gurung food. These are well worth a visit.

Continuing around the hill will bring you to the newest part of town, which is where you will find most of Ghandruk's many lodges, including the popular Hotel Trekker's Inn and the Hotel Milan. Several of the lodges here have rooms with private bathrooms. Unfortunately, most of the new lodges here have been built of cement in the ugly style of Pokhara's budget hotels. For more character, stick with the lodges in the older part of the village. The **Excellent View Lodge,** with a pretty garden, is a good choice, as is the **Snowland Lodge.** Ghandruk's nicest lodge is Ker & Downey's **Himalaya Lodge,** with its spacious gardens, cathedral-ceilinged dining hall, attractively decorated spacious rooms, and tiled private bathrooms. This lodge is used almost exclusively by organized teahouse trekking groups.

This is also where you'll find the headquarters of the Annapurna Conservation Area Project. Stop by to learn more about what ACAP is doing to preserve the culture and natural beauty of this spectacular region.

## DAY 10: GHANDRUK TO BIRETHANTI

Ghandruk to Shaule Bazaar: 3 hours; Shaule Bazaar to Birethanti: 2 hours; Birethanti to Naya Pul: 30 minutes; Naya Pul to Pokhara: 2–3 hours by bus or 1 hour by taxi. ELEVATION LOSS: 3,110 ft. (948m).

From Ghandruk, the trail descends gradually at first on a wide flagstone-paved trail that is the superhighway of this trek. The trail crosses open hillsides and is usually warm and sunny. Keep to the ridge and continue descending slowly, passing through the small village of **Kimche** (5,480 ft.; 1,670m). Near the village of Clue, the landscape becomes more lush. Eventually, the trail becomes steeper as it heads for the valley floor just below **Shaule Bazaar** (3,723 ft.; 1,135m). The trail finally reaches the river at a couple of lodges known as **Riverside**. From here the trail is once again quite level, but the going is rather difficult because you are walking on river rocks. Along this stretch of trail, you will pass Ker & Downey's Sanctuary Lodge (see above).

In another 30 minutes or so, you will be in **Birethanti** (3,640 ft.; 1,109m), which is the last village before Naya Pul and the road. Birethanti stands at the confluence of the Bhurungdi Khola and the Modi Khola and is a busy bazaar village on the trekking route to Jomosom. Because this is the most popular trekking route in the country, there are plenty of comfortable lodges here, including the upscale **Lakshmi Lodge,** which charges around $12 for an attractive room with a shared bathroom. If you aren't yet ready to leave the trails, this makes a pleasant place to spend 1 last night. Otherwise, it is just a 30- to 45-minute walk down the river to the road.

The trail to Naya Pul crosses the suspension bridge and immediately forks to the right, staying on the valley floor. Be sure to glance back over your shoulder at the excellent view of Machhapuchhare. The trail is now lined with small businesses selling supplies needed by villages up the trail, and although the view of the river is nice, this stretch of trail has the feel of a road-head boomtown. Things just get uglier and uglier and more and more packed with shops as you approach the road that connects Pokhara with Baglung. There will be buses (Rs26; 40¢) and taxis (Rs700; $10.60) waiting here to take you back to Pokhara.

An alternative to the easy Naya Pul route is to climb 1½ hours from Birethanti to **Chandrakot** (5,125 ft.; 1,562m). This is a more rigorous trail, but it cuts off almost an hour of the bus or truck ride and gives you a chance to visit one last village before ending your trek. Why rush back to the noise and pollution of civilization? To take this route, cross the suspension bridge and keep to the left; the trail immediately begins climbing steeply to Chandrakot, which is about 1,500 feet (457m) higher than Birethanti. From Chandrakot, it is just a few minutes downhill to the road where you can wait for a bus. If you are full of energy, you might just start walking along the road and flag down the next vehicle headed toward Pokhara.

## 5 The Langtang Valley

Due primarily to the crowds on the Everest and Annapurna treks, this trek has been gaining in popularity in the past few years. You certainly won't see as many other trekkers here, but likewise the accommodations are fewer, farther apart, and less comfortable. There are few teahouses between villages, which means you frequently will have to hike for 3 hours to reach the next village that has food and accommodations. However, the things that make this trek appealing are its long stretches of undisturbed forest where birds are plentiful; high-altitude meadows where you may see wild sheep; excellent mountain views; and Tibetan-like culture. If you bring along a tent, a stove, and food, you can even strike out on your own and do a bit of exploring at the upper end of the Langtang Valley, which is only a few miles from Tibet.

**Syabrubensi,** 2 hours beyond Dhunche on the road, is becoming an increasingly popular spot from which to start this trek, due in large part to the easy trail you can follow up the Langtang Khola at the start of the trek. However, because this option requires more time on a bus and bypasses the attractive village of Syabru, I don't recommend it.

### DAY 1: KATHMANDU TO DHUNCHE
Kathmandu to Dhunche: 9–13 hours.

Buses to Dhunche, the main Langtang trailhead village, leave from the Gongabu Bus Park on Ring Road north of Thamel. Buses leave daily between 6 and 8am and normally take between 9 and 13 grueling hours to reach Dhunche, and it's not unheard of for this trip to take 14 hours or longer. Be psychologically prepared. The fare is Rs100 ($1.50), and it is a good idea to buy your ticket the day before you intend to travel. Also, be sure to arrive early enough so you can find your bus amid the chaos of the bus park.

About 45 minutes out of Kathmandu, you pass through the town of Kakani, where there are great views of the Ganesh Himal, a grouping of peaks only partially visible from Kathmandu. Trisuli, on the river of the same name, is a busy bazaar town, often called Trisuli Bazaar. The river, which flows southwest, is very popular with rafting companies.

For many years, this was the start of the Langtang trek, but there is now a road to Dhunche that bypasses the old trail and reduces the number of days necessary for the trek. It is a rough road to Dhunche, and during the rainy season there are frequent landslides, which may keep the road closed until sometime in mid-October. For part of the way, the road clings to the edge of a steep mountain. Very scary!

Between Trisuli and Dhunche, you will be required to show your trekking permit at least once and possibly twice. Because you will be trekking through **Langtang National Park,** you will also have to check in at the park headquarters near the outskirts of Dhunche and show your park permit, which you should have acquired for Rs650 ($9.85) in Kathmandu (see "Other Fees" in chapter 9). You might also be subjected to an unexplained military inspection of your belongings. It is unclear what sort of contraband the soldiers are searching for, but only trekkers' bags are searched. Finally, on the edge of Dhunche, you will once again have to show your trekking permit.

**Dhunche** (6,400 ft.; 1,951m) is an attractive village with large stone houses. The older part of the village is below the road and is almost completely hidden from view by newer buildings that have been constructed along the road. Here you'll find several lodges. The **Hotel Langtang View** is a good choice. Be sure to take time to explore the narrow, winding stone footpaths of old Dhunche. Most of the houses have stone-walled first floors and wooden second floors, often with ornately carved walls and window frames. The view from Dhunche, which is high above the Trisuli River, is breathtaking.

## DAY 2: DHUNCHE TO SYABRU

Dhunche to Bharkhu: 2 hours; Bharkhu to Syabru: 3 hours. ELEVATION GAIN: 1,500 ft. (457m). ELEVATION LOSS: 950 ft. (290m).

The first 90-minute stretch of this day's hike is clearly visible from Dhunche; it is the road that angles across the far side of the valley to the north of town. Luckily, there is little traffic on this road, and it follows a much easier route than the old trail. To begin the trek from Dhunche, follow the gravel road out of town heading north. The road descends to a bridge over the Trisuli Khola, a stream flowing from the Gosainkund Lakes, which are a 2-day walk from here. The road then climbs steadily to round a ridge, at which point you lose sight of Dhunche. Ahead and below lies the village of **Bharkhu,** which is much smaller than Dhunche but features the same sort of attractive architecture. Both Dhunche and Bharkhu are Tamang villages. The Tamang people are primarily Buddhists and are often farmers or porters.

Pass through Bharkhu, and on the far side of the village, watch for a trail leading uphill to the right. It climbs a steep slope to the top of a ridge (7,550 ft.; 2,301m), where there is a good area to rest. You have now entered the Langtang Valley, and there are views of Ganesh Himal to the west, Tibet to the north, and Langtang Lirung to

# Langtang, Gosainkund & Helambu Trekking Routes

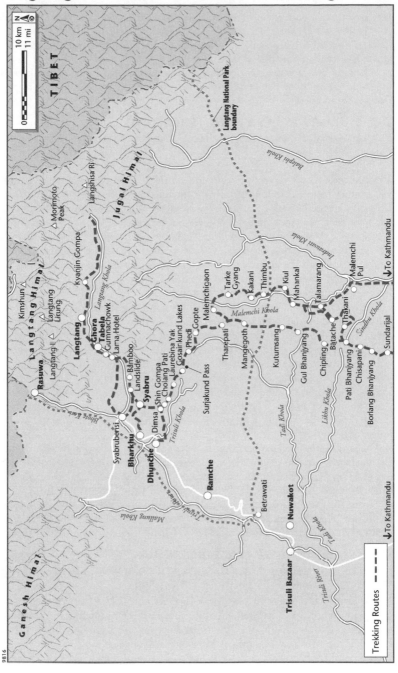

the east. After an hour, you will also be able to see, on a ridgetop below you, the village of **Syabru** (7,000 ft.; 2,134m). The trail contours around the ridge before descending a short, steep slope into this village. There are several lodges in Syabru, which is scattered across the ridge.

If you got an early start and feel like walking farther, you could continue to the lodges at Landslide or Bamboo. Syabru, however, makes a much more interesting place to spend the night.

## DAY 3: SYABRU TO LAMA HOTEL (CHONGONG)

Syabru to Landslide: 2 hours; Landslide to Bamboo: 1 hour; Bamboo to bridge: 30 minutes; bridge to Lama Hotel: 2 hours. ELEVATIION GAIN: 2,500 ft. (762m). ELEVATION LOSS: 1,700 ft. (518m).

Descend through the village of Syabru and continue down the ridge until you come to a trail to the east that drops sharply off the ridge and goes through a dense forest. Cross a bridge (6,400 ft.; 1,951m) over a tributary of the Langtang Khola, and then climb for a short distance through a dry forest. After rounding the ridge, you will come to a teahouse, beyond which the trail suddenly begins a steep and slippery descent to the floor of the Langtang Khola valley. This section of trail skirts the edge of a huge landslide until you are almost to the river and then cuts across the unstable slope to reenter a lush, damp forest. Not far beyond the landslide, you come to two simple lodges, which are known collectively as **Landslide.**

The valley, which runs east-west at this point, is very narrow and rarely receives much sunlight on the south bank, which is where the trail is located. However, the valley walls on the north bank receive considerably more sunshine and support a landscape of striking contrast to other parts of the valley. Instead of ferns, mosses, and tall trees, there are only grasses and cactuses. Such contrasts are typical of the Himalayas, where the orientation of the mountains plays a crucial role in modifying the climate.

An hour beyond Landslide, you will pass another small lodge deep in the forest at a spot known as **Bamboo.** Thirty minutes beyond this lodge, you cross a bridge (6,700 ft.; 2,042m) to the drier north side of the Langtang Khola. There are a couple of small lodges at this bridge.

The trail begins climbing up from the river at this point, passing through Rimche (where there are several lodges), and in an hour, shortly after the trail levels off at 7,800 feet (2,377m), you join the trail from Syarpagaon and Syabrubensi. Another hour from this trail junction brings you to the tiny village of **Chongong** (7,800 ft.; 2,377m), where there are several lodges including the **Lama Hotel,** which has long lent its name to this spot. Try the **Lama Guest House.** If you don't feel like stopping just yet, it is another hour or so to **Gumnachowk.** The Woodland Lodge is a good choice there.

## DAY 4: LAMA HOTEL TO LANGTANG VILLAGE

Lama Hotel to Gumnachowk: 1 hour; Gumnachowk to Ghora Tabela: 3 hours; Ghora Tabela to Langtang: 3 hours. ELEVATION GAIN: 3,675 ft. (1,121m).

It takes about 7 hours to reach Langtang Village from Lama Hotel, so you may want to get an early start. From Lama Hotel, the trail climbs steadily to Ghora Tabela with glimpses of Langtang Lirung (23,767 ft.; 7,244m) through the trees. Midway between Lama Hotel and Ghora Tabela, you pass by the lodges at Gumnachowk and Chhunama.

At times the trail becomes very steep, but only for short distances. At **Ghora Tabela** (9,850 ft.; 3,002m) the trail leaves the forest, and a spectacular view of Langtang Lirung appears. Ghora Tabela was once a Tibetan resettlement camp but is now an army post. There is a good lodge here where you can get lunch or stop for the day. You must show your trekking permit at the police checkpoint. Continue up the valley, leaving the forests behind.

In 30 to 45 minutes, you come to **Thangshyap** (10,754 ft.; 3,278m), where there are a couple of basic lodges and good views both up and down the valley. The trail climbs steadily up to **Langtang** village (11,475 ft.; 3,498m), passing below a monastery about 30 minutes before reaching the village. Langtang is another Tamang village with stone-and-wood houses and pastures in which you just might see yaks. There are several trekkers' lodges here.

## DAY 5: LANGTANG TO KYANJIN GOMPA
Langtang to Kyanjin Gompa: 3 hours. ELEVATION GAIN: 975 ft. (297m).

You may notice that the valley above this point is U-shaped, which indicates that it was carved by a glacier. Below Langtang, the valley has the characteristic V-shape of a river-carved valley. Leaving Langtang, you climb gradually to a chorten, behind which are several very long mani walls. You are now above the treeline, and low-growing shrubs dominate this alpine environment. As the valley widens, the trail passes the three villages of **Mundu, Sindum,** and **Yamfu,** all of which have small lodges.

You cross several streams and a moraine before arriving at **Kyanjin Gompa** (12,450 ft.; 3,795m). Between Langtang and Kyanjin Gompa, the views get better and better. You can see Yansa Tsenji (21,452 ft.; 6,539m) and Kimshun (22,123 ft.; 6,743m) to the north and the Langtang Himal to the northwest. Kyanjin Gompa is a small Buddhist monastery, but there are also numerous lodges and a cheese factory here. Try the **Snow View Hotel** or **Hotel Tibet.** Since you will probably arrive before lunch, you will have time to do some exploring in the afternoon, though you may be experiencing some discomfort from the altitude. One possibility is to climb the steep hill to the north of Kyanjin Gompa. This hill is more than 13,000 feet (3,962m) high and provides an excellent view of Langtang Lirung.

## DAY 6: KYANJIN GOMPA
Climbing one of the area's low peaks or taking a day hike farther up the valley past the airstrip will provide more spectacular views that include Langtang Lirung, Ganchenpo (20,950 ft.; 6,386m), Langshisa Ri (20,894 ft.; 6,368m), Dorje Lakpa (22,927 ft.; 6,988m), Lenpo Gang (23,232 ft.; 7,081m), and Urkinmang (20,175 ft.; 6,149m). One popular excursion is to climb the lateral moraine north of Kyanjin Gompa for a close view of the Lirung Glacier and icefall. Alternatively, if you have more energy, you can climb to the top of what is known as Kyanjin Ri (15,665 ft.; 4,775m), the prayer flag–topped peak directly north of Kyanjin Gompa. There is also another cheese factory in the village of Yala, which can be reached in about 3 hours if you are acclimatized. Another 2 hours above Yala is the summit of 16,348-foot (4,983m) Tserko Ri. If you start early in the morning and are acclimatized, you should be able to climb this peak and return to Kyanjin Gompa in 1 long day. If you have mountaineering experience and have come equipped for a difficult climb, it is possible to cross the Ganja La, a 16,800-foot (5,121m) pass, to Helambu. This crossing is not possible in the winter months when the pass is closed by snow. You will need a guide, tents, food, fuel, an axe, and crampons to cross the Ganja La, and it is essential that you spend a day acclimatizing at Kyanjin Gompa.

## DAY 7: KYANJIN GOMPA TO LAMA HOTEL
Kyanjin Gompa to Lama Hotel: 5 hours. ELEVATION LOSS: 4,750 ft. (1,448m).

Since you will be acclimatized and will be descending, you should be able to reach Lama Hotel in a short day's walk from Kyanjin Gompa. If you reach Lama Hotel by lunch and don't feel like stopping so early, consider continuing to Bamboo or Landslide.

## DAY 8: ONWARD FROM LAMA HOTEL

Lama Hotel to Syabrubensi (old route): 7 hours; Lama Hotel to Syabrubensi (new route): 5 hours; Lama Hotel to Dhunche: 8 hours; Lama Hotel to Shin Gompa: 8 hours. To Dunche: ELEVATION GAIN: 2,650 ft. (808m). ELEVATION LOSS: 4,000 ft. (1,219m). To Syabrubensi: ELEVATION LOSS: 3,040 ft. (427m).

Beyond Lama Hotel there are several possible routes, depending on where you are headed and how much time you have. If your goal is to reach Dhunche as quickly as possible, you should be able to get there after a long day's hike from Lama Hotel. You can shorten this route by continuing to Landslide or Bamboo on the day you leave Kyanjin Gompa.

There are also two routes to the village of **Syabrubensi,** which is on the road north of Bharkhu. To reach Syabrubensi in a long day, take the old trail that forks off the main trail at Rimche, 15 minutes below Lama Hotel. This route stays high above the river, does a bit of climbing, and has some good views. A newer alternative route to Syabrubensi leaves the main trail beyond Landslide. This latter route takes about 2 hours less than the old route. From Syabrubensi, you can either catch the bus to Kathmandu or hike along the road to Dhunche and then catch the bus.

If you are on your way to Gosainkund, you would definitely do better to continue past Lama Hotel on the day you leave Kyanjin. From Lama Hotel, it would be a long day's hike to **Shin Gompa,** but this day would be a bit more bearable if you started from Bamboo or Landslide. See the "Gosainkund" section, below, for details on continuing the trek through that region.

## DAY 9: DHUNCHE (OR SYABRUBENSI) TO KATHMANDU

Dhunche to Kathmandu: 9–13 hours.

Since you will arrive in Dhunche or Syabrubensi too late to catch a bus to Trisuli, you will have to spend the night in town and take the bus the next morning.

# 6  Gosainkund

Each summer during the August full moon, Hindu pilgrims from all over Nepal and India make the trek up to Gosainkund's sacred high-altitude lakes. Legends say that these lakes were formed when the god Shiva pierced a glacier with his trident. Local legends also claim that the water from Gosainkund, the main lake, flows underground to emerge from a spring at the Kumbeshwar Temple in Patan. There is a large white stone in the middle of the Gosainkund Lake that is believed to be the remains of a Shiva temple, and on the lake's shore, there is a shrine containing a large stone Shiva lingam.

This trek connects the Helambu and Langtang treks by way of the trail over the Surjakund pass, and it can be done in either direction. It is a good idea to have a guide for the section over the pass. During the warmer months of the main trekking seasons, there are lodges all along the route over Surjakund Pass. However, after late November, when snow begins to accumulate at the higher elevations, the lodges shut down. If you're planning to do this trek in the colder months, be sure to find out about trail conditions and whether lodges are open. For a truly fascinating experience, make this trek during the annual pilgrimage in August, which is in the middle of the monsoon season—expect to stay wet for most of the trek.

I describe the trek starting on the Langtang side and proceeding to Tharepati on the Helambu trek. (See "The Langtang Valley," above, and "Helambu," below, for descriptions of these two treks.) Keep in mind that this trek does a lot of climbing very quickly, so it is both a strenuous trek and one on which you should be alert for symptoms of altitude sickness.

## DAY 1: DHUNCHE (OR SYABRU) TO SHIN GOMPA

Dhunche to Dimsa: 4 hours; Dimsa to Shin Gompa: 1 hour; Sybaru to Shin Gompa: 4 hours.
ELEVATION GAIN: From Dhunche, 4,550 ft. (1,388m); from Syabru, 3,950 ft. (1,204m).

The trail to Shin Gompa leaves the road through Dhunche on the far side of town from the police checkpoint. The trail crosses through terraced fields before descending to the Trisuli Khola, a stream that has its origin in Gosainkund Lake. The path keeps close to the right bank for a while but then begins climbing steadily through forests of oak and, at higher elevations, fir and rhododendron. This is a long, steep climb with only a few lodges between Dhunche and Shin Gompa, so carry plenty of water and some snacks. Because this stretch of trail is so sparsely populated, it is the most likely place for you to spot wildlife, including langurs (long-tailed monkeys), martens, and many species of birds.

It is a sweaty 3 hours before you reach the first teahouse and another hour or so to the lodges at **Dimsa,** which is above the point where a trail from Bharkhu joins this trail. In another hour of climbing through forest from Dimsa, you come to the small Buddhist monastery of **Shin Gompa** (10,950 ft.; 3,338m) in a large clearing on the side of a steep slope. This clearing was caused by a fire more than a decade ago, and the skeletal tree trunks that rise from the hillside frequently serve as perches for large hawks. Shin Gompa is also the site of a large government cheese factory and a couple of good lodges.

If you are coming from **Syabru,** walk uphill through the village. Just past the army post, take the trail that forks to the right. This trail leads very steeply uphill and continues to climb sharply for several hours. For the first 2 hours, the trail climbs up an open hillside with good views. There are several teahouses along this stretch of trail. The trail then enters a thick wood filled with huge old trees. After hiking through this forest for an hour or more, you come to a lodge on a cleared ridge (10,492 ft.; 3,198m). There are excellent views from here, and this makes a great lunch spot. Beyond this teahouse, the trail is much less steep. Short climbs alternate with fairly flat sections of trail, and forests alternate with pastures. After passing through the last bit of enchanting forest, you come to **Shin Gompa.**

## DAY 2: SHIN GOMPA TO LAUREBINA YAK

Shin Gompa to Cholang Pati: 1½ hours; Cholang Pati to Laurebina Yak: 1½ hours. ELEVATION GAIN: 1,837 ft. (560m).

Although this is a short day, you still manage to ascend 1,837 feet (560m), which is as much as you should attempt at this altitude. If you aren't planning on going over the Surjakund Pass, you might consider hiking up to Gosainkund Lake in the afternoon and then returning to Laurebina Yak. If you are feeling any discomfort from the altitude, consider spending an acclimatization day at Shin Gompa before moving on.

From Shin Gompa, the wide, well-trodden trail continues climbing steadily through rhododendron forest with the Trisuli Khola far below. The trail crosses over to the Langtang side of the ridge shortly before reaching the lodges at **Cholang Pati** (11,751 ft.; 3,582m).

Above Cholang Pati, you leave the forest and pass through a landscape of rhododendron shrubs. You are now above the treeline, and as you continue to climb, the vegetation becomes more and more stunted.

An hour and a half above Cholang Pati, you come to the stone lodges at **Laurebina Yak** (12,787 ft.; 3,897m). This barren ridgeline, with no protection from the fierce winds, is always cold, but it offers one of the most stunning vistas in Nepal. Visible are Langtang Lirung (23,767 ft.; 7,244m) to the north; a mountain range in Tibet to the northwest; and the Ganesh Himal (24,357 ft.; 7,424m), Himalchuli (25,879 ft.; 7,888m), and Manaslu (26,764 ft.; 8,158m) all to the west. For this reason alone (regardless of the need to stop due to the elevation gain), it is worth spending a night here. The views are best in the early morning, when the skies are cloud free. By late afternoon, this ridge is often socked in by dense clouds and can be very cold and damp.

## DAY 3: LAUREBINA YAK TO GOPTE

Laurebina Yak to Gosainkund Lake: 2 hours; Gosainkund to Surjakund Pass: 1½ hours; Surjakund Pass to Gopte: 4 hours. ELEVATION GAIN: 2,463 FT. (751m). ELEVATION LOSS: 3,550 ft. (1,082m).

Because you must get up and over the Surjakund Pass and then descend a long way to the first lodges, be sure to get an early start, but don't leave before you catch the sunrise. Also be sure to have lunch at Gosainkund Lake before heading over the pass.

Above Laurebina Yak, the trail climbs steeply to a grassy ridge, where there is a small Buddhist shrine just off the trail. Beyond this shrine, the trail ascends more gradually but clings to a vertiginous mountainside. This area is used in the summer months as high-altitude grazing land for flocks of sheep and goats. From here you will finally be able to see the Gosainkund lakes. The first two lakes lay far below the trail, which begins to descend when the third lake comes into view. This third lake is the holy **Gosainkund Lake** (14,350 ft.; 4,374m), and it has a Shiva shrine and some guest houses on its shores.

The trail then skirts the north shore of Gosainkund Lake before climbing toward the pass. As you climb this easy slope, you will see four more lakes. You will know you have reached **Surjakund Pass** (15,100 ft.; 4,602m) when you see the many cairns that have been built over the years. The trail then descends, steeply at first but then more gradually, to the southeast on a rocky path. In about an hour you will come to an area known as **Phedi,** where during the trekking seasons there is usually a primitive lodge. From here the trail descends another ridge, crossing several streams and passing two waterfalls. After passing another stone hut, the trail climbs to another ridge and **Gopte** (11,700 ft.; 3,566m), where overhanging rocks form a cave that is also used as a trekkers' lodge.

## DAY 4: GOPTE TO MALEMCHIGAON OR KUTUMSANG

Gopte to Tharepati: 2 hours; Tharepati to Malemchigaon: 4 hours; Tharepati to Kutumsang: 5 hours. To Melemchigaon: ELEVATION GAIN: 3,400 ft. (1,036m). To Kutumsang: ELEVATION LOSS: 3,603 ft. (1,098m).

From Gopte, the trail descends to more caves and enters a thick forest of rhododendrons. The trail crosses a stream, which is dry for part of the year, before climbing through the forest to **Tharepati** (11,500 ft.; 3,505m), a grouping of small stone huts used in the summer months by herders. During trekking season, there is usually a very basic lodge here.

From the ridge above Tharepati, there are two choices for your onward path. Both trails will get you back to Kathmandu in 3 to 4 days. The trail through **Tarke Gyang** is the more interesting route, though the first day of this trail entails a steep and difficult descent and an equally steep ascent. To take this route, head southeast and descend to **Malemchigaon** near the floor of the Malemchi Khola Valley. You will be able to see Tarke Gyang high up on the far side of the valley. The other route back to Kathmandu stays high on a system of ridges that leads from here to the Kathmandu Valley. This trail follows a ridge to the south and leads to **Kutumsang.** (For detailed descriptions of these two routes, see "Helambu," below, in this chapter.)

# 7 Helambu

The Helambu trek, though not the easiest or most spectacular, is certainly the most accessible—the trailhead lies within the Kathmandu Valley. You can be on the trail within an hour of leaving your hotel in downtown Kathmandu. Perhaps because of its location, the trail is rarely used by trekkers. In addition, the existing trails are badly eroded, poorly maintained, and often difficult to follow. Hiring a guide is highly advisable if you plan to do this trek.

## DAY 1: KATHMANDU TO PATI BHANJYANG

Kathmandu to Sundarijal by taxi and bus: 1 hour; Sundarijal to Borlang Bhanjyang: 4 hours; Borlang Bhanjyang to Chisapani: 1 hour; Chisapani to Pati Bhanjyang: 1½ hours. ELEVATION GAIN: 3,200 ft. (975m). ELEVATION LOSS: 2,200 ft. (671m).

You should be able to hire a taxi for around Rs 500 ($7.60) to take you all the way to the trailhead at Sundarijal, which is beyond Boudha on the north side of the Kathmandu Valley. You can also take a taxi to Boudha (Rs 100 [$1.50]) and then take one of the minibuses that operate from there to Sundarijal. If a minibus is not available at a convenient time, you can walk to Sundarijal (and the trailhead) from Boudha in 2 to 3 hours.

Sundarijal (4,800 ft.; 1,463m) is at the foot of Shivapuri Ridge, the long hill that forms the north side of the Kathmandu Valley. This ridge is now part of the **Shivapuri Watershed and Wildlife Reserve,** and a Rs250 ($3.80) admission is charged. The trail begins at the north end of town near a water treatment plant and parallels a large water pipe that brings water down to the plant. In about 45 minutes you cross a small dam. The trail climbs alternately through forest and terraced fields to the village of **Mulkharka** (5,800 ft.; 1,768m). After another 2 hours on a steep and badly eroded trail, you reach the top of the Shivapuri Ridge and the small village of **Borlang Bhanjyang** (8,000 ft.; 2,438m), which is just over the pass on the north side of the ridge. From the pass you get your first view of the Langtang and Jugal Himal, the mountains you are hiking toward.

The trail descends through sparsely populated scrubby forests. After an hour or so, you cross a dirt road in a closely cropped pasture near the village of **Chisapani.** About 100 yards beyond the road, there is a lodge that takes good advantage of the view from here. This is a better place to stop than the village of **Pati Bhanjyang** (5,800 ft.; 1,768m), which is in a ridge saddle another 1½ hours farther down the trail and doesn't have such a spectacular view. There are a couple of lodges in Pati Bhanjyang and a police checkpoint.

## DAY 2: PATI BHANJYANG TO TALAMARANG

Pati Bhanjyang to Thakani: 1½ hours; Thakani to Batache: 1 hour; Batache to Talamarang: 3 hours. ELEVATION LOSS: 2,653 ft. (808m).

From Pati Bhanjyang you have a choice of two routes. One stays high on the ridge, whereas the other descends steeply to the valley floor. I prefer the lower route, since it makes the trek a bit easier and gives you a few days to develop your trekking muscles before making the ascent to Tharepati. The trail to the Malemchi Khola and Talamarang begins north of town near the top of a hill with a few houses on it. Take a right to head east at these houses, and you will see the trail ascending to a notch in a ridge. It is about an hour to the notch and another 30 minutes to the village of **Thakani.** The trail stays above the village and then passes through a meadow. In another hour you will come to **Batache.** Here the trail turns northward and begins its steep descent to the river. This trail may be difficult to find. If you are trekking without a guide, ask directions frequently. It is 3 hours to **Talamarang** (3,147 ft.; 960m), which has several lodges and is now on a dirt road that is an extension of the road to Malemchi Pul, an alternative starting or finishing point for this trek.

## DAY 3: TALAMARANG TO LOWER THIMBU

Talamarang to Mahankal: 2 hours; Mahankal to Kiul: 1 hour; Kiul to Thimbu: 1½ hours. ELEVATION GAIN: 2,032 ft. (620m).

The trail from Talamarang to Thimbu is fairly flat and easy to walk, a welcome relief after the previous 2 days' steep ascent and descent. The villages along the Malemchi Khola are prosperous and attractive, and all of them have lodges. If you decide to stop early, you should have no problem securing a room. The elevation here is quite low, only about 3,000 feet (914m), so bananas line the trail. It can be warm hiking even in December. It is about 2 hours along the dirt road to the lodges in **Mahankal** village, beyond which the road reverts to trail and crosses the Malemchi Khola on a suspension bridge. An hour from Mahankal you will reach **Kiul,** where there are several lodges. From Kiul, it is 1½ hours to **Thimbu** (5,179 ft.; 1,580m), which is a scattered village covering a very steep hillside. At the foot of the mountainside on which Thimbu is built, there are a couple of lodges beside a stream (4,500 ft.; 1,372m). These are your only choices for a place to stay in Thimbu, and they are not very luxurious accommodations, even by trekking standards.

## DAY 4: LOWER THIMBU TO TARKE GYANG

Thimbu to Kakani: 2½ hours; Kakani to Tarke Gyang: 4 hours. ELEVATION GAIN: 3,821 ft. (1,163m).

This day starts out with a grueling climb up from the river on a bad trail that seems to go straight up the mountainside. However, once the trail gets above upper **Thimbu,** it is a fairly gradual ascent, with a few short climbs, to **Tarke Gyang** (9,000 ft.; 2,743m). There are few houses or villages along this section of trail, so be sure to carry some food with you for lunch. Chapati and egg sandwiches, made up in the morning at your lodge, are an easy trail meal. In 2½ hours you pass through the village of **Kakani** (7,850 ft.; 2,393m). Several lodges and a gompa (Buddhist monastery) are located here. Beware of begging children, who have been known to throw rocks at trekkers who do not give in to their demands.

You are now entering the region inhabited by the Helambu Sherpas, who are only distantly related to the famous Sherpas of the Solu-Khumbu region. As in Solu-Khumbu, the Sherpas of this region build both mani walls (walls of stones that have had prayers carved onto them) and chortens (small stupalike shrines). Remember to keep these mani walls and chortens on your right side as you pass them. It is considered disrespectful to have your left side to one of these structures.

Beyond Kakani, the trail enters a large valley created by a tributary of the Malemchi Khola. There is a hydroelectric project in this valley, and electric power lines stretch from here to Tarke Gyang. From Kakani it is about 3 hours to the hydroelectric project and another hour to Tarke Gyang, the largest and most important village in the region. After the many small and scattered villages you pass on the way here, Tarke Gyang is like an oasis. There is a large gompa surrounded by the densely packed stone houses of the village. On the steep slopes above the village there is a dark forest of rhododendrons and fir trees. Five minutes before town, there is a large lodge, but I prefer the smaller **Lama Lodge** beside the gompa. Local entrepreneurs may want to sell you curios, but most of the items they have for sale are available in Kathmandu at lower prices. The genuinely valuable pieces offered for sale carry steep price tags.

## DAY 5: TARKE GYANG TO THAREPATI

Tarke Gyang to Malemchi Khola: 2 hours; Malemchi Khola to Malemchigaon: 2 hours; Malemchigaon to Tharepati: 4 hours. ELEVATION GAIN: 5,300 ft. (1,615m). ELEVATION LOSS: 2,800 ft. (853m).

If you aren't looking forward to the long and arduous trek up to Tharepati, you might want to spend a few days in Tarke Gyang, making day trips up to some of the high pastures above the village. There are excellent views to the north from within a few hours of Tarke Gyang.

If you feel like moving on from Tarke Gyang, descend to reach the river (6,200 ft.; 1,890m) in about 2 hours. Cross the bridge and climb the steep trail to **Malemchigaon** (8,300 ft.; 2,530m), which takes about 2 hours also. Here in Malemchigaon, you will have to show your Langtang National Park entry permit (which you purchased for Rs650 [$9.85] when you got your trekking permit in Kathmandu) before continuing into the park to Tharepati. There are lodges in Malemchigaoun if you prefer to postpone the final push to Tharepati.

From Malemchigaon, the trail leads up a very steep mountainside. This trail is often hard to follow and can be slippery. It takes at least 4 hours to reach the **Tharepati Pass** (11,500 ft.; 3,505m). This climb of more than 5,000 feet (1,524m) in 1 day is grueling. In the winter, snow makes the going even more difficult, and the trail becomes even harder to follow. Prayer flags mark the pass, where there are several lodges.

## DAY 6: THAREPATI TO KUTUMSANG

Tharepati to Mangegoth: 2 hours; Mangegoth to Kutumsang: 4 hours. ELEVATION GAIN: 1,375 ft. (419m). ELEVATION LOSS: 3,675 ft. (1,120m).

From Tharepati, there are two possible routes. The trail north climbs up to the 15,100-foot (4,602m) Surjakund Pass and links the Helambu trek with the Langtang trek by way of Gosainkund. This route is usually not passable in winter and is even difficult during the rest of the year. Though it is possible to cross the Surjakund Pass without a guide, it is not recommended. See "Gosainkund," above, for details about that trekking route.

If you are only making a circuit of Helambu, follow the ridge to the south, and in an hour you will pass the lodges at **Mangegoth.** This is a very remote area of high pastures and oak and rhododendron forests. If you are going to see any wildlife other than birds, this is probably the most likely area. For the first 3 hours the trail descends gradually, but the second half of the day's trek is a steep descent to **Kutumsang** (8,097 ft.; 2,470m), a small village on a windy ridge saddle. The Langtang National Park office here will probably check your national park permit. There are a couple of lodges beside the park office and several more as you head south out of the village and up the ridge.

## DAY 7: KUTUMSANG TO PATI BHANJYANG

Kutumsang to Gul Bhanjyang: 2 hours; Gul Bhanjyang to Chipling: 2 hours; Chipling to Pati Bhanjyang: 2 hours. ELEVATION GAIN: 1,375 ft. (419m). ELEVATION LOSS: 3,675 ft. (1,120m).

From Kutumsang, the trail climbs the ridge before making a steep descent to **Gul Bhanjyang,** which has several lodges and is also in a saddle. Climb up the ridge from Gul Bhanjyang, continuing to head south, and in 2 hours you will reach **Chipling,** where there are some teahouses. A steep and rocky trail descends from Chipling to another saddle, where there are a few lodges. The trail then ascends another ridge before dropping down to the saddle on which **Pati Bhanjyang** is built.

## DAY 8: PATI BHANJYANG TO KATHMANDU

Pati Bhanjyang to Sundarijal: 5½ hours.

From Pati Bhanjyang, retrace your steps back to **Sundarijal.**

## 8 Less-Traveled Treks

If you have already done the more popular treks in Nepal or want to avoid the more crowded ones (even though they are the most spectacular routes), consider getting off the beaten path. For the most part, these are not treks that can be done on your own, and in fact, the Nepali government requires that you go with a licensed trekking company on the Mustang, Dolpo, around Manaslu, and Kanchenjunga treks. Special high-priced trekking permits are also levied on people who trek these routes. The reason for the restrictions is to limit the number of trekkers visiting these regions. Hordes of trekkers have made lasting changes on areas such as Annapurna and Solu-Khumbu, and these changes are not necessarily for the good. If you do one of these restricted treks, you will be experiencing Nepali culture that has been less tainted by contact with the outside world. With any luck you won't see a single Chicago Bulls T-shirt on a trek through Mustang or Dolpo. In my opinion, the benefits of trekking through regions rarely visited by foreigners is well worth the costs (financial, physical, and time).

## MUSTANG

Anyone who has ever trekked through the village of Kagbeni on the Jomosom or Annapurna Circuit trek has likely gazed up the barren valley of the Kali Gandaki and longed to visit Mustang. This remote and barren region of Nepal was for decades thought of as a forbidden kingdom. No trekkers were allowed into the area due to its sensitive position along the Tibetan border. A glance at a map shows that this region actually juts into Tibet, and both culturally and geographically, Mustang has far more in common with Tibet than with Nepal. Mustang was a stronghold of Tibetan resistance after the Chinese invaded Tibet, and Nepal's support of Tibet in the conflict with China caused tension between Nepal and China. These tensions left most of Nepal's Tibetan border areas off-limits to trekkers. Today, relations between China and Nepal are stable, and Nepal has opened up many of its border areas, including ♦ Upper Mustang, to trekkers.

The Kali Gandaki valley, which passes through Mustang, has been a trans-Himalayan trading route for thousands of years and is a natural route into Tibet. Trade along this route was very important, and anyone who could control passage along the Kali Gandaki could become very wealthy. Consequently, several small kingdoms developed throughout the Mustang region. *Dzongs* (castles) and *gompas* (Buddhist temples) were built in the densely packed earth-and-stone villages. These villages still stand and are today little changed by the passing of centuries. Mustang today is what Tibet must have been like before the coming of the Chinese. Meager harvests of barley are still coaxed from the barren, rocky soil with the help of irrigation waters from the river, and yaks, goats, and stocky ponies provide labor, butter, wool, and transportation in the region. These are the reasons so many trekkers have longed to visit Mustang—to catch a fleeting glimpse of an ancient Tibetan Buddhist culture.

Should you decide you must trek into Mustang to the ancient walled village of **Lo Manthang,** a fleeting and expensive glimpse is all you will get. Special regulations apply to this region, and a trekking permit, valid for 10 days, will cost you $700 per person ($70 per day after 10 days). All treks must be organized by a licensed trekking company, and groups must be self-sufficient during their trek. This trek can be combined with either the Jomosom trek or the trek around Annapurna. However, if you have limited time, it is also possible to fly into Jomosom and begin trekking from there. It is only a few hours' hike from Jomosom to Kagbeni, which marks the edge of the once-forbidden district.

## DOLPO

Nearly as fabled as Mustang, Dolpo is a rugged and remote region to the west of Mustang. The region was made famous by Peter Matthiessen in his book *The Snow Leopard*, a chronicle of a trip made with animal-behaviorist George Schaller. *Remote* is the key word in describing Dolpo. If you wish to explore this region, with its ancient villages, high passes, beautiful lakes, isolated Buddhist monasteries, and relatively plentiful wildlife, you will have to have plenty of time available. Before reaching the spectacular settings described in Matthiessen's book, you'll spend several days hiking through low-elevation forests with few views. Most treks into Dolpo take **20 to 30 days,** and because winter comes early to the high passes, the best time to trek in Dolpo is toward the end of the monsoon season, since heat and leeches can be a problem at lower elevations during the monsoon season. You can make shorter Dolpo treks by flying into the airstrip at Jumla.

Trekking permits for lower Dolpo cost $10 per week for the first month and $20 per week after that. To visit the more spectacular region of upper Dolpo, you will have to pay the same $700 trekking permit fee that is charged for Mustang. After 10 days, you'll have to pay an additional $70 per day. You will also have to arrange a fully organized trek with an established trekking company. If you book your trek in Nepal, you will likely have to pay between $50 and $60 per day of your trek.

## OTHER AREAS

While Mustang and Dolpo are prohibitively expensive to visit, there are remote treks with more reasonably priced trekking fees. Again, these are treks that must be done on an organized camping trek due to the lack of lodges along the trekking routes. For this reason, you will see fewer trekkers and will experience more authentic Nepali hill life.

**The Kanchenjunga Area**    Located in far-eastern Nepal on the border with India, Kanchenjunga (28,200 ft.; 8,595m) is the world's third-highest peak. A trek to Kanchenjunga entails crossing one or two high passes, and that fact, plus the length of a trek here, makes this a choice only for the very fit. Along the way you pass through villages of the Limbu people, who live only here in eastern Nepal. Treks in the Kanchenjunga region generally take 3 to 4 weeks.

**Makalu**    Mount Makalu (27,759 ft.; 8,461m) lies just to the east of Mount Everest within the **Makalu Barun National Park.** A trek in this region provides excellent views and passes through landscapes similar to those of the crowded Khumbu region south of Everest. Treks in the Makalu region take 3 weeks or more.

**Around Manaslu**    Lying just to the east of the Annapurna Himal, Manaslu (26,775 ft.; 8,161m), the eighth-highest peak in the world, can be circled in the same way that the Annapurnas can be circled, and just as on the Annapurna Circuit, there is a high pass to be crossed—the Larkya La (17,100 ft.; 5,212m). This trek, which begins in Gorkha, links up with the Annapurna Circuit, providing the option of circling both Manaslu and Annapurna in one long trek.

**Jumla to Rara Lake**    Lying at an elevation of 9,775 feet (2,979m) in far-western Nepal, Rara Lake is the largest lake in Nepal and is surrounded by pine, spruce, and juniper forests. Protected within **Rara Lake National Park,** this remote region does not have the spectacular mountain views of other regions, but there is generally more wildlife than in other parts of the country. A trek here generally takes about 10 days.

**Simikot**    This area of far-western Nepal, only recently opened up to trekking, lies close to the Tibetan border, and the people of the region have much in common with

Tibetans. From this area it is also now possible to trek into Tibet and then continue onward by vehicle to **Mount Kailash,** the holiest mountain in Asia. A trek through the Simikot region will take around 10 days, and continuing to Mount Kailash adds another 10 days or so.

**Alternative Annapurna Treks** Even in the popular Annapurna region, there are treks that avoid the main trails. These are generally short treks that take in excellent views. One such trek leads up to the Mardi Himal and the base of Machhapuchhare, providing the most close-up view of the stunning **"Fish Tail Peak."** Another even-shorter trek leads up above the village of Sikles, which is north of Pokhara in the drainage of the Mardi Khola. Again, there are great views on this trek.

# Appendix

## A Basic Phrases & Vocabulary

### CONVERSATIONAL PHRASES

Hello/Good-bye  *Na*maste
How are you?  *Kasto* chha?
Fine  *San*chaai
Please (give me)  *Khaa*nuhos
Thank you  *Dhany*abad
Yes (it is)  **Ho**
Yes (it exists)  **Chha**
OK  *Hun*chha
No (it is not)  *Hoi*na
No (it does not exist)  *Chaai*na
Excuse me  *Hajur*
Give me  *Malaai . . . di*nos
Where is?  *. . . ka*haa chha?
A hospital  *aas*pital
A hotel  *ho*tel
The toilet  *chhar*pi
Straight ahead  *Sojhai jaa*nus
Turn left  *Baayaa mod*nos
Turn right  *Daayaa mod*nos
Do you have a?  *Tapaai . . .
  san*ga?
Room  *ko*thaa
How much is this?  *Yesko kati?*
(or *Kati parch*ha?)
When?  *Kahile?*
Where?  *Kahaan?*
How?  *Kasari?*
Why?  *Kina?*
What?  *Ke?*
How much?  *Kati?*
Today  *Aa*ja
Tomorrow  *Bho*li

Yesterday  *Hi*jo
Minute  *Mi*nut
Hour  *Ghan*taa
Day  **Din**
Good  *Raam*ro
Bad  *Naraam*ro
May I please take your picture?
  *Tapaaiko pho*to *khi*chu?
How old are you?  *Tapaaiko
  u*mer *kati bha*yo?
What is your name?  *Tapaaiko
  naam ke ho?*
My name is . . .  *Mero naam . . .
  ho.*
Where are you from?
*Tapaaiko
  ghar ka*ha ho?
I come from . . .  *Mero* ghar *. . .
  ma.*
What is the name of this?
  *Yes*ko naam ko ho?
I don't speak Nepali.  **Ma
  Ne***paali* bol*dina.
I only speak a little Nepali.  **Ma
  al***i al*i Ne*paali* maatrai
  bolchhu.
I don't understand.  *Maile*
  bu*jhi*na.
What time is it?  *Kati baj*yo?
It is four o'clock.  **Char** *baj*yo.
I will stay for 1 day.  **Ek din**
  *bas*ne.

## TREKKING PHRASES

Which is the way to . . . ?
   **. . . *jaa*ne *baat*o kun ho?**
How much for 1 night?
   **Ek raat ko *ka*ti?**
How many hours to . . . ?
   **. . . *ka*ti *ghant*aa *laag*chha?**
Is there a lodge in . . . ?
   **. . . maa *bhaa*tti chha?**
Can we get food in . . . ?
   **. . . maa *khaa*naa *paain*cha?**

Is food available?
   ***Khaa*na *paain*chha?**
Please give me . . .   **. . . *di*nos.**
Food   **khaa**na
Tea   ***chi*yaa**
Shelter   **baas**
Where is the . . . ?   **. . . *ka*haa chha?**
Inn   ***bha*tti**
Village   **gaau**
Where are you going?   **Ta*pai ka*haa** ***janne?***

## NUMBERS

| | | | |
|---|---|---|---|
| 1 | ek | 21 | *ek*kaais |
| 2 | dui | 22 | *ba*ais |
| 3 | teen | 23 | teis |
| 4 | char | 24 | *chau*bis |
| 5 | panch | 25 | *paa*chis |
| 6 | chha | 26 | *chha*bis |
| 7 | saat | 27 | *sat*thaais |
| 8 | aath | 28 | *at*thaais |
| 9 | nau | 29 | *un*antis |
| 10 | das | 30 | tis |
| 11 | *eg*haara | 40 | chaa*lis* |
| 12 | *baah*ra | 50 | pa*chaas* |
| 13 | *teh*ra | 60 | *saa*thi |
| 14 | *chau*dha | 70 | *sat*tari |
| 15 | *pan*dhra | 80 | *ash*i |
| 16 | *soh*ra | 90 | *nab*be |
| 17 | *sat*ra | 100 | ek say |
| 18 | *at*haara | 101 | ek say ek |
| 19 | *un*naais | 200 | dui say |
| 20 | bis | 1000 | ek *ha*jaar |

## B  Menu Items

**Bhat**   Rice usually served with dal—the mainstay of the Nepali diet
**Chang**   Home-brewed rice, barley, or millet beer
*Chi*ya   Tea
**Dal**   Watery lentil soup served over rice; the mainstay of the Nepali diet
**Hot lemon**   Usually listed as a tea but consists only of lemon and water
*Ko*thay   Tibetan fried dumpling similar to a Chinese potsticker
*Mo*mos   Tibetan steamed dumplings stuffed with either meat or vegetables
Si*karn*i   Dessert made from yogurt and spices
*Thuk*pa   Tibetan noodle and vegetable soup

## C  Glossary of Terms

### ARCHITECTURAL TERMS
**Bahal**   Buddhist monastery
**Chaitya**   Small stupa
**Chorten**   Tibetan Buddhist term for *chaitya* (see above)
**Dharmasala**   Resting house for pilgrims
**Ghat**   Stone platform used for performing cremations beside rivers
**Gompa**   Tibetan Buddhist temple or monastery
**Hiti**   Bathing and washing fountain, usually with ornate water spouts
**Jhya**   Carved window
**Mandir**   Temple
**Math**   Hindu priest's house
**Pagoda**   Tower-shaped building, usually a temple, with several roofs
**Stupa**   Large hemispherical Buddhist shrine
**Torana**   Semicircular and ornately decorated panel usually found over temple
entrances; depicts the deities housed within the temple
**Tympanum**   Similar to a torana but not as large; usually hangs above windows,
leaning out slightly from the building
**Vihara (Viharn)**   Buddhist monastery

### RELIGIOUS SYMBOLS
**Dorje**   Tibetan name for *vajra* (see below)
**Ghanta**   Buddhist ritual bell representing wisdom and the female aspect; used in
conjunction with the vajra, it is always held in the left hand
**Lingam**   Phallic symbol that represents the Hindu god Shiva
**Lotus**   Called also *padma,* the lotus is associated with the Buddha and symbolizes
self-creation
**Kailash**   Holy water pitcher
**Mandala**   Tantric symbol representing meditation; it consists of circles enclosing
squares and is used in meditation
**Prayer Wheel**   Wheels filled with prayers that are spun by hand, by the wind, or
by water, thus saying the prayers housed inside the wheel
**Sankha**   Conch shell symbolizing the Hindu god Vishnu and used as a trumpet at
religious services
**Shirivasta**   Endless knot; one of the eight primary Buddhist symbols, it is a symbol
of luck
**Swastika**   Symbol of the law in both Hindu and Buddhist doctrine; also a symbol
of well-being

**Trisul**   Trident, a symbol of Shiva

**Vajra**   Buddhist symbol (called *dorje* in Tibetan) that represents the thunderbolt or diamond that destroys all ignorance and is itself indestructible; it represents power (or method) and the male aspect; used in conjunction with the *ghanta* (bell) and always held in the right hand

**Yoni**   Represents the female genitals and is used in conjunction with the lingam to symbolize Shiva

## MYTHOLOGICAL FIGURES

**Ashta Matrikas**   The eight mother goddesses

**Avalokiteshwara**   A bodhisattva and the Buddhist deity of compassion (known as Chenrezig in Tibet)

**Bhairav**   Ferocious aspect of Shiva

**Bodhisattva**   Enlightened being or Buddha who chooses to remain on earth to help others become enlightened

**Brahma**   One of the Hindu trinity of the most powerful gods; the creator

**Buddha**   Prince Siddhartha Gautama, born in Lumbini, which is now in Nepal; he became the Buddha after meditating under a boddhi tree and discovering the way to transcend all suffering

**Dhyani Buddhas**   Five Buddhas, symbolic of five aspects of Buddhahood that are found on stupas

**Durga**   Frightening incarnation of Parvati

**Ganesh**   The elephant-headed son of Shiva and Parvati; a widely worshiped god said to bring good luck and remove impediments

**Garuda**   Half-man, half-bird vehicle upon which the Hindu god Vishnu travels

**Green Tara**   Buddhist goddess who embodies all that is good in women and who is credited with introducing Buddhism to Tibet

**Hanuman**   White-monkey god who helped rescue Sita, Rama's wife, from Ravana in the epic *Ramayana*

**Indra**   Hindu god of rain and king of heaven

**Kali**   Another wrathful incarnation of Parvati, worshiped at Dakshinkali in Kathmandu Valley

**Krishna**   Well-loved incarnation of Vishnu; his skin is usually blue

**Kumari**   The living goddess; the most famous kumari lives on Kathmandu's Durbar Square

**Laxmi**   Hindu goddess of wealth

**Macchendranath**   Incarnation of Avalokiteshwara and a highly revered god in Kathmandu Valley

**Maitreya**   Future Buddha

**Manjushri**   Buddhist god of knowledge who, according to legend, drained the lake that once filled the Kathmandu Valley by slicing through the surrounding mountains with his sword

**Milaropa**   Famous 12th-century Buddhist monk who wrote thousands of songs and is always depicted with his right hand to his ear

**Naga**   Guardian serpent

**Nandi**   Bull upon which Shiva rides; stands in front of temples containing statues of Shiva lingam

**Narayan**   Most common incarnation of Vishnu in Nepal; considered the creator of life

**Narsimha**   Half-man, half-lion incarnation of Vishnu who killed the demon Hiranya Kashiapu

**Padmasambhawa**   Buddhist saint of northern India who brought Buddhism to Tibet
**Parvati**   Shiva's wife
**Saraswati**   Hindu goddess of learning and Brahma's consort
**Shiva**   One of the Hindu trinity of most-powerful gods; the destroyer of all things
**Vishnu**   One of the Hindu trinity of highest gods; the preserver
**White Tara**   Consort of Avalokiteshwara and Buddhist goddess who protects human beings as they cross the ocean of existence

## D  Useful Web Sites

### VISITOR INFORMATION

www.travel-nepal.com
www.webnepal.com
www.south-asia.com
www.visitnepal.com
www.info-nepal.com
www.catmando.com

Center for Disease Control **www.cdc.gov**
**U.S. Department of State travel warnings** travel.state.gov/nepal
**Visa Application Forms** www.undp.org/mission/nepal/visa_app.htm

### ADVENTURE TRAVEL COMPANIES IN THE U.S.

**Above the Clouds** www.gorp.com/abvclds.htm
**Adventure Center** www.adventure-center.com
**Geographic Expeditions** www.geoex.com
**Himalayan Travel** www.gorp.com/himtravel/htm
**Journeys** www.journeys-intl.com

**KE Adventure** www.keadventure.com
**Mountain Madness** www.mountainmadness.com
**Mountain Travel Sobek** www.mtsobek.com
**Snow Lion Expeditions** www.snowlion.com
**Wilderness Travel** www.wildernesstravel.com

### ADVENTURE TRAVEL COMPANIES ON THE U.K.

**Classic Nepal** www.himalaya.co.uk
**Crusaders** www.crusadertravel.com
**Encounter Overland Expeditions** www.encounter.co.uk

**Exodus** www.exodustravels.co.uk
**Explore Worldwide** www.explore.co.uk
**Himalayan Kingdom Expeditions** www.hkexpeds.demon.co.uk

### YOGA AND MEDITATION CENTERS

**Kathmandu Center of Healing** www.ancientmassage,com

**Himalayan Buddhist Meditation Centre** www.dharmatours.com/hbmc

# Index

# NOTES

## FROMMER'S® COMPLETE TRAVEL GUIDES

Alaska
Amsterdam
Arizona
Atlanta
Australia
Austria
Bahamas
Barcelona, Madrid & Seville
Beijing
Belgium, Holland & Luxembourg
Bermuda
Boston
Budapest & the Best of Hungary
California
Canada
Cancún, Cozumel &
  the Yucatán
Cape Cod, Nantucket & Martha's Vineyard
Caribbean
Caribbean Cruises & Ports of Call
Caribbean Ports of Call
Carolinas & Georgia
Chicago
China
Colorado
Costa Rica
Denmark
Denver, Boulder & Colorado Springs
England
Europe
Florida
France
Germany
Greece
Greek Islands
Hawaii
Hong Kong
Honolulu, Waikiki & Oahu
Ireland
Israel
Italy
Jamaica & Barbados
Japan
Las Vegas
London
Los Angeles
Maryland & Delaware
Maui
Mexico
Miami & the Keys

Montana & Wyoming
Montréal & Québec City
Munich & the Bavarian Alps
Nashville & Memphis
Nepal
New England
New Mexico
New Orleans
New York City
Nova Scotia, New Brunswick &
  Prince Edward Island
Oregon
Paris
Philadelphia & the
  Amish Country
Portugal
Prague & the Best of the Czech Republic
Provence & the Riviera
Puerto Rico
Rome
San Antonio & Austin
San Diego
San Francisco
Santa Fe, Taos &
  Albuquerque
Scandinavia
Scotland
Seattle & Portland
Singapore & Malaysia
South Africa
Southeast Asia
South Pacific
Spain
Sweden
Switzerland
Thailand
Tokyo
Toronto
Tuscany & Umbria
USA
Utah
Vancouver & Victoria
Vermont, New Hampshire
  & Maine
Vienna & the Danube Valley
Virgin Islands
Virginia
Walt Disney World & Orlando
Washington, D.C.
Washington State

## FROMMER'S® DOLLAR-A-DAY GUIDES

Australia from $50 a Day
California from $60 a Day
Caribbean from $70 a Day
England from $70 a Day
Europe from $60 a Day
Florida from $60 a Day

Hawaii from $70 a Day
Ireland from $50 a Day
Israel from $45 a Day
Italy from $70 a Day
London from $85 a Day
New York from $80 a Day

New Zealand from $50 a Day
Paris from $85 a Day
San Francisco from $60 a Day
Washington, D.C.,
  from $60 a Day

## FROMMER'S® PORTABLE GUIDES

Acapulco, Ixtapa &
  Zihuatanejo
Alaska Cruises & Ports of Call
Bahamas
Baja & Los Cabos
Berlin
California Wine Country
Charleston & Savannah
Chicago

Dublin
Hawaii: The Big Island
Las Vegas
London
Maine Coast
Maui
New Orleans
New York City
Paris

Puerto Vallarta, Manzanillo
  & Guadalajara
San Diego
San Francisco
Sydney
Tampa & St. Petersburg
Venice
Washington, D.C.

## FROMMER'S® NATIONAL PARK GUIDES

Family Vacations in the
  National Parks
Grand Canyon

National Parks of the
  American West
Rocky Mountain

Yellowstone & Grand Teton
Yosemite & Sequoia/
  Kings Canyon
Zion & Bryce Canyon

## FROMMER'S® GREAT OUTDOOR GUIDES

New England
Northern California

Southern California & Baja
Washington & Oregon

## FROMMER'S® MEMORABLE WALKS

Chicago
London

New York
Paris

San Francisco
Washington D.C.

## FROMMER'S® IRREVERENT GUIDES

Amsterdam
Boston
Chicago
Las Vegas

London
Los Angeles
Manhattan

New Orleans
Paris
San Francisco

Seattle & Portland
Vancouver
Walt Disney World
Washington, D.C.

## FROMMER'S® BEST-LOVED DRIVING TOURS

America
Britain
California

Florida
France
Germany

Ireland
Italy
New England

Scotland
Spain
Western Europe

## THE COMPLETE IDIOT'S TRAVEL GUIDES

Boston
Chicago
Cruise Vacations
Planning Your Trip to Europe
Florida
Hawaii

Ireland
Las Vegas
London
Mexico's Beach Resorts
New Orleans
New York City

Paris
San Francisco
Spain
Walt Disney World
Washington, D.C.

## THE UNOFFICIAL GUIDES®

Bed & Breakfast in
  New England
Bed & Breakfast in
  the Northwest
Beyond Disney
Branson, Missouri
California with Kids
Chicago

Cruises
Florida with Kids
The Great Smoky &
  Blue Ridge
  Mountains
Inside Disney
Las Vegas

London
Miami & the Keys
Mini Las Vegas
Mini-Mickey
New Orleans
New York City
Paris

San Francisco
Skiing in the West
Walt Disney World
Walt Disney World
  for Grown-ups
Walt Disney World
  for Kids
Washington, D.C.

## SPECIAL-INTEREST TITLES

Born to Shop: France
Born to Shop: Hong Kong
Born to Shop: Italy
Born to Shop: New York
Born to Shop: Paris
Frommer's Britain's Best Bike Rides
The Civil War Trust's Official Guide
  to the Civil War Discovery Trail
Frommer's Caribbean Hideaways
Frommer's Europe's Greatest Driving Tours
Frommer's Food Lover's Companion to France
Frommer's Food Lover's Companion to Italy
Frommer's Gay & Lesbian Europe
Israel Past & Present
Monks' Guide to California

Monks' Guide to New York City
The Moon
New York City with Kids
Unforgettable Weekends
Outside Magazine's Guide
  to Family Vacations
Places Rated Almanac
Retirement Places Rated
Road Atlas Britain
Road Atlas Europe
Washington, D.C., with Kids
Wonderful Weekends from Boston
Wonderful Weekends from New York City
Wonderful Weekends from San Francisco
Wonderful Weekends from Los Angeles

# WHEREVER YOU TRAVEL, *H*ELP IS NEVER FAR AWAY.

From planning your trip to providing travel assistance along the way, American Express® Travel Service Offices are always there to help you do more.

---

## *Nepal*

---

Yeti Travels (R)
Hotel Mayalu, Jamal Tole
Durbar Marg
Kathmandu
(977) (1) 227635, 226172

**do more** AMERICAN EXPRESS
**Travel**
www.americanexpress.com/travel

**American Express Travel Service Offices are found in central locations throughout Nepal.**